Shojo Beat

W9-CDV-624

ORESAMA TEACHER

prince complex

Vol. 14

Story & Art by
Izumi Tsubaki

ORESAMA TEACHER

CHARACTERS AND THE STORY THUS FAR

● PUBLIC MORALS CLUB ●

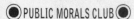

Mafuyu Kurosaki

THE FORMER BANCHO OF SAITAMA EAST HIGH. SHE ALSO PLAYS THE PARTS OF NATSUO AND SUPER BUN. SHE IS CONCERNED BY THE FACT THAT SHE HAS NO FEMALE FRIENDS.

 NATSUO

Same Person →

 SUPER BUN

Takaomi Saeki

THE ONE RESPONSIBLE FOR TURNING MAFUYU INTO A TERRIFYING PERSON. HE'S NOW MAFUYU'S HOMEROOM TEACHER AND THE ADVISOR OF THE PUBLIC MORALS CLUB.

PUBLIC MORALS CLUB

Shinobu Yui

A FORMER MEMBER OF THE STUDENT COUNCIL AND A SELF-PROCLAIMED NINJA. HE JOINED THE PUBLIC MORALS CLUB TO SPY ON THEM.

Hayasaka

MAFUYU'S CLASSMATE. HE ADMIRES SUPER BUN. HE IS A PLAIN AND SIMPLE DELINQUENT.

Aki Shibuya

A TALKATIVE AND WOMANIZING UNDERCLASSMAN. HIS NICKNAME IS AKKI.

Kyotaro Okegawa

THE BANCHO OF MIDORIGAOKA. HE FLUNKED A YEAR, SO HE'S A SUPER SENIOR THIS YEAR. HE TENTATIVELY JOINED THE PUBLIC MORALS CLUB TO HELP MAFUYU AND HER FRIENDS.

STUDENT COUNCIL

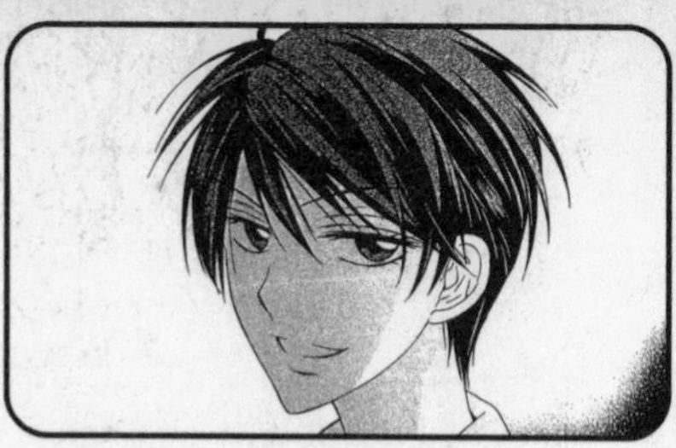

Miyabi Hanabusa

THE SCHOOL DIRECTOR'S SON AND THE PRESIDENT OF THE STUDENT COUNCIL. HE HAS THE POWER TO CAPTIVATE ANYONE WHO LOOKS AT HIM.

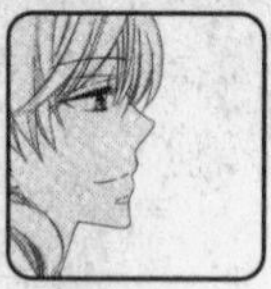

Runa Momochi

THIRD YEAR, CLASS THREE. HANABUSA'S CLASSMATE.

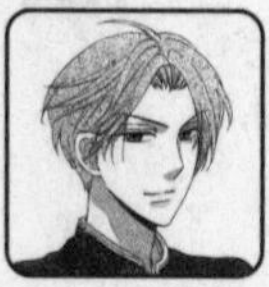

Shuntaro Kosaka

HE'S OBSESSED WITH MANUALS. HE DOESN'T HANDLE UNEXPECTED EVENTS WELL.

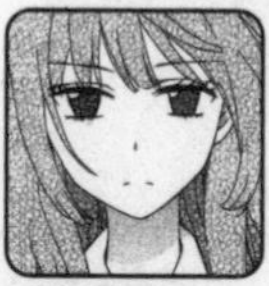

Komari Yukioka

SECOND YEAR, CLASS THREE. KOSAKA'S CLASSMATE.

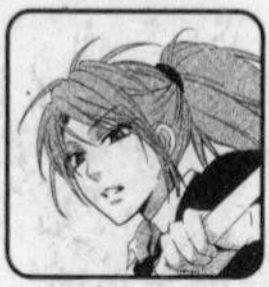

Wakana Hojo

SHE HAS A STOIC ATTITUDE AND WATCHES OVER HANABUSA. SHE HAS FEELINGS FOR YUI.

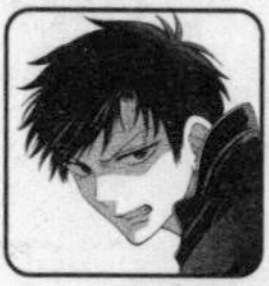

Reito Ayabe

HE LOVES CLEANING AND DIRTY ENVIRONMENTS MAKE HIM STRONGER. HE'S A STUDENT COUNCIL OFFICER, BUT ALSO FRIENDS WITH MAFUYU.

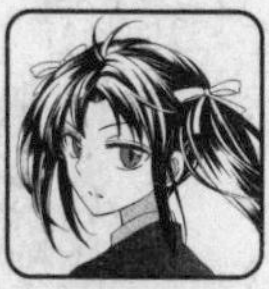

Kanon Nonoguchi

SHE HATES MEN. HER FAMILY RUNS A DOJO, SO SHE'S STRONG. SHE PLANS TO DESTROY THE PUBLIC MORALS CLUB OUT OF GRATITUDE TO MIYABI.

KIYAMA HIGH SCHOOL

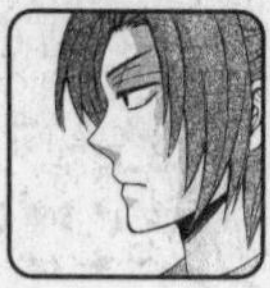

Nogami

THE BANCHO OF KIYAMA HIGH WHO ORDERED KANON'S ABDUCTION. WHAT IS HE REALLY UP TO?

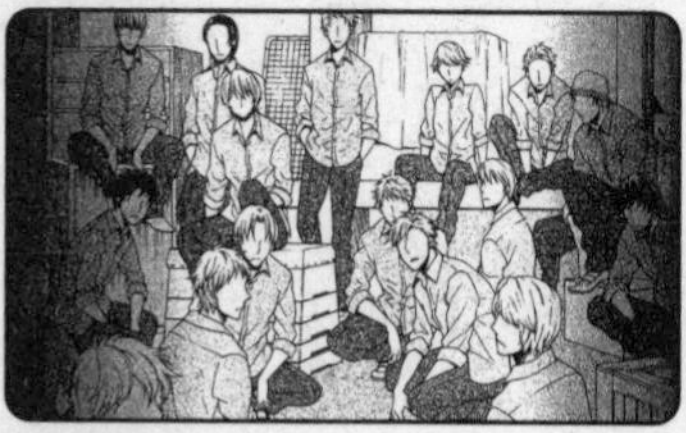

Kiyama Delinquents

THEY HAVE BAD ATTITUDES AND AREN'T VERY SMART.

story

★ MAFUYU KUROSAKI WAS ONCE THE BANCHO WHO CONTROLLED ALL OF SAITAMA, BUT WHEN SHE WAS TRANSFERRED TO MIDORIGAOKA ACADEMY, SHE CHANGED COMPLETELY AND BECAME A NORMAL (BUT SPIRITED) HIGH SCHOOL GIRL...OR AT LEAST SHE WAS SUPPOSED TO! TAKAOMI SAEKI, MAFUYU'S CHILDHOOD FRIEND AND HOMEROOM TEACHER, FORCED HER TO JOIN THE PUBLIC MORALS CLUB, THUS MAKING SURE HER LIFE CONTINUED TO BE FAR FROM AVERAGE.

★ THE PUBLIC MORALS CLUB IS FIGHTING THE STUDENT COUNCIL FOR CONTROL OF MIDORIGAOKA ACADEMY, AND HAVE ALREADY BESTED STUDENT COUNCIL MEMBERS KOSAKA, AND AYABE. AND NOW THEY HAVE A NEW MEMBER NAMED SHIBUYA. THE NEXT STUDENT COUNCIL MEMBER TO OPPOSE THEM IS KANON NONOGUCHI, WHO CONTROLS THE GIRLS-ONLY CLASS, OTHERWISE KNOWN AS G-CLASS. KANON TRIES TO DISCOVER THE TRUE IDENTITIES OF THE PUBLIC MORALS CLUB'S MYSTERIOUS NATSUO AND SUPER BUN. IN ORDER TO GET NATSUO TO REVEAL HIMSELF, KANON SPREADS A RUMOR ABOUT THE INFAMOUS KIYAMA HIGH SCHOOL, BUT KIYAMA HIGH SCHOOL RETALIATES FOR THE SMEAR ON THEIR REPUTATION BY ABDUCTING HER! MAFUYU AND HER FRIENDS CHARGE INTO KIYAMA HIGH SCHOOL TO SAVE KANON, BUT...

ORESAMA TEACHER

Volume 14
CONTENTS

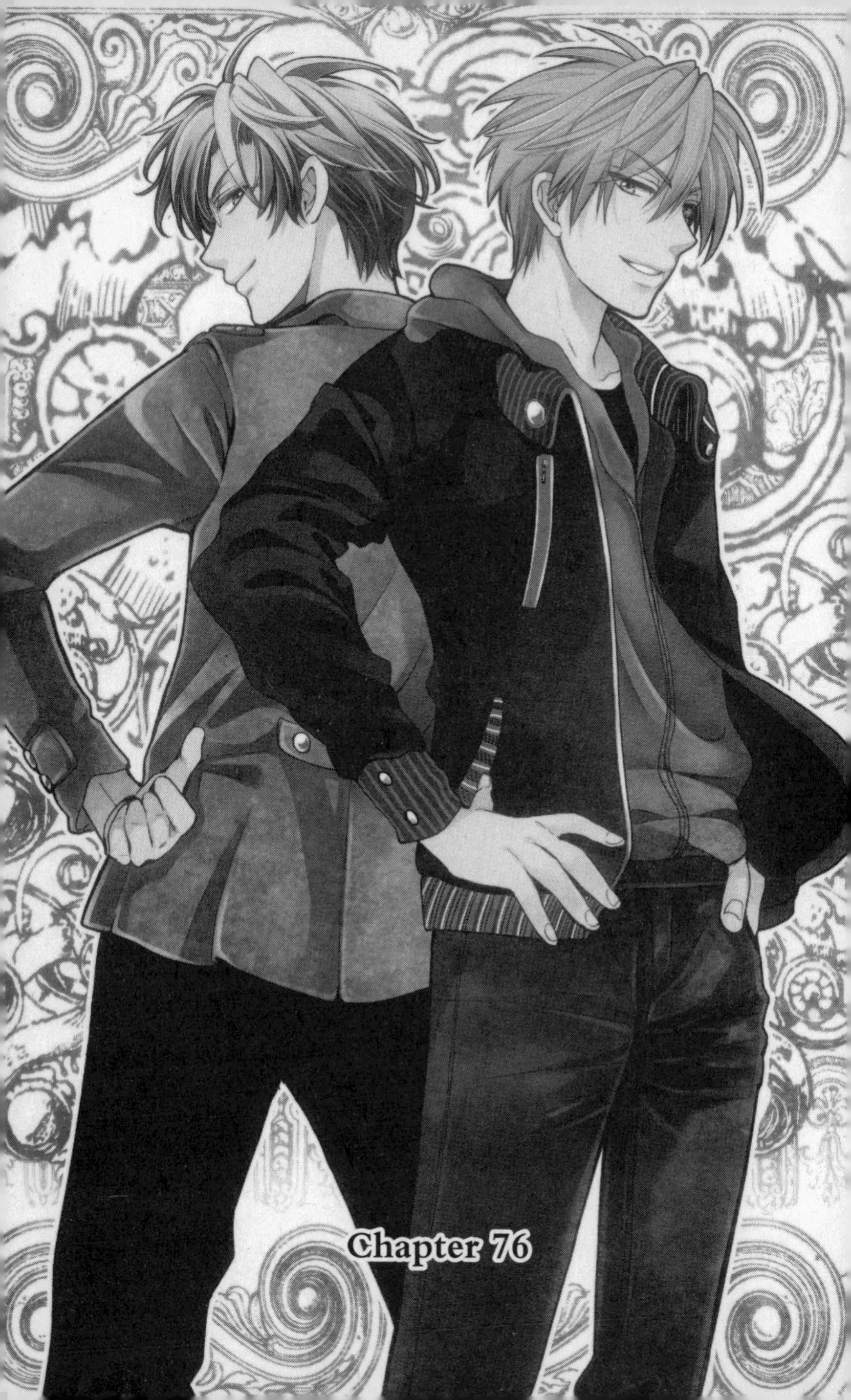
Chapter 76

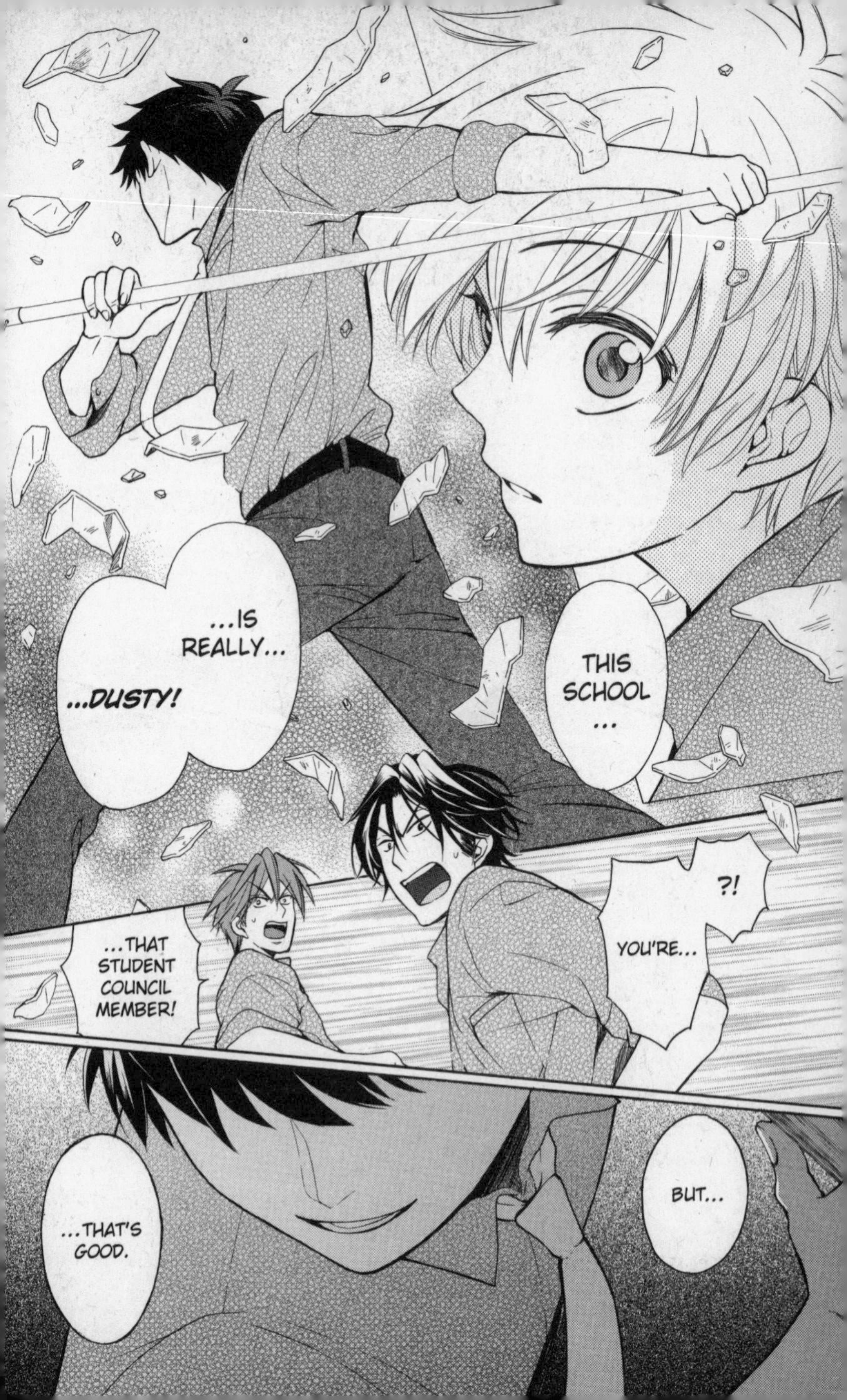
THIS SCHOOL ...
...IS REALLY...
...DUSTY!
?!
YOU'RE...
...THAT STUDENT COUNCIL MEMBER!
BUT...
...THAT'S GOOD.

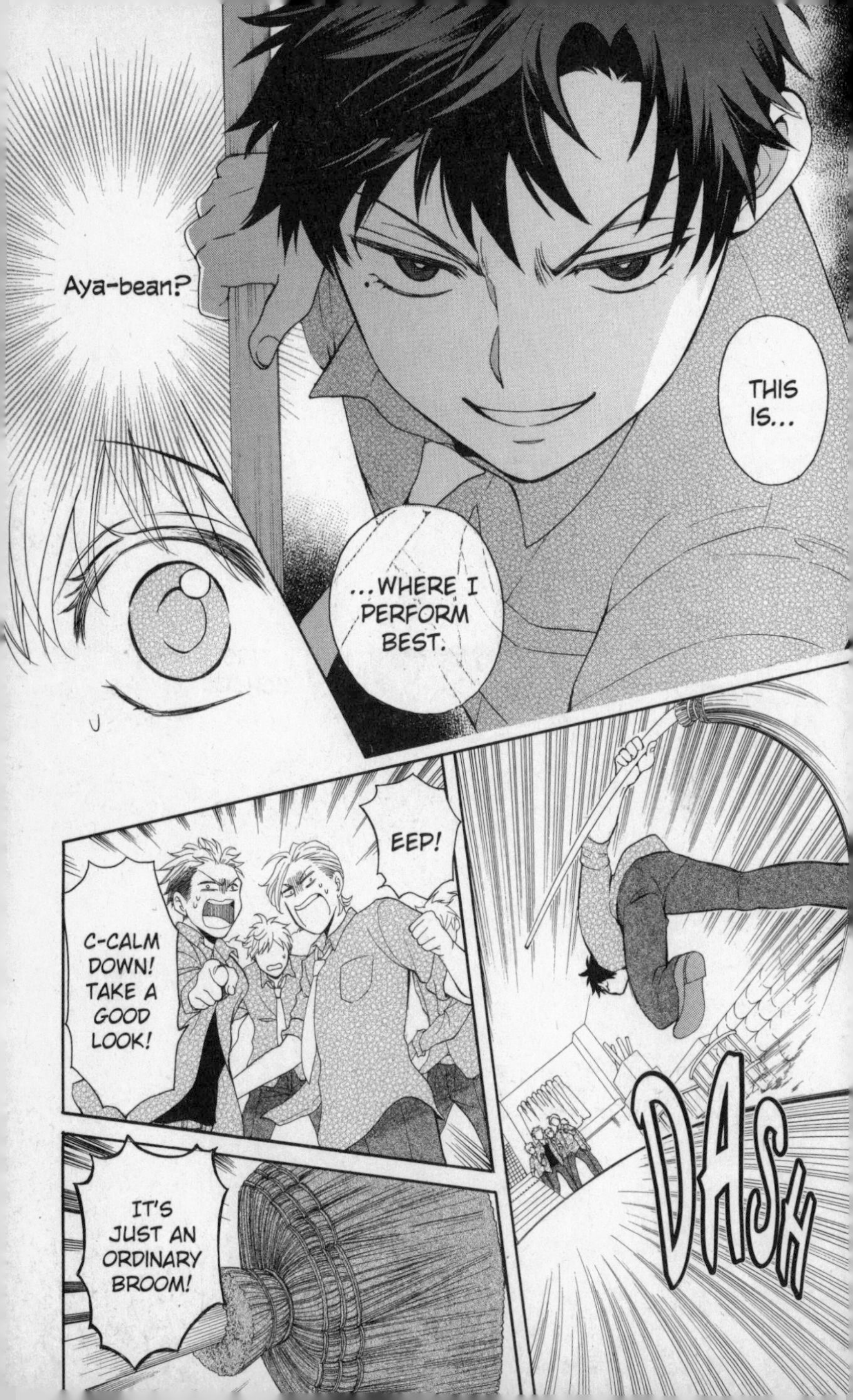
THIS IS...
...WHERE I PERFORM BEST.
Aya-bean?
DASH
EEP!
C-CALM DOWN! TAKE A GOOD LOOK!
IT'S JUST AN ORDINARY BROOM!

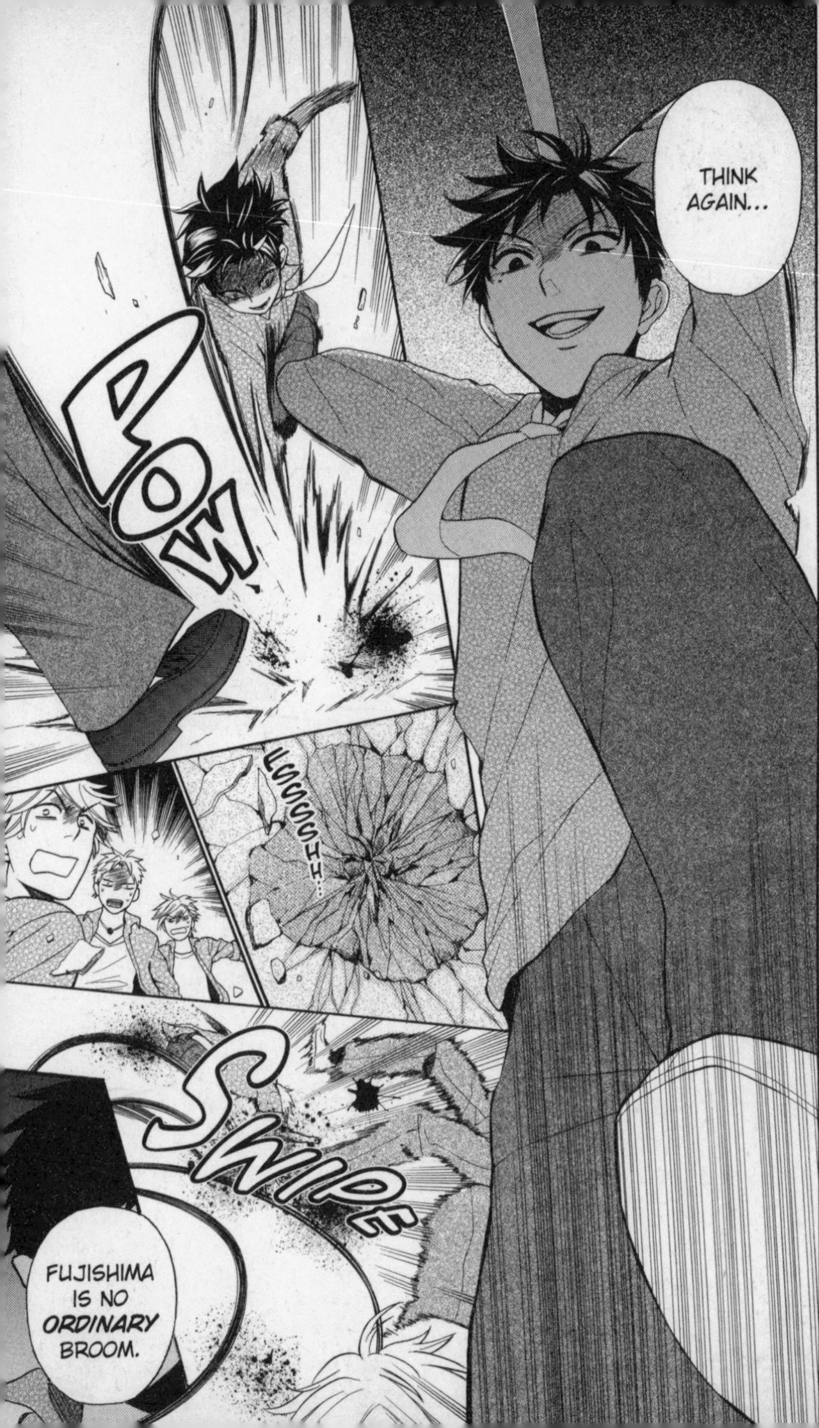
THINK AGAIN...
POW
ESSSSHH...
SWIPE
FUJISHIMA IS NO *ORDINARY* BROOM.

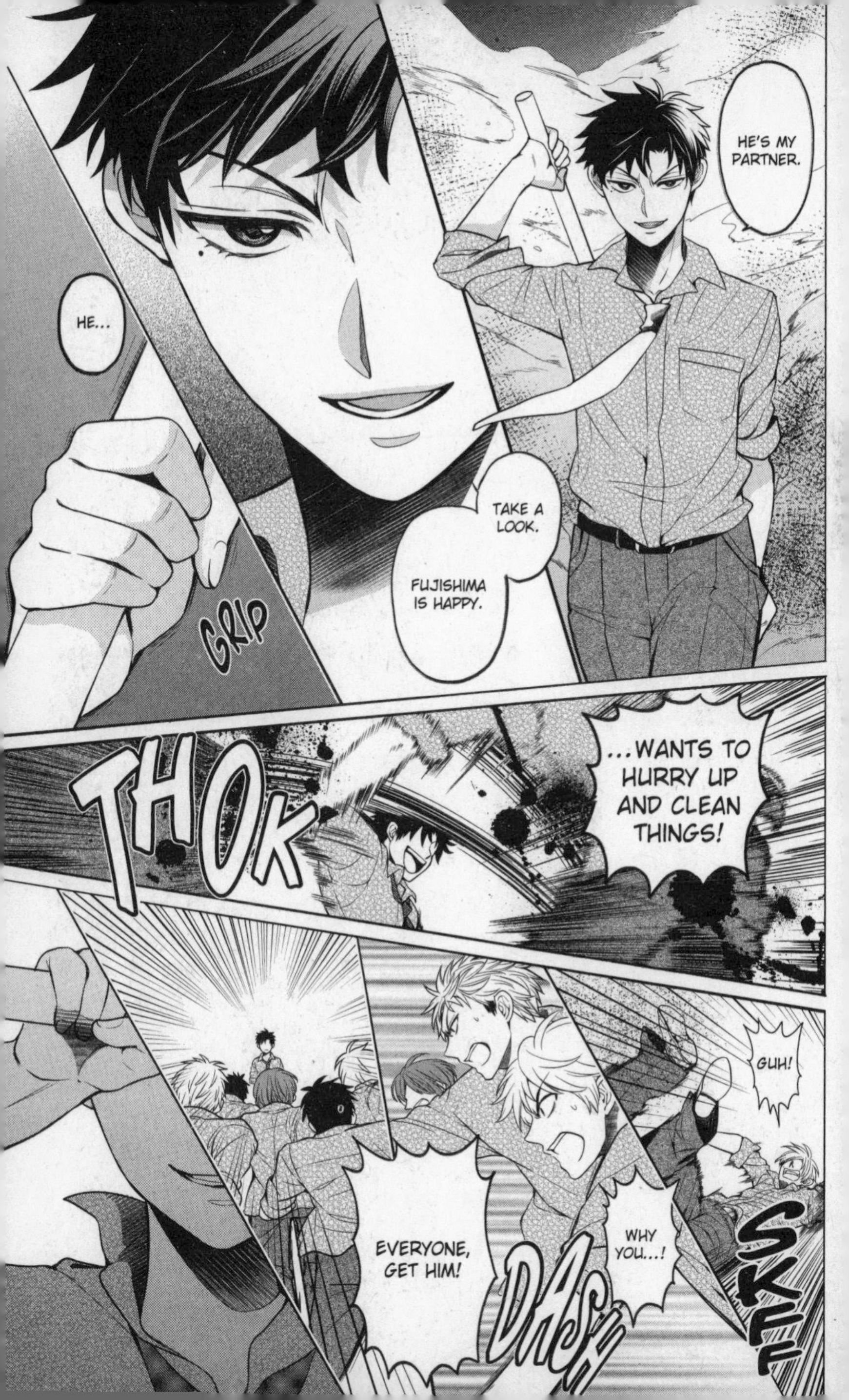
HE'S MY PARTNER.
TAKE A LOOK.
FUJISHIMA IS HAPPY.
HE...
GRIP
...WANTS TO HURRY UP AND CLEAN THINGS!
THOK
GUH!
SKFF
WHY YOU...!
DASH
EVERYONE, GET HIM!

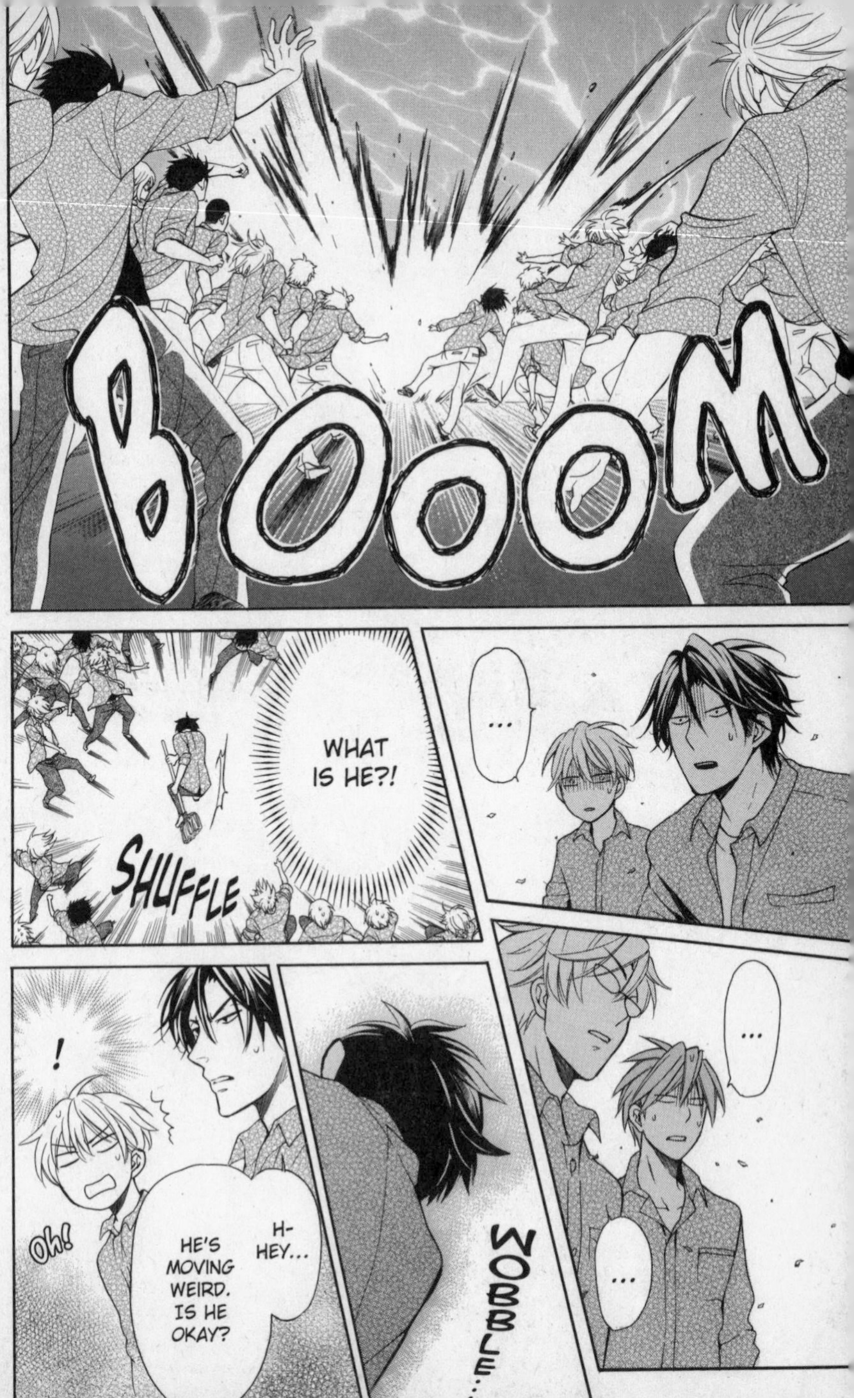
BOOOM
...
WHAT IS HE?!
SHUFFLE
...
...
WOBBLE...
!
H- HEY...
HE'S MOVING WEIRD. IS HE OKAY?
Oh!

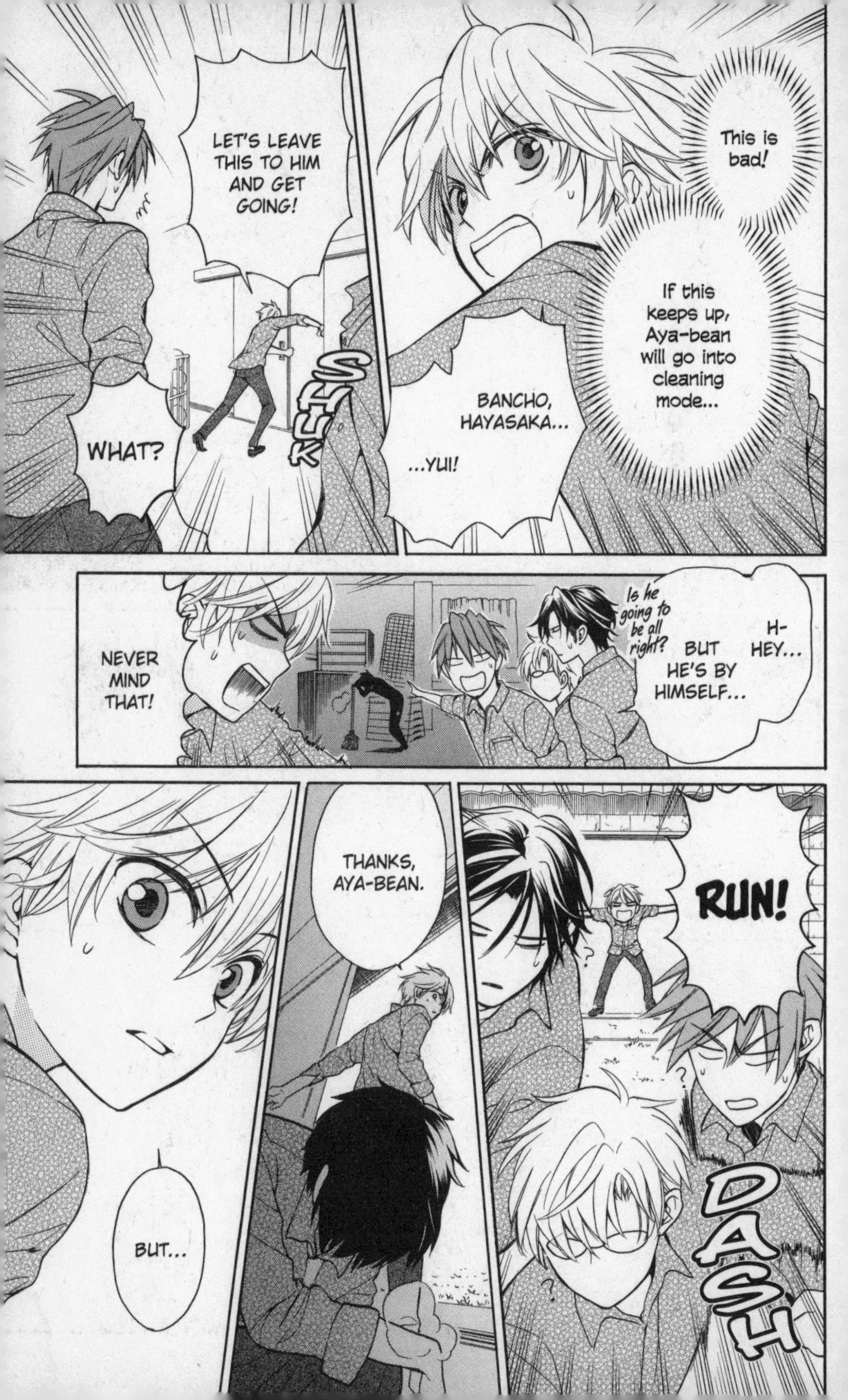
This is bad!
If this keeps up, Aya-bean will go into cleaning mode...
BANCHO, HAYASAKA...
...YUI!
LET'S LEAVE THIS TO HIM AND GET GOING!
SHUK
WHAT?
H-HEY...
BUT HE'S BY HIMSELF...
Is he going to be all right?
NEVER MIND THAT!
RUN!
DASH
THANKS, AYA-BEAN.
BUT...

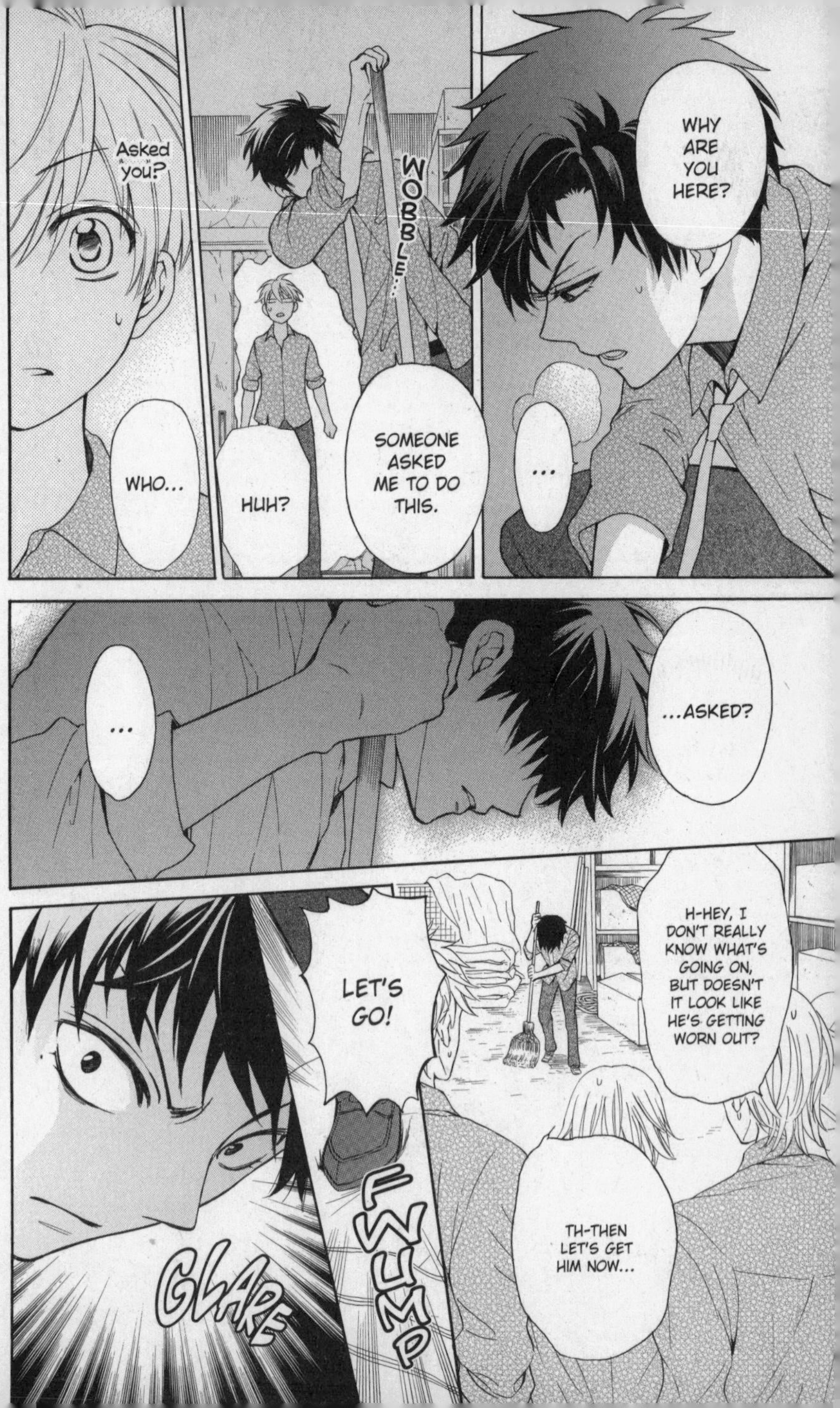
WHY ARE YOU HERE?
...
WOBBLE...
SOMEONE ASKED ME TO DO THIS.
HUH?
Asked you?
WHO...
...ASKED?
...
H-HEY, I DON'T REALLY KNOW WHAT'S GOING ON, BUT DOESN'T IT LOOK LIKE HE'S GETTING WORN OUT?
TH-THEN LET'S GET HIM NOW...
LET'S GO!
FWUMP
GLARE

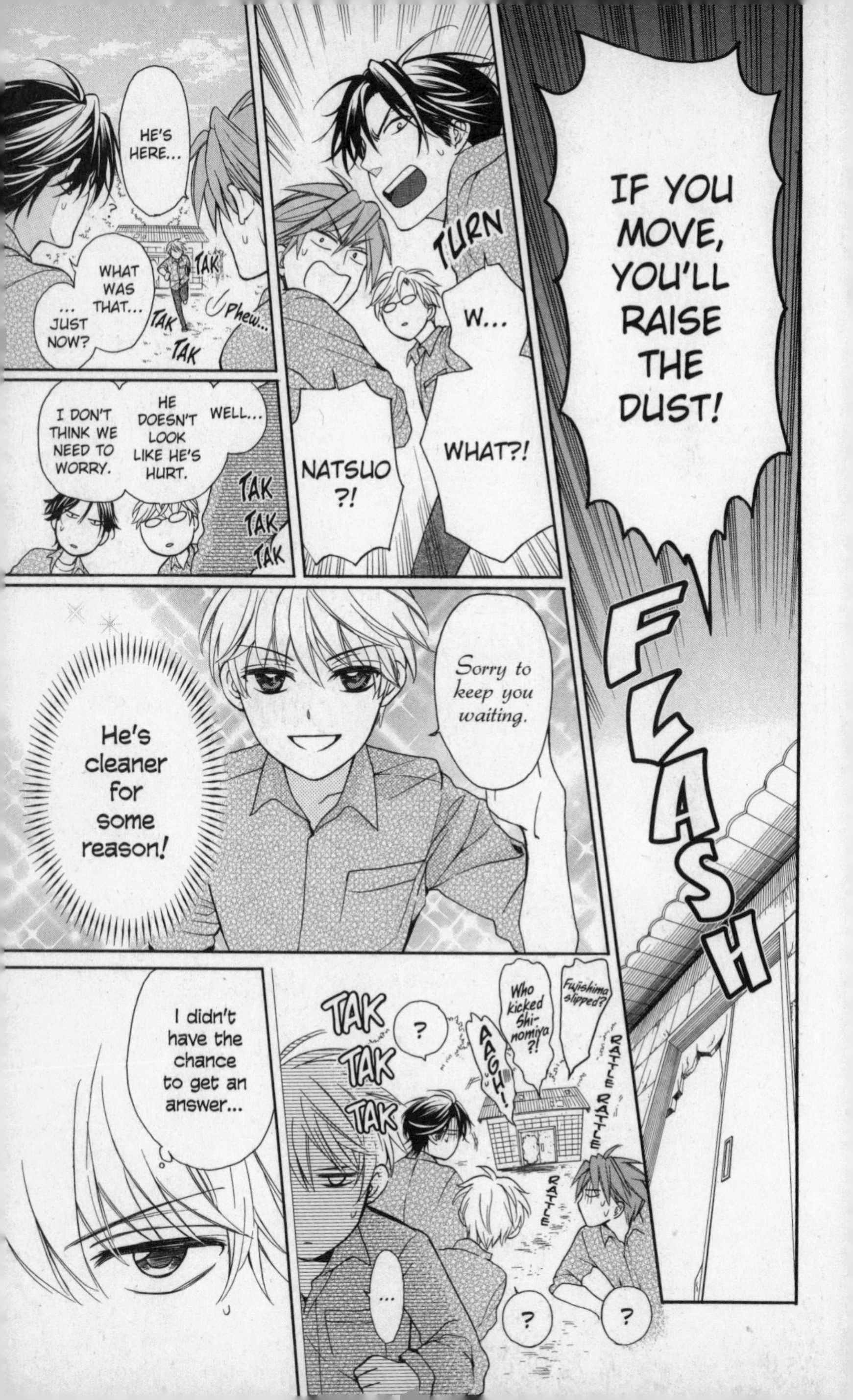
IF YOU MOVE, YOU'LL RAISE THE DUST!
FLASH
TURN
W...
WHAT?!
NATSUO?!
HE'S HERE...
?
TAK
Phew...
TAK
TAK
WHAT WAS THAT... ...JUST NOW?
WELL...
HE DOESN'T LOOK LIKE HE'S HURT.
I DON'T THINK WE NEED TO WORRY.
TAK
TAK
TAK
Sorry to keep you waiting.
He's cleaner for some reason!
Fujishima slipped?
RATTLE RATTLE
Who kicked Shi-nomiya?!
AAGH!
RATTLE
?
TAK
TAK
TAK
...
?
?
I didn't have the chance to get an answer...

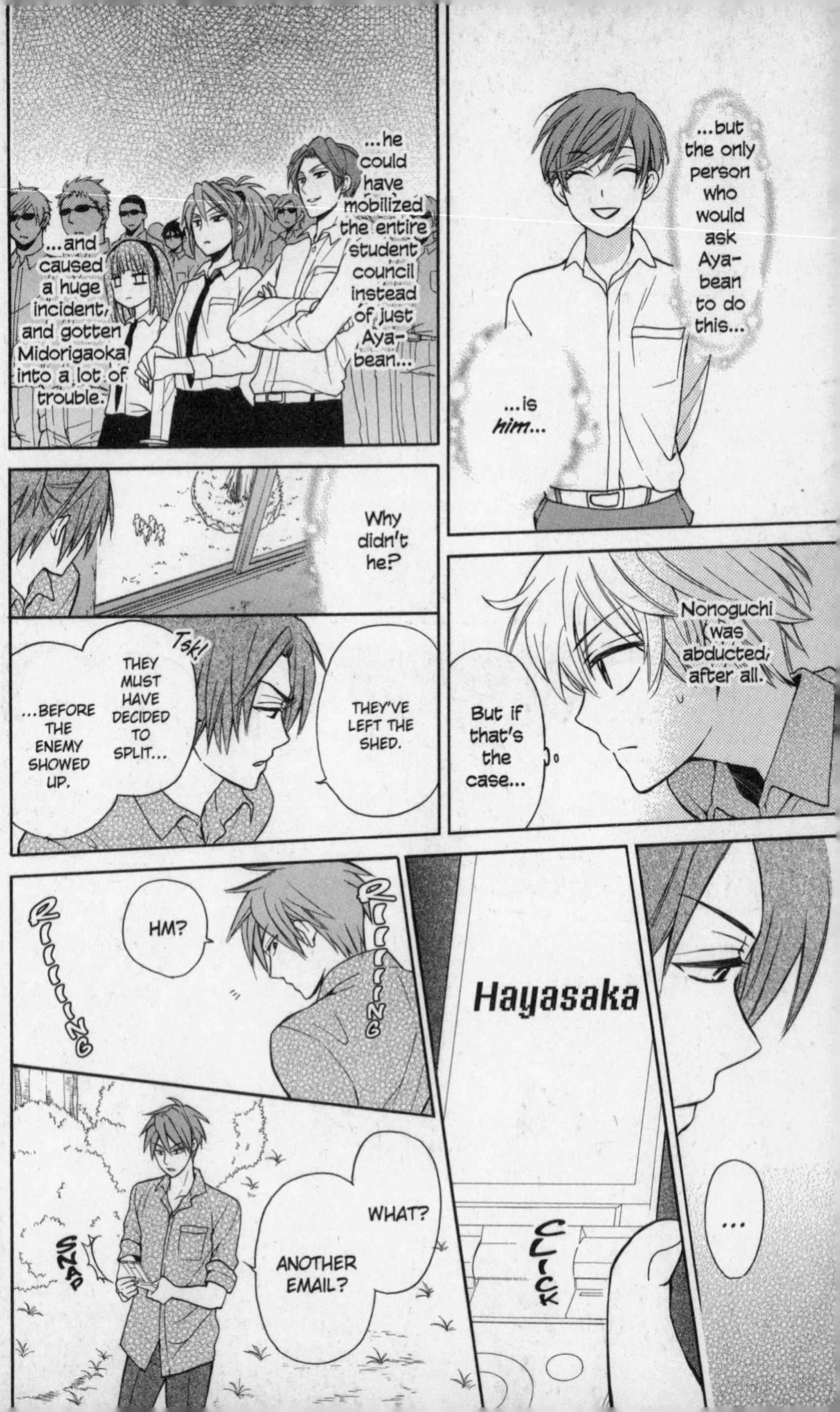

...but the only person who would ask Aya-bean to do this...
...is *him*...
...he could have mobilized the entire student council instead of just Aya-bean...
...and caused a huge incident, and gotten Midorigaoka into a lot of trouble.
Why didn't he?
Nonoguchi was abducted, after all.
But if that's the case...
THEY'VE LEFT THE SHED.
Tsk!
THEY MUST HAVE DECIDED TO SPLIT...
...BEFORE THE ENEMY SHOWED UP.
...
Hayasaka
CLICK
RIIIING
HM?
RIIIING
WHAT?
ANOTHER EMAIL?
SNAP

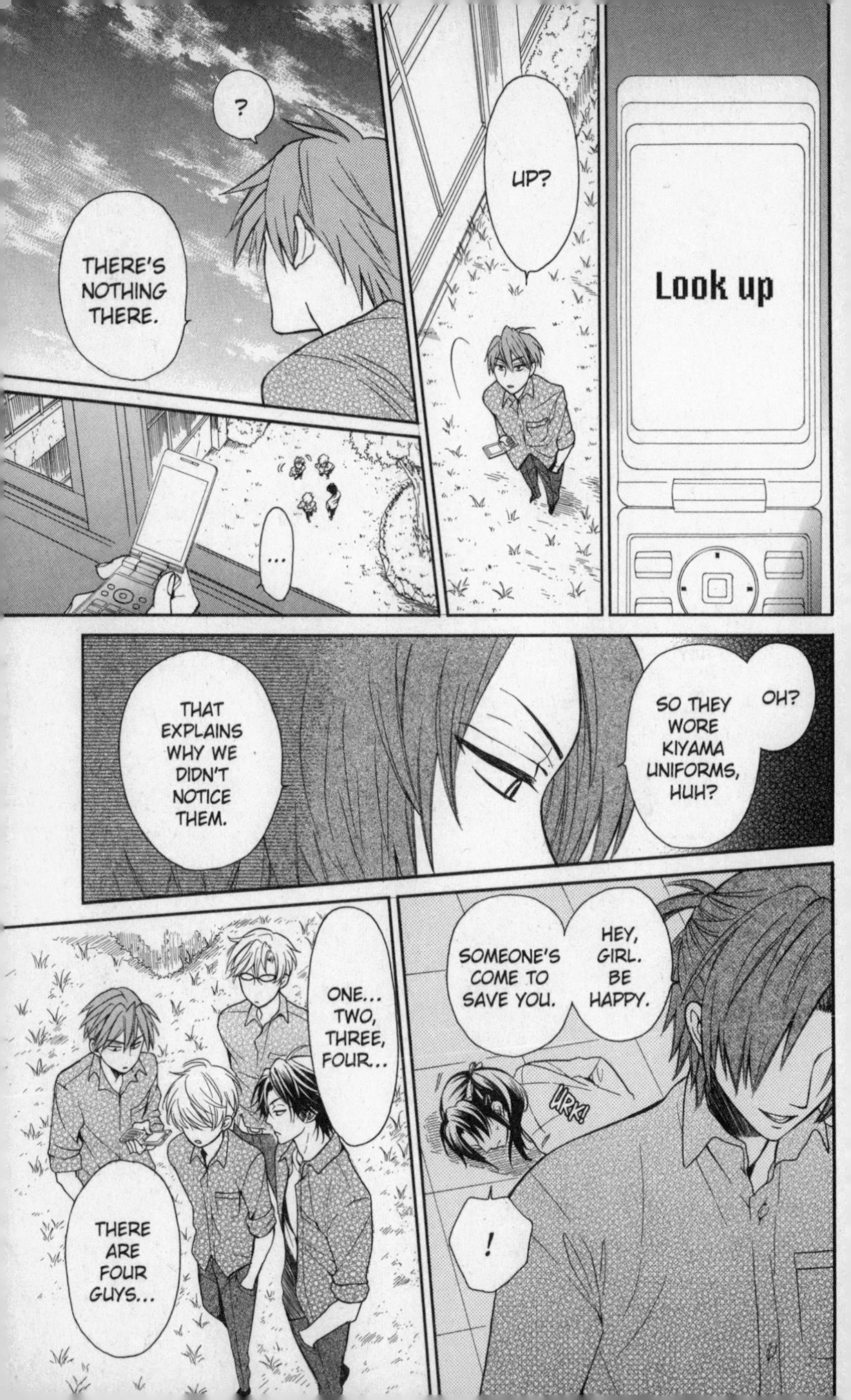
Look up
UP?
?
THERE'S NOTHING THERE.
...
OH?
SO THEY WORE KIYAMA UNIFORMS, HUH?
THAT EXPLAINS WHY WE DIDN'T NOTICE THEM.
HEY, GIRL. BE HAPPY.
SOMEONE'S COME TO SAVE YOU.
URK!
!
ONE... TWO, THREE, FOUR...
THERE ARE FOUR GUYS...

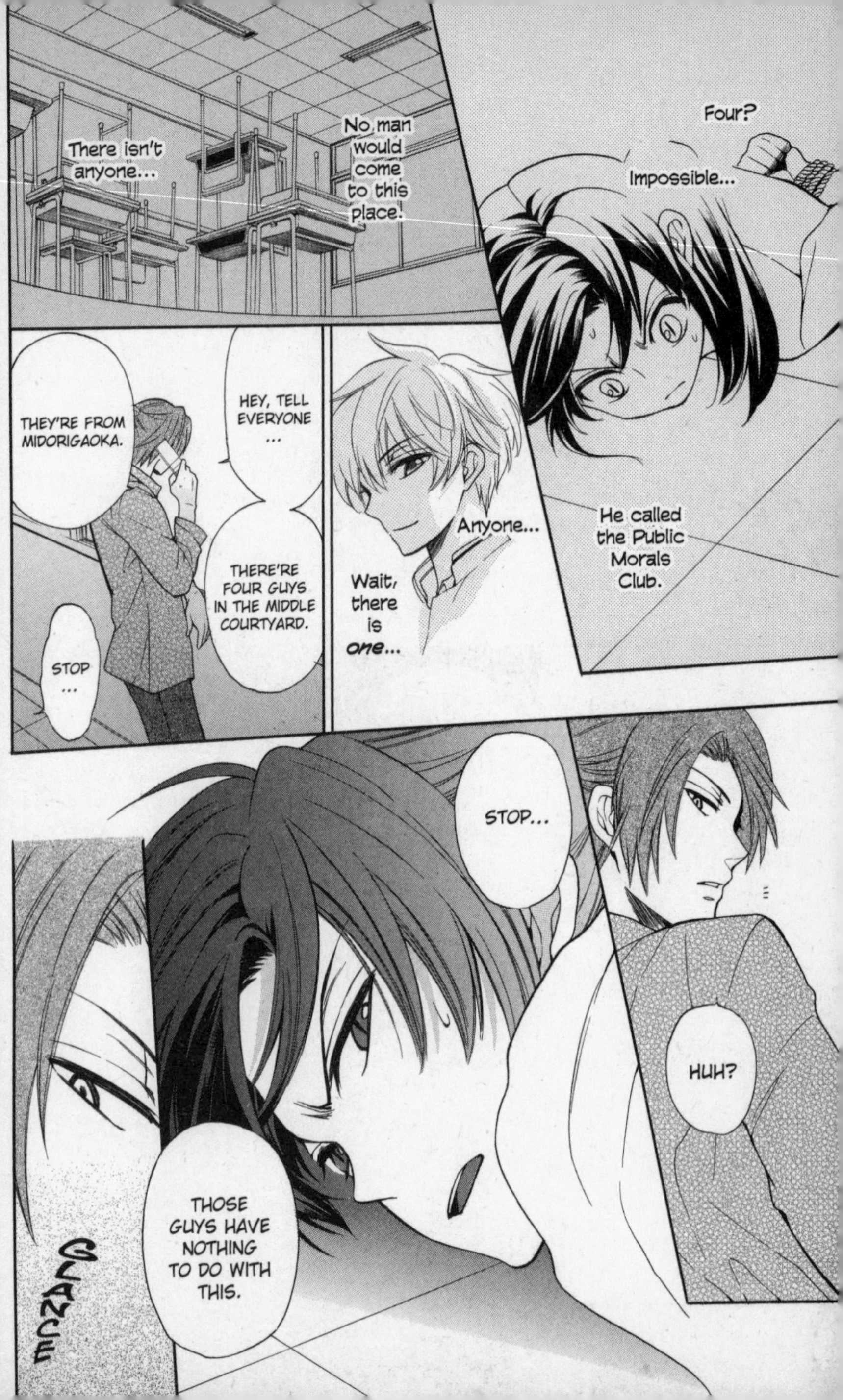
Four?
Impossible...
He called the Public Morals Club.
No man would come to this place.
There isn't anyone...
Anyone...
Wait, there is *one*...
HEY, TELL EVERYONE ...
THERE'RE FOUR GUYS IN THE MIDDLE COURTYARD.
THEY'RE FROM MIDORIGAOKA.
STOP ...
STOP...
HUH?
THOSE GUYS HAVE NOTHING TO DO WITH THIS.
GLANCE

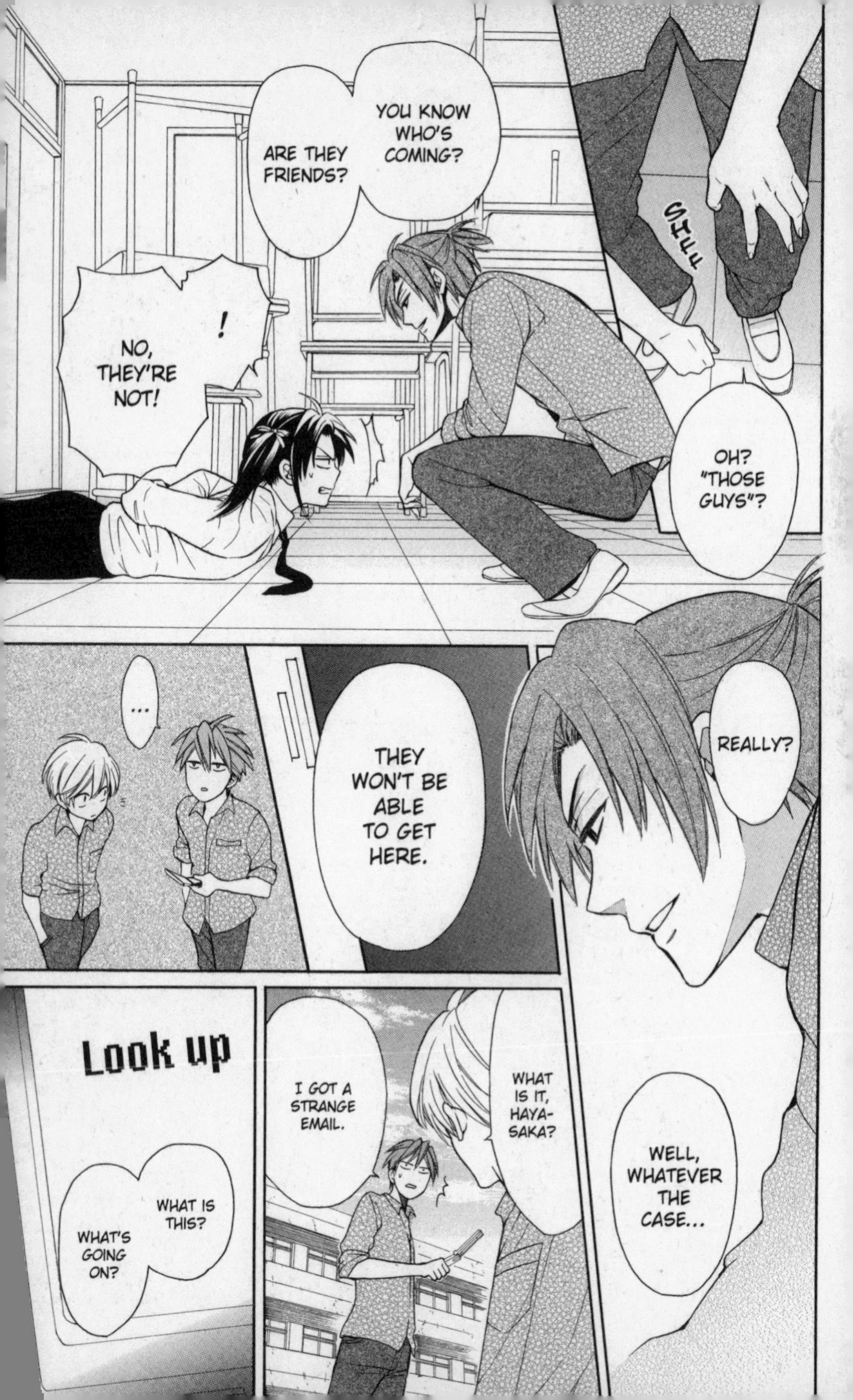
SHFF
OH? "THOSE GUYS"?
YOU KNOW WHO'S COMING?
ARE THEY FRIENDS?
!
NO, THEY'RE NOT!
REALLY?
THEY WON'T BE ABLE TO GET HERE.
...
WELL, WHATEVER THE CASE...
WHAT IS IT, HAYA-SAKA?
I GOT A STRANGE EMAIL.
Look up
WHAT IS THIS?
WHAT'S GOING ON?

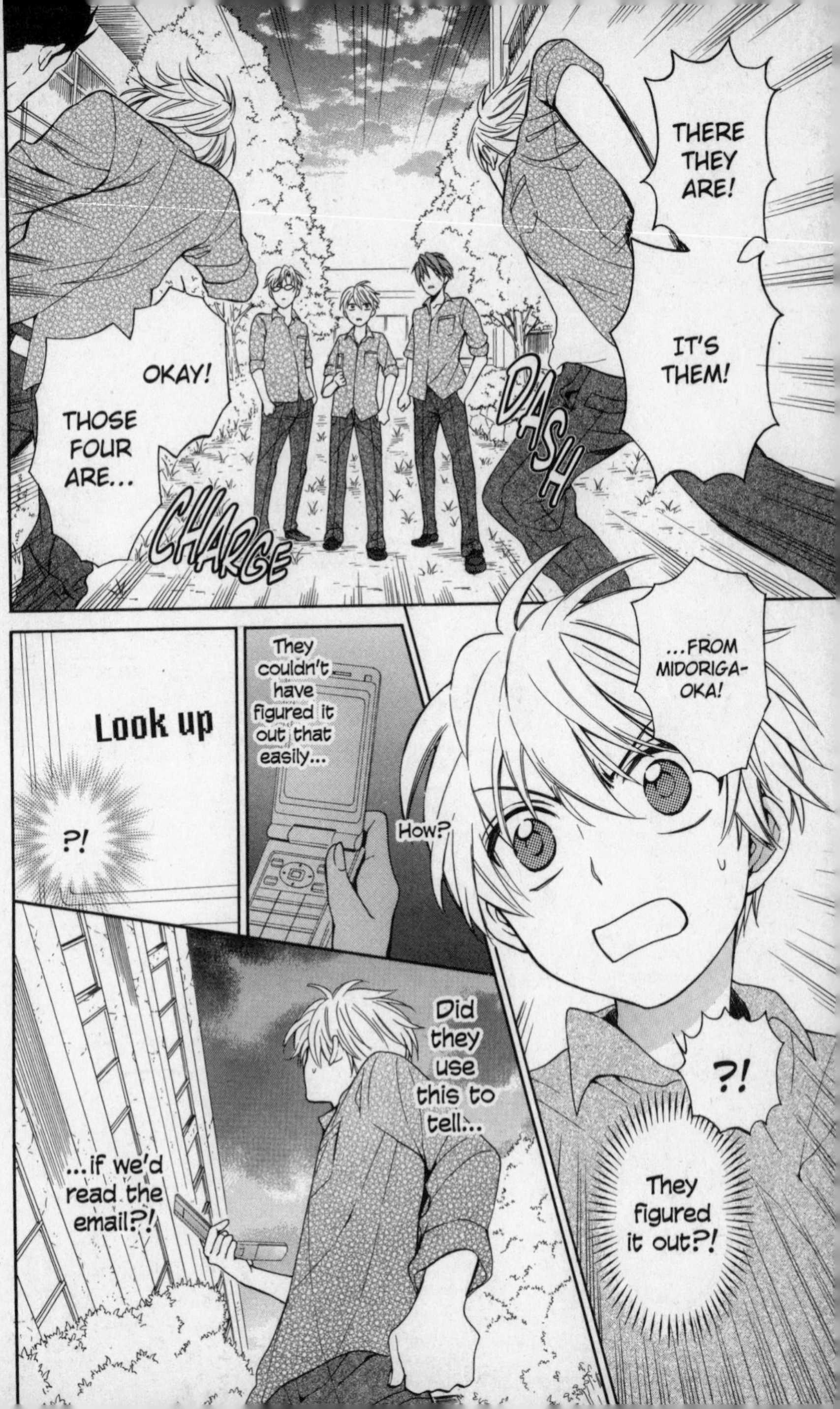
THERE THEY ARE!
IT'S THEM!
DASH
OKAY!
THOSE FOUR ARE...
CHARGE
...FROM MIDORIGA-OKA!
?!
They figured it out?!
They couldn't have figured it out that easily...
How?
Look up
?!
Did they use this to tell...
...if we'd read the email?!

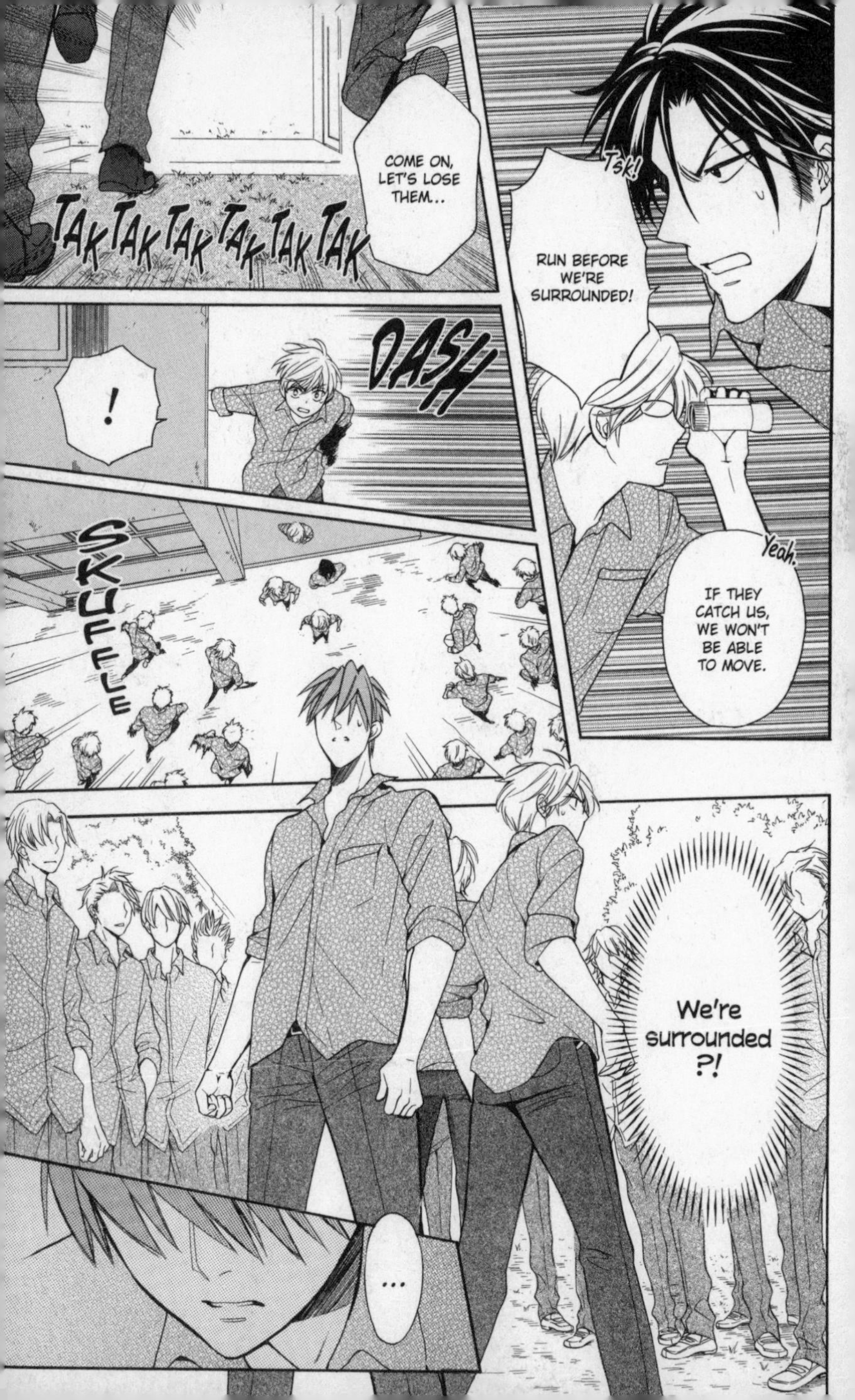
Tsk!
RUN BEFORE WE'RE SURROUNDED!
Yeah.
IF THEY CATCH US, WE WON'T BE ABLE TO MOVE.
COME ON, LET'S LOSE THEM...
TAK TAK TAK TAK TAK TAK
DASH
!
SKUFFLE
We're surrounded ?!
...

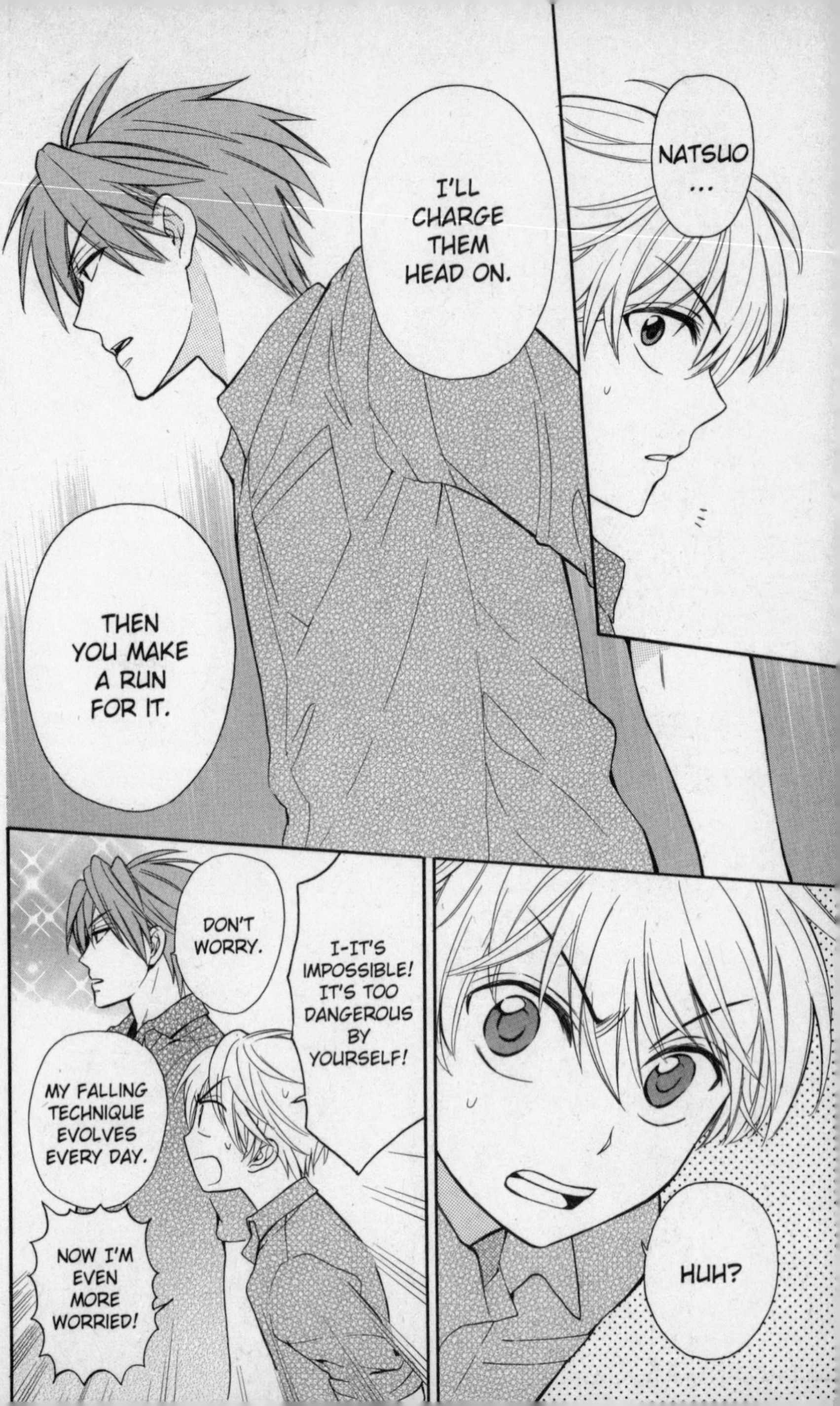
I'LL CHARGE THEM HEAD ON.
THEN YOU MAKE A RUN FOR IT.
NATSUO ...
HUH?
I-IT'S IMPOSSIBLE! IT'S TOO DANGEROUS BY YOURSELF!
DON'T WORRY.
MY FALLING TECHNIQUE EVOLVES EVERY DAY.
NOW I'M EVEN MORE WORRIED!

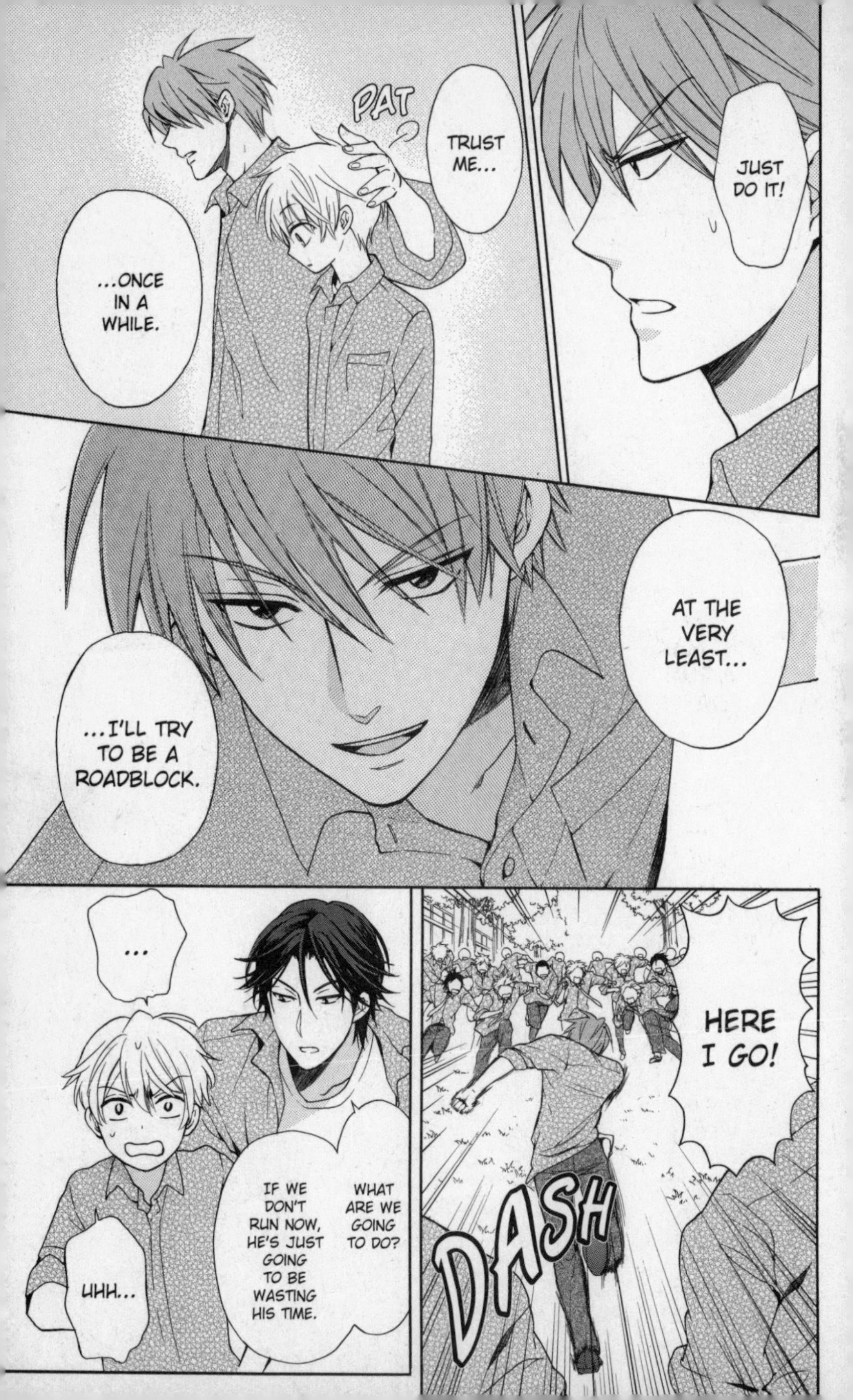
JUST DO IT!
PAT
TRUST ME...
...ONCE IN A WHILE.
AT THE VERY LEAST...
...I'LL TRY TO BE A ROADBLOCK.
HERE I GO!
DASH
...
WHAT ARE WE GOING TO DO?
IF WE DON'T RUN NOW, HE'S JUST GOING TO BE WASTING HIS TIME.
UHH...

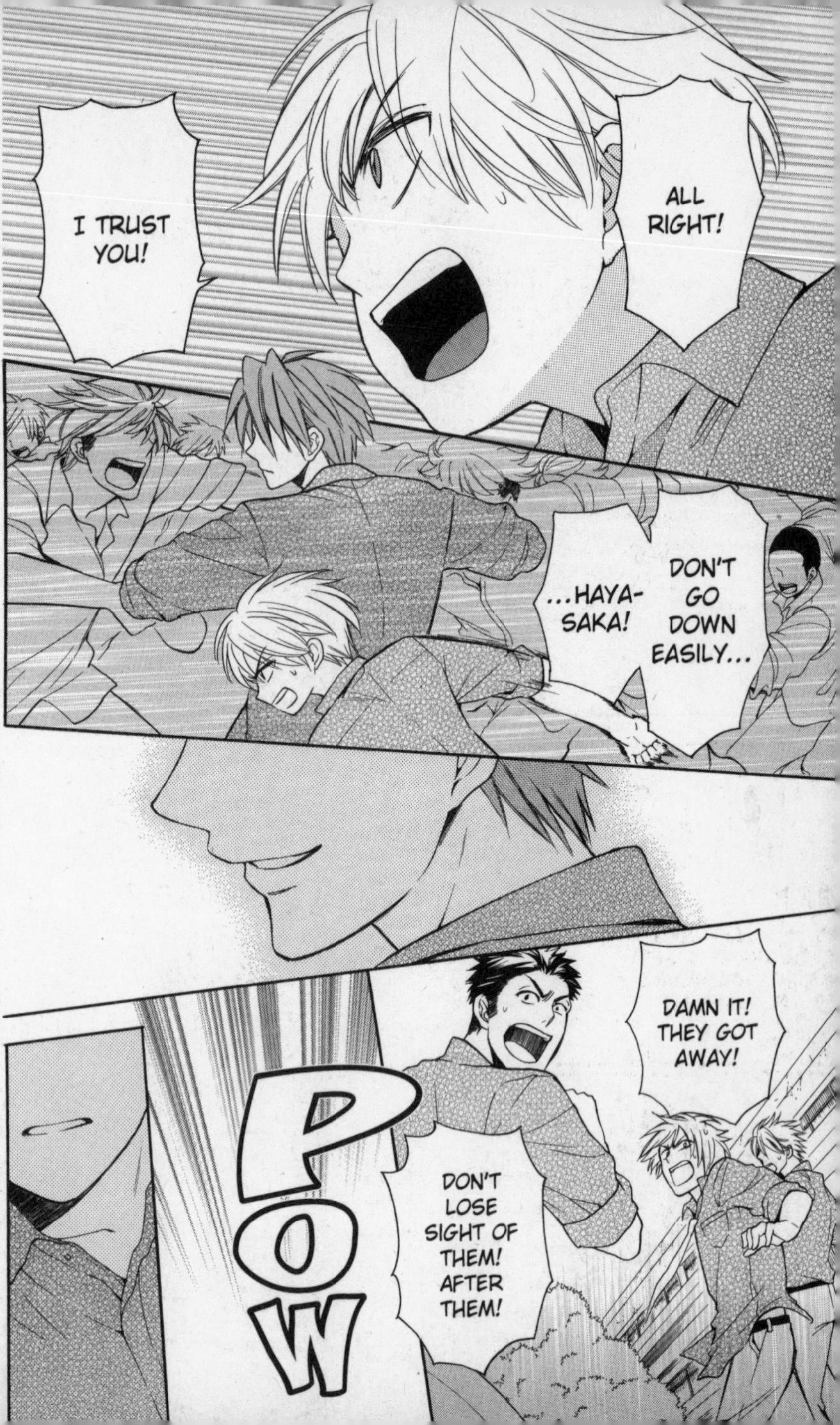
ALL RIGHT!
I TRUST YOU!
DON'T GO DOWN EASILY...
...HAYA-SAKA!
DAMN IT! THEY GOT AWAY!
DON'T LOSE SIGHT OF THEM! AFTER THEM!
POW

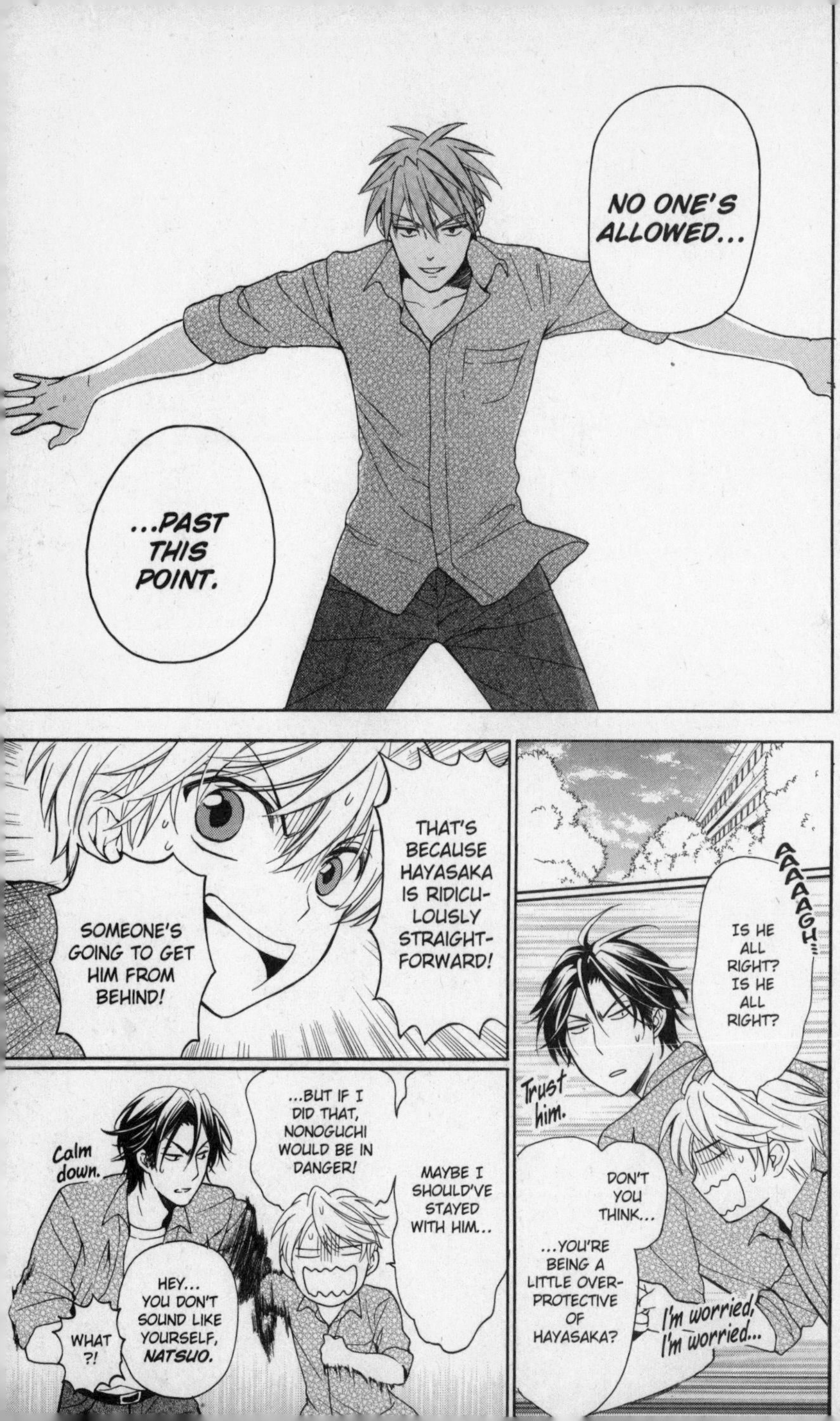
NO ONE'S ALLOWED...
...PAST THIS POINT.
AAAAAGH!!
IS HE ALL RIGHT? IS HE ALL RIGHT?
Trust him.
DON'T YOU THINK...
...YOU'RE BEING A LITTLE OVER-PROTECTIVE OF HAYASAKA?
I'm worried, I'm worried...
THAT'S BECAUSE HAYASAKA IS RIDICULOUSLY STRAIGHT-FORWARD!
SOMEONE'S GOING TO GET HIM FROM BEHIND!
...BUT IF I DID THAT, NONOGUCHI WOULD BE IN DANGER!
MAYBE I SHOULD'VE STAYED WITH HIM...
Calm down.
HEY... YOU DON'T SOUND LIKE YOURSELF, **NATSUO.**
WHAT?!

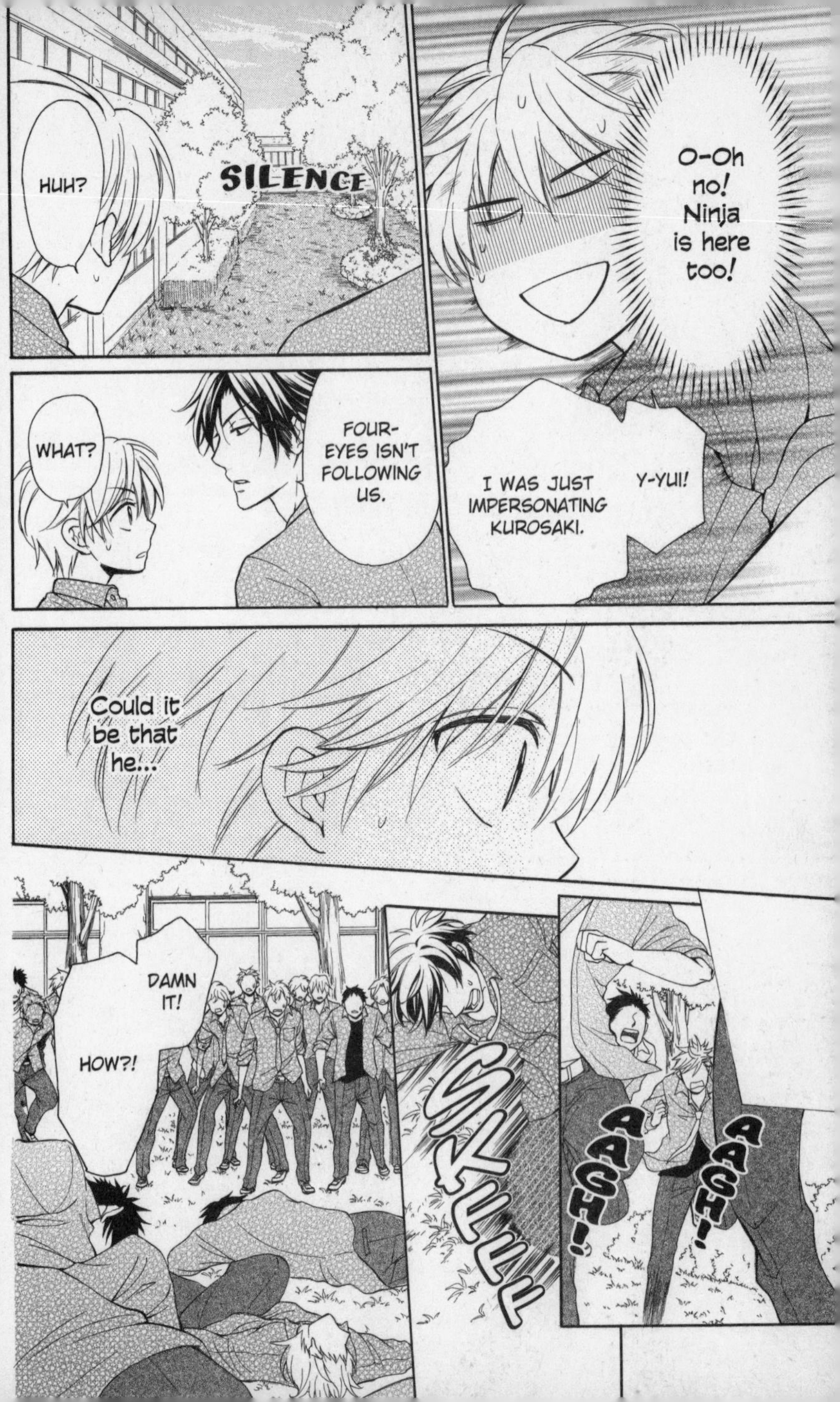
O-Oh no! Ninja is here too!
Y-YUI!
I WAS JUST IMPERSONATING KUROSAKI.
HUH?
SILENCE
FOUR-EYES ISN'T FOLLOWING US.
WHAT?
Could it be that he...
AACH!
AACH!
SKFFF
DAMN IT!
HOW?!

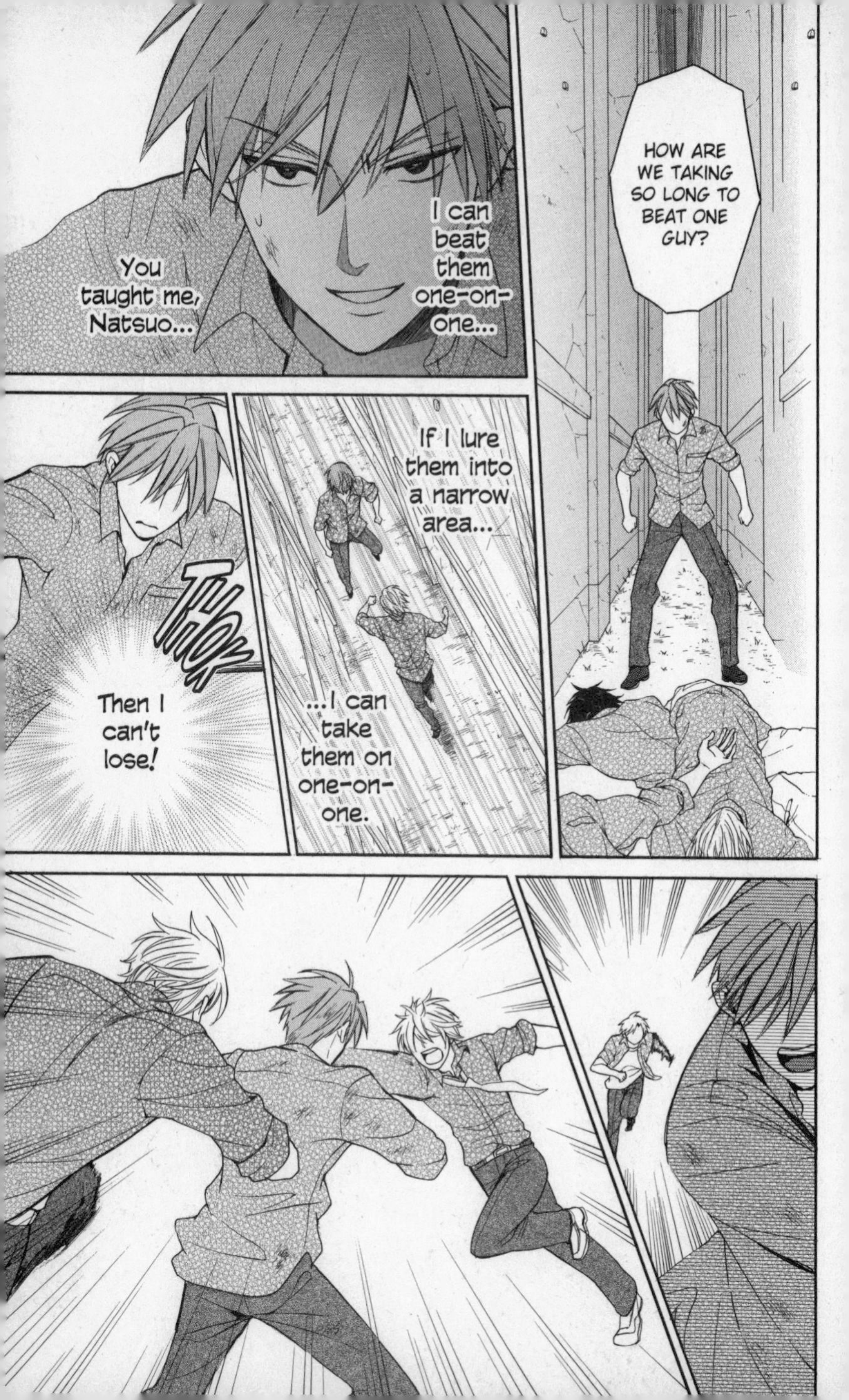
HOW ARE WE TAKING SO LONG TO BEAT ONE GUY?
I can beat them one-on-one...
You taught me, Natsuo...
If I lure them into a narrow area...
...I can take them on one-on-one.
THOK
Then I can't lose!

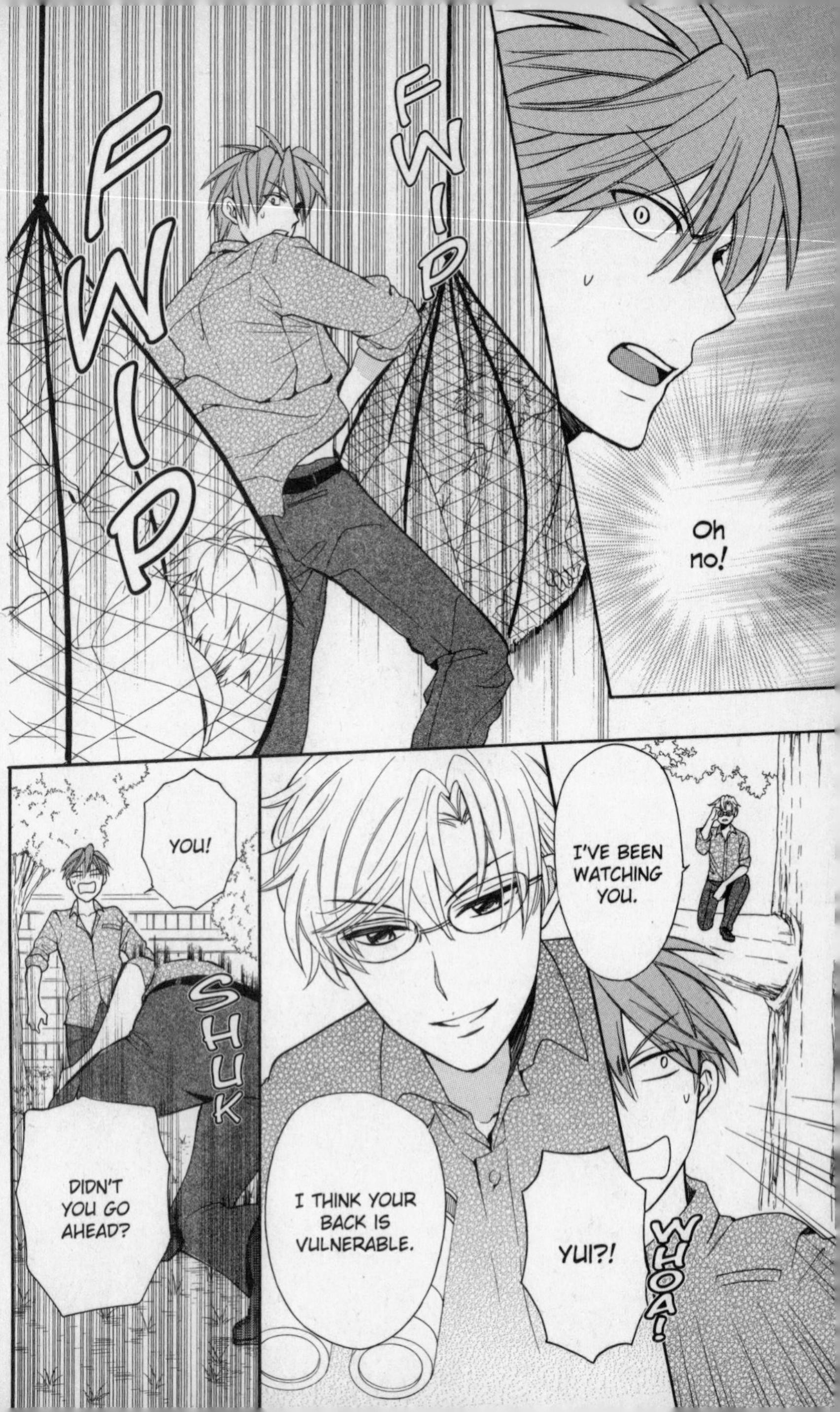
Oh no!
FWIP
FWIP
I'VE BEEN WATCHING YOU.
WHOA!
YUI?!
I THINK YOUR BACK IS VULNERABLE.
YOU!
SHUK
DIDN'T YOU GO AHEAD?

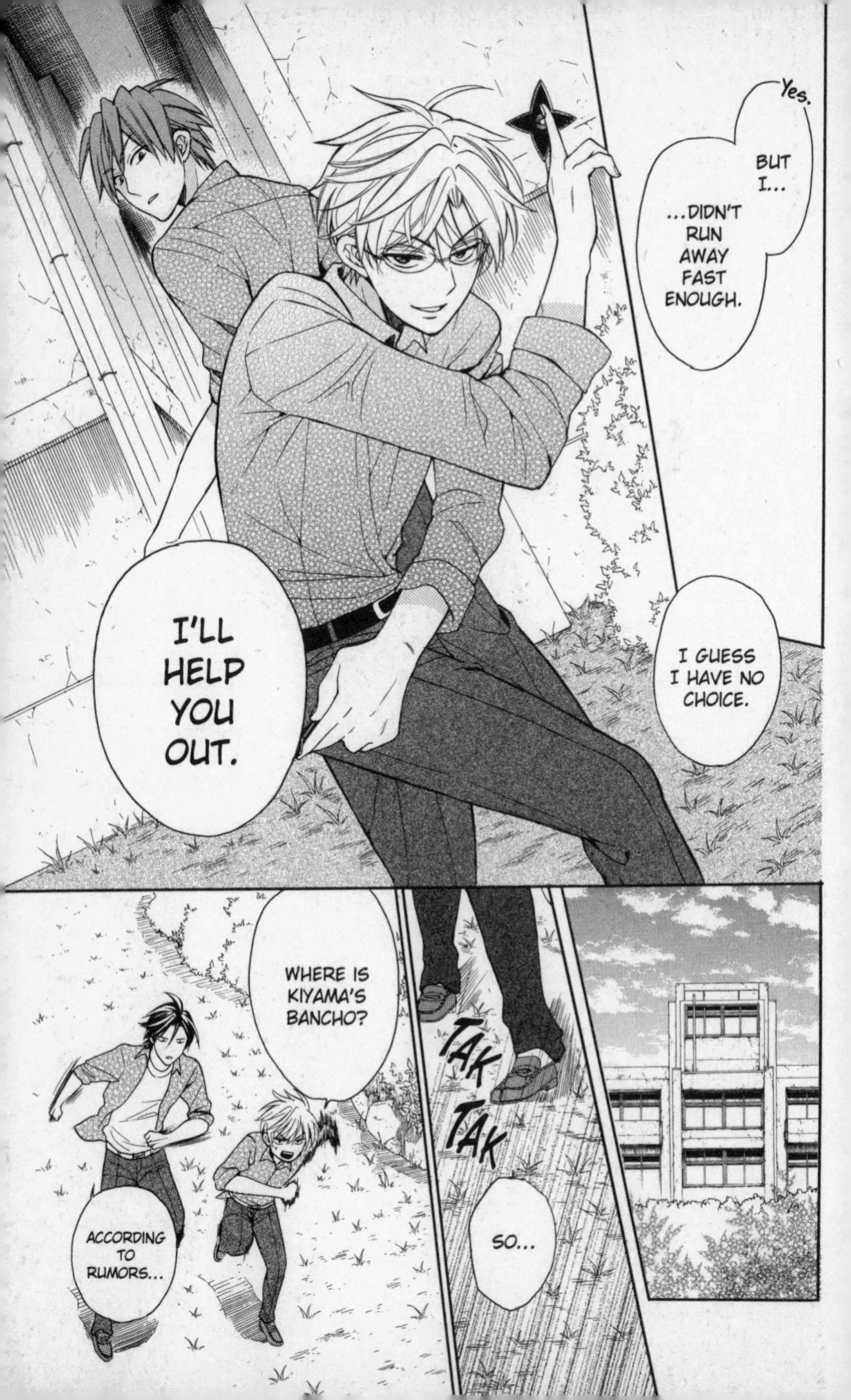
Yes.
BUT I...
...DIDN'T RUN AWAY FAST ENOUGH.
I GUESS I HAVE NO CHOICE.
I'LL HELP YOU OUT.
TAK TAK
SO...
WHERE IS KIYAMA'S BANCHO?
ACCORDING TO RUMORS...

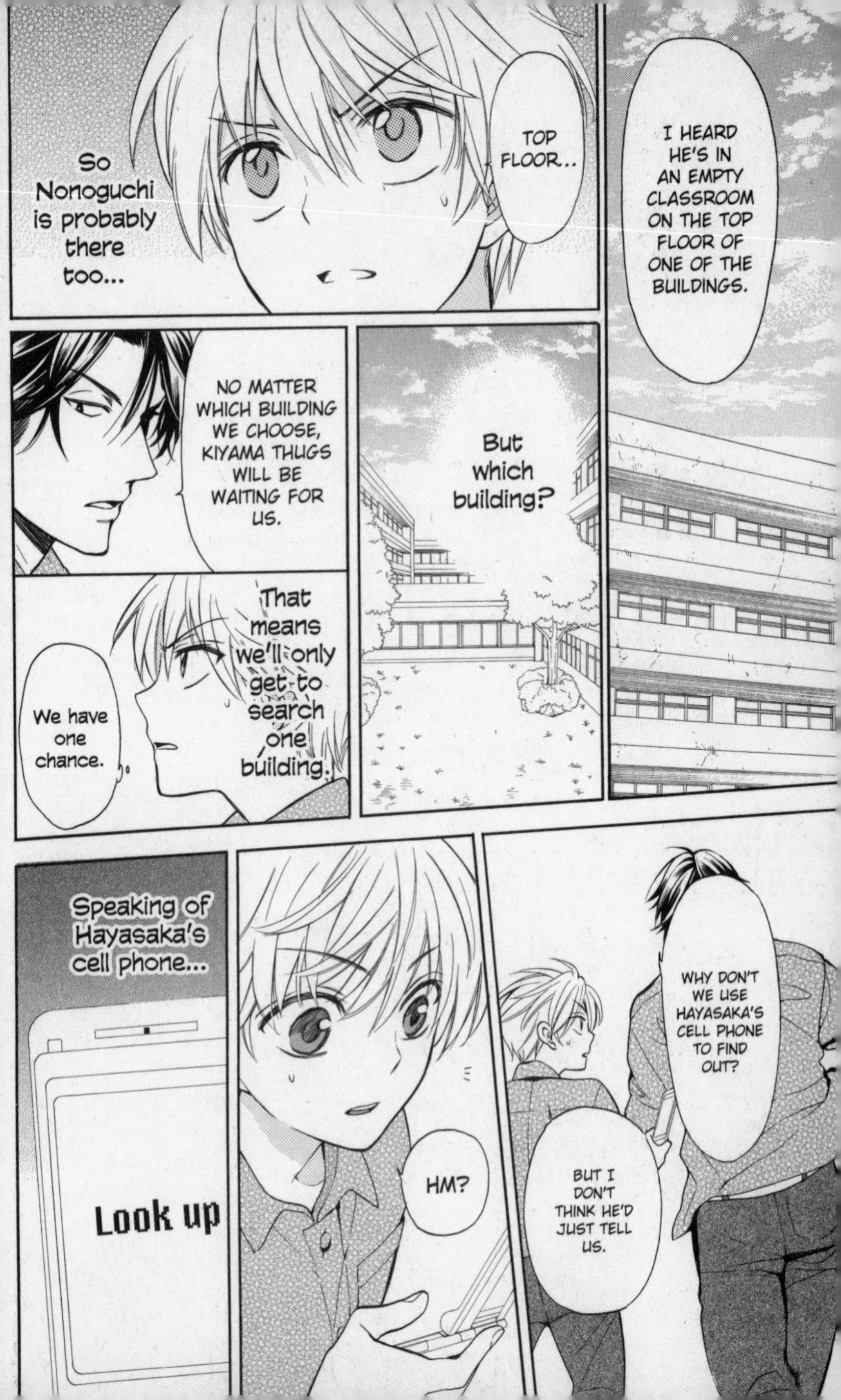
I HEARD HE'S IN AN EMPTY CLASSROOM ON THE TOP FLOOR OF ONE OF THE BUILDINGS.
TOP FLOOR...
So Nonoguchi is probably there too...
But which building?
NO MATTER WHICH BUILDING WE CHOOSE, KIYAMA THUGS WILL BE WAITING FOR US.
That means we'll only get to search one building.
We have one chance.
WHY DON'T WE USE HAYASAKA'S CELL PHONE TO FIND OUT?
BUT I DON'T THINK HE'D JUST TELL US.
HM?
Speaking of Hayasaka's cell phone...
Look up

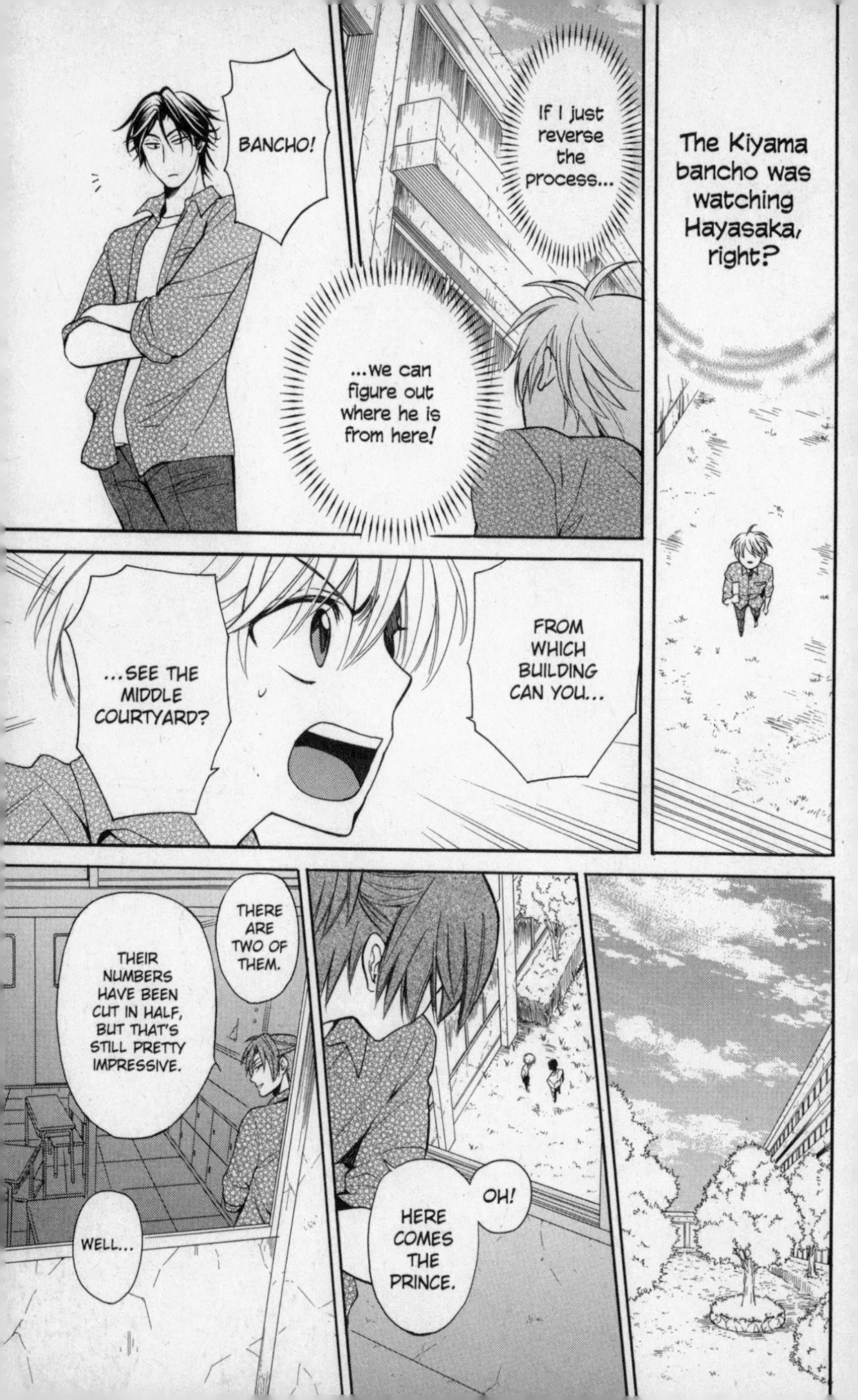
The Kiyama bancho was watching Hayasaka, right?
If I just reverse the process...
...we can figure out where he is from here!
BANCHO!
FROM WHICH BUILDING CAN YOU...
...SEE THE MIDDLE COURTYARD?
OH!
HERE COMES THE PRINCE.
THERE ARE TWO OF THEM.
THEIR NUMBERS HAVE BEEN CUT IN HALF, BUT THAT'S STILL PRETTY IMPRESSIVE.
WELL...

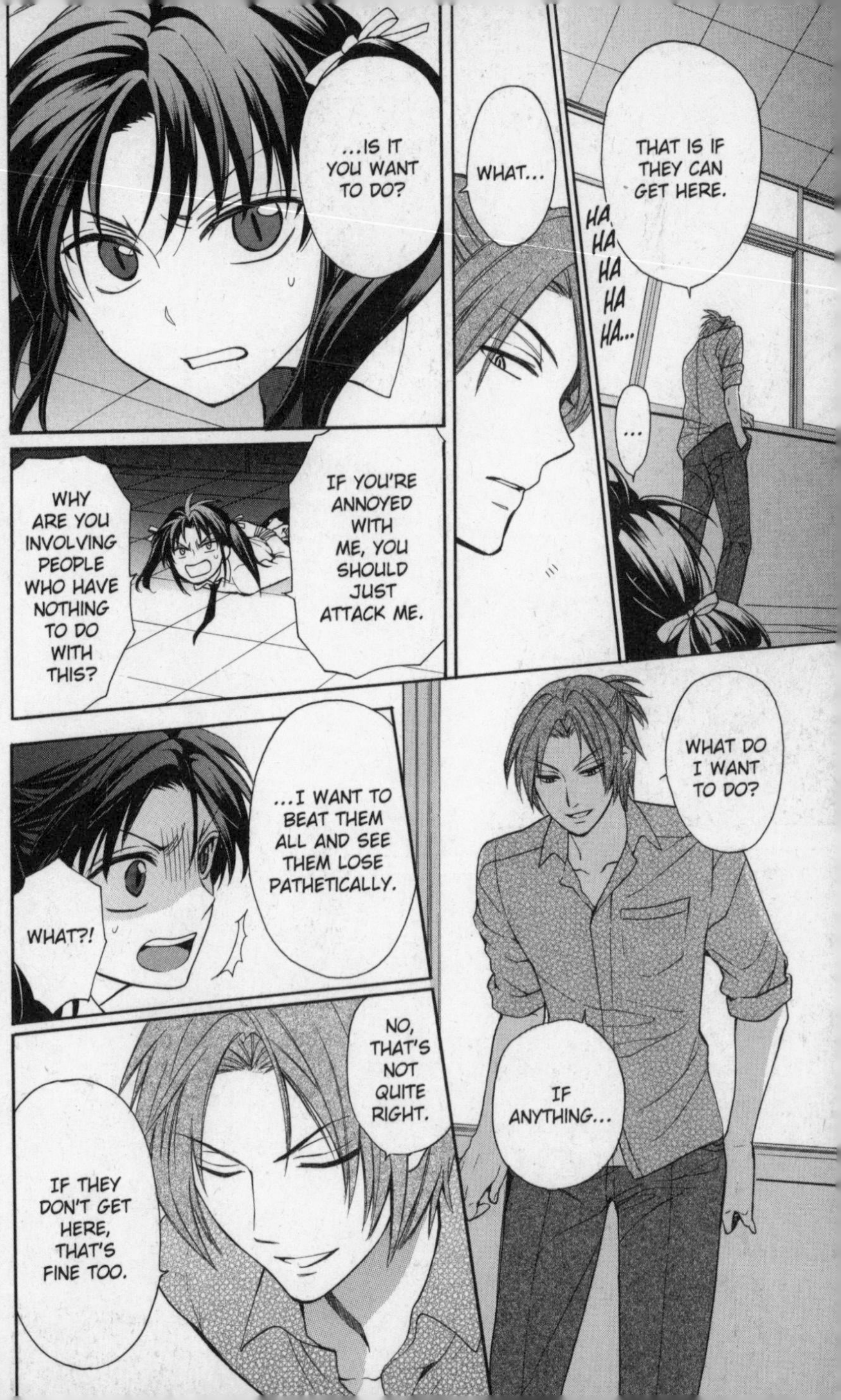
THAT IS IF THEY CAN GET HERE.
HA HA HA HA HA...
...
WHAT...
...IS IT YOU WANT TO DO?
IF YOU'RE ANNOYED WITH ME, YOU SHOULD JUST ATTACK ME.
WHY ARE YOU INVOLVING PEOPLE WHO HAVE NOTHING TO DO WITH THIS?
WHAT DO I WANT TO DO?
IF ANYTHING...
...I WANT TO BEAT THEM ALL AND SEE THEM LOSE PATHETICALLY.
WHAT?!
NO, THAT'S NOT QUITE RIGHT.
IF THEY DON'T GET HERE, THAT'S FINE TOO.

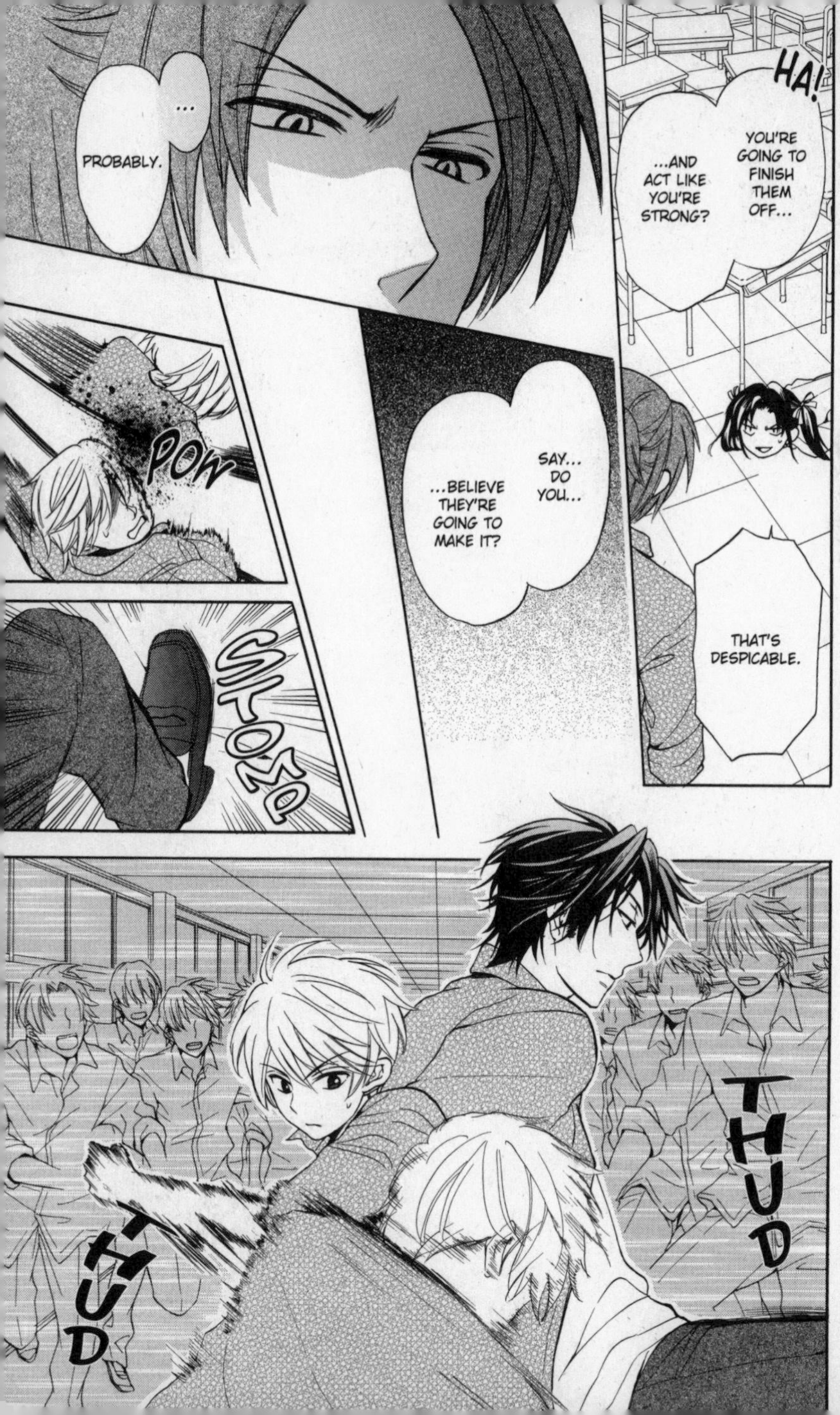
HA!
YOU'RE GOING TO FINISH THEM OFF...
...AND ACT LIKE YOU'RE STRONG?
THAT'S DESPICABLE.
...
PROBABLY.
SAY... DO YOU...
...BELIEVE THEY'RE GOING TO MAKE IT?
POW
STOMP
THUD
THUD

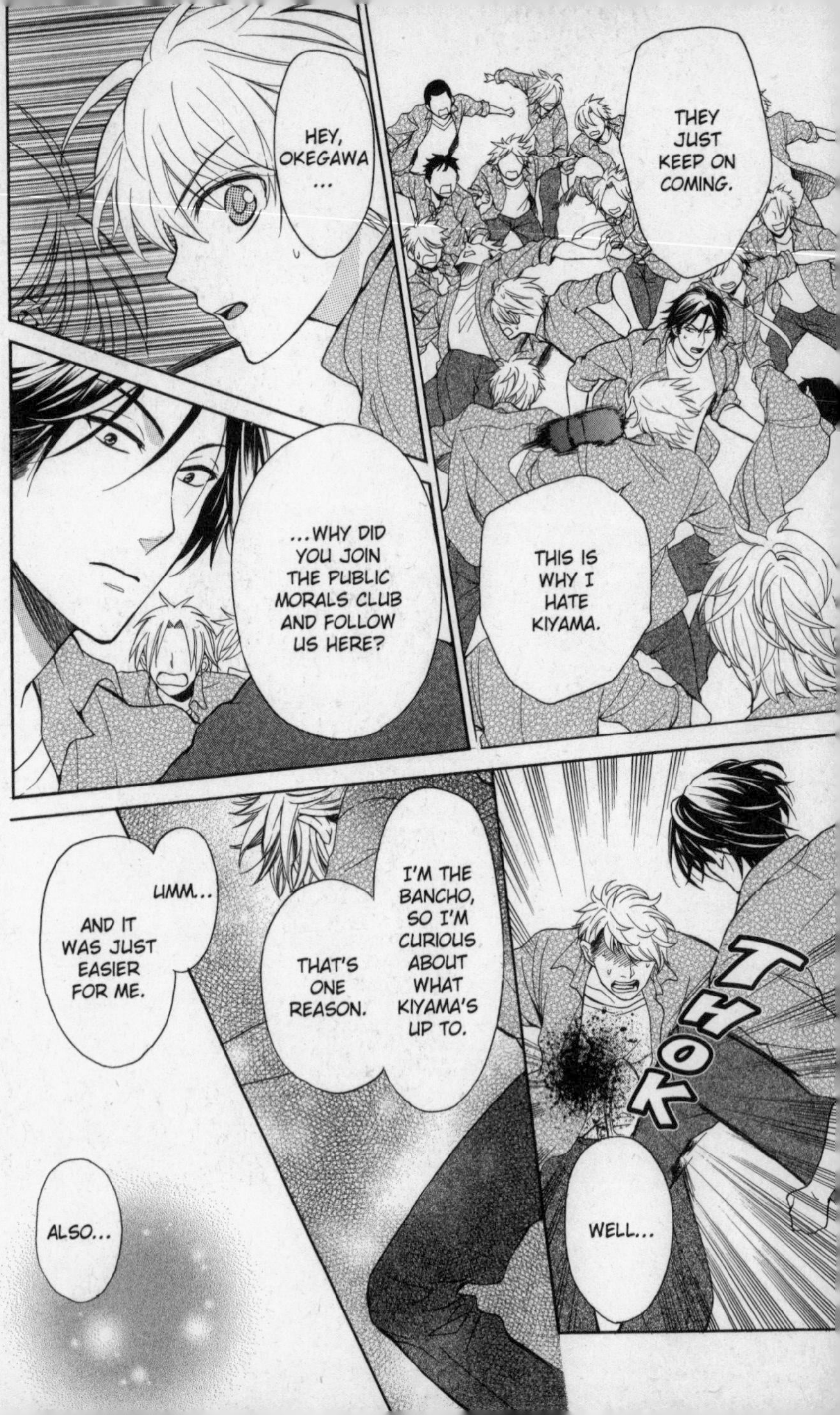
THEY JUST KEEP ON COMING.
THIS IS WHY I HATE KIYAMA.
HEY, OKEGAWA...
...WHY DID YOU JOIN THE PUBLIC MORALS CLUB AND FOLLOW US HERE?
THOK
WELL...
I'M THE BANCHO, SO I'M CURIOUS ABOUT WHAT KIYAMA'S UP TO.
THAT'S ONE REASON.
UMM...
AND IT WAS JUST EASIER FOR ME.
ALSO...

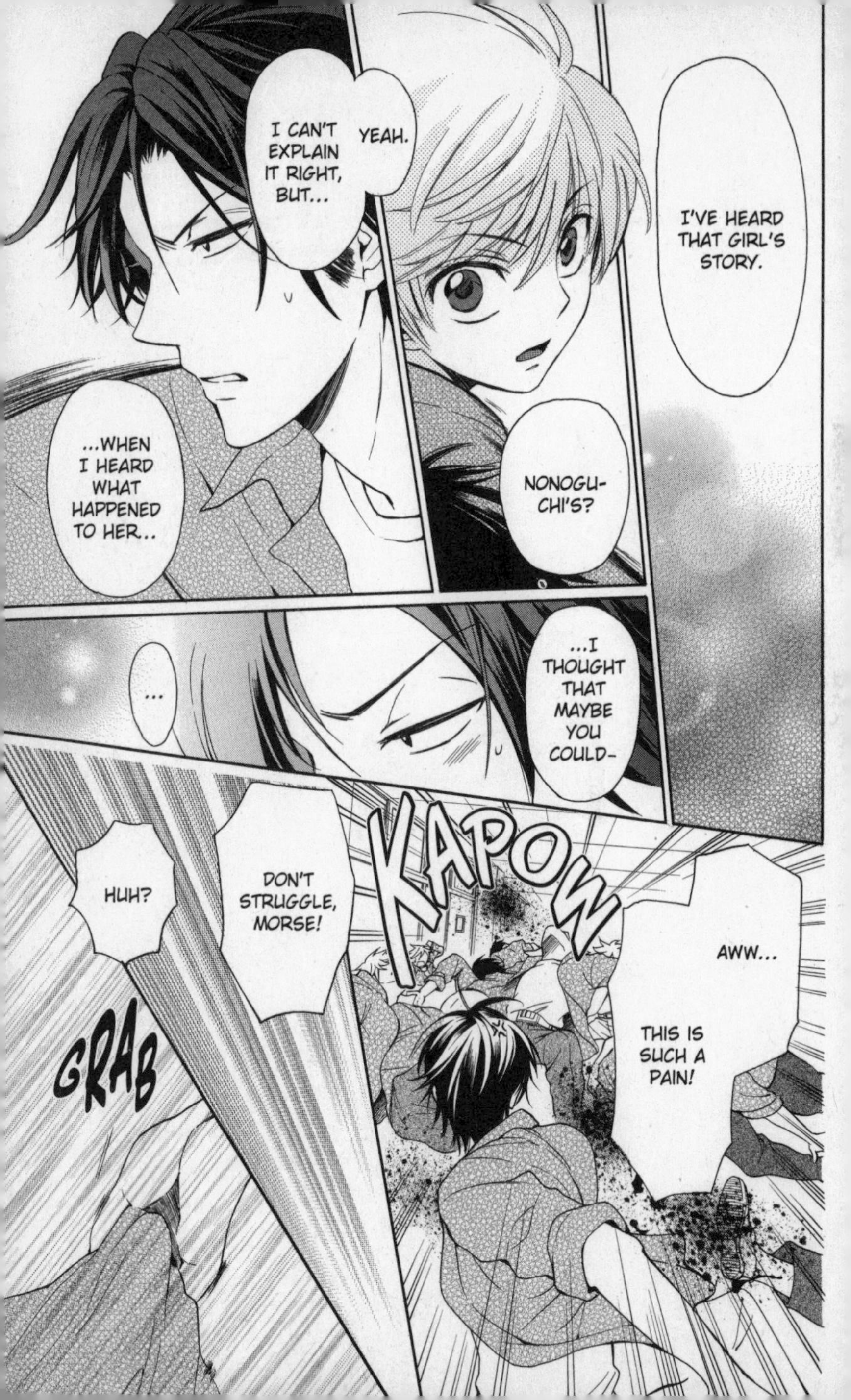
I'VE HEARD THAT GIRL'S STORY.
NONOGU-CHI'S?
YEAH.
I CAN'T EXPLAIN IT RIGHT, BUT...
...WHEN I HEARD WHAT HAPPENED TO HER...
...I THOUGHT THAT MAYBE YOU COULD-
...
AWW...
THIS IS SUCH A PAIN!
KAPOW
DON'T STRUGGLE, MORSE!
HUH?
GRAB

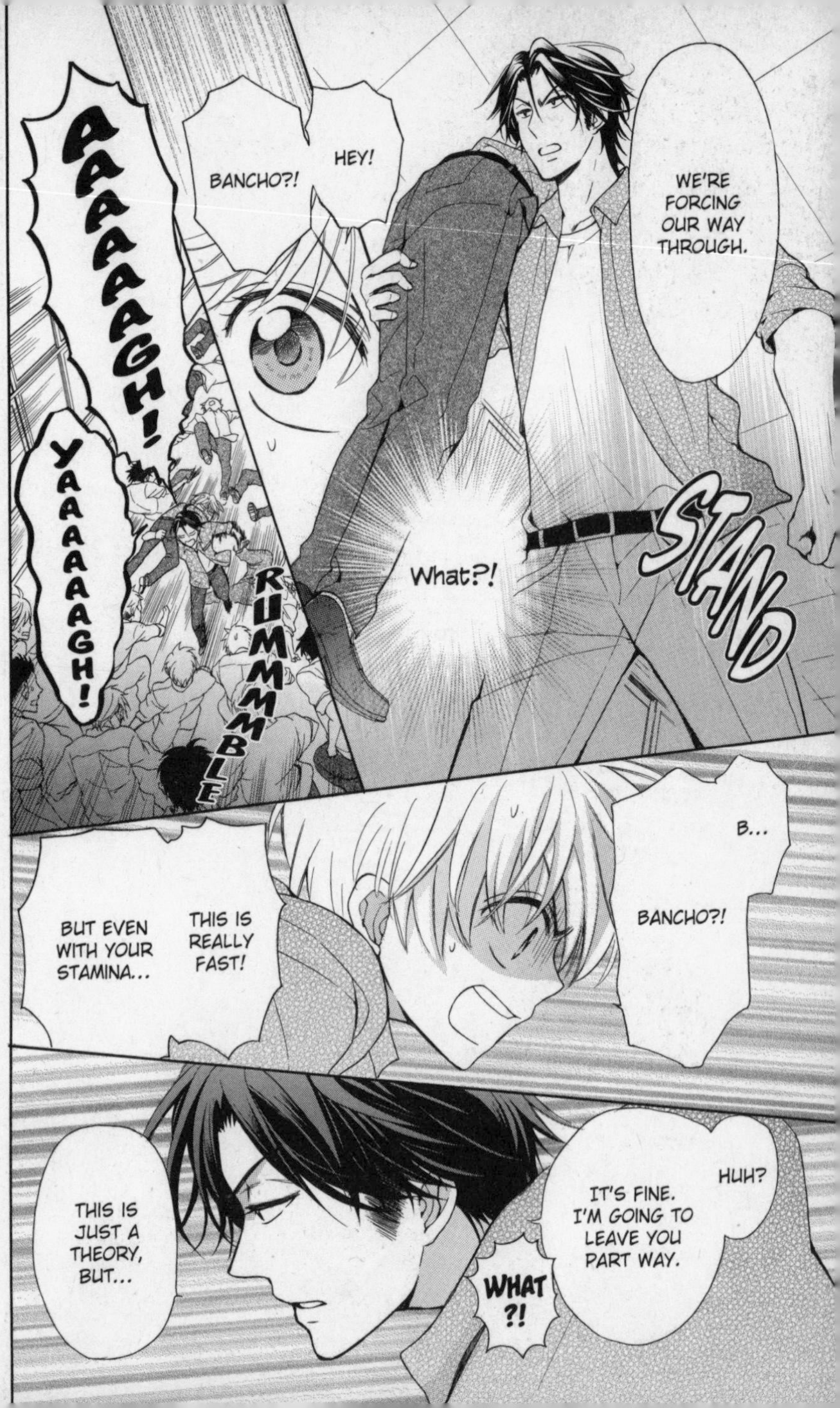
WE'RE FORCING OUR WAY THROUGH.
STAND
What?!
HEY!
BANCHO?!
AAAAAAAGH!
YAAAAAAAGH!
RUMMMBLE
B...
BANCHO?!
THIS IS REALLY FAST!
BUT EVEN WITH YOUR STAMINA...
HUH?
IT'S FINE. I'M GOING TO LEAVE YOU PART WAY.
WHAT?!
THIS IS JUST A THEORY, BUT...

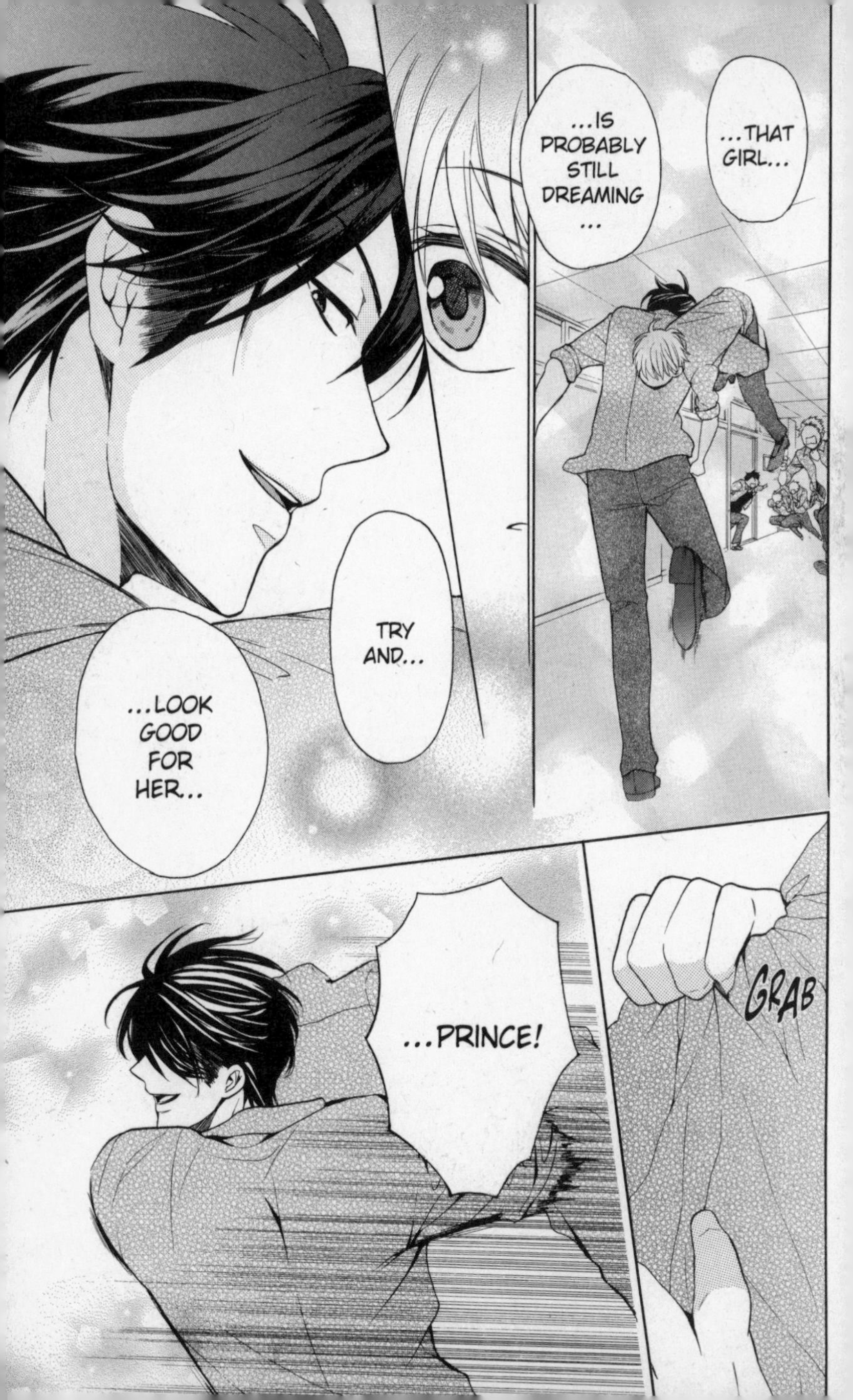
...THAT GIRL...
...IS PROBABLY STILL DREAMING...
TRY AND...
...LOOK GOOD FOR HER...
GRAB
...PRINCE!

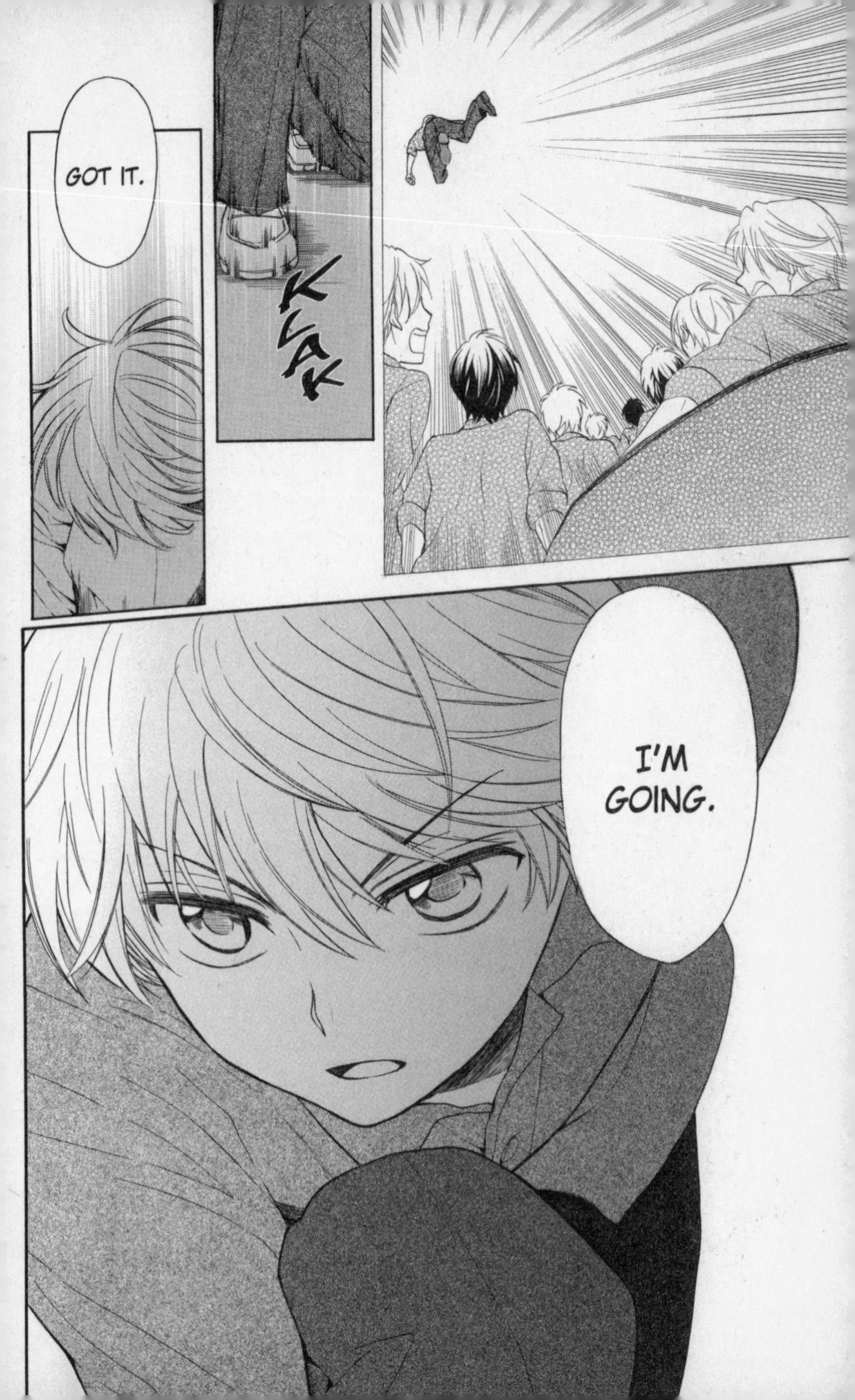
KLAK
GOT IT.
I'M GOING.

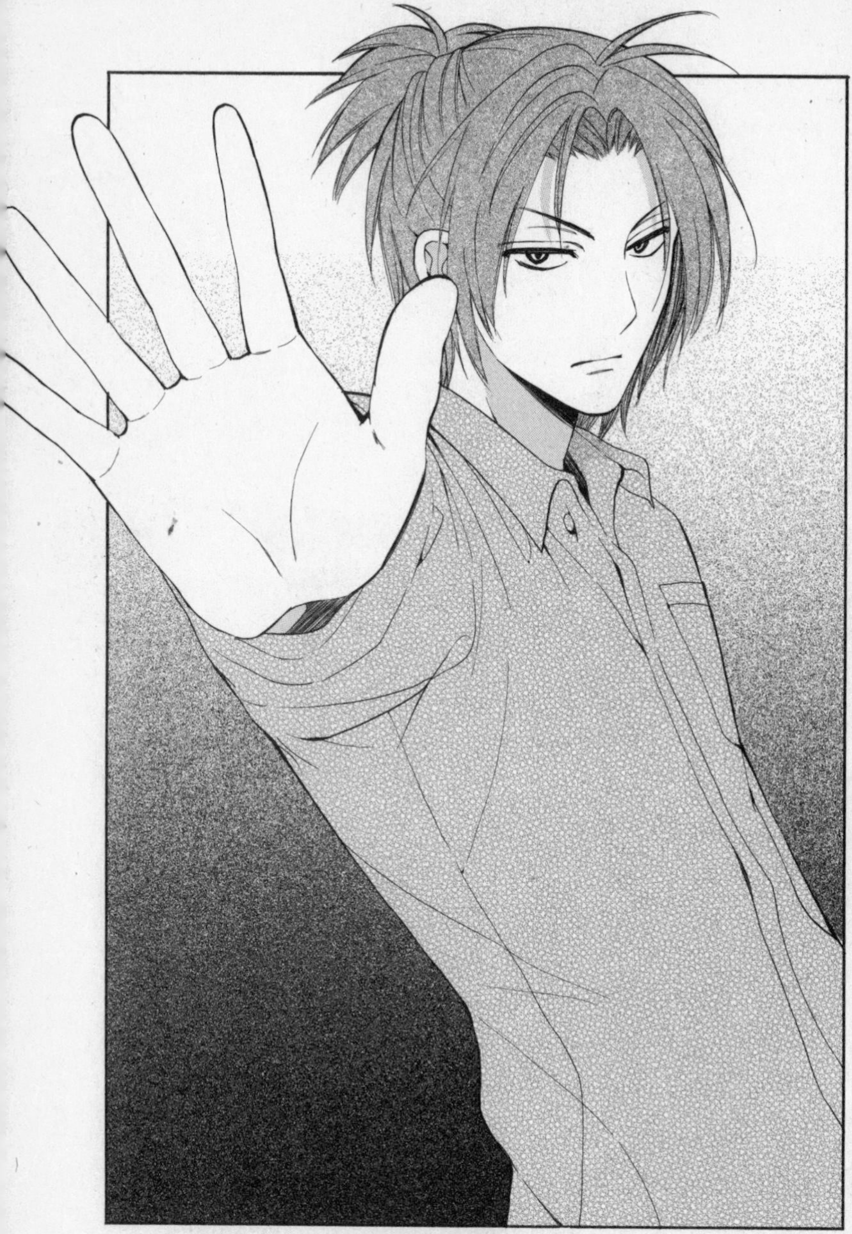

Chapter 77

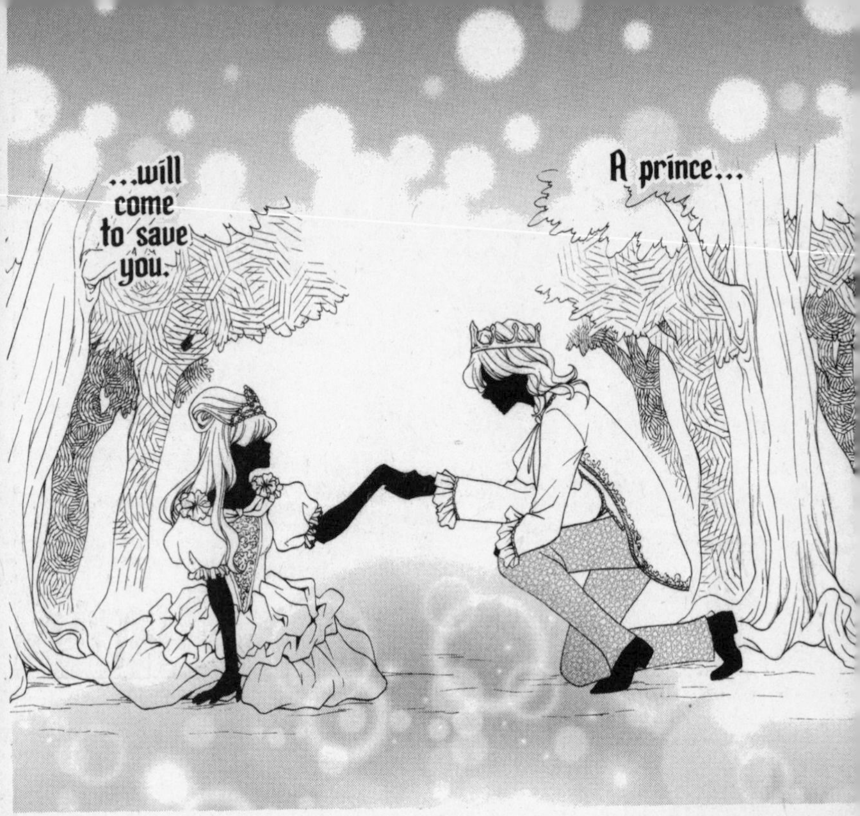
A prince...
...will come to save you.
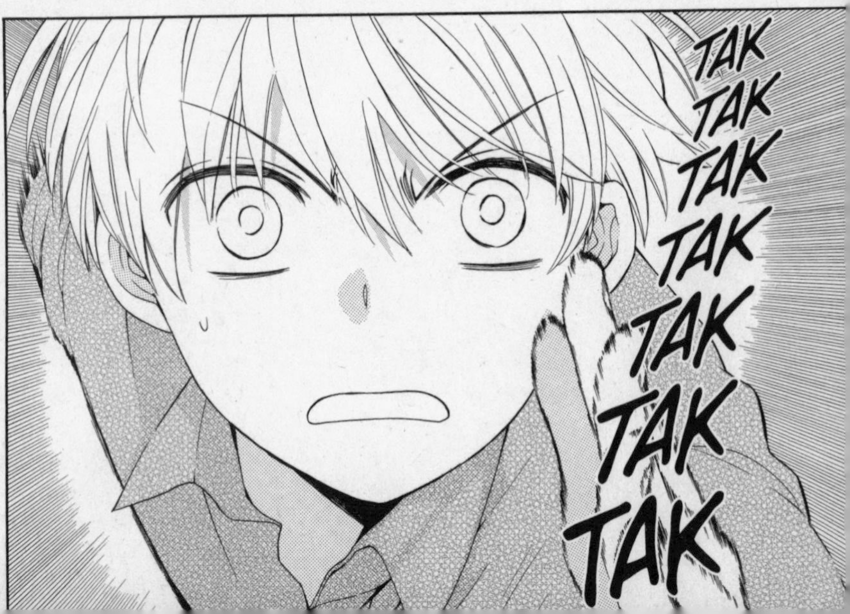
TAK TAK TAK TAK TAK TAK TAK TAK

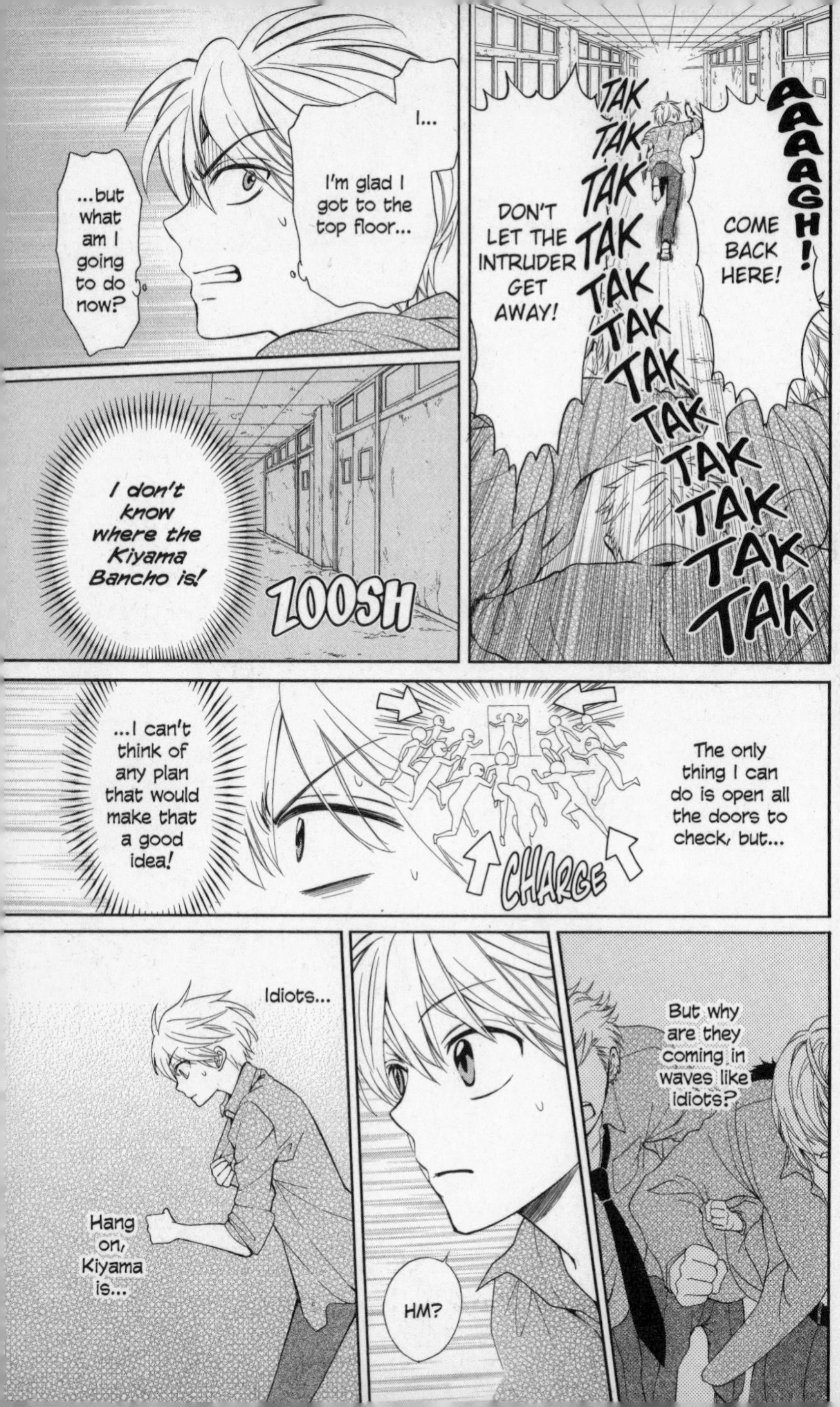
AAAAGH!
COME BACK HERE!
DON'T LET THE INTRUDER GET AWAY!
TAK TAK TAK TAK TAK TAK TAK TAK TAK TAK TAK TAK TAK
I...
I'm glad I got to the top floor...
...but what am I going to do now?
I don't know where the Kiyama Bancho is!
ZOOSH
The only thing I can do is open all the doors to check, but...
CHARGE
...I can't think of any plan that would make that a good idea!
But why are they coming in waves like idiots?
HM?
Idiots...
Hang on, Kiyama is...

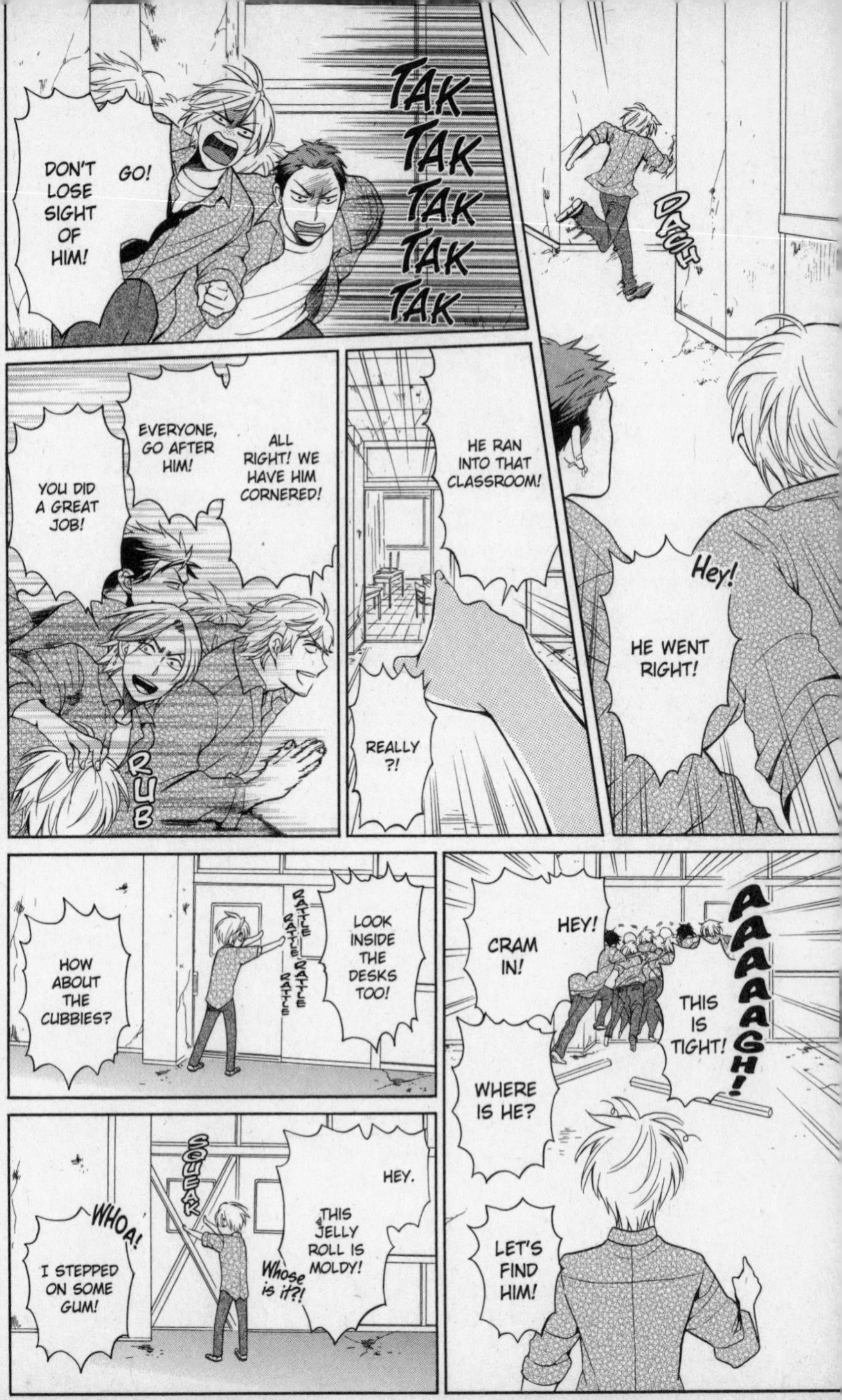
DASH
TAK TAK TAK TAK TAK
GO!
DON'T LOSE SIGHT OF HIM!
Hey!
HE WENT RIGHT!
HE RAN INTO THAT CLASSROOM!
REALLY ?!
ALL RIGHT! WE HAVE HIM CORNERED!
EVERYONE, GO AFTER HIM!
YOU DID A GREAT JOB!
RUB
HEY!
CRAM IN!
AAAAAGH!
THIS IS TIGHT!
WHERE IS HE?
LET'S FIND HIM!
LOOK INSIDE THE DESKS TOO!
RATTLE RATTLE RATTLE
HOW ABOUT THE CUBBIES?
HEY.
THIS JELLY ROLL IS MOLDY!
Whose is it?!
SQUEAK
WHOA!
I STEPPED ON SOME GUM!

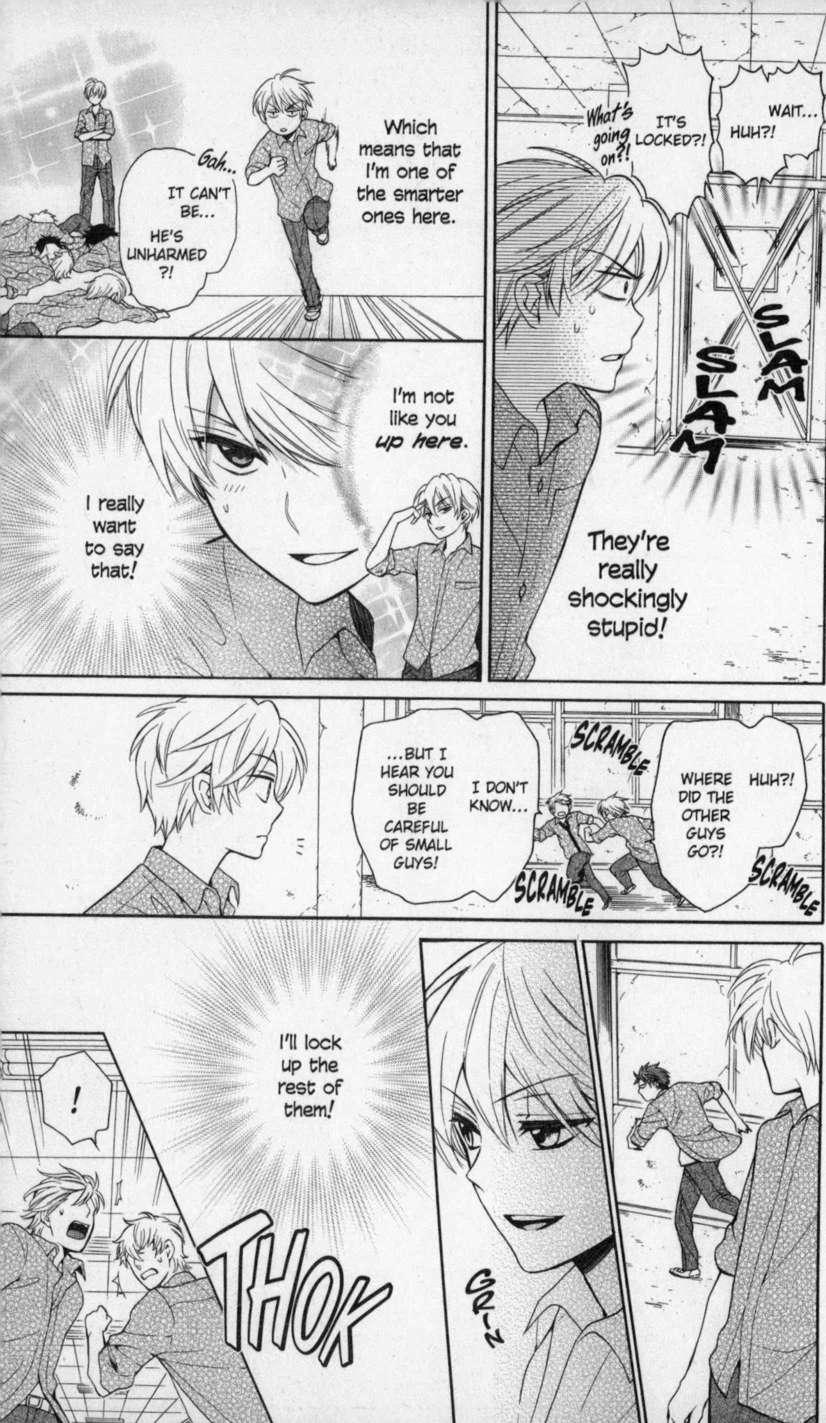
WAIT... HUH?!
IT'S LOCKED?!
What's going on?!
SLAM
SLAM
They're really shockingly stupid!
Which means that I'm one of the smarter ones here.
Gah...
IT CAN'T BE... HE'S UNHARMED?!
I'm not like you *up here*.
I really want to say that!
HUH?!
WHERE DID THE OTHER GUYS GO?!
SCRAMBLE
I DON'T KNOW...
...BUT I HEAR YOU SHOULD BE CAREFUL OF SMALL GUYS!
SCRAMBLE
SCRAMBLE
GRIN
I'll lock up the rest of them!
THOK
!

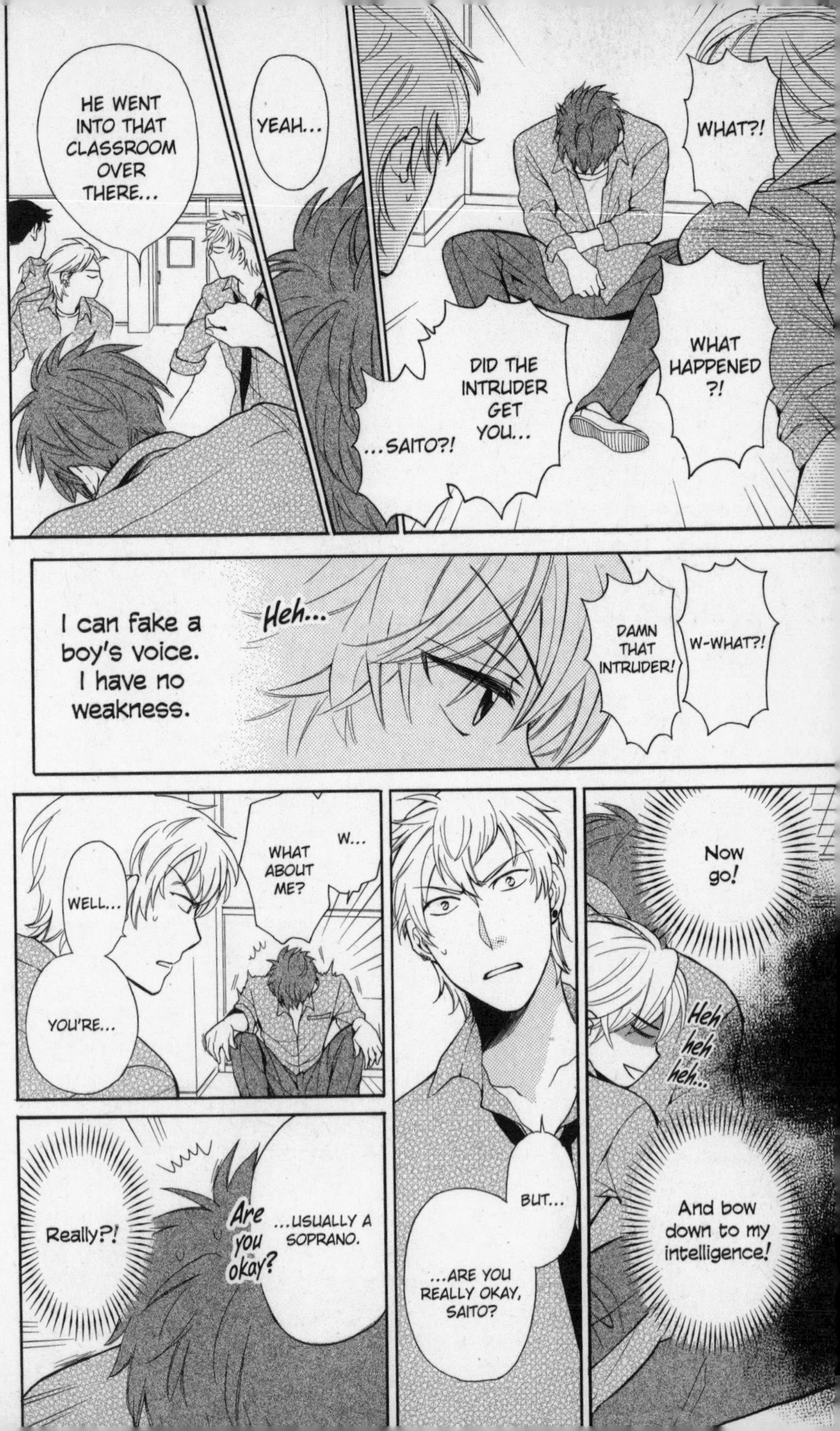
WHAT?!
WHAT HAPPENED?!
DID THE INTRUDER GET YOU...
...SAITO?!
YEAH...
HE WENT INTO THAT CLASSROOM OVER THERE...
W-WHAT?!
DAMN THAT INTRUDER!
Heh...
I can fake a boy's voice. I have no weakness.
Now go!
Heh heh heh...
And bow down to my intelligence!
BUT...
...ARE YOU REALLY OKAY, SAITO?
W...
WHAT ABOUT ME?
WELL...
YOU'RE...
Really?!
Are you okay?
...USUALLY A SOPRANO.

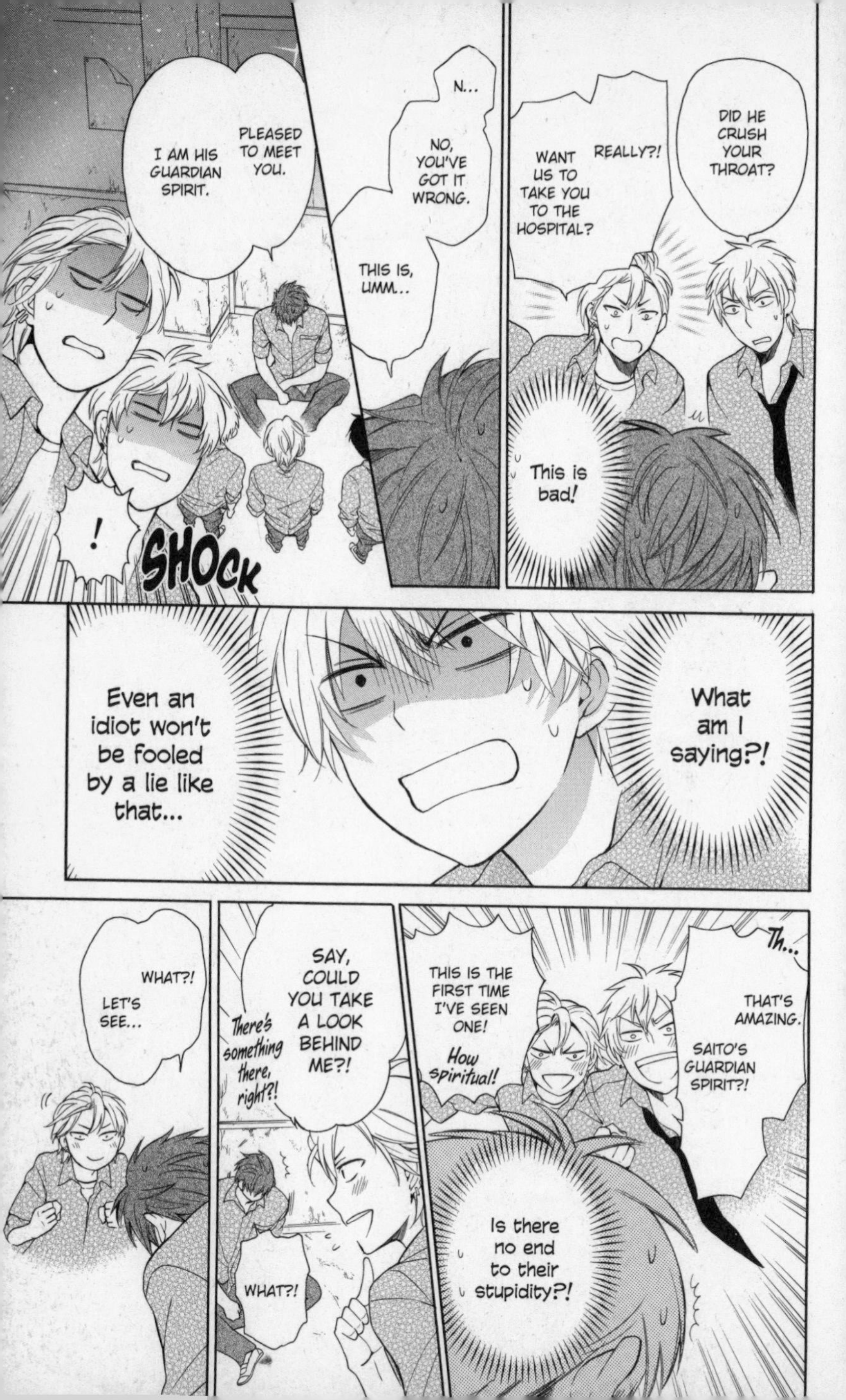
DID HE CRUSH YOUR THROAT?
REALLY?!
WANT US TO TAKE YOU TO THE HOSPITAL?
This is bad!
N...
NO, YOU'VE GOT IT WRONG.
THIS IS, UMM...
PLEASED TO MEET YOU.
I AM HIS GUARDIAN SPIRIT.
!
SHOCK
What am I saying?!
Even an idiot won't be fooled by a lie like that...
Th...
THAT'S AMAZING.
SAITO'S GUARDIAN SPIRIT?!
THIS IS THE FIRST TIME I'VE SEEN ONE!
How spiritual!
Is there no end to their stupidity?!
SAY, COULD YOU TAKE A LOOK BEHIND ME?!
There's something there, right?!
WHAT?!
WHAT?!
LET'S SEE...

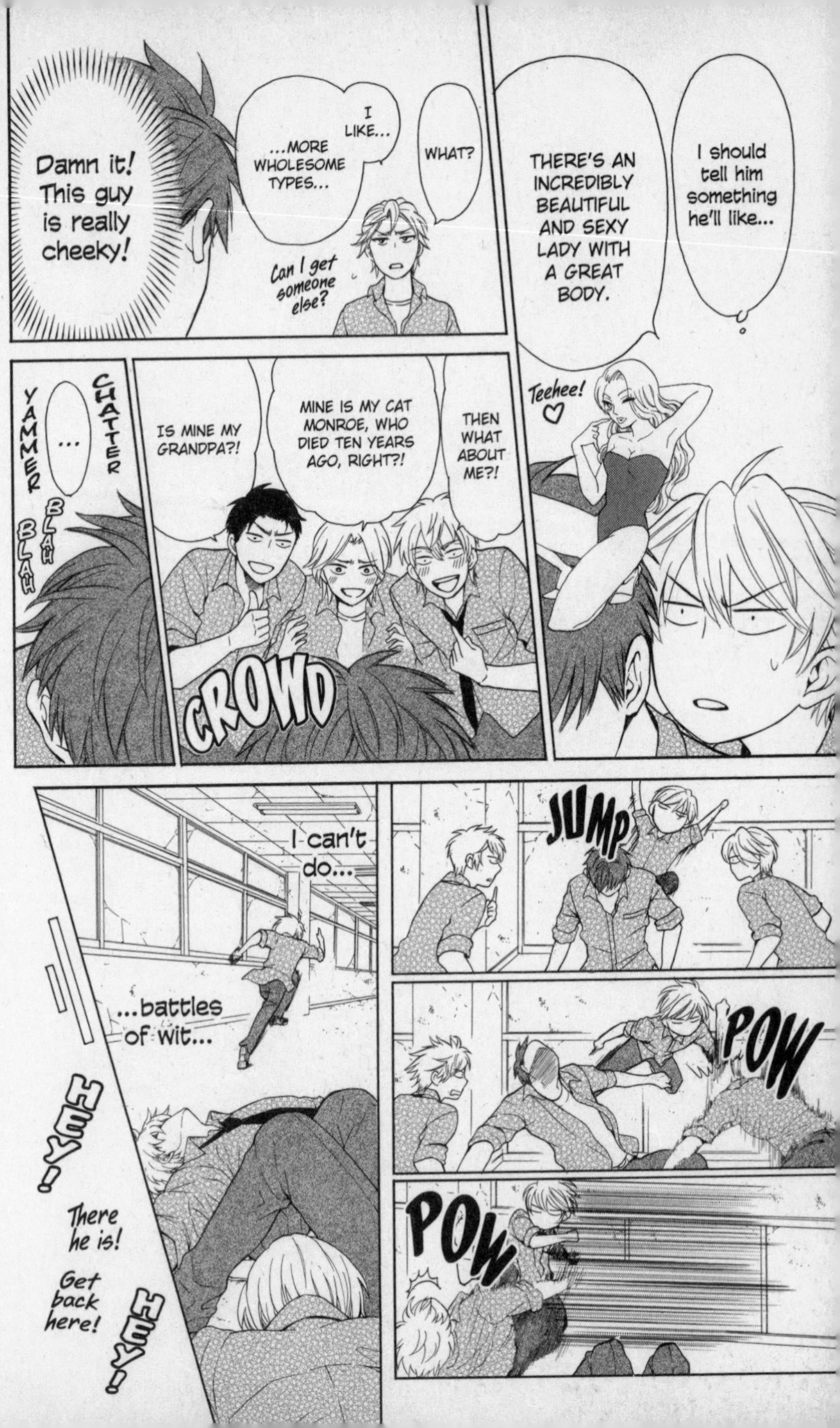
I should tell him something he'll like...
THERE'S AN INCREDIBLY BEAUTIFUL AND SEXY LADY WITH A GREAT BODY.
Teehee! ♡
I LIKE...
...MORE WHOLESOME TYPES...
WHAT?
Can I get someone else?
Damn it! This guy is really cheeky!
THEN WHAT ABOUT ME?!
MINE IS MY CAT MONROE, WHO DIED TEN YEARS AGO, RIGHT?!
IS MINE MY GRANDPA?!
CROWD
CHATTER
...
YAMMER
BLAH BLAH
JUMP
POW
POW
I can't do...
...battles of wit...
HEY! HEY!
There he is!
Get back here!
HEY! HEY!

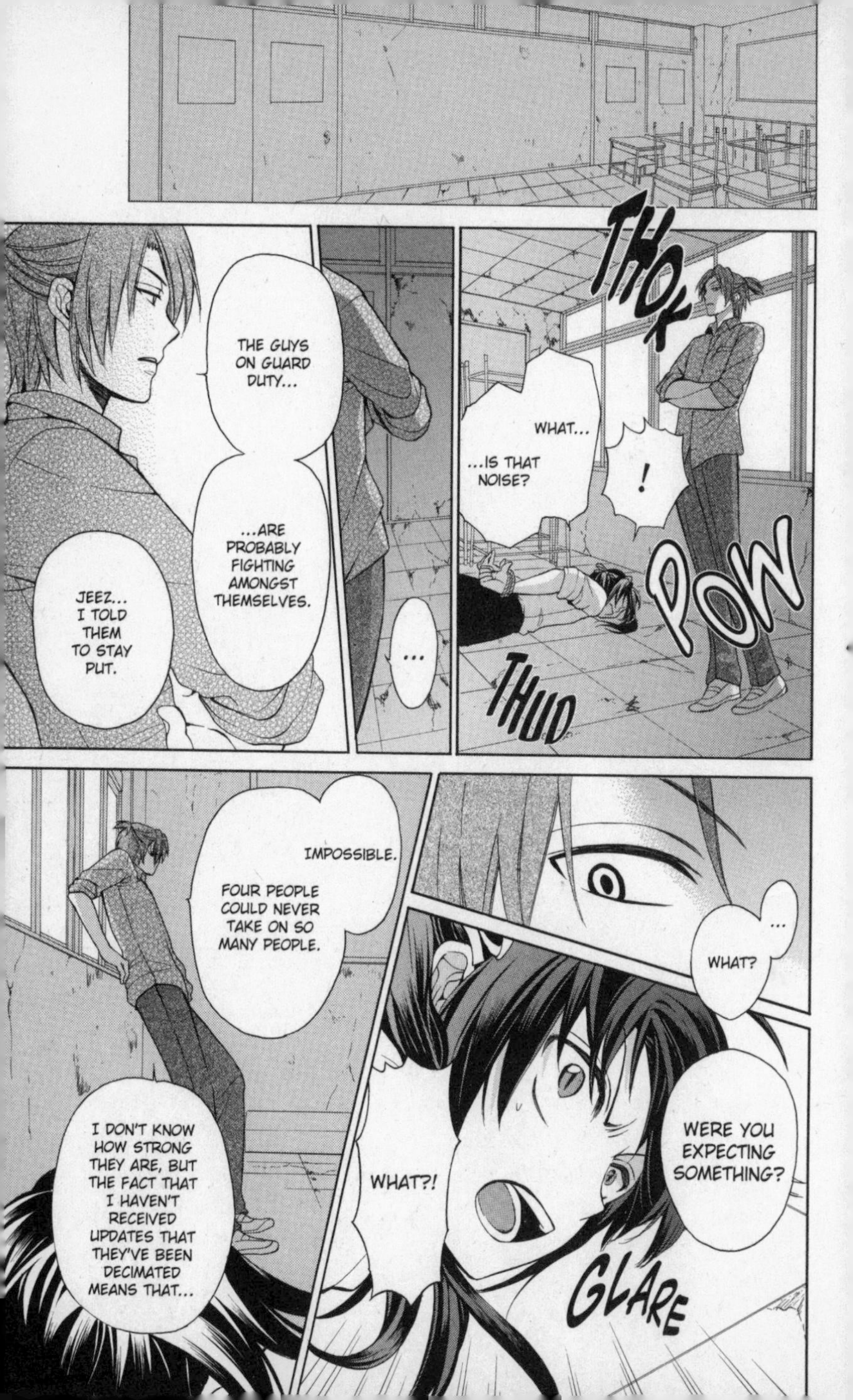
THOK
WHAT...
...IS THAT NOISE?
!
POW
THUD
...
THE GUYS ON GUARD DUTY...
...ARE PROBABLY FIGHTING AMONGST THEMSELVES.
JEEZ... I TOLD THEM TO STAY PUT.
...
WHAT?
WERE YOU EXPECTING SOMETHING?
WHAT?!
GLARE
IMPOSSIBLE.
FOUR PEOPLE COULD NEVER TAKE ON SO MANY PEOPLE.
I DON'T KNOW HOW STRONG THEY ARE, BUT THE FACT THAT I HAVEN'T RECEIVED UPDATES THAT THEY'VE BEEN DECIMATED MEANS THAT...

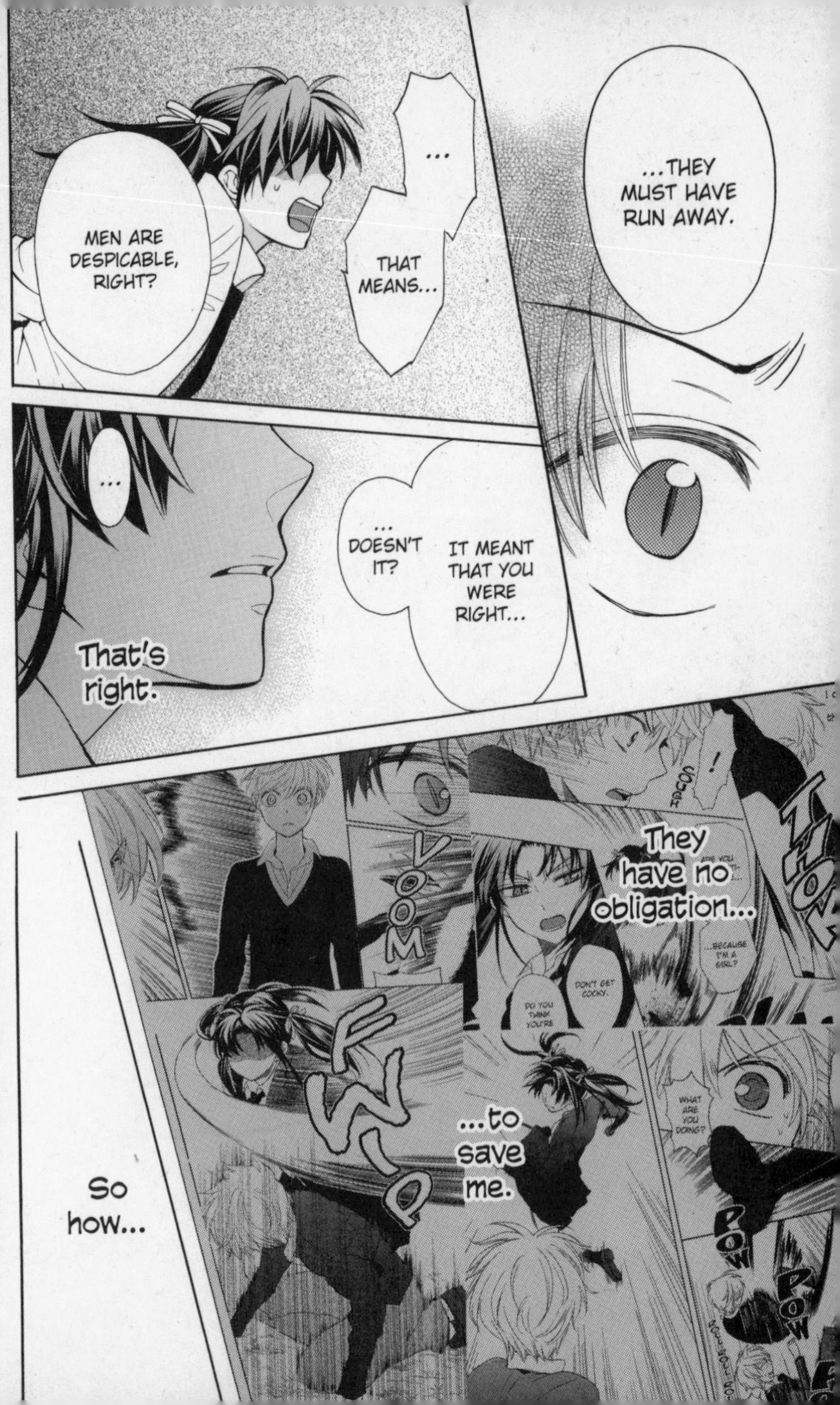
...THEY MUST HAVE RUN AWAY.
...
THAT MEANS...
MEN ARE DESPICABLE, RIGHT?
IT MEANT THAT YOU WERE RIGHT...
...DOESN'T IT?
...
That's right.
COUGH
They have no obligation...
...BECAUSE I'M A GIRL?
DON'T GET COCKY.
DO YOU THINK YOU'RE
VOOM
...to save me.
WHAT ARE YOU DOING?
POW
POW
POW
FWOO
So how...

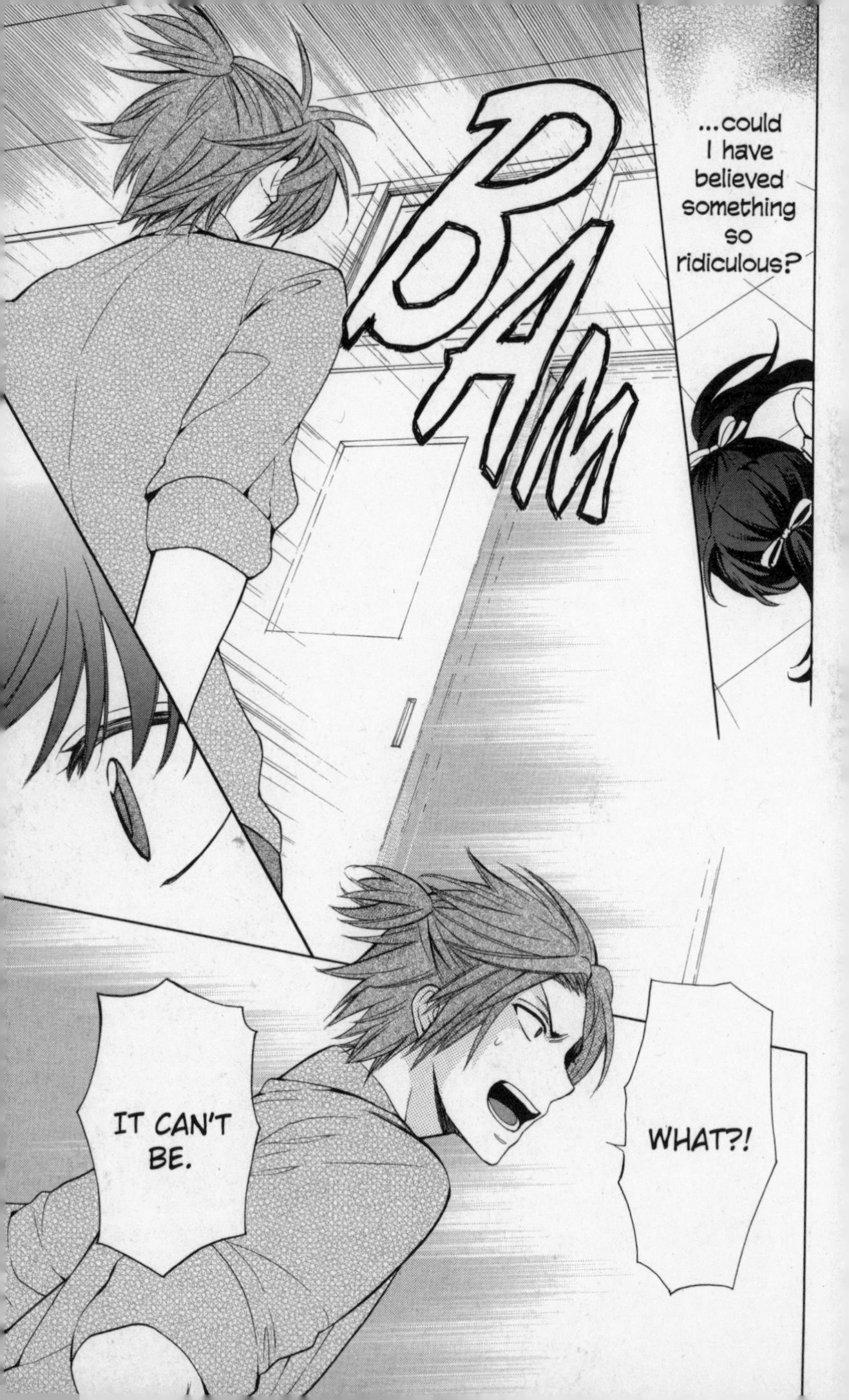
...could I have believed something so ridiculous?
PAM
WHAT?!
IT CAN'T BE.

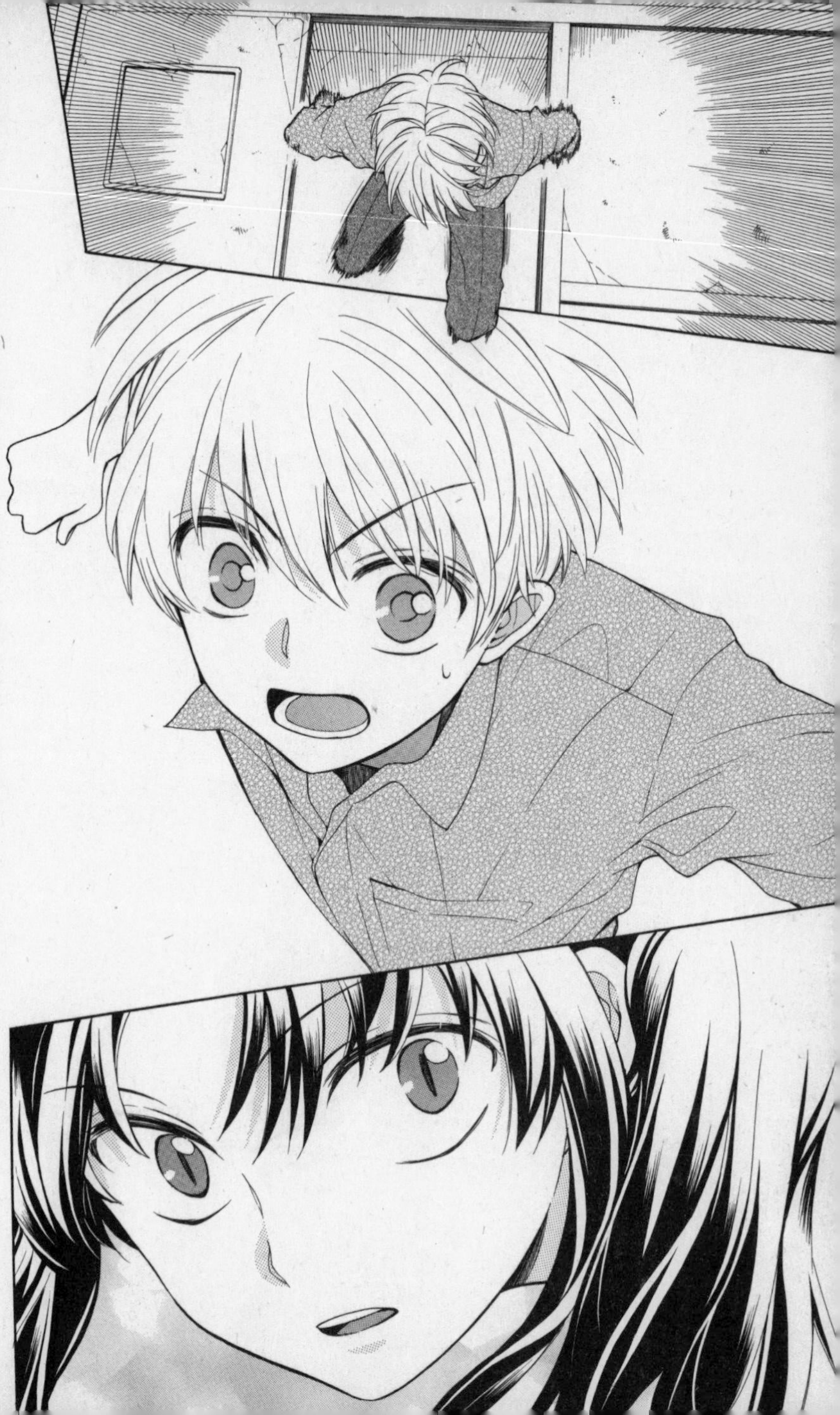

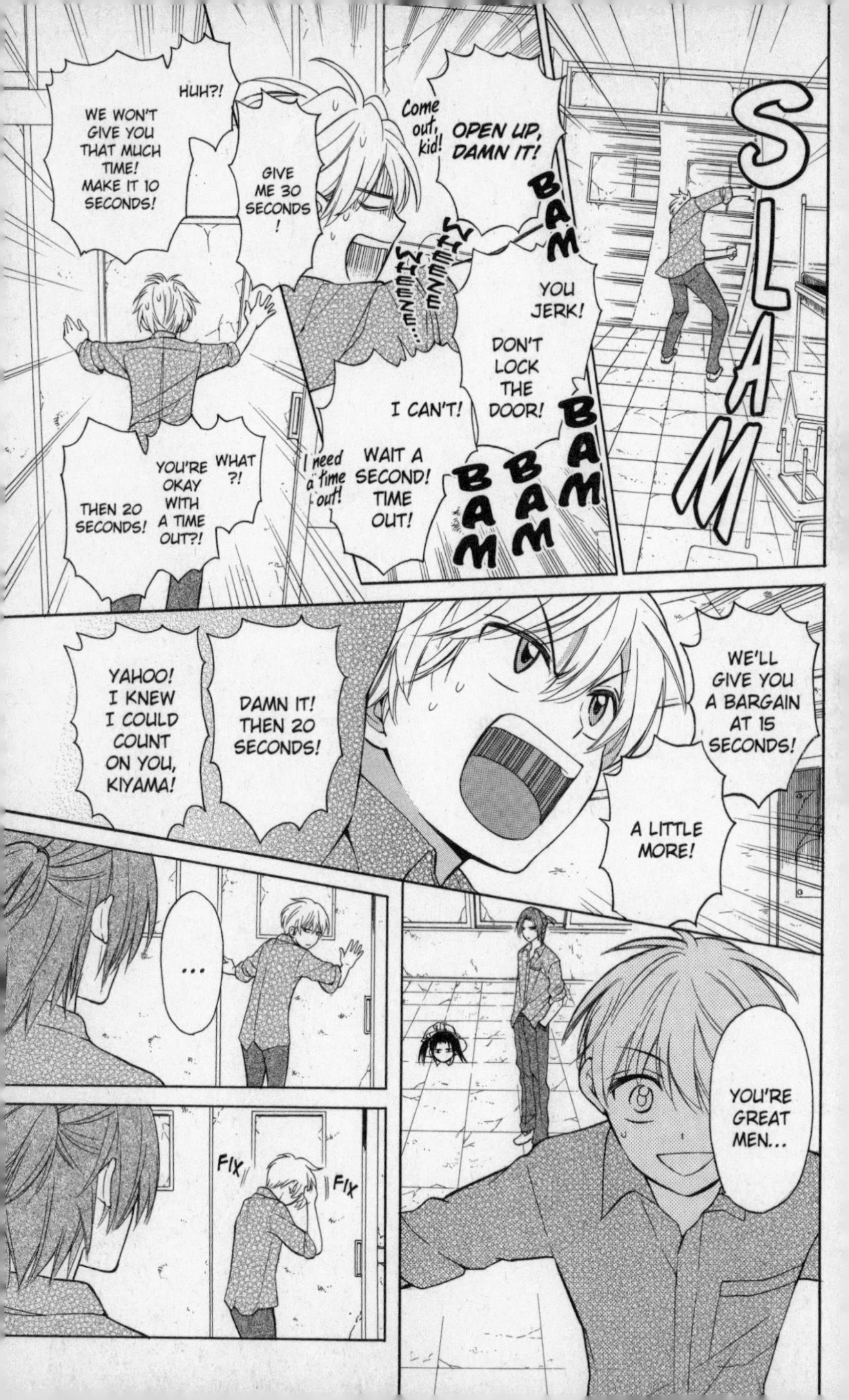
SLAM
Come out, kid!
OPEN UP, DAMN IT!
BAM BAM
YOU JERK!
DON'T LOCK THE DOOR!
BAM BAM BAM BAM
I CAN'T!
WAIT A SECOND! TIME OUT!
I need a time out!
WHEEZE WHEEZE...
GIVE ME 30 SECONDS!
HUH?!
WE WON'T GIVE YOU THAT MUCH TIME! MAKE IT 10 SECONDS!
WHAT?!
YOU'RE OKAY WITH A TIME OUT?!
THEN 20 SECONDS!
WE'LL GIVE YOU A BARGAIN AT 15 SECONDS!
A LITTLE MORE!
DAMN IT! THEN 20 SECONDS!
YAHOO! I KNEW I COULD COUNT ON YOU, KIYAMA!
YOU'RE GREAT MEN...
...
FIX
FIX

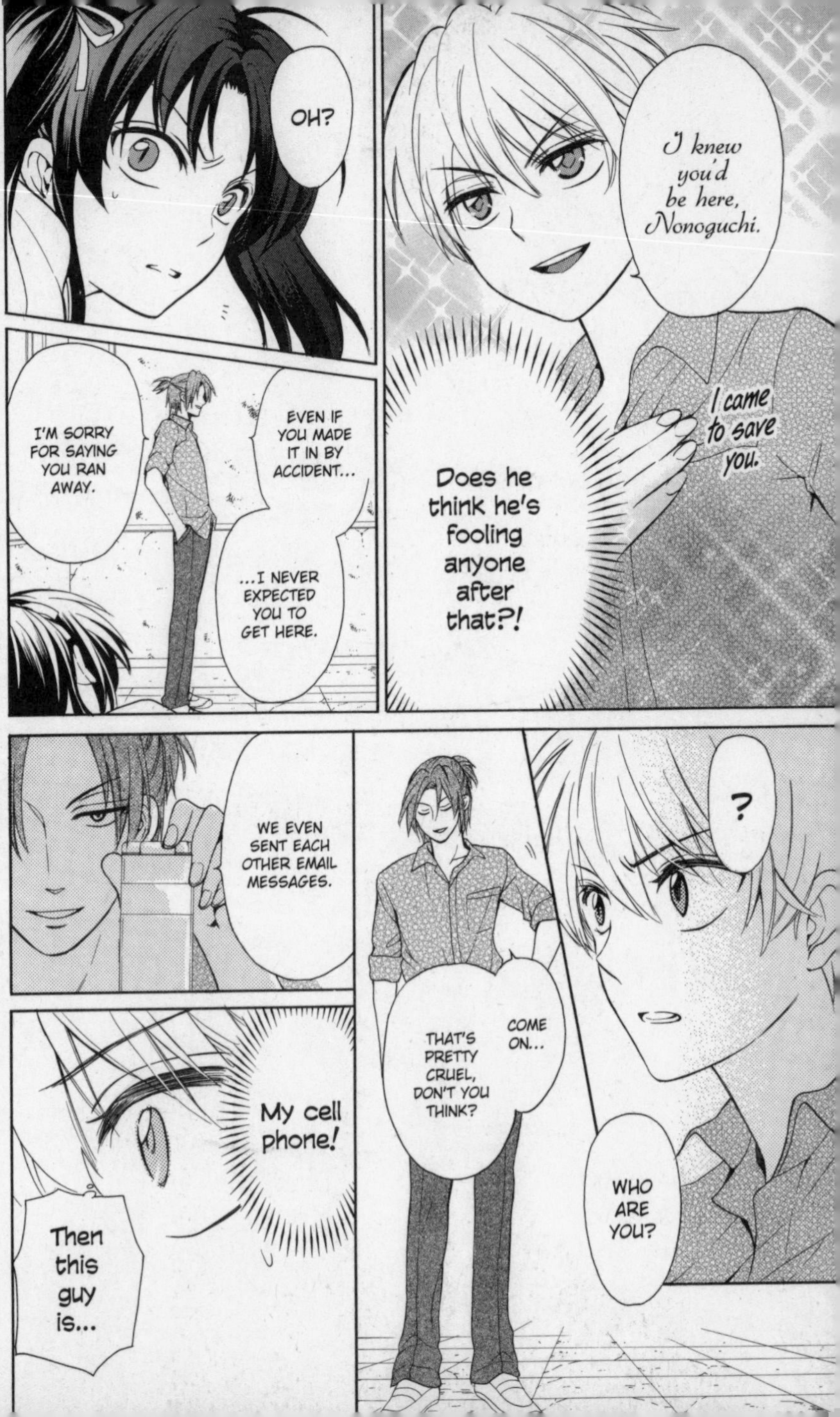
I knew you'd be here, Nonoguchi.
I came to save you.
Does he think he's fooling anyone after that?!
OH?
EVEN IF YOU MADE IT IN BY ACCIDENT...
...I NEVER EXPECTED YOU TO GET HERE.
I'M SORRY FOR SAYING YOU RAN AWAY.
?
WHO ARE YOU?
COME ON...
THAT'S PRETTY CRUEL, DON'T YOU THINK?
WE EVEN SENT EACH OTHER EMAIL MESSAGES.
My cell phone!
Then this guy is...

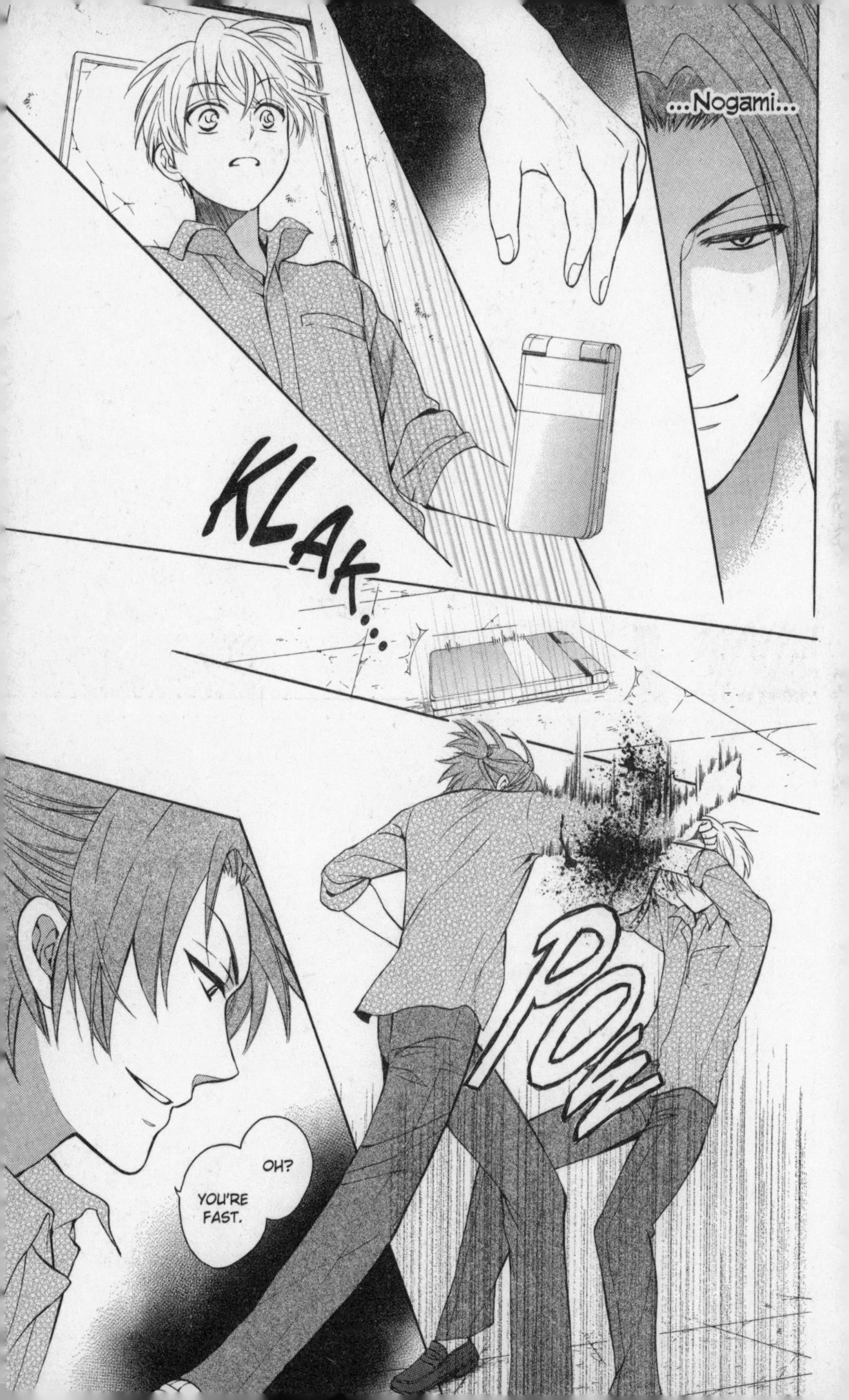
...Nogami...
KLAK...
POW
OH?
YOU'RE FAST.

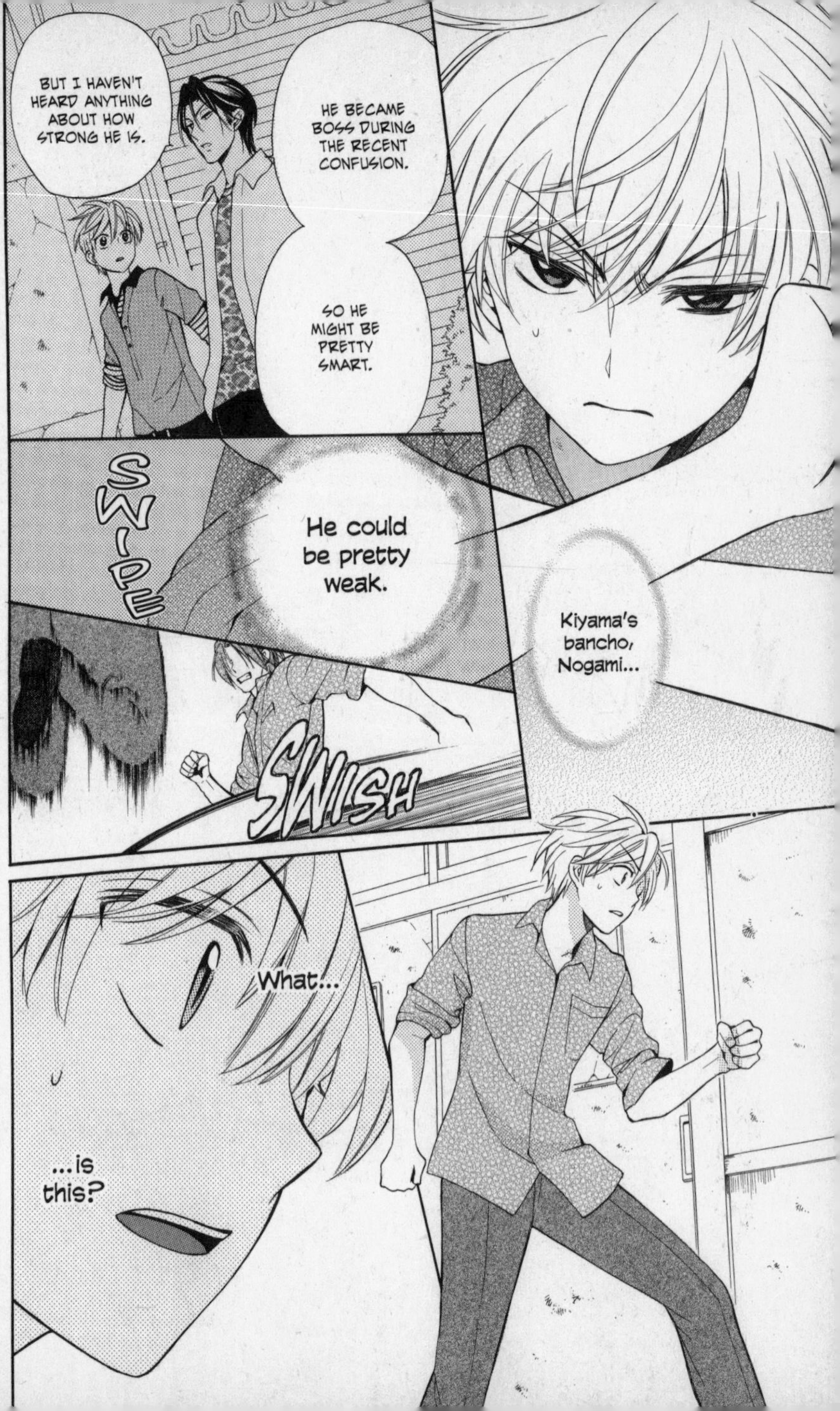
HE BECAME BOSS DURING THE RECENT CONFUSION.
SO HE MIGHT BE PRETTY SMART.
BUT I HAVEN'T HEARD ANYTHING ABOUT HOW STRONG HE IS.
SWIPE
He could be pretty weak.
Kiyama's bancho, Nogami...
SWISH
What...
...is this?

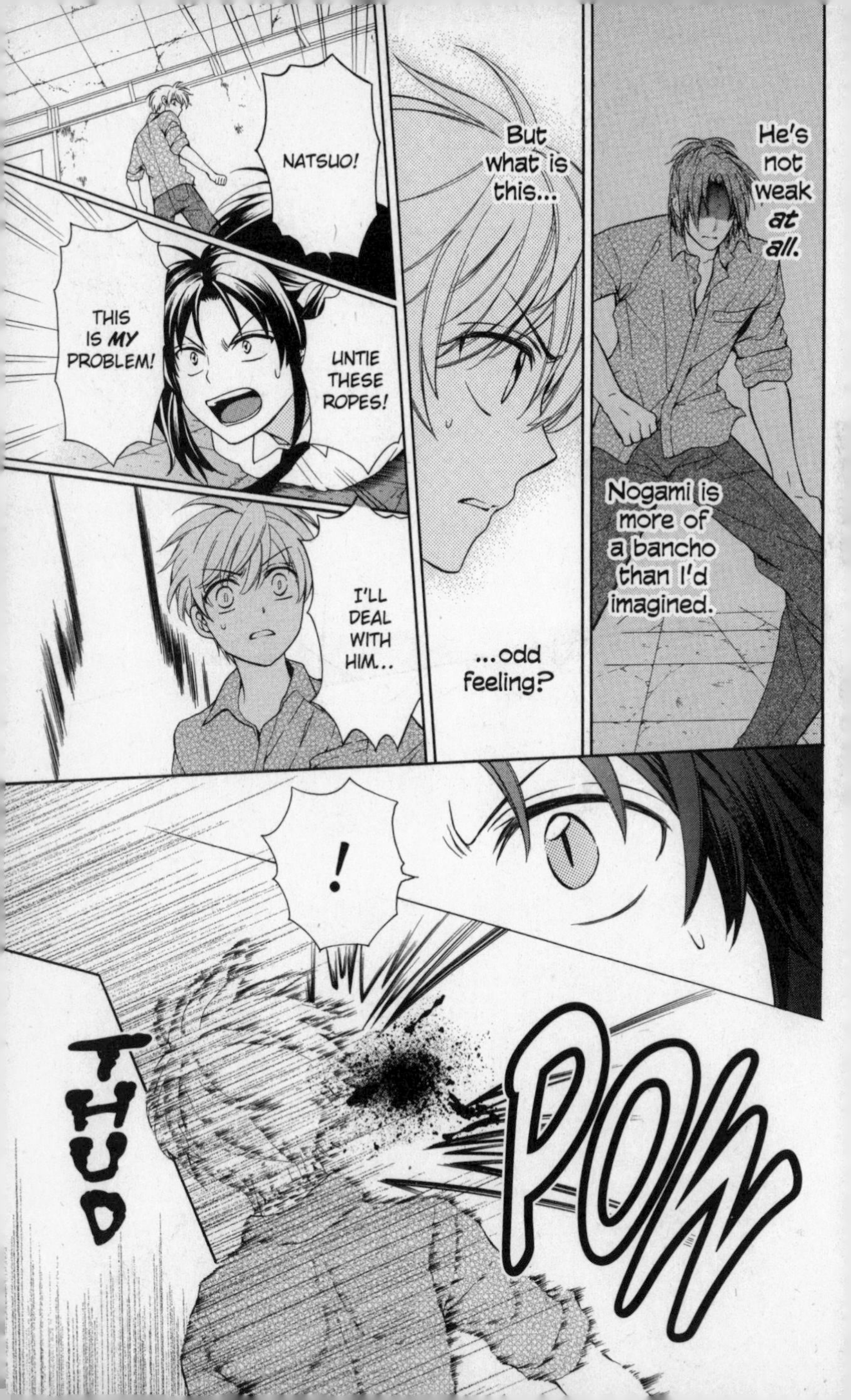
He's not weak at all.
Nogami is more of a bancho than I'd imagined.
But what is this...
...odd feeling?
NATSUO!
THIS IS MY PROBLEM!
UNTIE THESE ROPES!
I'LL DEAL WITH HIM...
!
POW
THUD

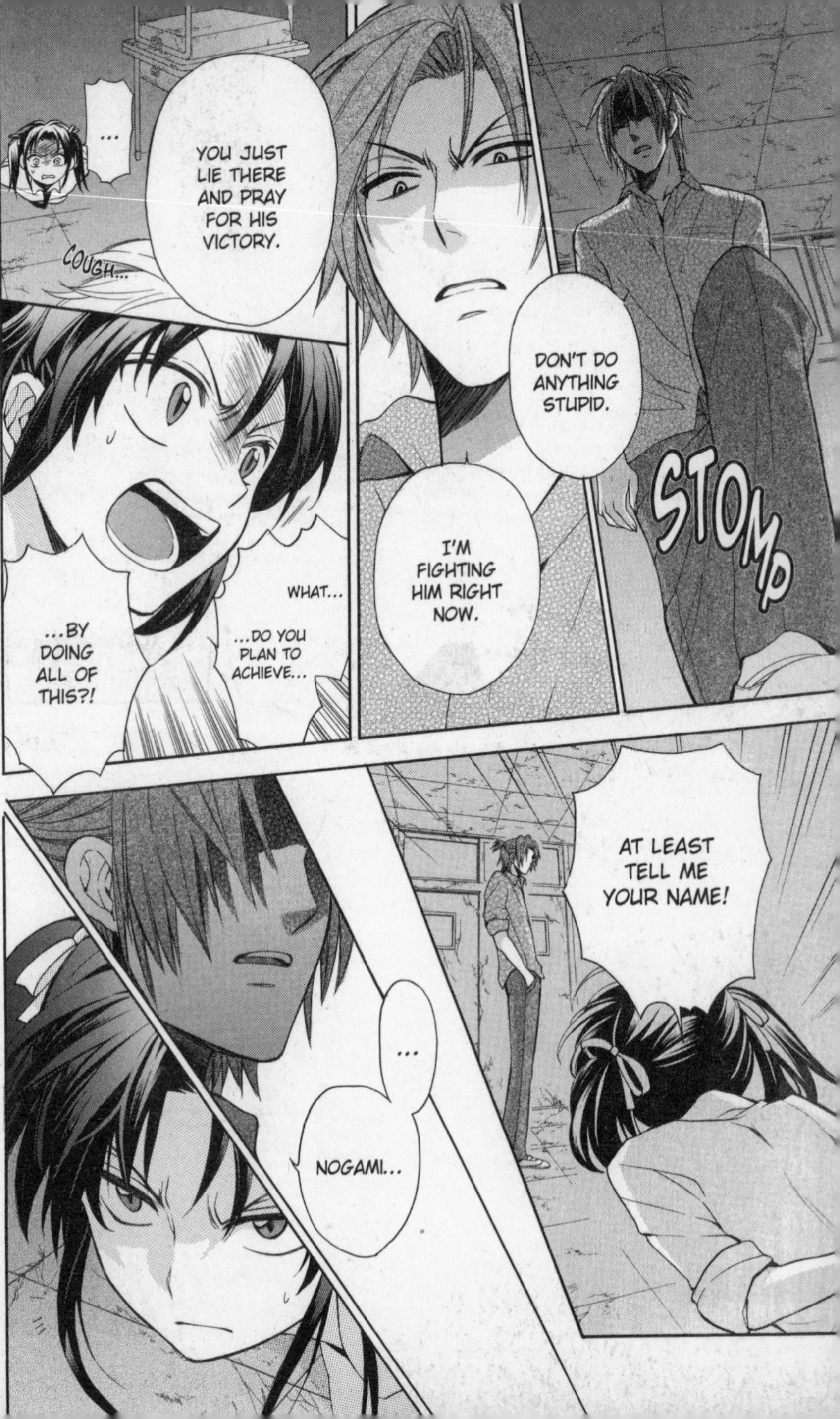
STOMP
DON'T DO ANYTHING STUPID.
I'M FIGHTING HIM RIGHT NOW.
...
YOU JUST LIE THERE AND PRAY FOR HIS VICTORY.
COUGH...
WHAT...
...DO YOU PLAN TO ACHIEVE...
...BY DOING ALL OF THIS?!
AT LEAST TELL ME YOUR NAME!
...
NOGAMI...

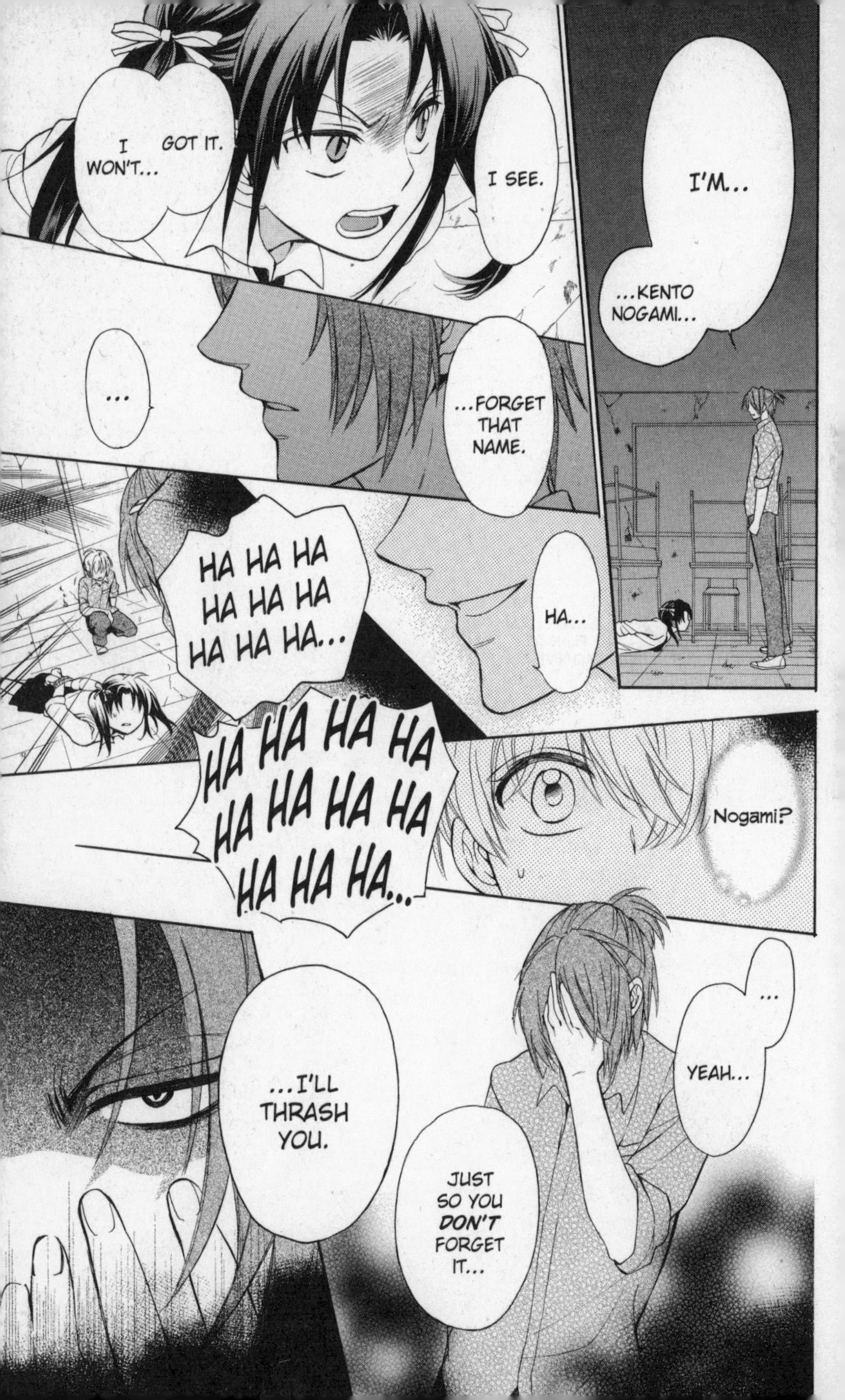
I'M...
...KENTO NOGAMI...
I SEE.
I WON'T... GOT IT.
...FORGET THAT NAME.
...
HA...
HA HA HA HA HA HA HA HA HA...
Nogami?
HA HA HA HA HA HA HA HA HA HA HA HA...
...
YEAH...
...I'LL THRASH YOU.
JUST SO YOU *DON'T* FORGET IT...

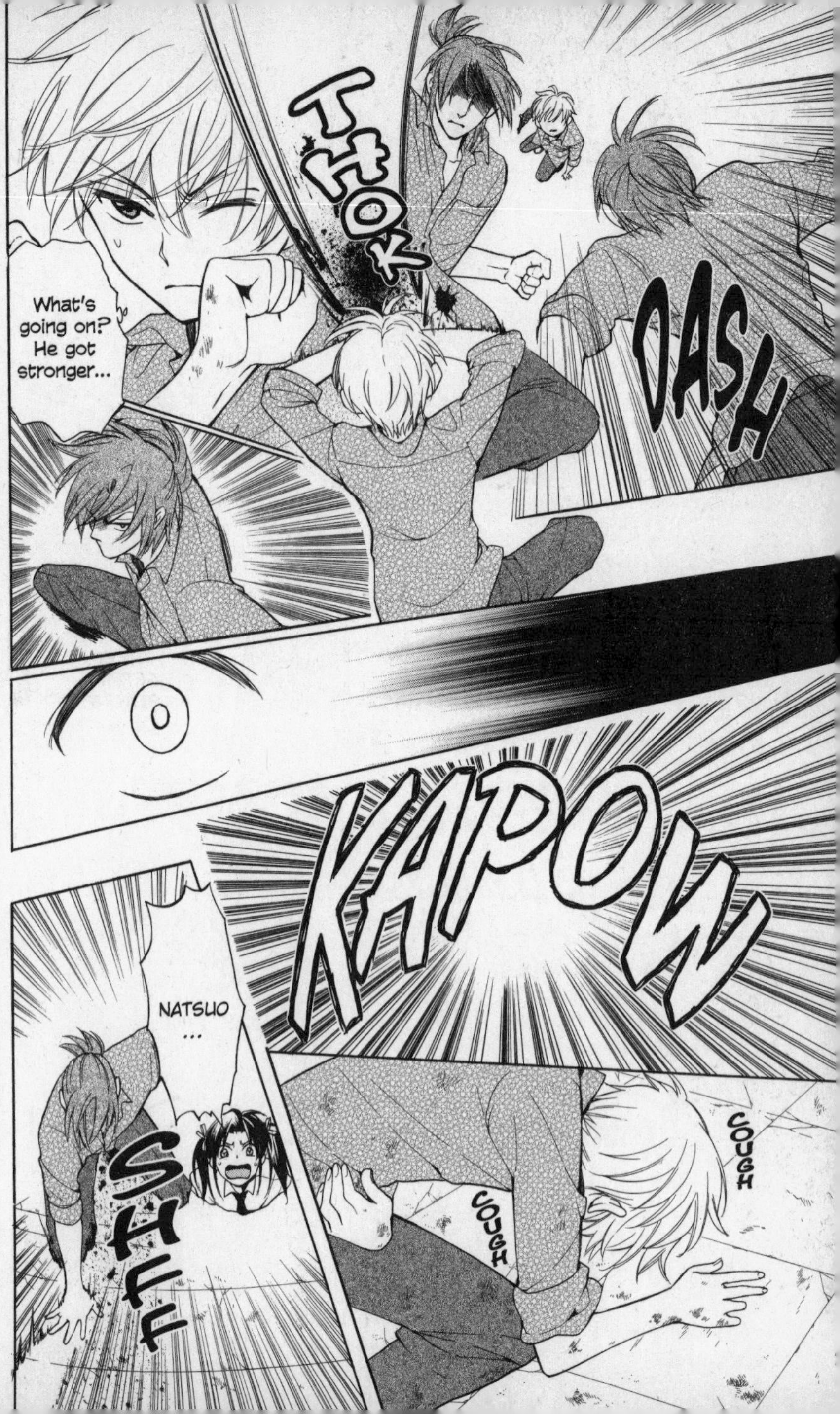
THOK
DASH
What's going on? He got stronger...
KAPOW
COUGH
COUGH
NATSUO ...
SHFF

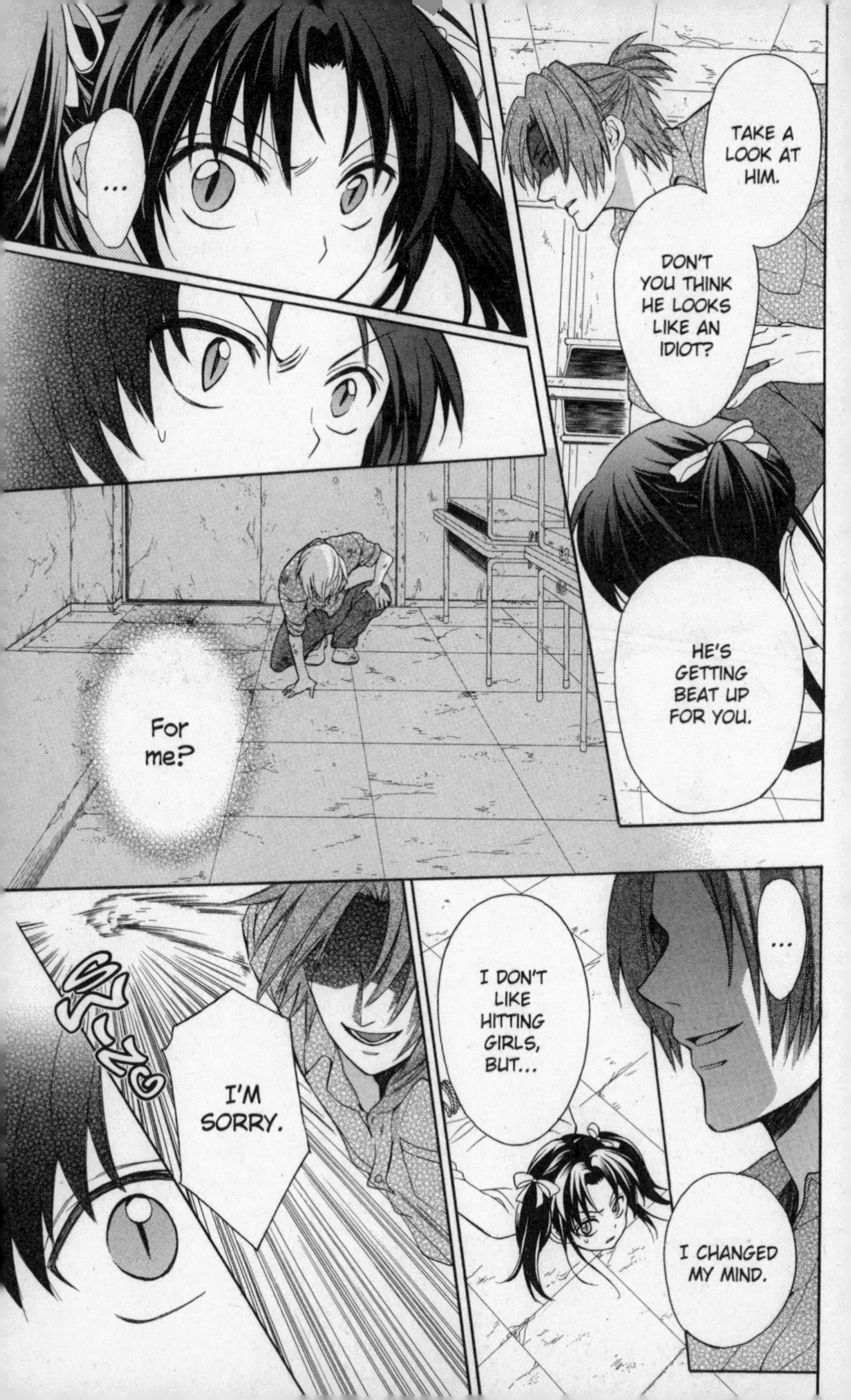
TAKE A LOOK AT HIM.
DON'T YOU THINK HE LOOKS LIKE AN IDIOT?
HE'S GETTING BEAT UP FOR YOU.
...
For me?
...
I DON'T LIKE HITTING GIRLS, BUT...
I CHANGED MY MIND.
I'M SORRY.

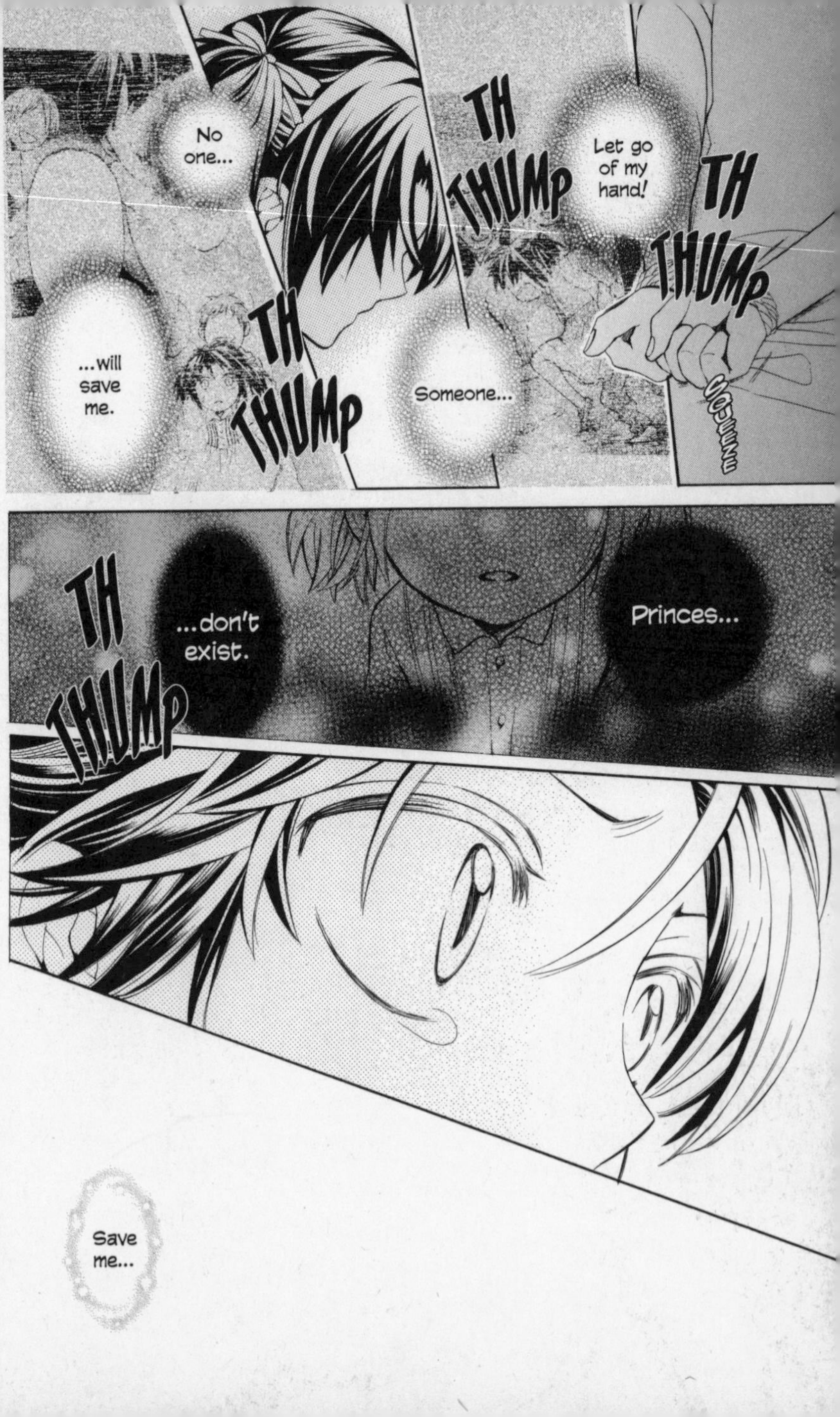
Let go of my hand!
TH THUMP
TH THUMP
Someone...
TH THUMP
No one...
...will save me.
Princes...
...don't exist.
TH THUMP
Save me...

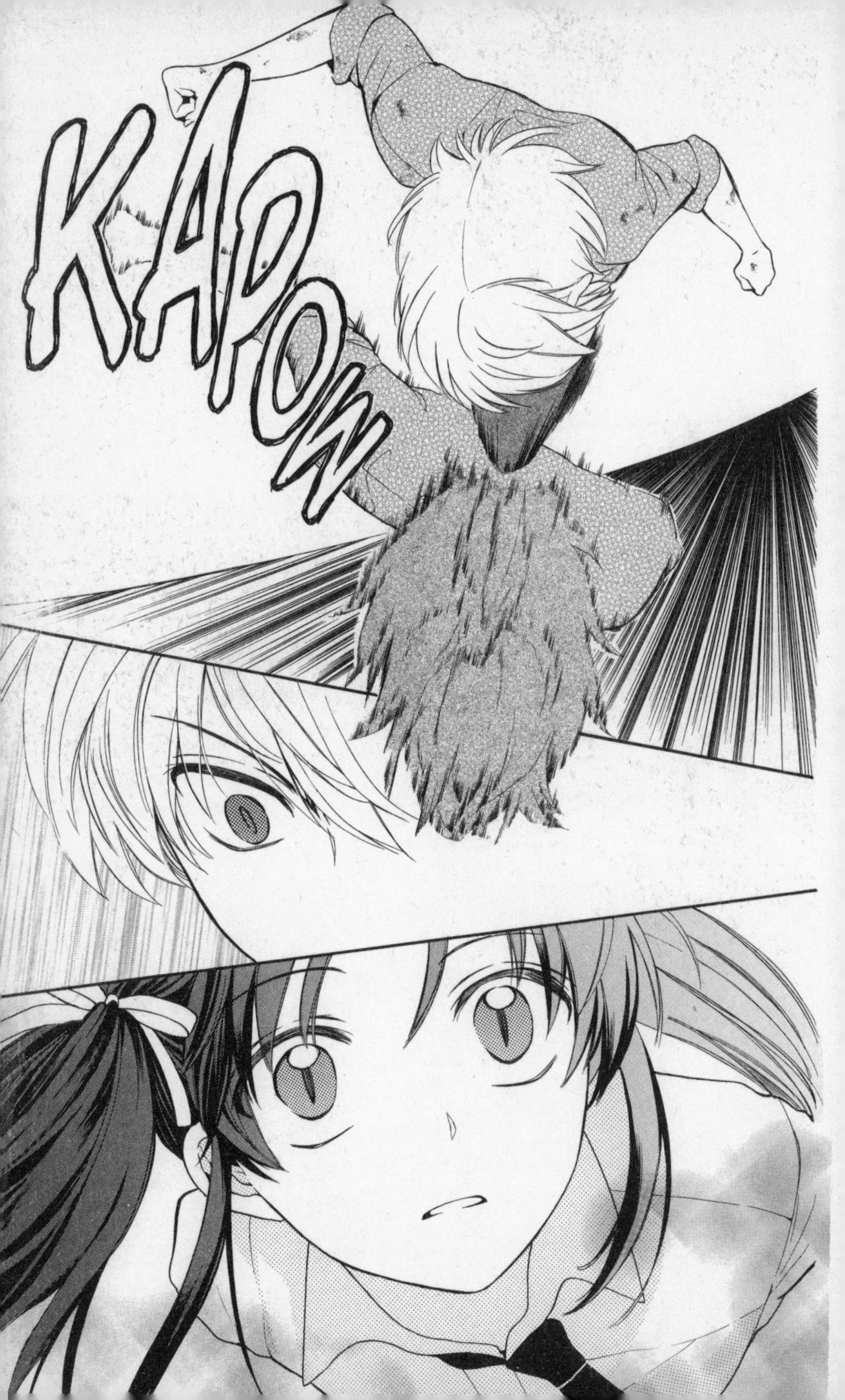
KAPOW

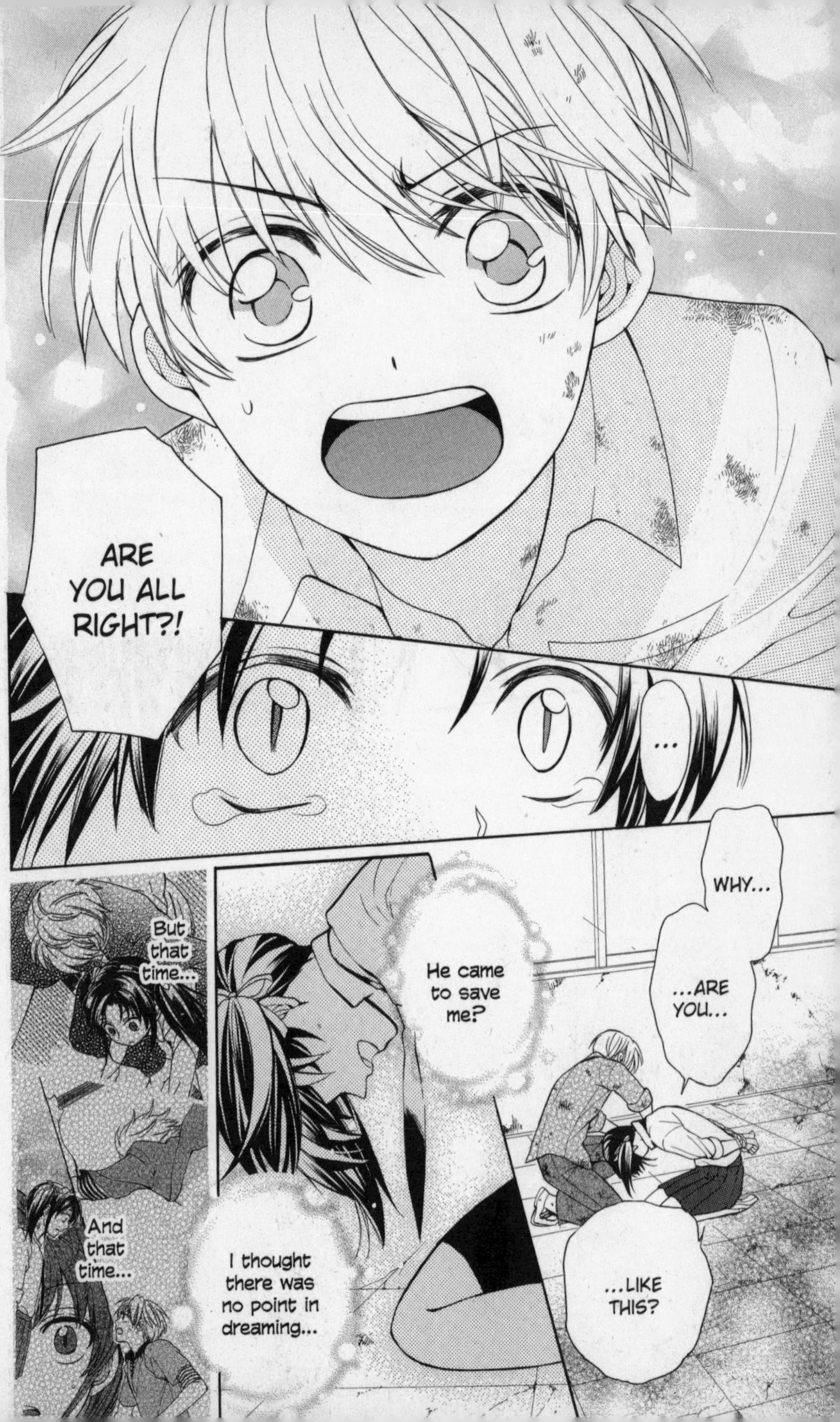
ARE YOU ALL RIGHT?!
...
WHY...
...ARE YOU...
...LIKE THIS?
He came to save me?
But that time...
And that time...
I thought there was no point in dreaming...

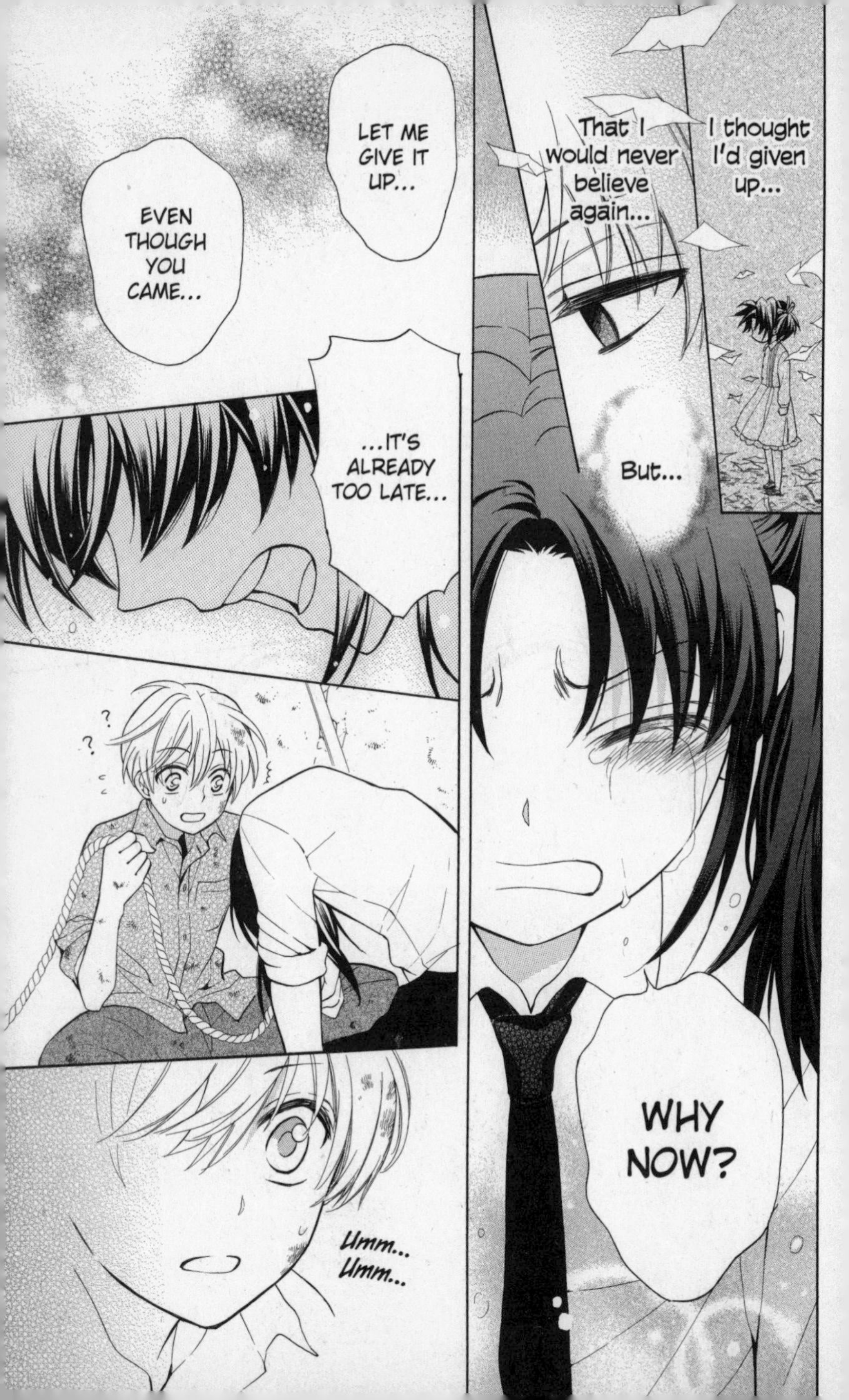
I thought I'd given up...
That I would never believe again...
But...
WHY NOW?
LET ME GIVE IT UP...
EVEN THOUGH YOU CAME...
...IT'S ALREADY TOO LATE...
Umm... Umm...

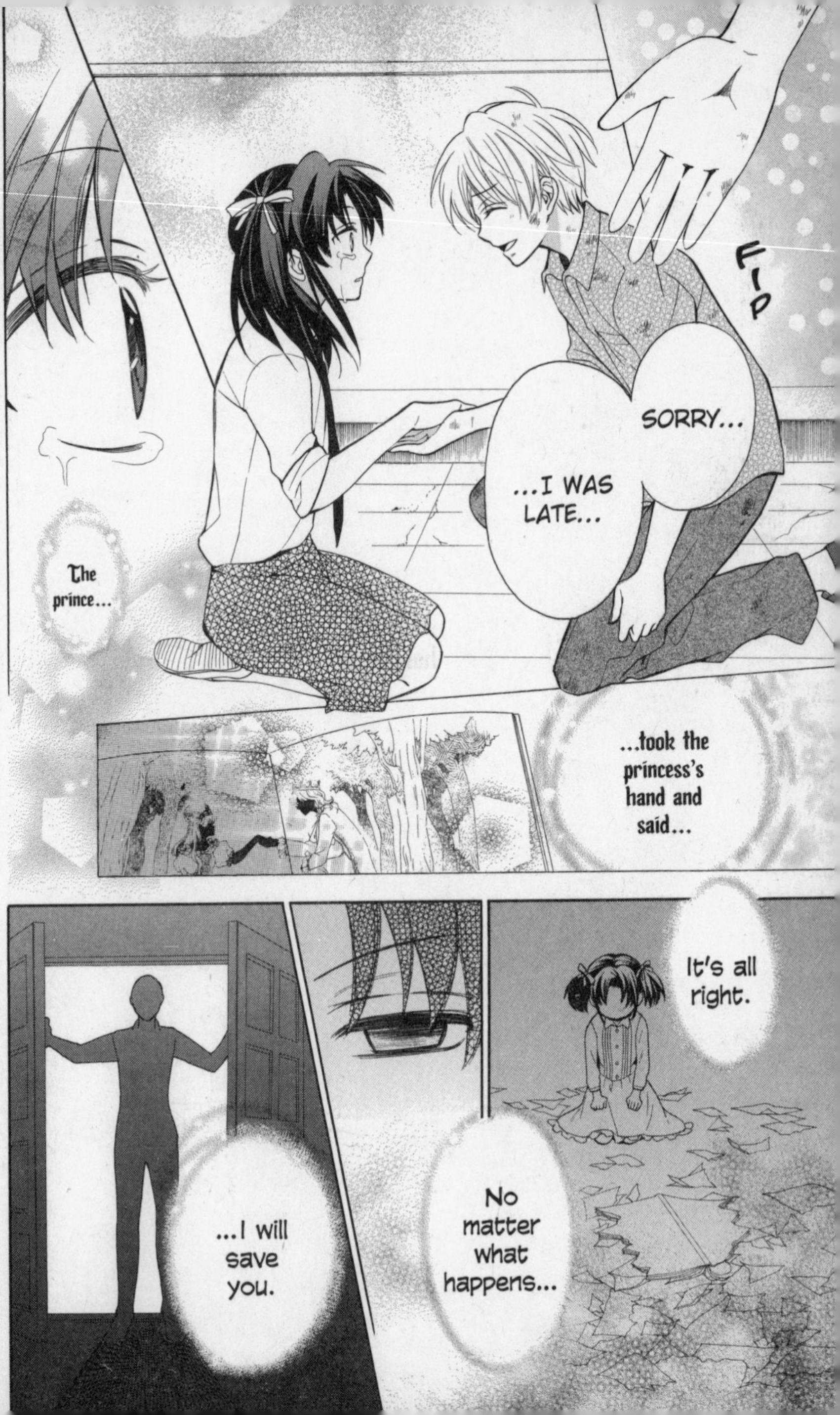
FIP
SORRY...
...I WAS LATE...
The prince...
...took the princess's hand and said...
It's all right.
No matter what happens...
...I will save you.

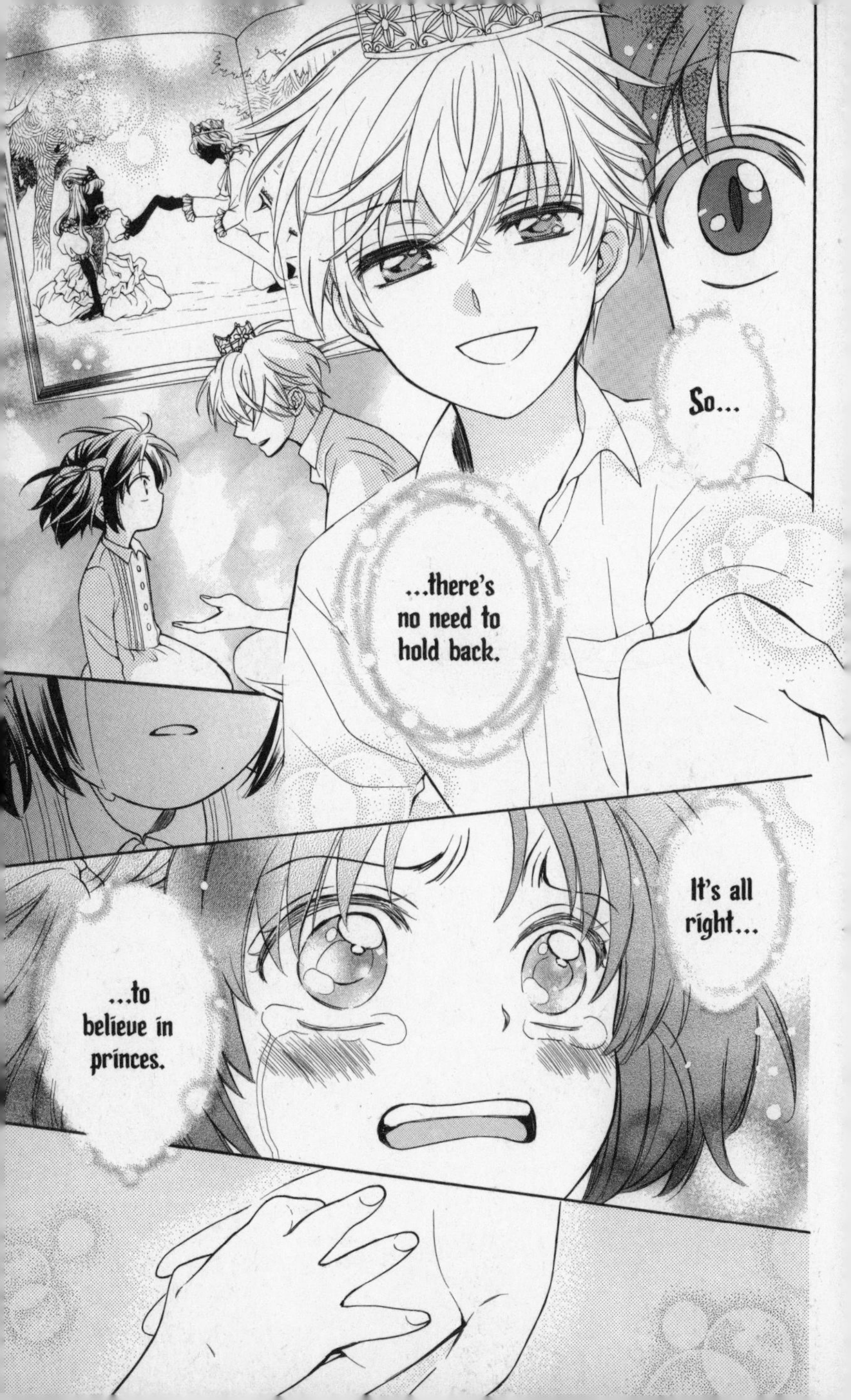
So...
...there's no need to hold back.
It's all right...
...to believe in princes.

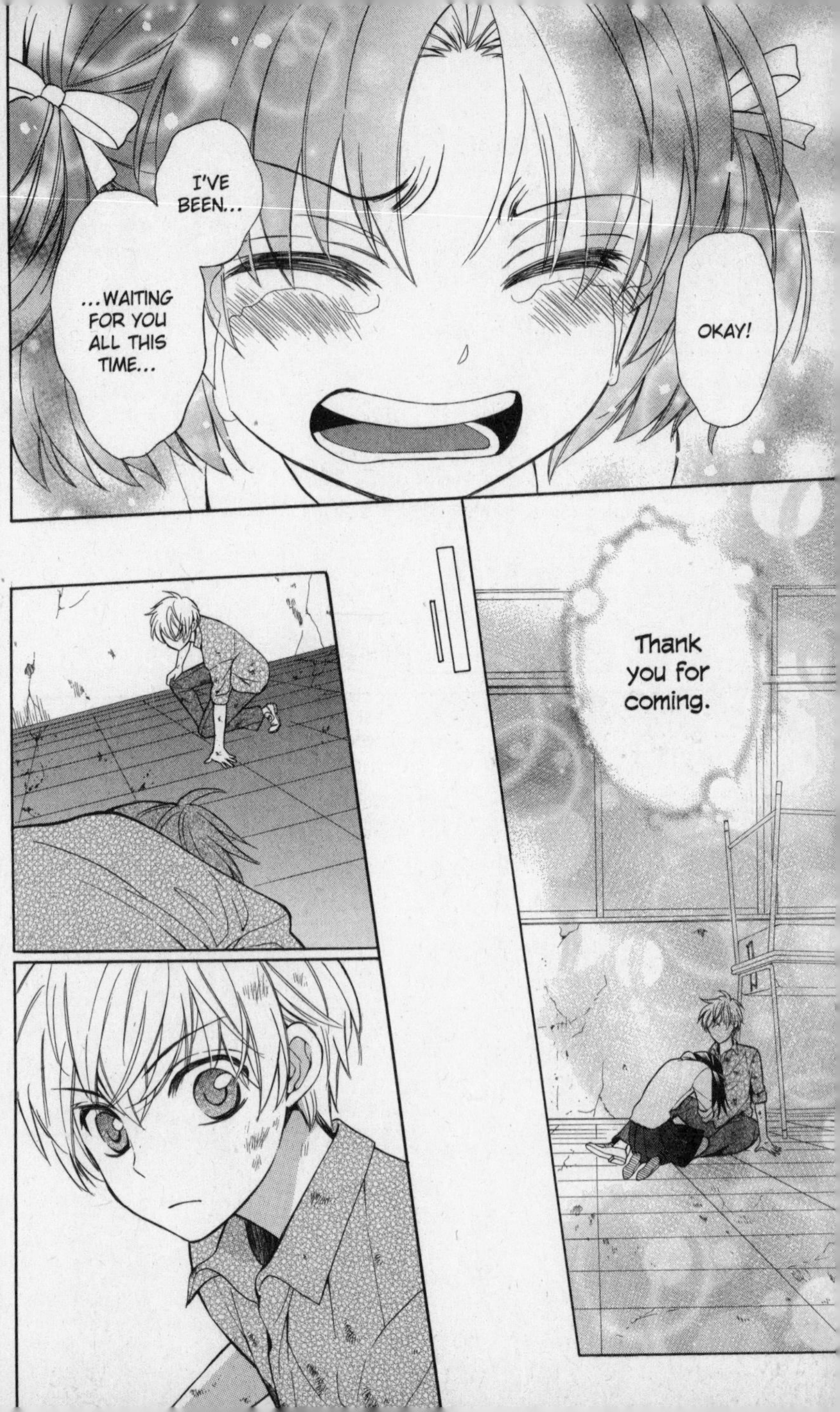
OKAY!
I'VE BEEN...
...WAITING FOR YOU ALL THIS TIME...
Thank you for coming.

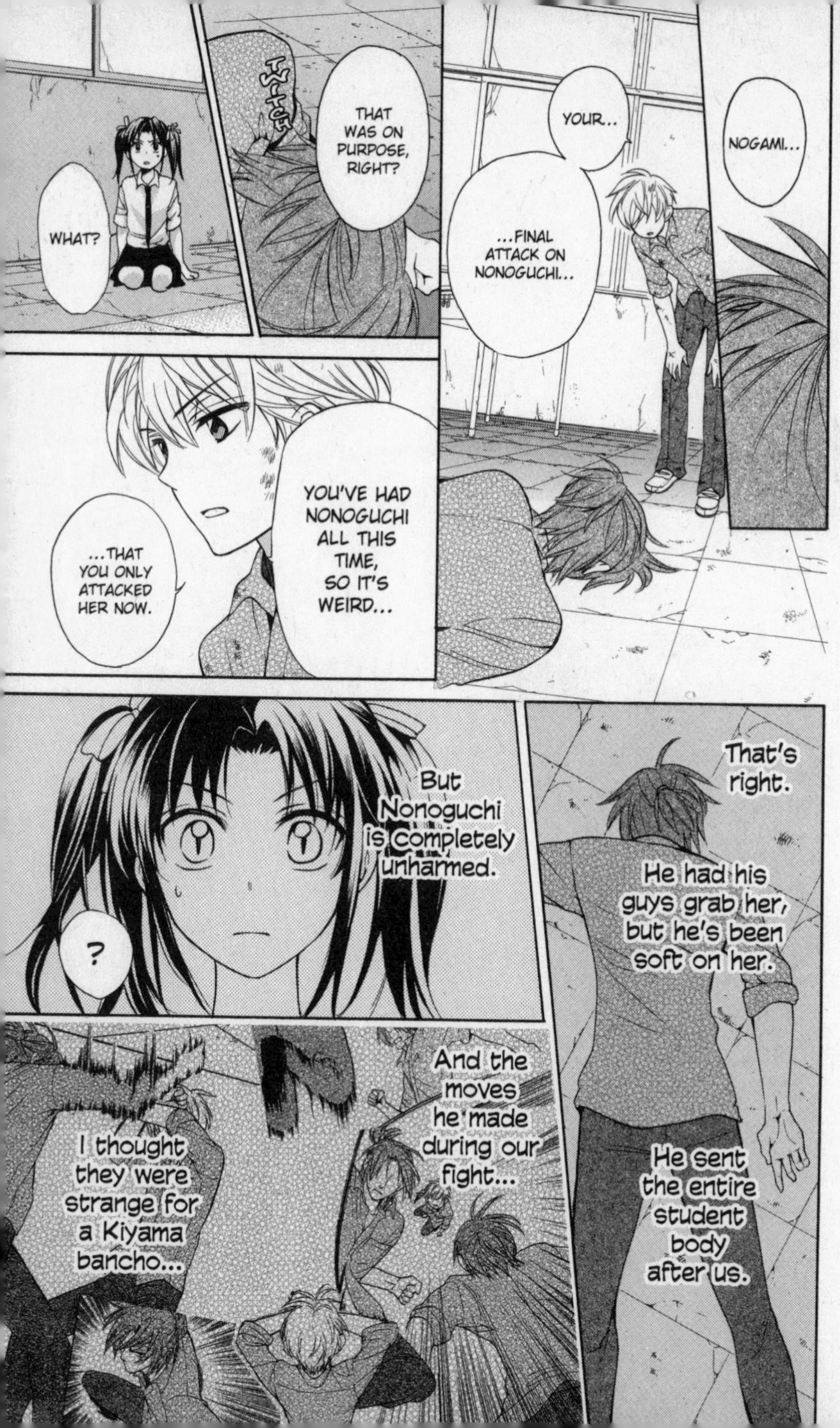

NOGAMI...
YOUR...
...FINAL ATTACK ON NONOGUCHI...
TWITCH
THAT WAS ON PURPOSE, RIGHT?
WHAT?
YOU'VE HAD NONOGUCHI ALL THIS TIME, SO IT'S WEIRD...
...THAT YOU ONLY ATTACKED HER NOW.
That's right.
He had his guys grab her, but he's been soft on her.
He sent the entire student body after us.
But Nonoguchi is completely unharmed.
?
And the moves he made during our fight...
I thought they were strange for a Kiyama bancho...

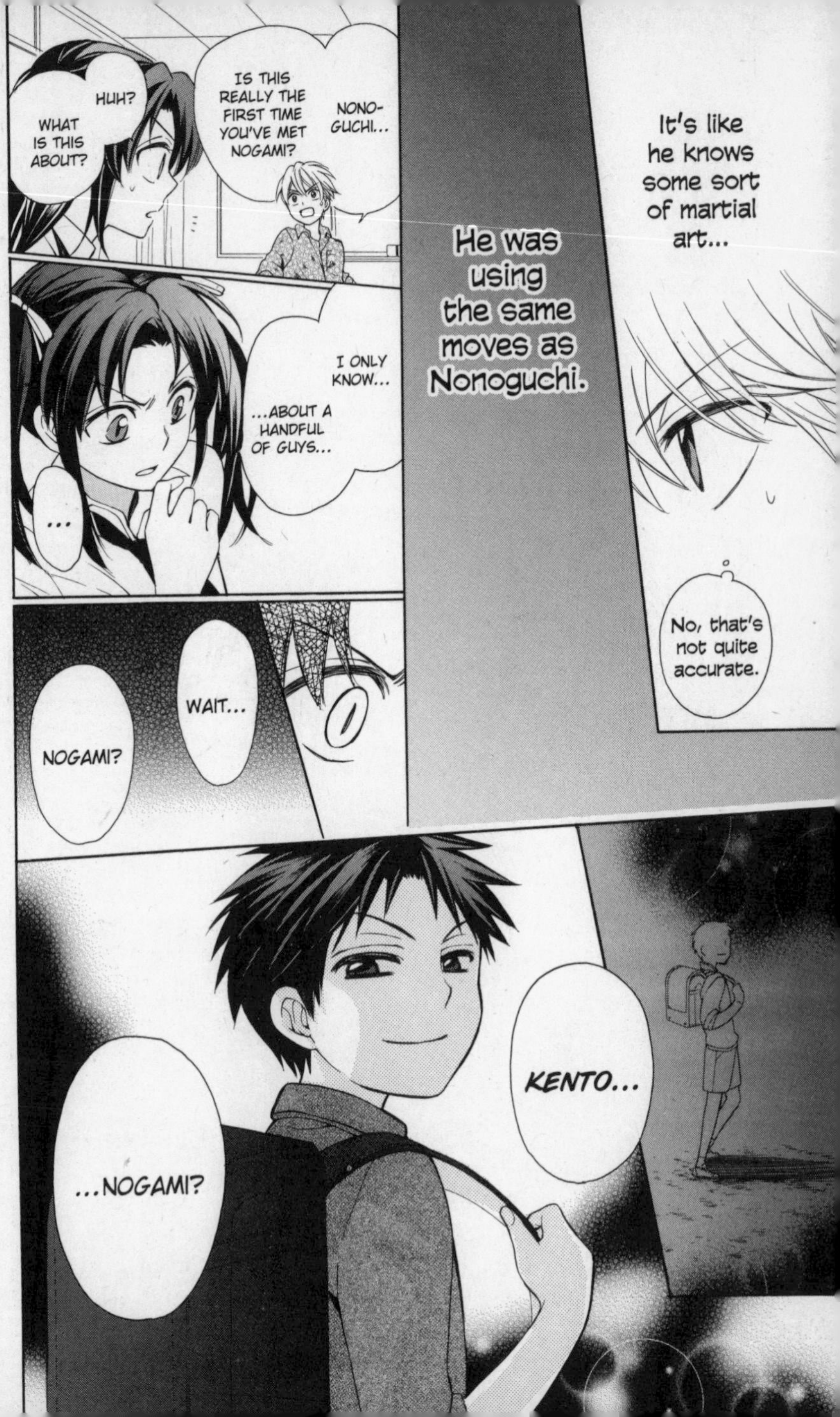
It's like he knows some sort of martial art...
No, that's not quite accurate.
He was using the same moves as Nonoguchi.
NONO-GUCHI...
IS THIS REALLY THE FIRST TIME YOU'VE MET NOGAMI?
HUH?
WHAT IS THIS ABOUT?
I ONLY KNOW...
...ABOUT A HANDFUL OF GUYS...
...
WAIT...
NOGAMI?
KENTO...
...NOGAMI?

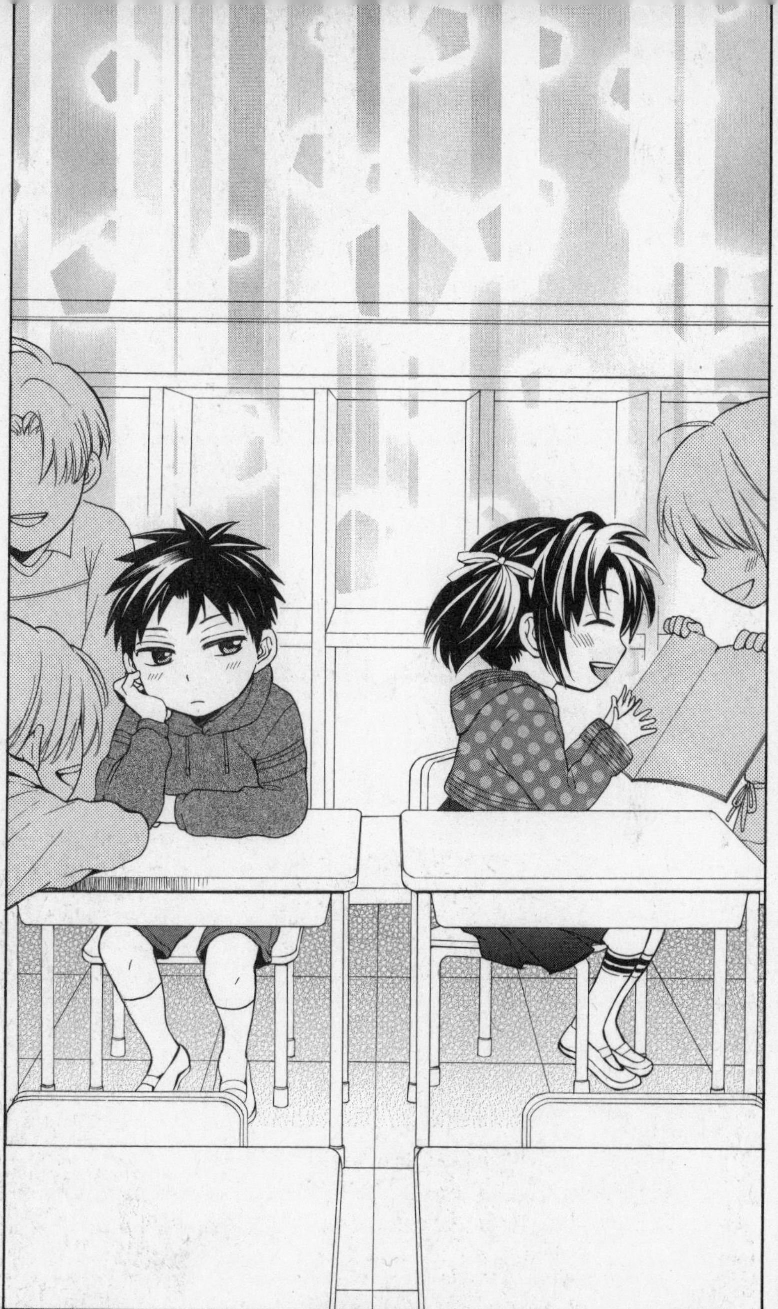

Chapter 78

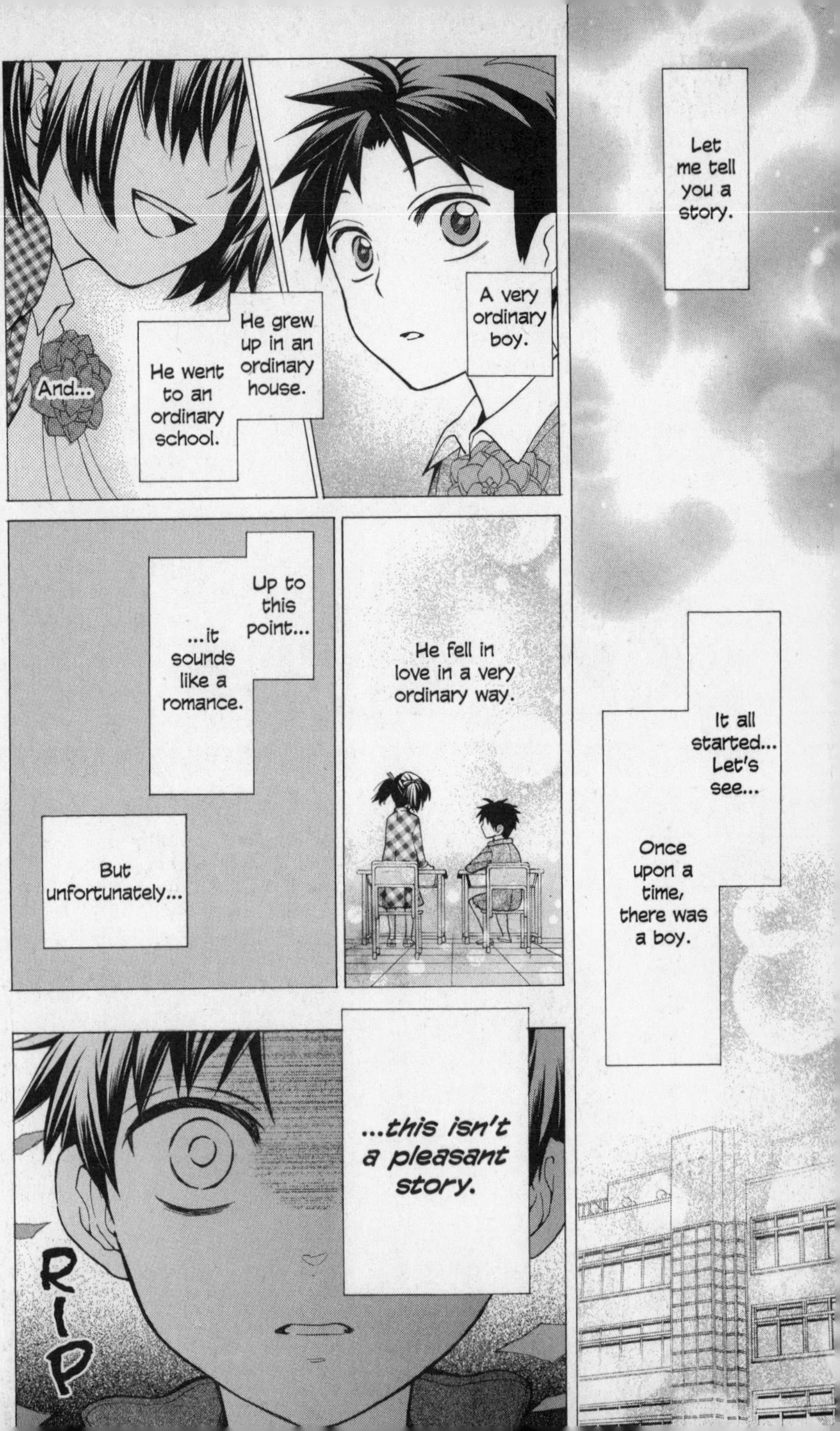
Let me tell you a story.
It all started... Let's see...
Once upon a time, there was a boy.
A very ordinary boy.
He grew up in an ordinary house.
He went to an ordinary school.
And...
He fell in love in a very ordinary way.
Up to this point...
...it sounds like a romance.
But unfortunately...
...this isn't a pleasant story.
RIP

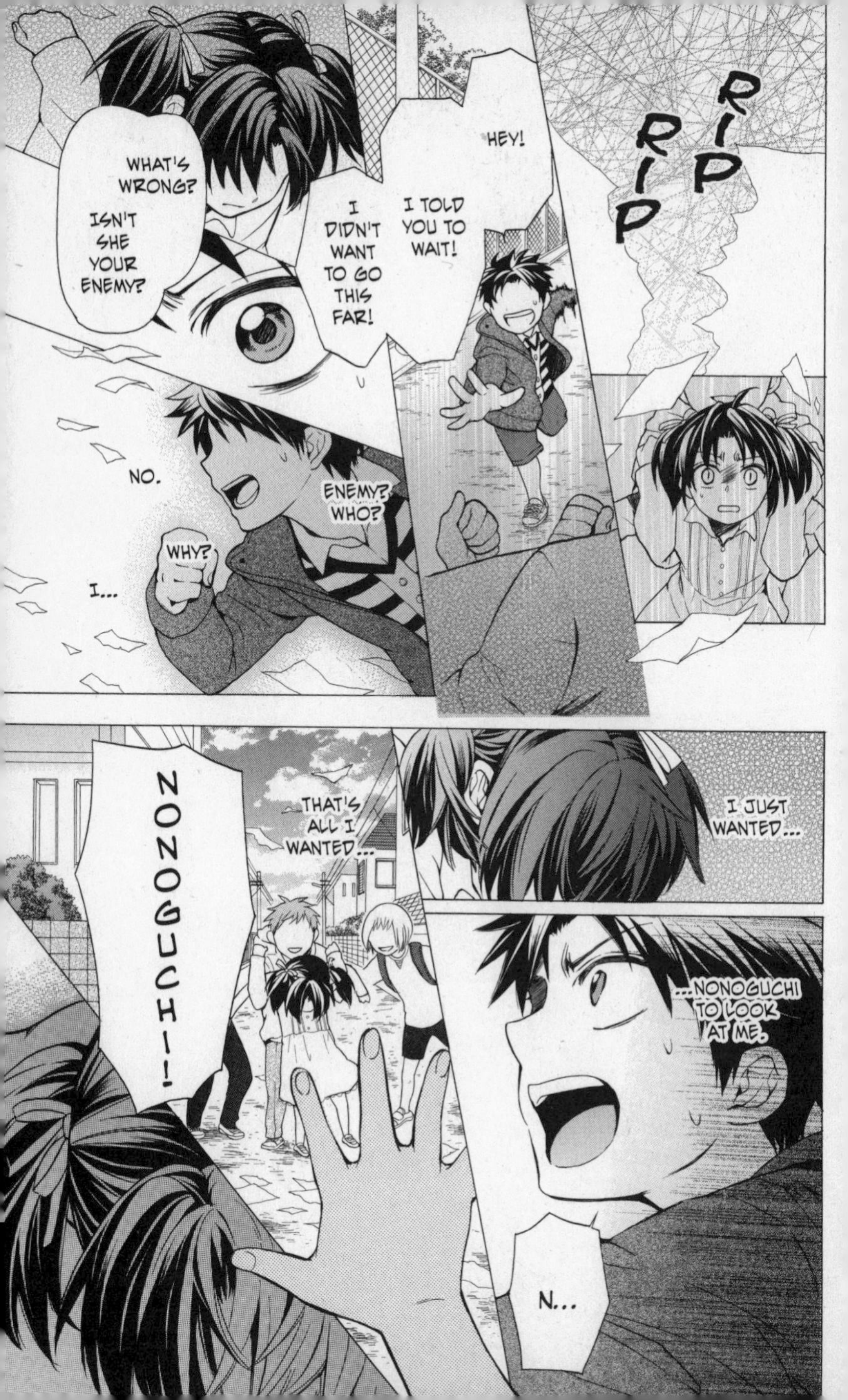
RIP RIP
HEY!
I TOLD YOU TO WAIT!
I DIDN'T WANT TO GO THIS FAR!
WHAT'S WRONG?
ISN'T SHE YOUR ENEMY?
ENEMY? WHO?
NO.
WHY?
I...
I JUST WANTED...
...NONOGUCHI TO LOOK AT ME.
N...
THAT'S ALL I WANTED...
NONOGUCHI!

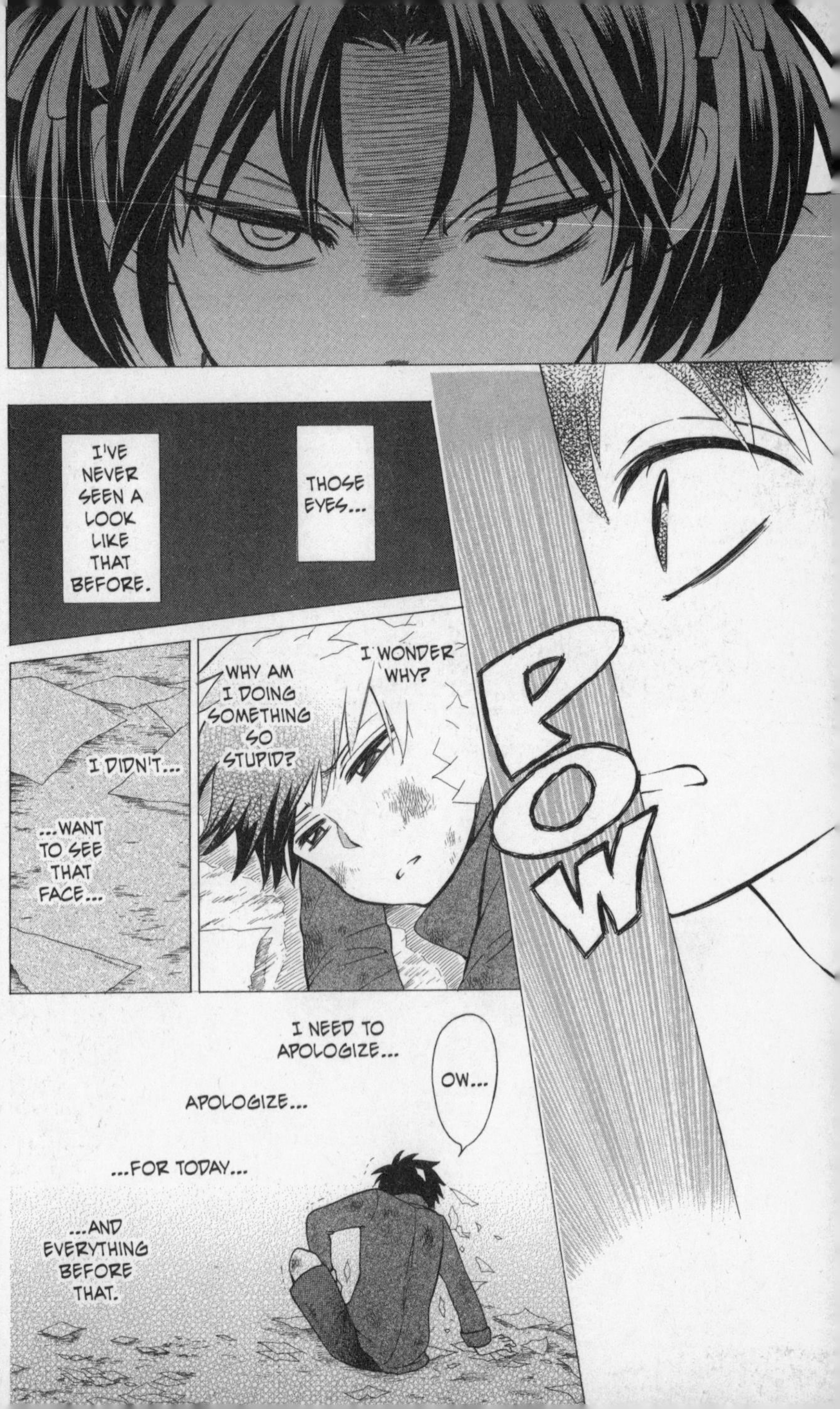
POW
THOSE EYES...
I'VE NEVER SEEN A LOOK LIKE THAT BEFORE.
I WONDER WHY?
WHY AM I DOING SOMETHING SO STUPID?
I DIDN'T...
...WANT TO SEE THAT FACE...
OW...
I NEED TO APOLOGIZE...
APOLOGIZE...
...FOR TODAY...
...AND EVERYTHING BEFORE THAT.

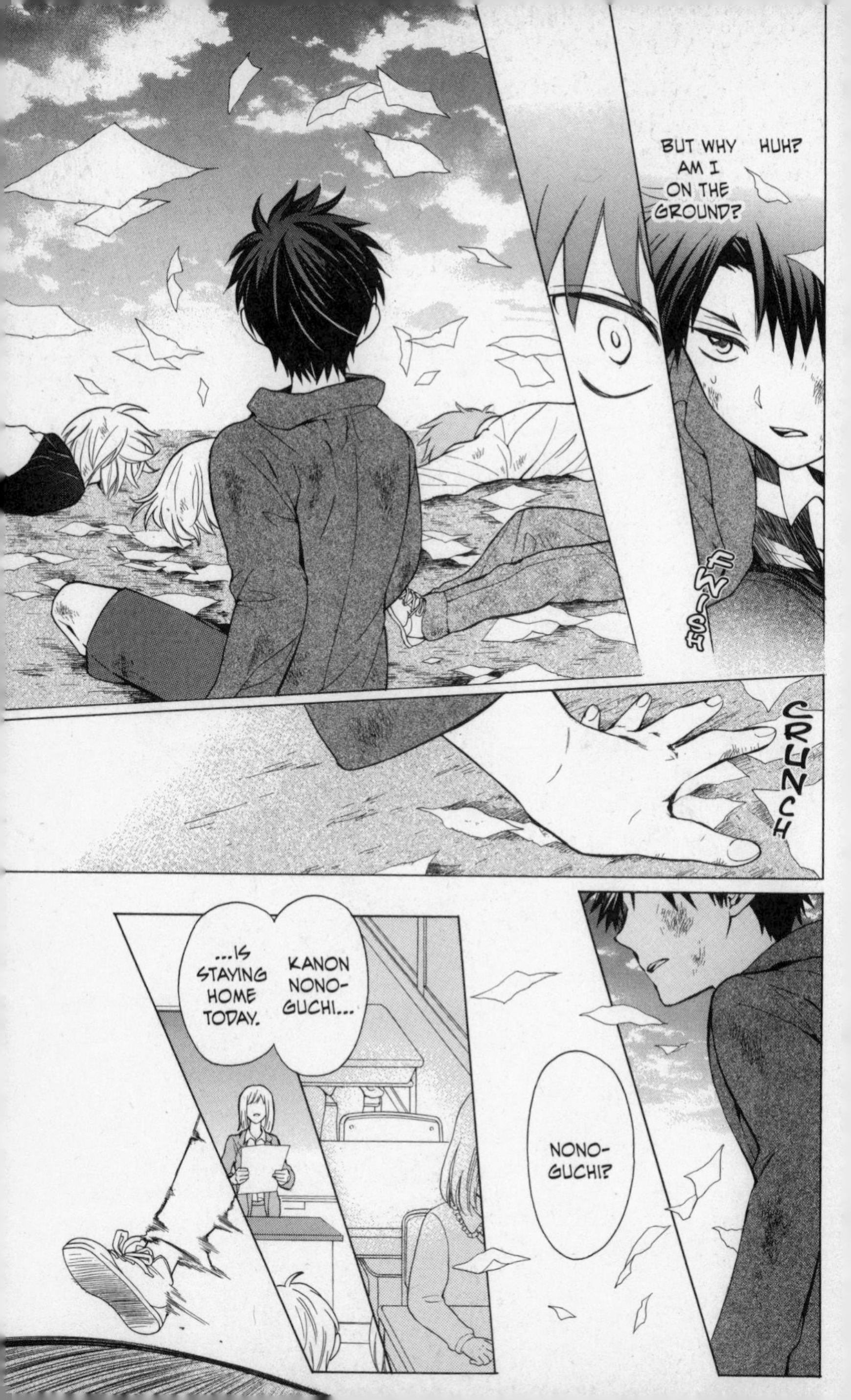
HUH?
BUT WHY AM I ON THE GROUND?
FWISH
CRUNCH
NONO-GUCHI?
KANON NONO-GUCHI...
...IS STAYING HOME TODAY.

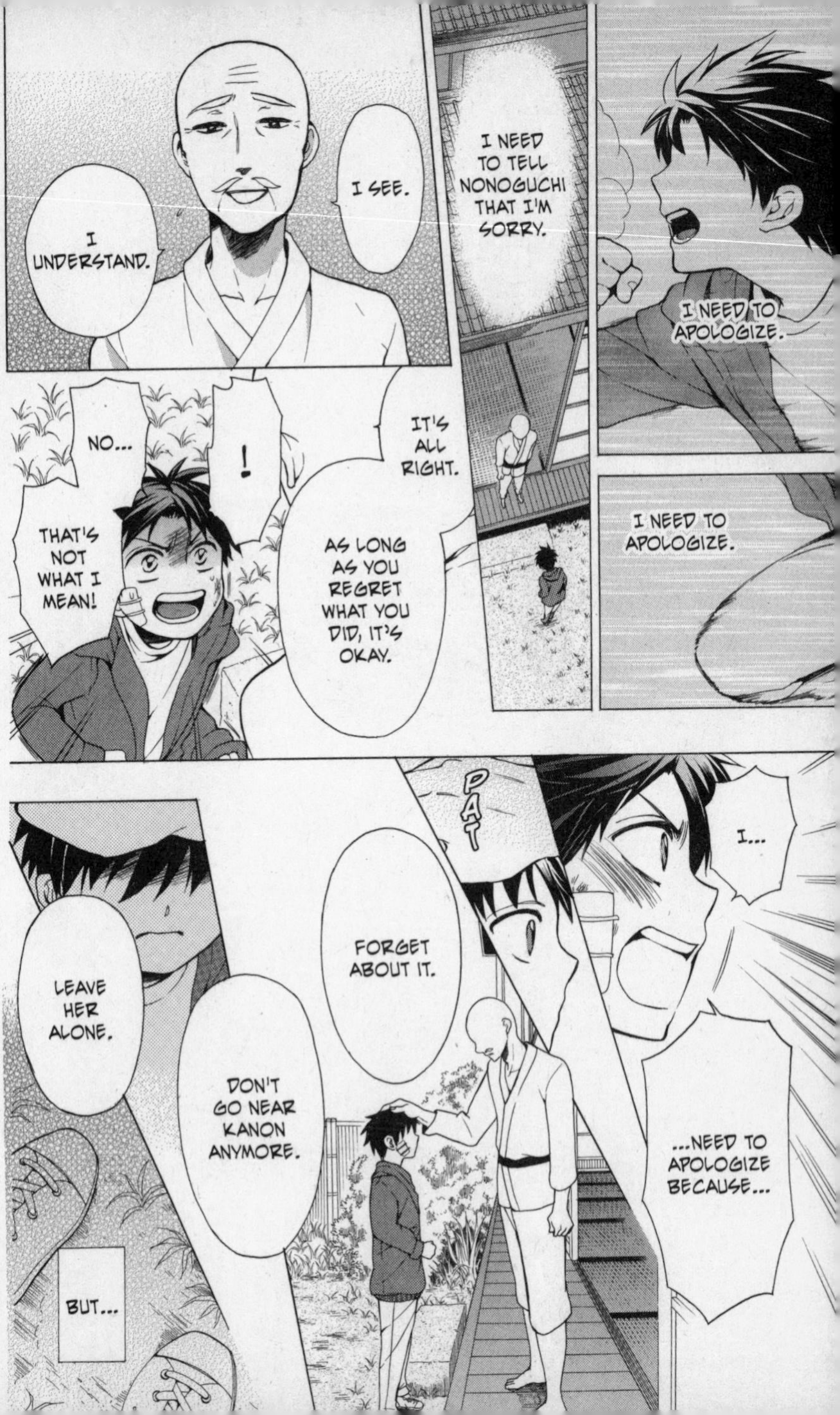
I NEED TO APOLOGIZE.
I NEED TO APOLOGIZE.
I NEED TO TELL NONOGUCHI THAT I'M SORRY.
I SEE.
I UNDERSTAND.
IT'S ALL RIGHT.
AS LONG AS YOU REGRET WHAT YOU DID, IT'S OKAY.
!
NO...
THAT'S NOT WHAT I MEAN!
I...
...NEED TO APOLOGIZE BECAUSE...
PAT
FORGET ABOUT IT.
DON'T GO NEAR KANON ANYMORE.
LEAVE HER ALONE.
BUT...

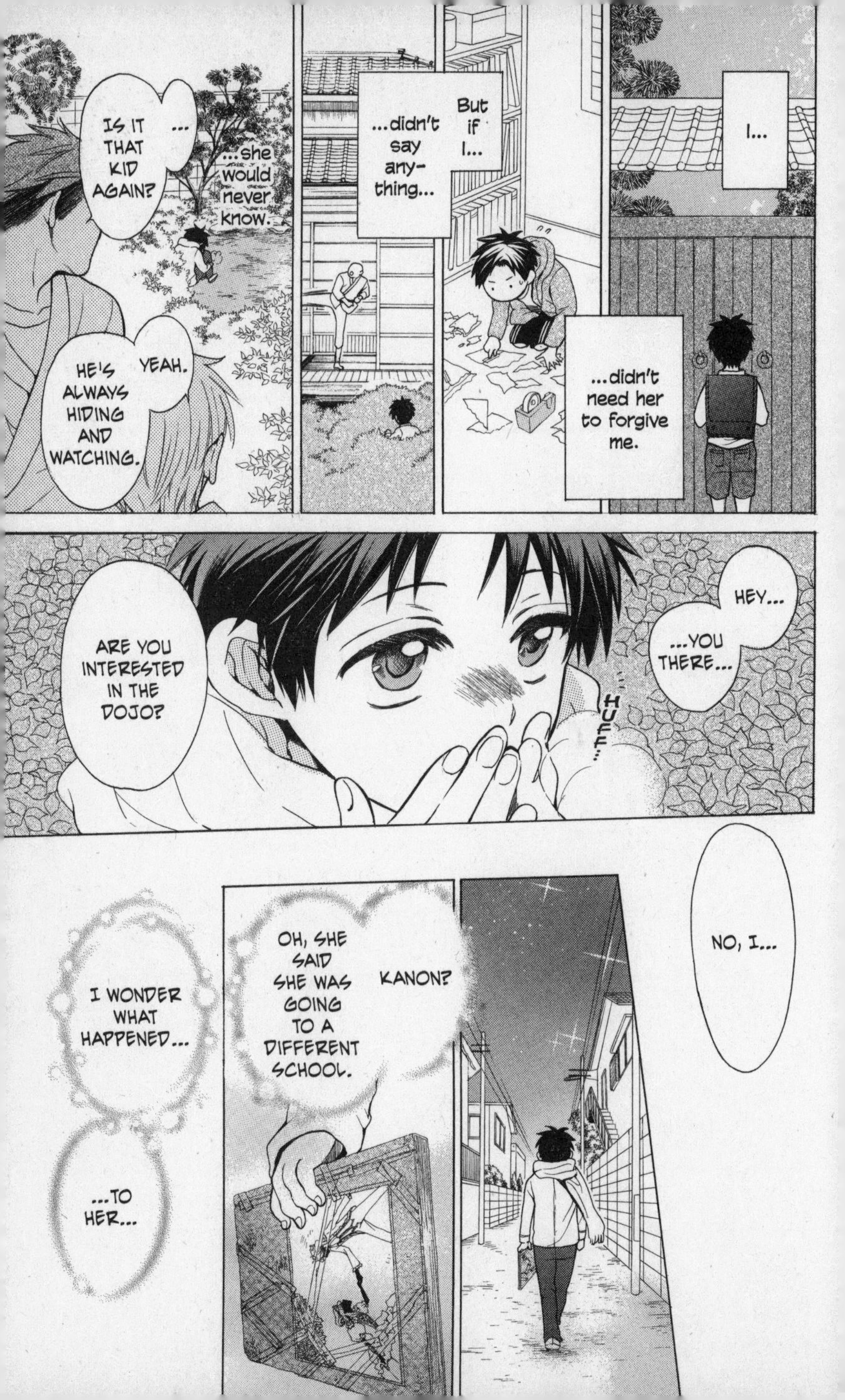
I...
...didn't need her to forgive me.
But if I...
...didn't say anything...
...she would never know.
...
IS IT THAT KID AGAIN?
YEAH.
HE'S ALWAYS HIDING AND WATCHING.
HEY...
...YOU THERE...
HUFF...
ARE YOU INTERESTED IN THE DOJO?
NO, I...
KANON?
OH, SHE SAID SHE WAS GOING TO A DIFFERENT SCHOOL.
I WONDER WHAT HAPPENED...
...TO HER...

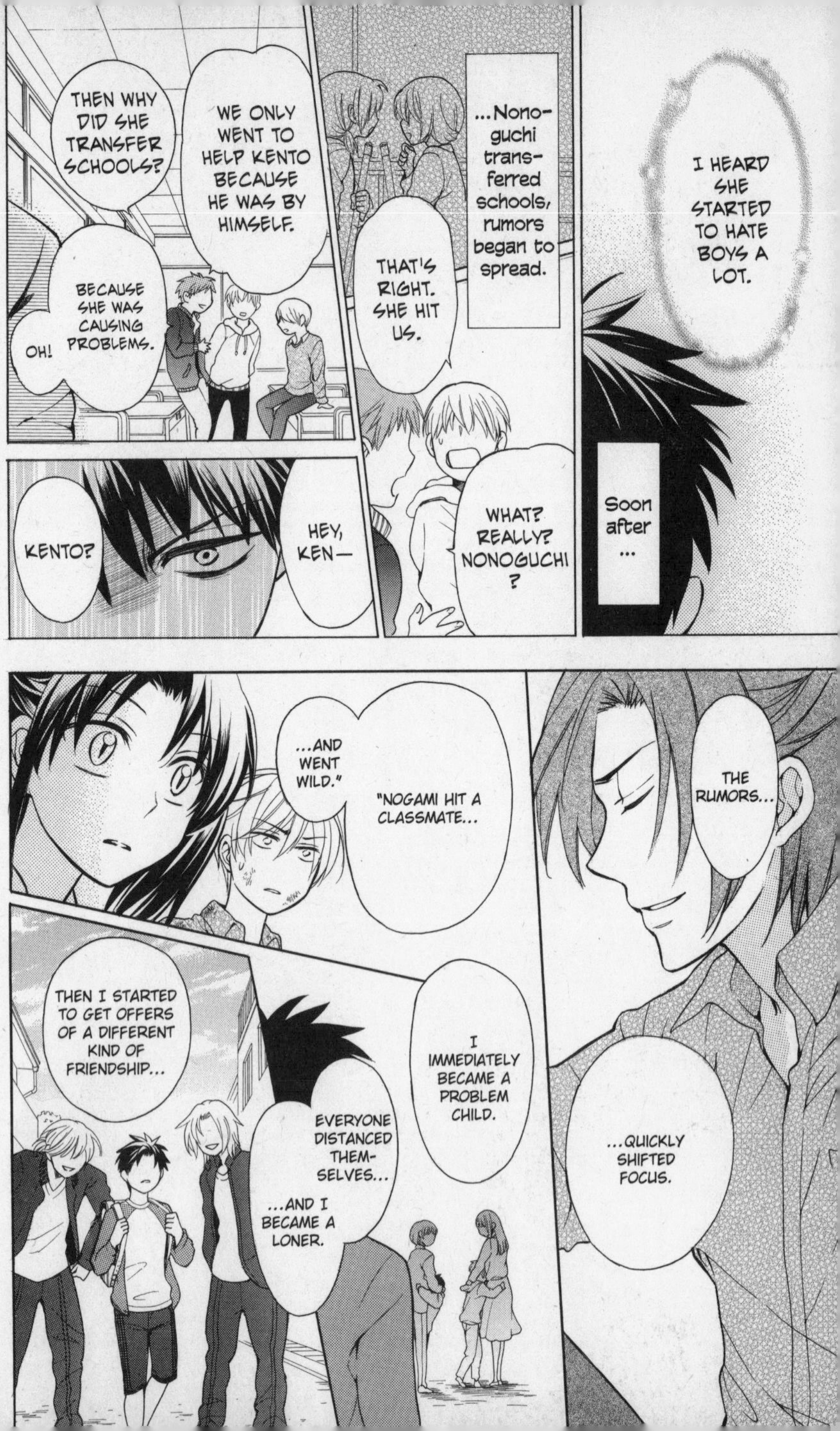
I HEARD SHE STARTED TO HATE BOYS A LOT.
Soon after ...
...Nonoguchi transferred schools, rumors began to spread.
THAT'S RIGHT. SHE HIT US.
WE ONLY WENT TO HELP KENTO BECAUSE HE WAS BY HIMSELF.
THEN WHY DID SHE TRANSFER SCHOOLS?
BECAUSE SHE WAS CAUSING PROBLEMS.
OH!
WHAT? REALLY? NONOGUCHI?
HEY, KEN—
KENTO?
THE RUMORS...
...QUICKLY SHIFTED FOCUS.
"NOGAMI HIT A CLASSMATE...
...AND WENT WILD."
I IMMEDIATELY BECAME A PROBLEM CHILD.
EVERYONE DISTANCED THEMSELVES...
...AND I BECAME A LONER.
THEN I STARTED TO GET OFFERS OF A DIFFERENT KIND OF FRIENDSHIP...

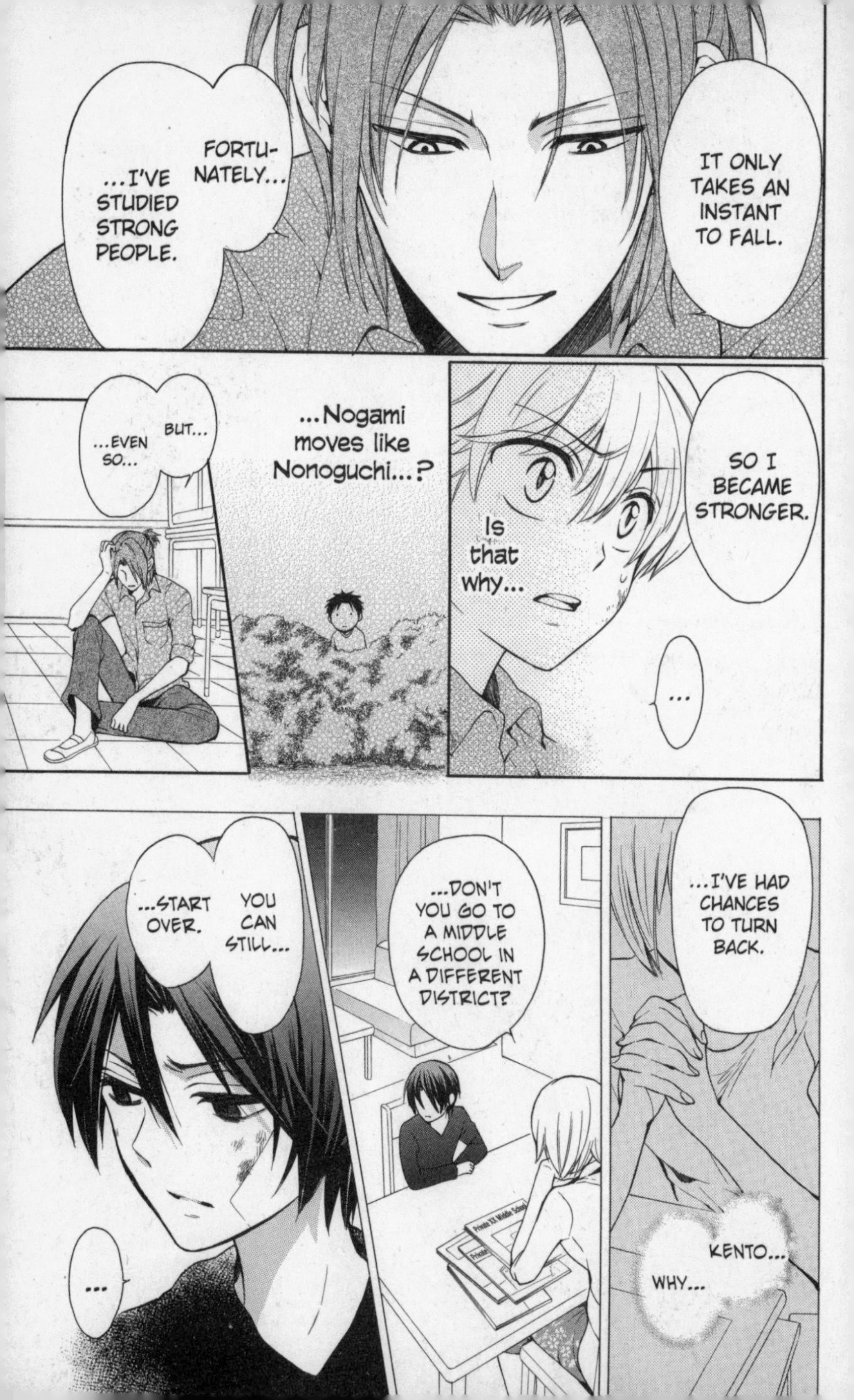
IT ONLY TAKES AN INSTANT TO FALL.
FORTUNATELY...
...I'VE STUDIED STRONG PEOPLE.
SO I BECAME STRONGER.
Is that why...
...
...Nogami moves like Nonoguchi...?
BUT...
...EVEN SO...
...I'VE HAD CHANCES TO TURN BACK.
KENTO...
WHY...
...DON'T YOU GO TO A MIDDLE SCHOOL IN A DIFFERENT DISTRICT?
YOU CAN STILL...
...START OVER.
...

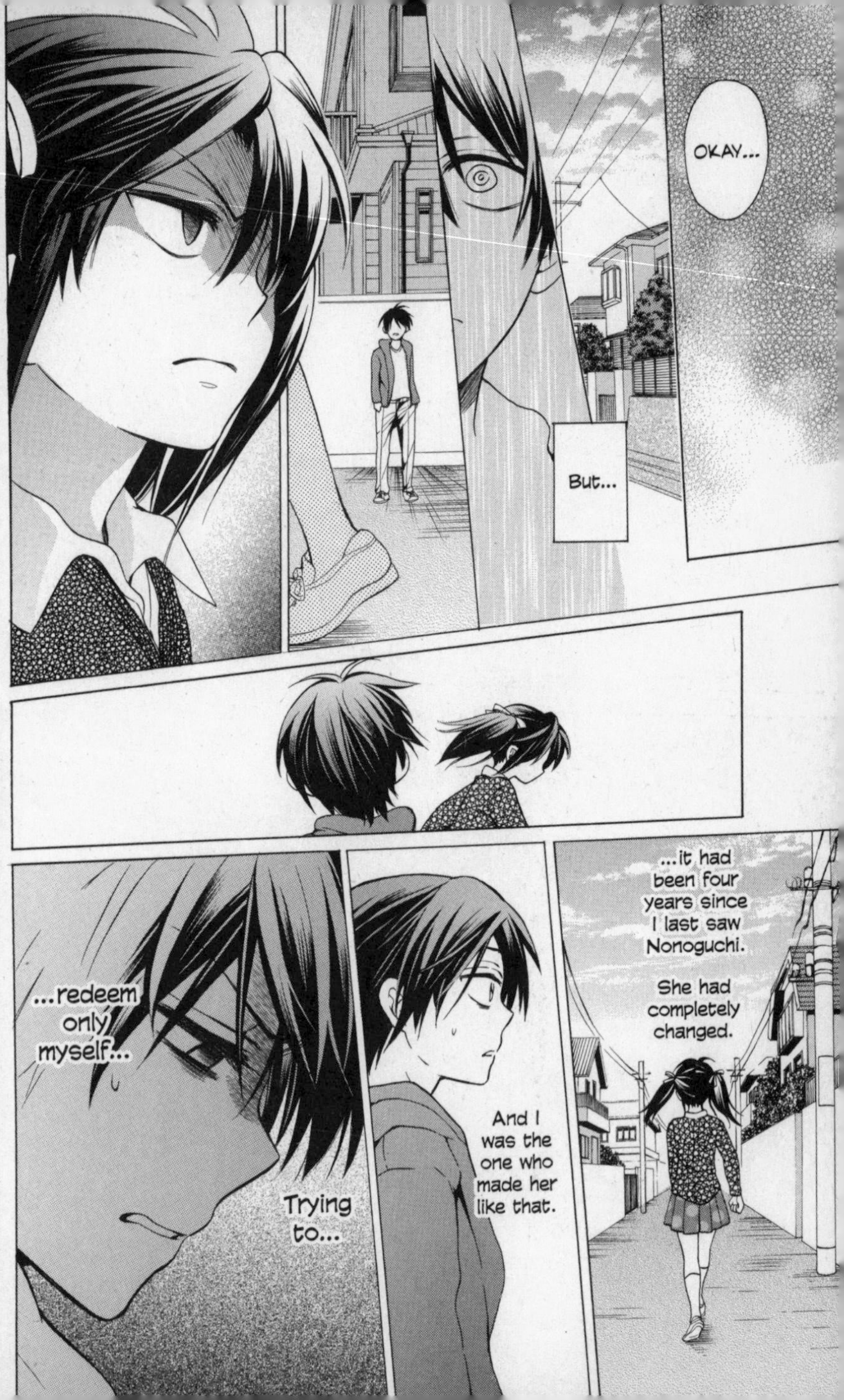
OKAY...
But...
...it had been four years since I last saw Nonoguchi.
She had completely changed.
And I was the one who made her like that.
Trying to...
...redeem only myself...

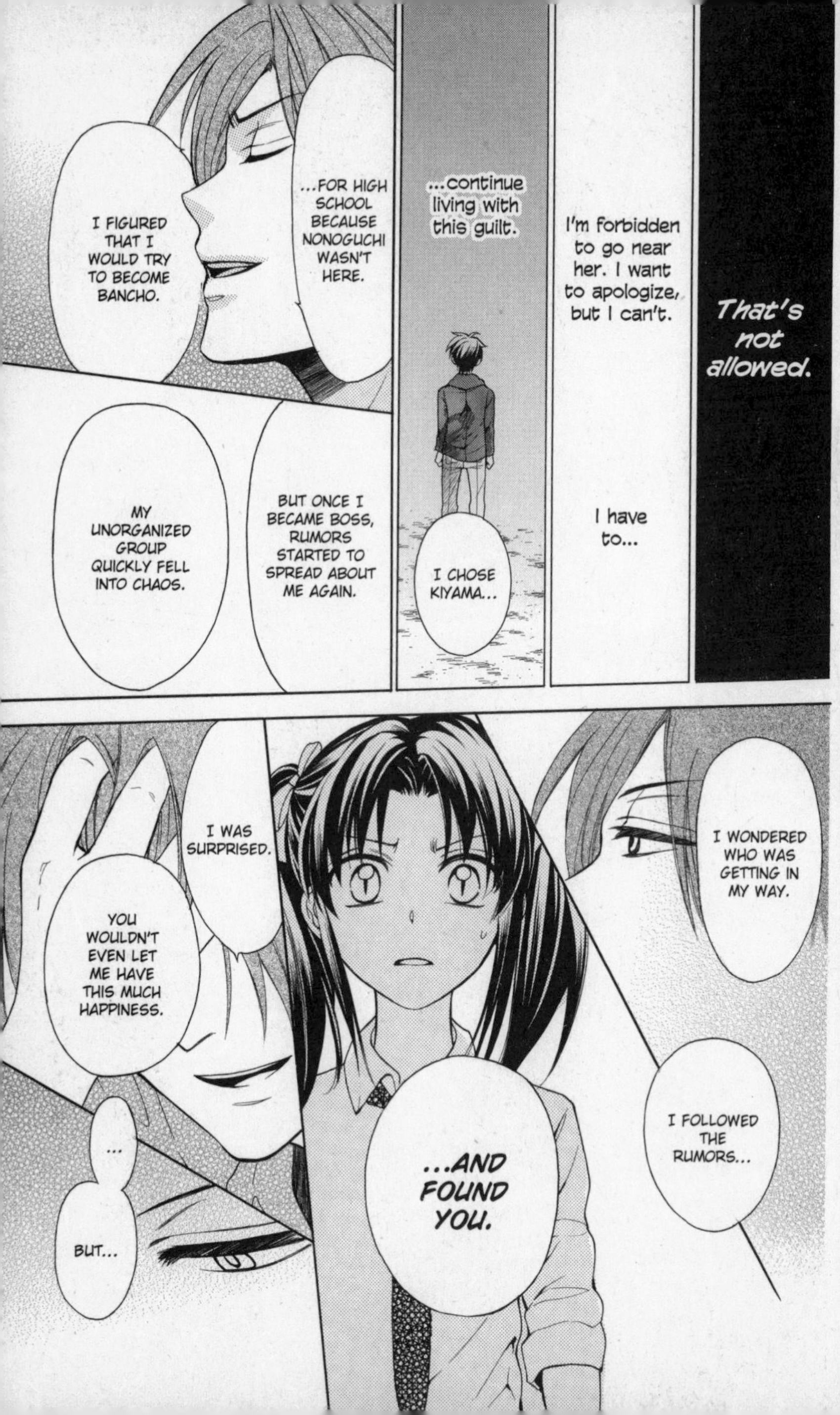
That's not allowed.
I'm forbidden to go near her. I want to apologize, but I can't.
I have to...
...continue living with this guilt.
I CHOSE KIYAMA...
...FOR HIGH SCHOOL BECAUSE NONOGUCHI WASN'T HERE.
I FIGURED THAT I WOULD TRY TO BECOME BANCHO.
BUT ONCE I BECAME BOSS, RUMORS STARTED TO SPREAD ABOUT ME AGAIN.
MY UNORGANIZED GROUP QUICKLY FELL INTO CHAOS.
I WONDERED WHO WAS GETTING IN MY WAY.
I FOLLOWED THE RUMORS...
...AND FOUND YOU.
I WAS SURPRISED.
YOU WOULDN'T EVEN LET ME HAVE THIS MUCH HAPPINESS.
...
BUT...

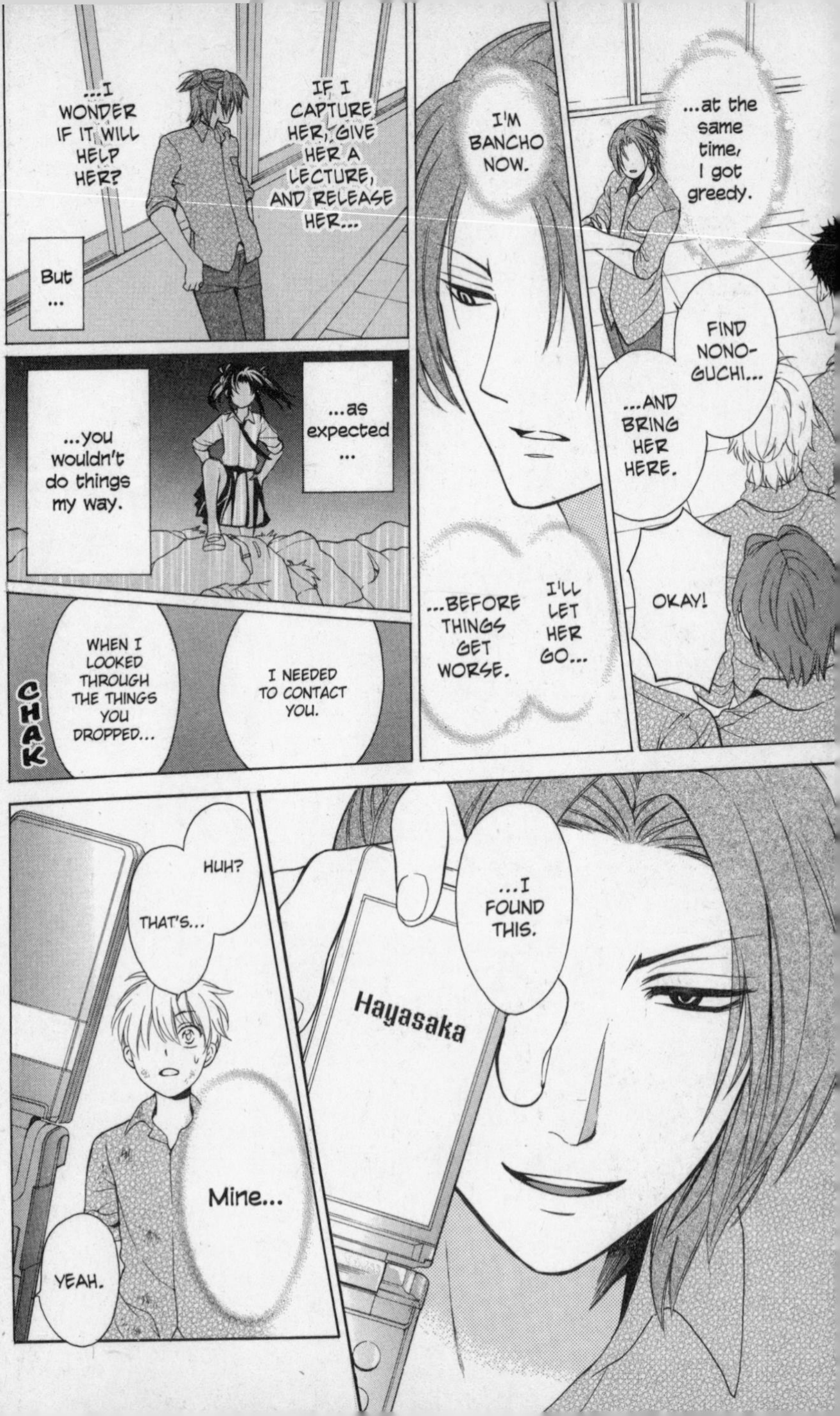
...at the same time, I got greedy.
FIND NONO-GUCHI...
...AND BRING HER HERE.
OKAY!
I'M BANCHO NOW.
I'LL LET HER GO...
...BEFORE THINGS GET WORSE.
IF I CAPTURE HER, GIVE HER A LECTURE, AND RELEASE HER...
...I WONDER IF IT WILL HELP HER?
But...
...as expected...
...you wouldn't do things my way.
I NEEDED TO CONTACT YOU.
WHEN I LOOKED THROUGH THE THINGS YOU DROPPED...
CHAK
...I FOUND THIS.
Hayasaka
HUH?
THAT'S...
Mine...
YEAH.

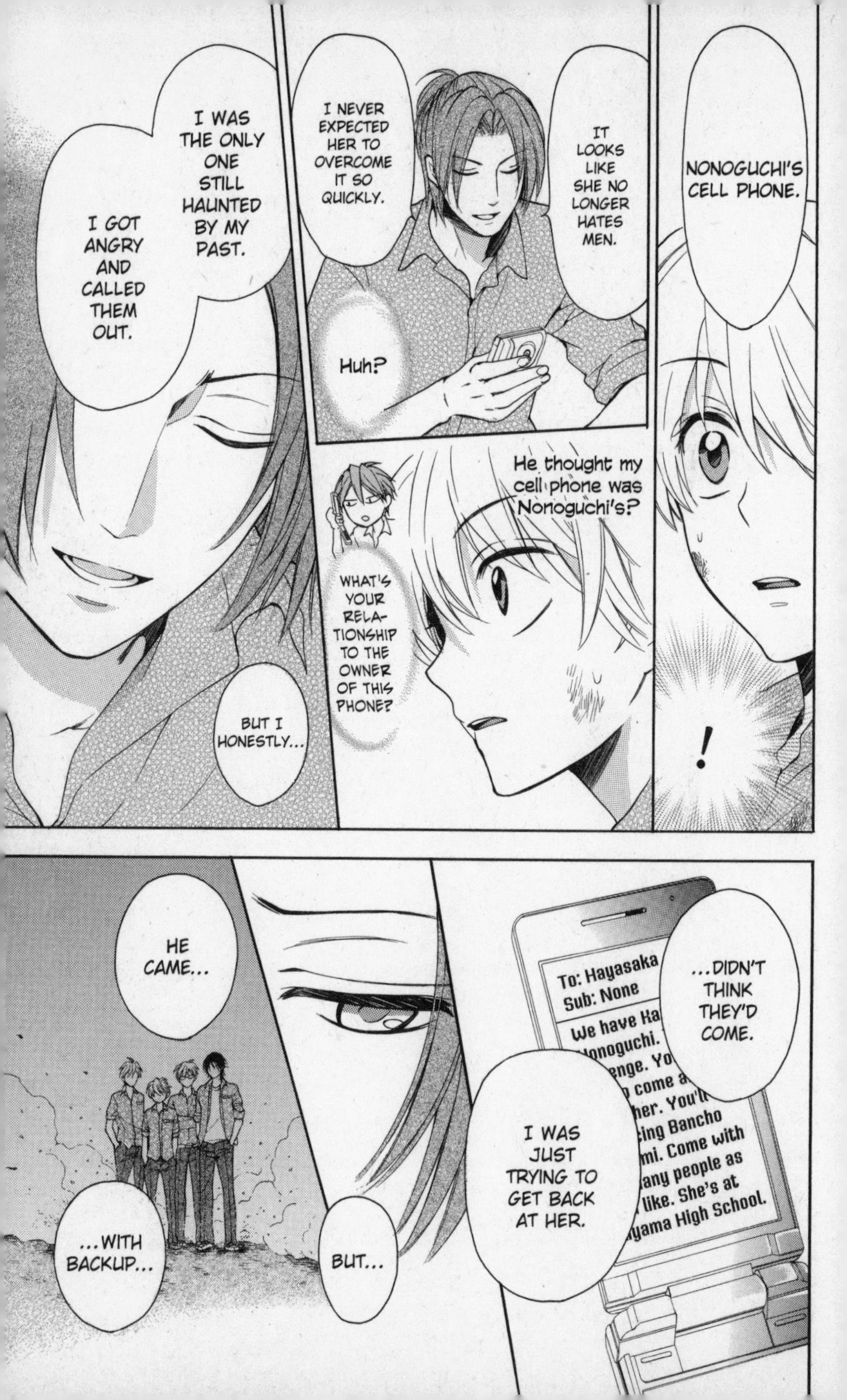
NONOGUCHI'S CELL PHONE.
!
IT LOOKS LIKE SHE NO LONGER HATES MEN.
I NEVER EXPECTED HER TO OVERCOME IT SO QUICKLY.
Huh?
He thought my cell phone was Nonoguchi's?
WHAT'S YOUR RELATIONSHIP TO THE OWNER OF THIS PHONE?
I WAS THE ONLY ONE STILL HAUNTED BY MY PAST.
I GOT ANGRY AND CALLED THEM OUT.
BUT I HONESTLY...
...DIDN'T THINK THEY'D COME.
To: Hayasaka
Sub: None
We have
Bancho
Come with
many people as
like. She's at
High School.
I WAS JUST TRYING TO GET BACK AT HER.
BUT...
HE CAME...
...WITH BACKUP...

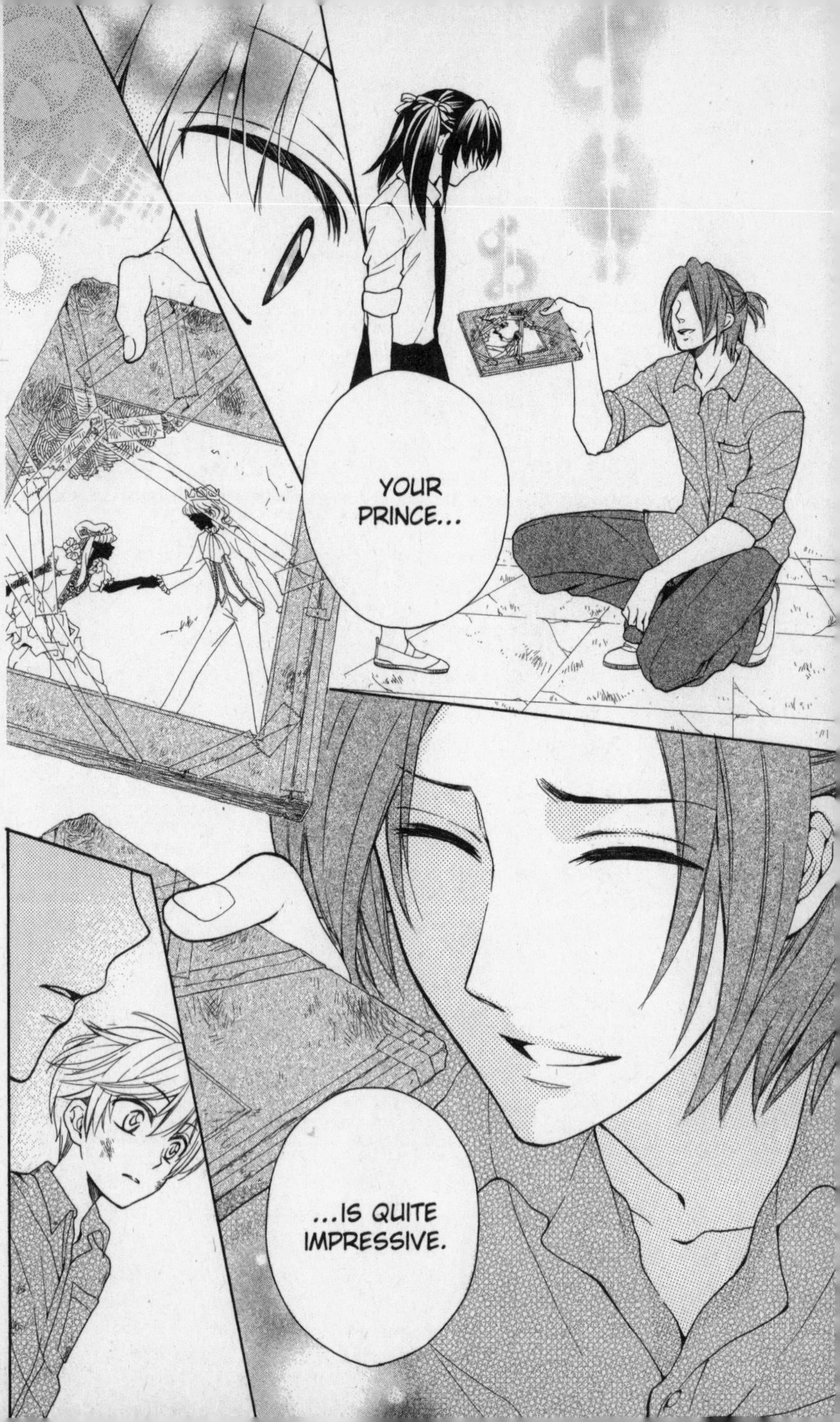
YOUR PRINCE...
...IS QUITE IMPRESSIVE.

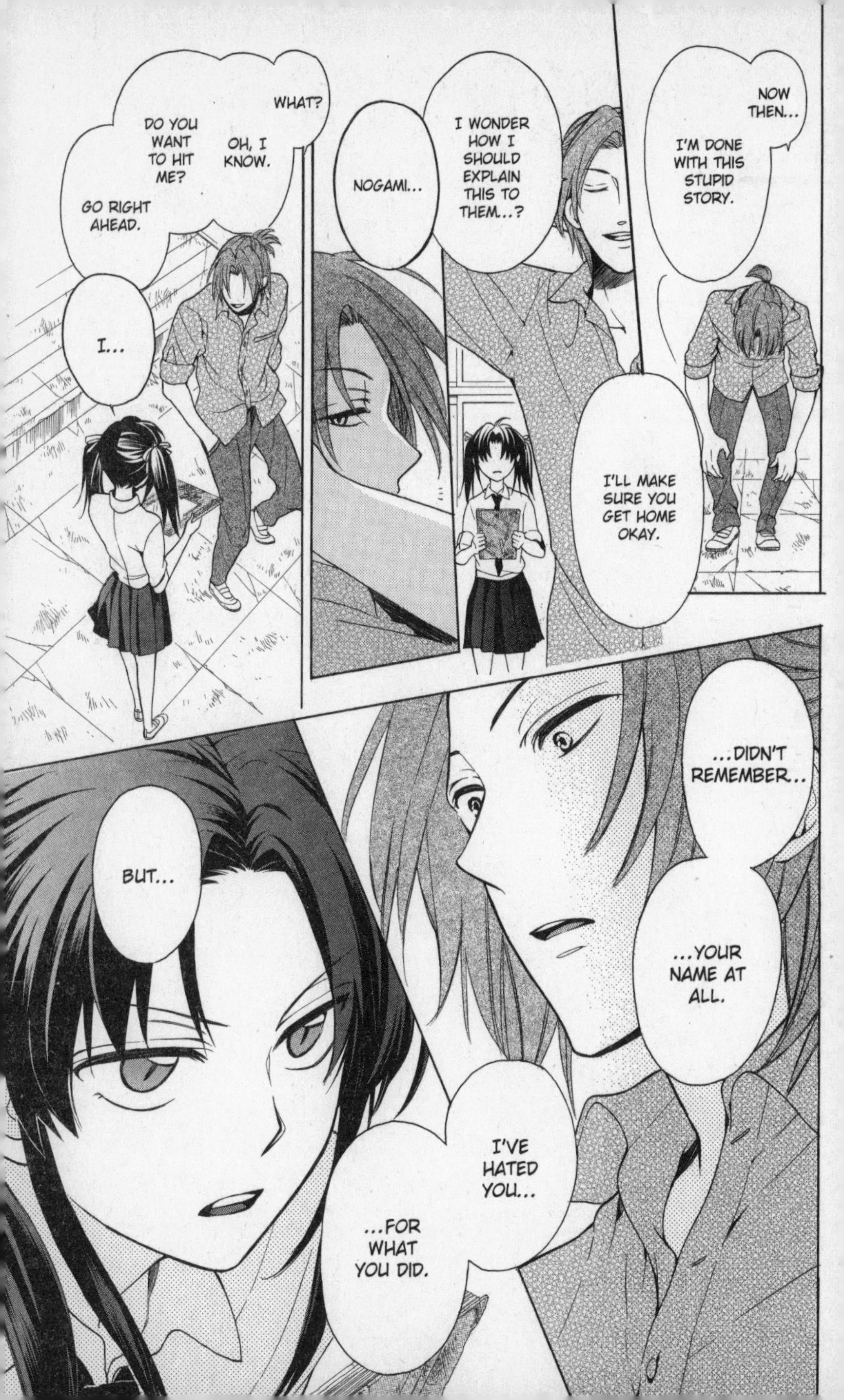
NOW THEN...
I'M DONE WITH THIS STUPID STORY.
I'LL MAKE SURE YOU GET HOME OKAY.
I WONDER HOW I SHOULD EXPLAIN THIS TO THEM...?
NOGAMI...
WHAT?
OH, I KNOW.
DO YOU WANT TO HIT ME?
GO RIGHT AHEAD.
I...
...DIDN'T REMEMBER...
...YOUR NAME AT ALL.
BUT...
I'VE HATED YOU...
...FOR WHAT YOU DID.

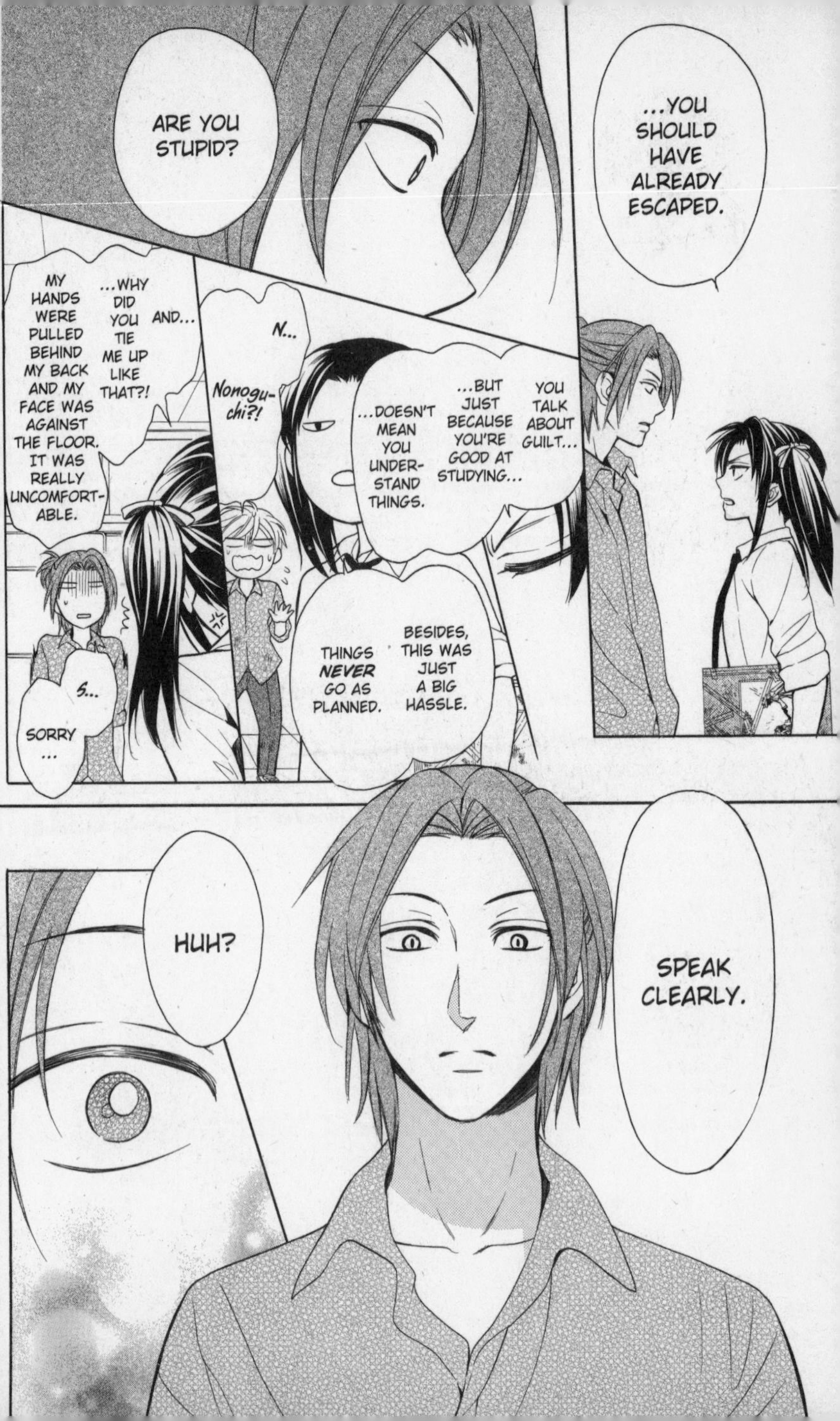
...YOU SHOULD HAVE ALREADY ESCAPED.
ARE YOU STUPID?
YOU TALK ABOUT GUILT...
...BUT JUST BECAUSE YOU'RE GOOD AT STUDYING...
...DOESN'T MEAN YOU UNDER-STAND THINGS.
BESIDES, THIS WAS JUST A BIG HASSLE.
THINGS *NEVER* GO AS PLANNED.
N...
Nonoguchi?!
...WHY DID YOU TIE ME UP LIKE THAT?!
AND...
MY HANDS WERE PULLED BEHIND MY BACK AND MY FACE WAS AGAINST THE FLOOR. IT WAS REALLY UNCOMFORT-ABLE.
S...
SORRY ...
SPEAK CLEARLY.
HUH?

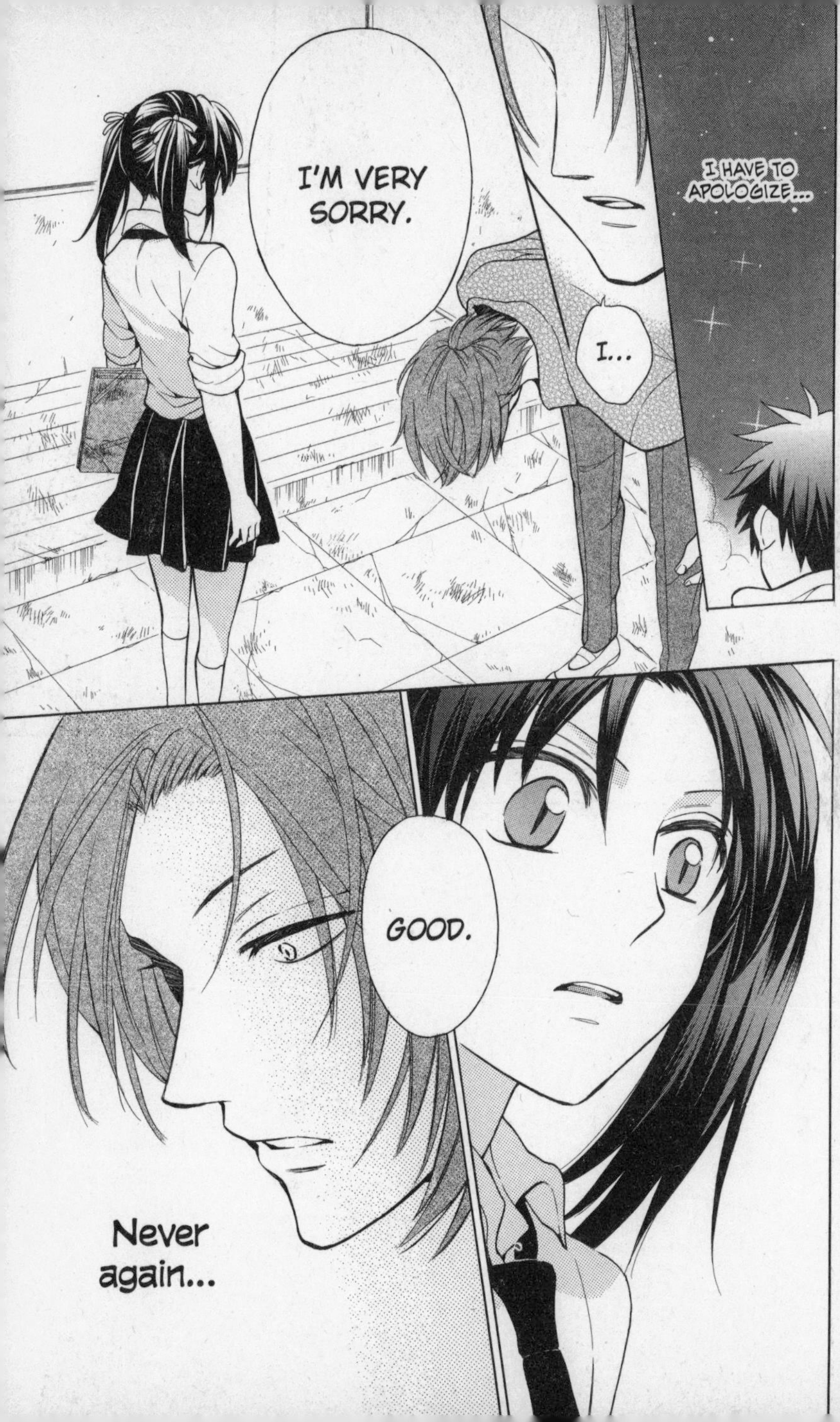
I HAVE TO APOLOGIZE...
I...
I'M VERY SORRY.
GOOD.
Never again...

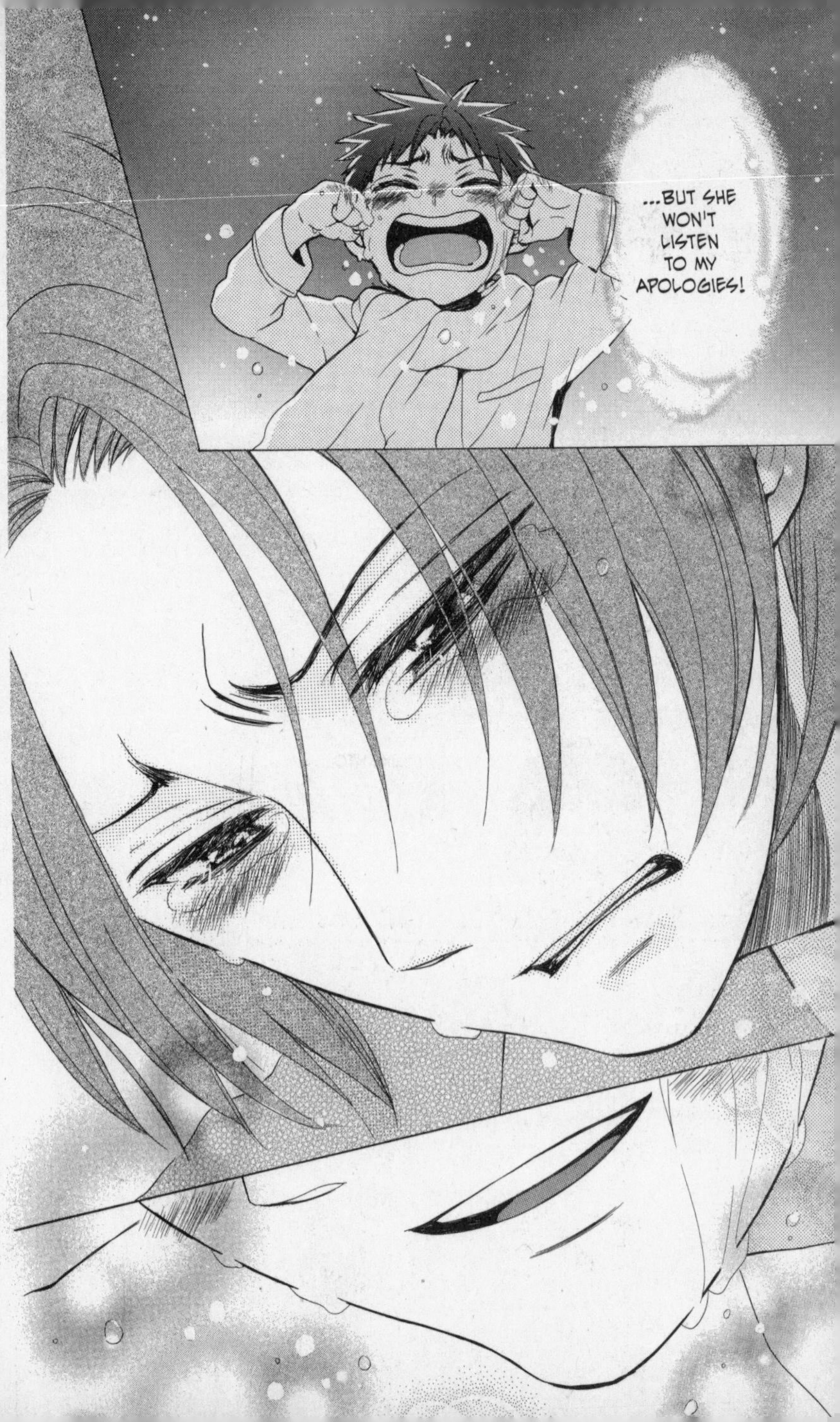
...BUT SHE WON'T LISTEN TO MY APOLOGIES!

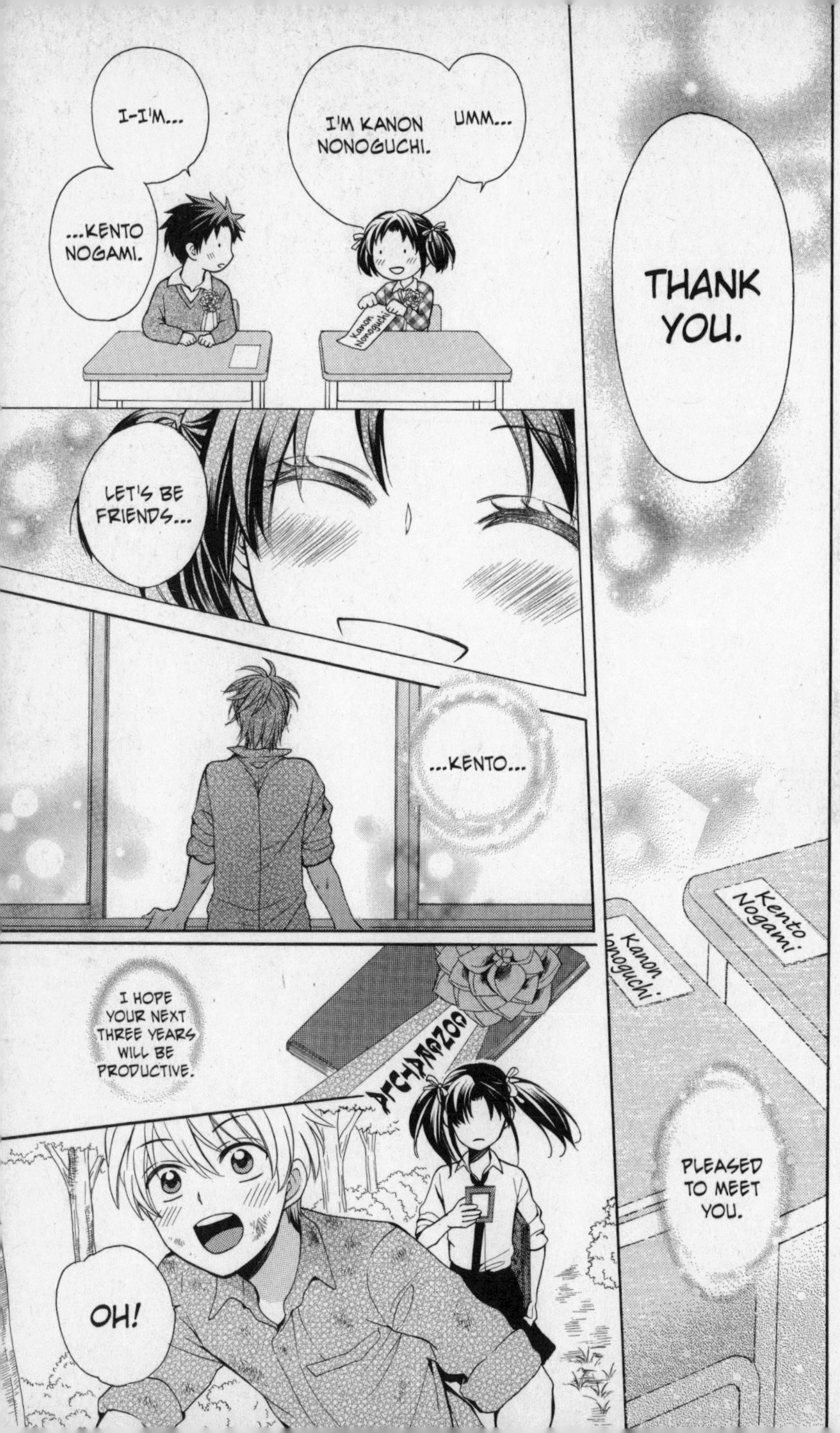
THANK YOU.
Kento Nogami
Kanon Nonoguchi
PLEASED TO MEET YOU.
UMM...
I'M KANON NONOGUCHI.
I-I'M...
...KENTO NOGAMI.
Kanon Nonoguchi
LET'S BE FRIENDS...
...KENTO...
I HOPE YOUR NEXT THREE YEARS WILL BE PRODUCTIVE.
OH!

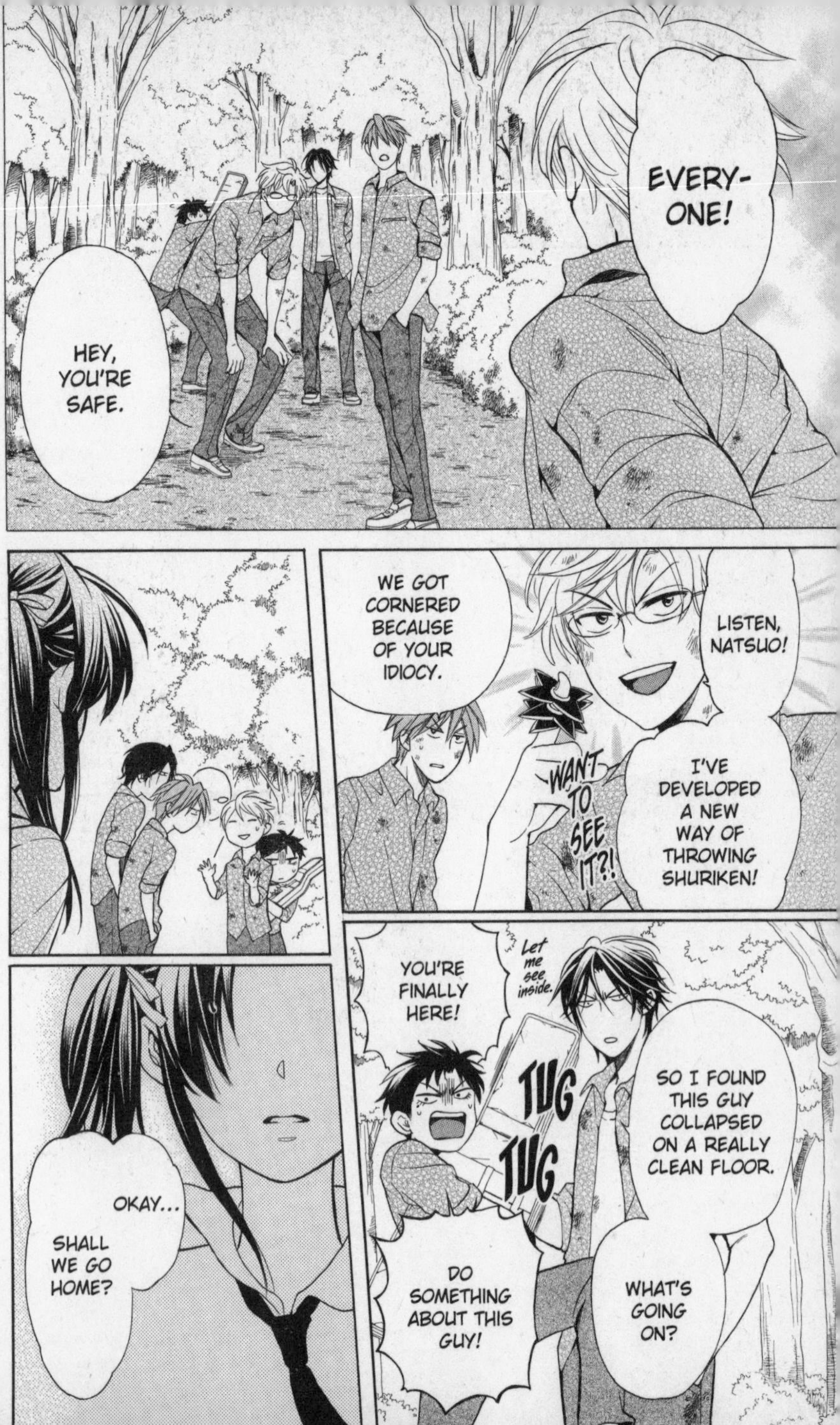
EVERY-ONE!
HEY, YOU'RE SAFE.
LISTEN, NATSUO!
I'VE DEVELOPED A NEW WAY OF THROWING SHURIKEN!
WANT TO SEE IT?!
WE GOT CORNERED BECAUSE OF YOUR IDIOCY.
SO I FOUND THIS GUY COLLAPSED ON A REALLY CLEAN FLOOR.
Let me see inside.
YOU'RE FINALLY HERE!
TUG TUG
WHAT'S GOING ON?
DO SOMETHING ABOUT THIS GUY!
OKAY...
SHALL WE GO HOME?

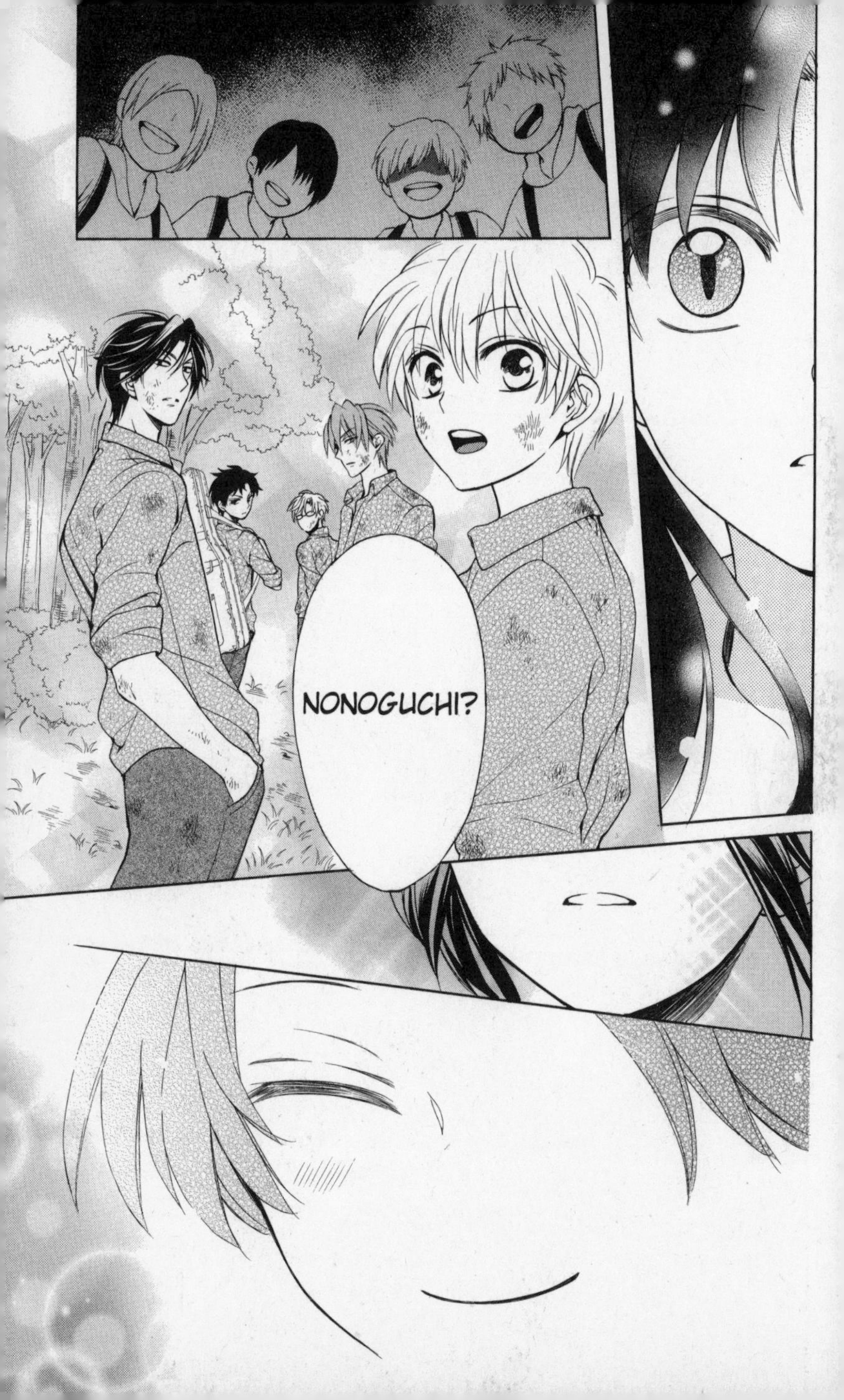
NONOGUCHI?

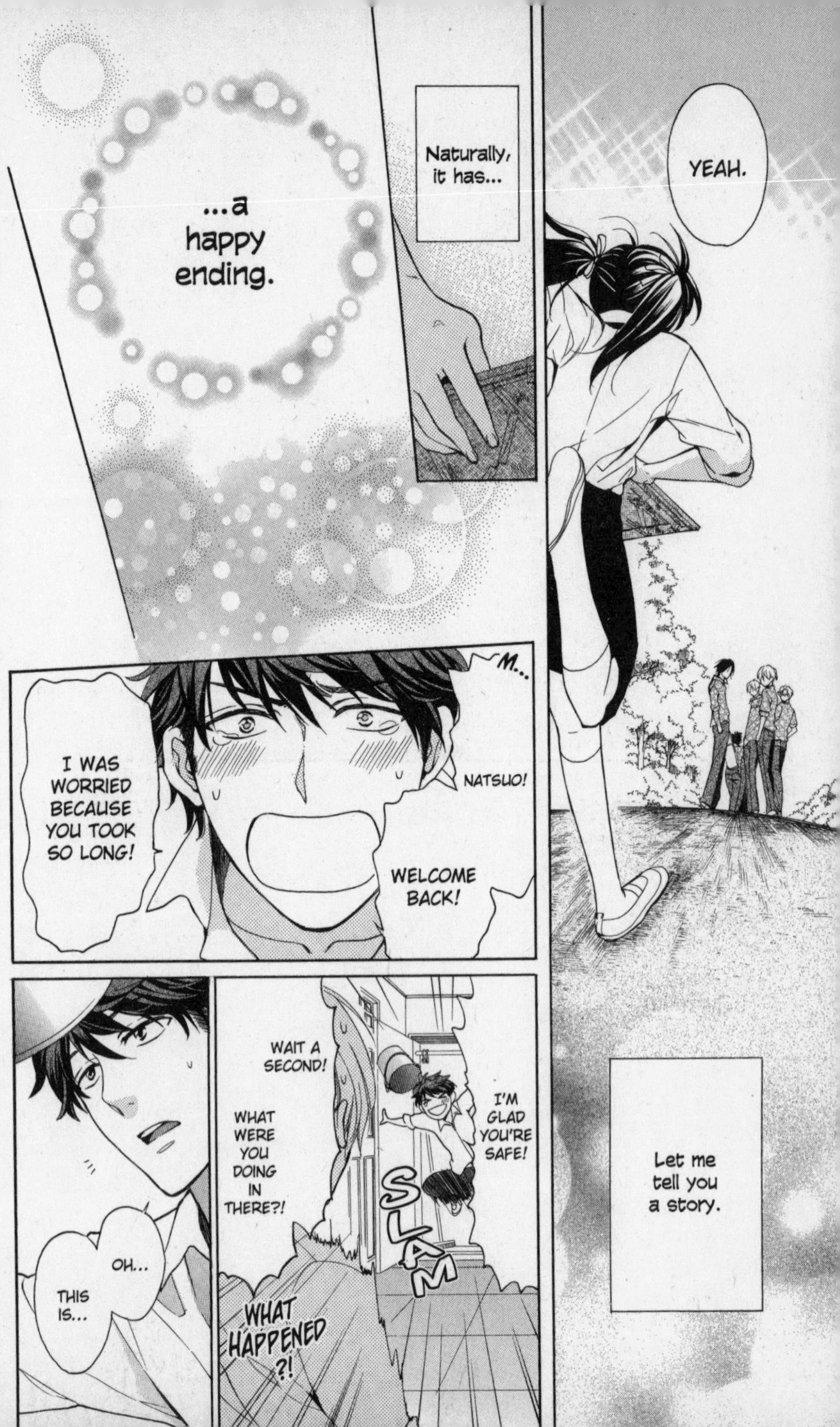
YEAH.
Let me tell you a story.
Naturally, it has...
...a happy ending.
M...
NATSUO!
WELCOME BACK!
I WAS WORRIED BECAUSE YOU TOOK SO LONG!
I'M GLAD YOU'RE SAFE!
WAIT A SECOND!
WHAT WERE YOU DOING IN THERE?!
SLAM
WHAT HAPPENED?!
OH...
THIS IS...

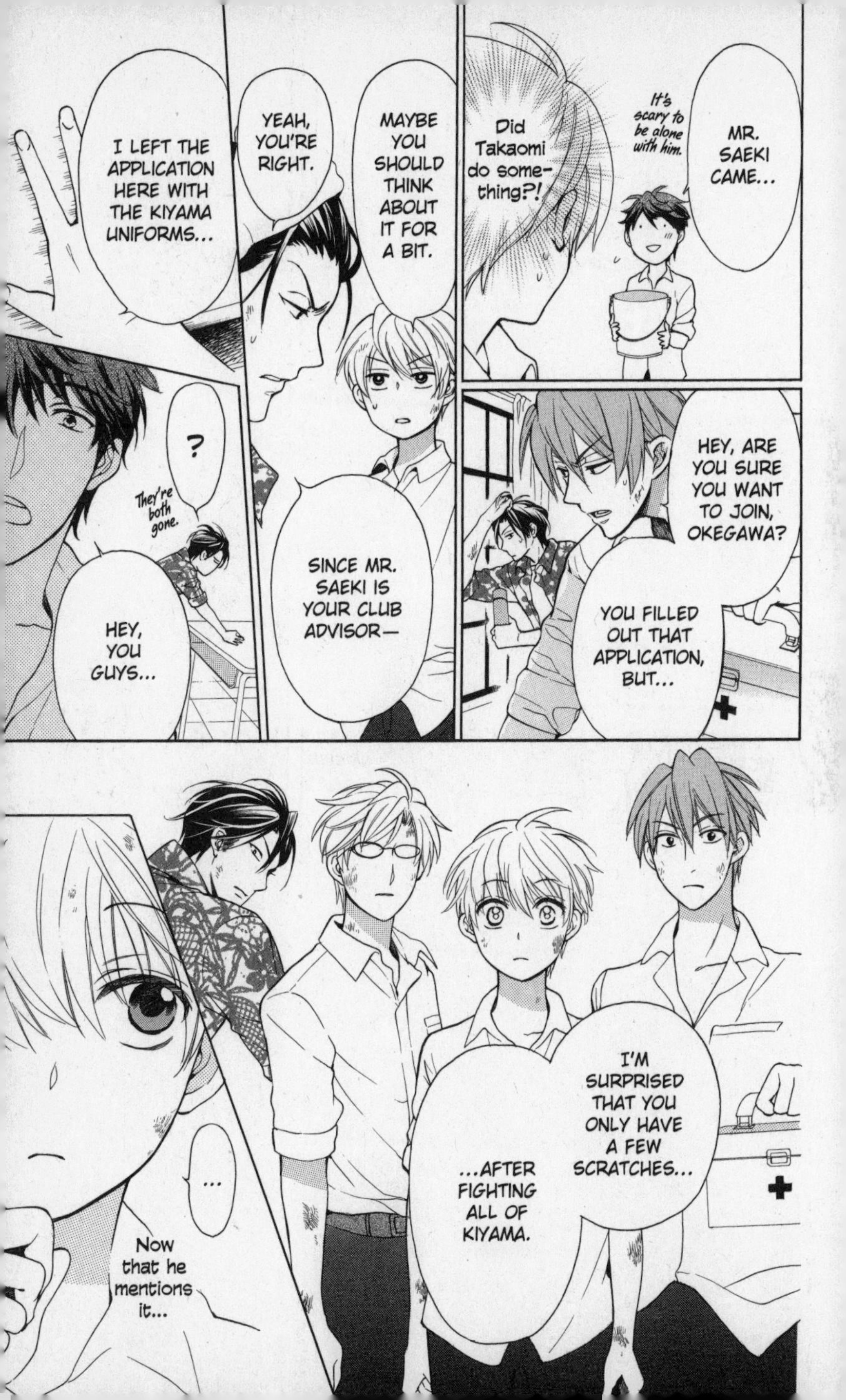
MR. SAEKI CAME...
It's scary to be alone with him.
Did Takaomi do some-thing?!
HEY, ARE YOU SURE YOU WANT TO JOIN, OKEGAWA?
YOU FILLED OUT THAT APPLICATION, BUT...
MAYBE YOU SHOULD THINK ABOUT IT FOR A BIT.
YEAH, YOU'RE RIGHT.
SINCE MR. SAEKI IS YOUR CLUB ADVISOR—
I LEFT THE APPLICATION HERE WITH THE KIYAMA UNIFORMS...
?
They're both gone.
HEY, YOU GUYS...
I'M SURPRISED THAT YOU ONLY HAVE A FEW SCRATCHES...
...AFTER FIGHTING ALL OF KIYAMA.
...
Now that he mentions it...

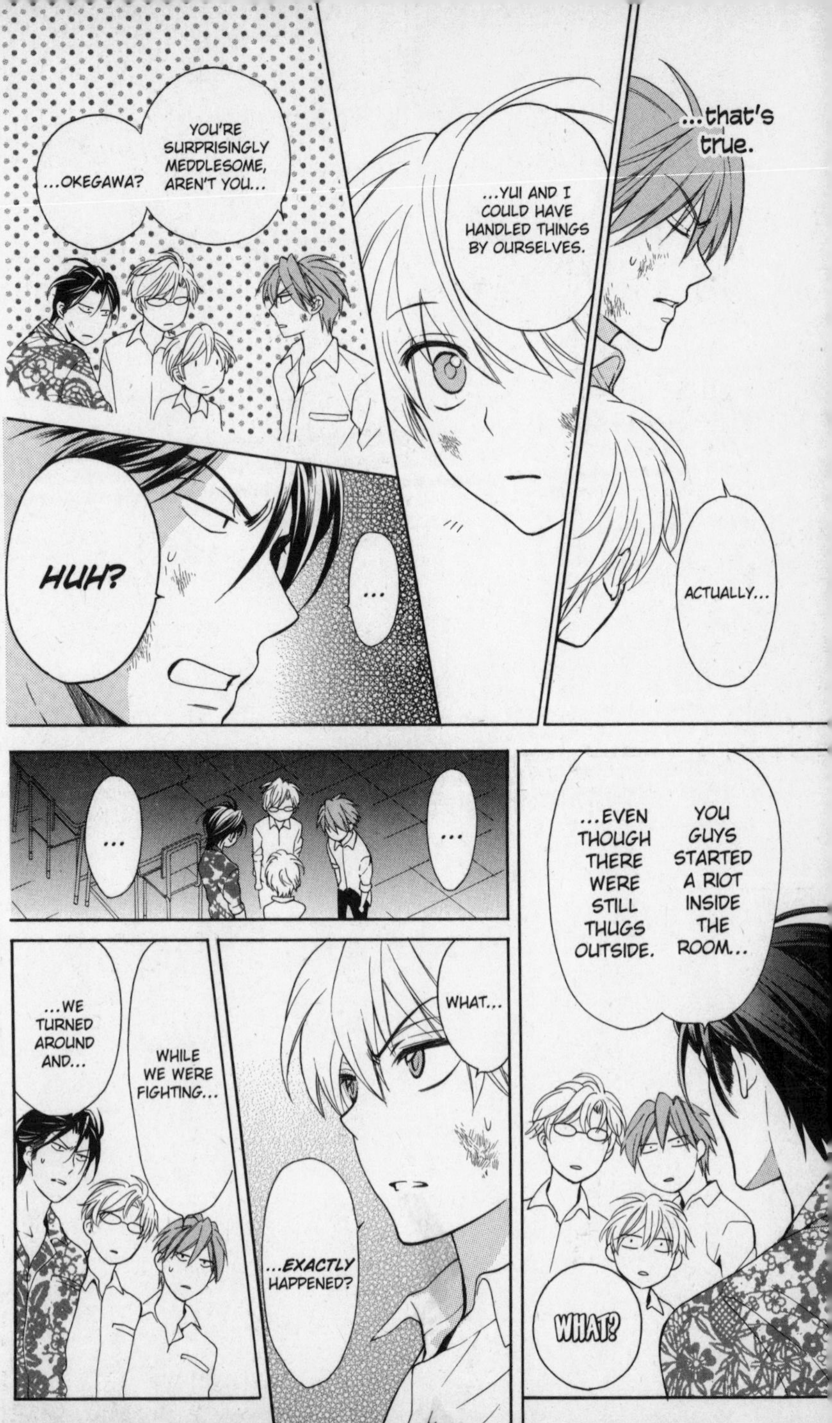
...that's true.
ACTUALLY...
...YUI AND I COULD HAVE HANDLED THINGS BY OURSELVES.
YOU'RE SURPRISINGLY MEDDLESOME, AREN'T YOU...
...OKEGAWA?
...
HUH?
YOU GUYS STARTED A RIOT INSIDE THE ROOM...
...EVEN THOUGH THERE WERE STILL THUGS OUTSIDE.
WHAT?
...
...
WHAT...
...EXACTLY HAPPENED?
WHILE WE WERE FIGHTING...
...WE TURNED AROUND AND...

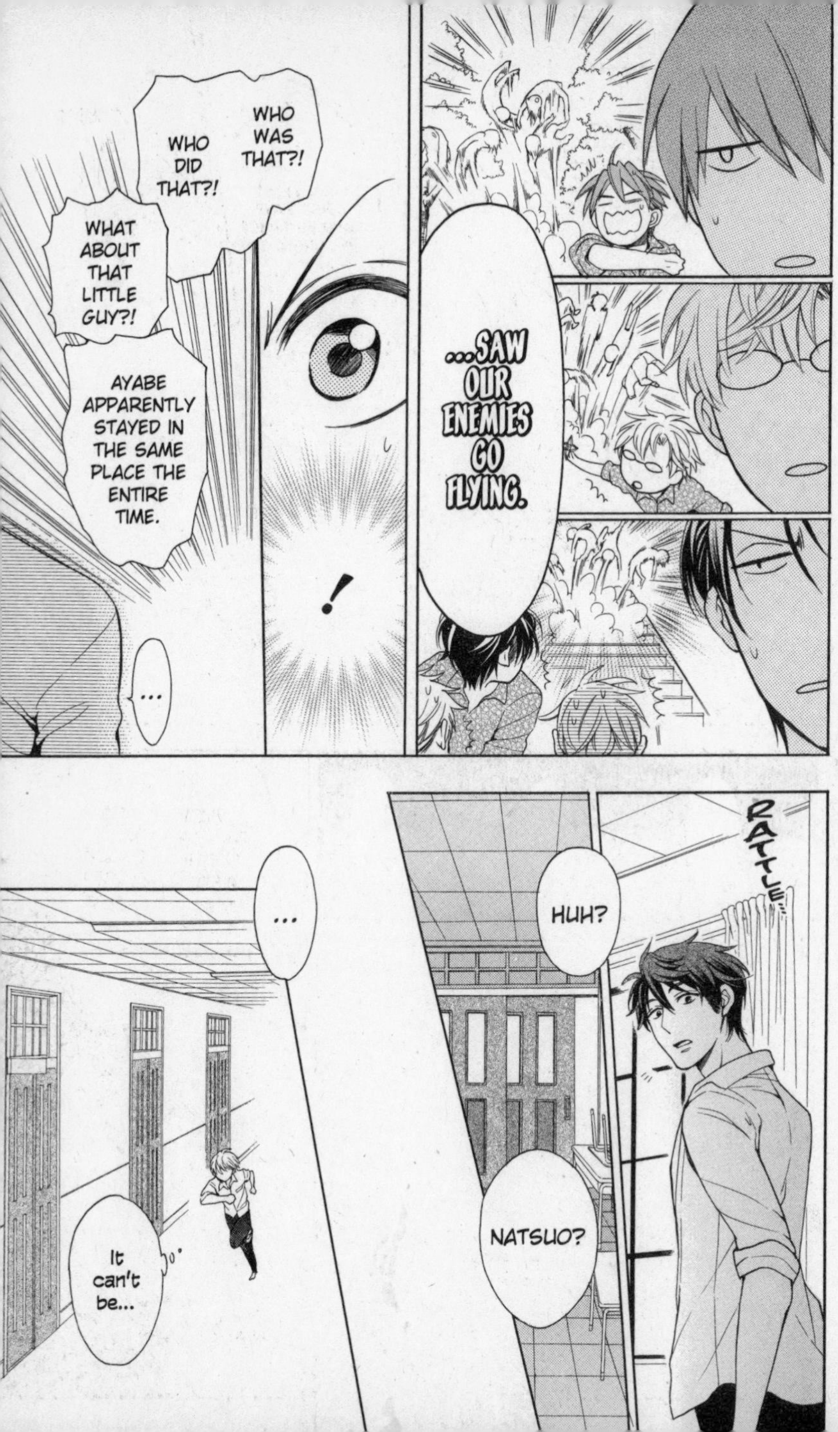
...SAW OUR ENEMIES GO FLYING.
!
WHO WAS THAT?!
WHO DID THAT?!
WHAT ABOUT THAT LITTLE GUY?!
AYABE APPARENTLY STAYED IN THE SAME PLACE THE ENTIRE TIME.
...
RATTLE...
HUH?
NATSUO?
...
It can't be...

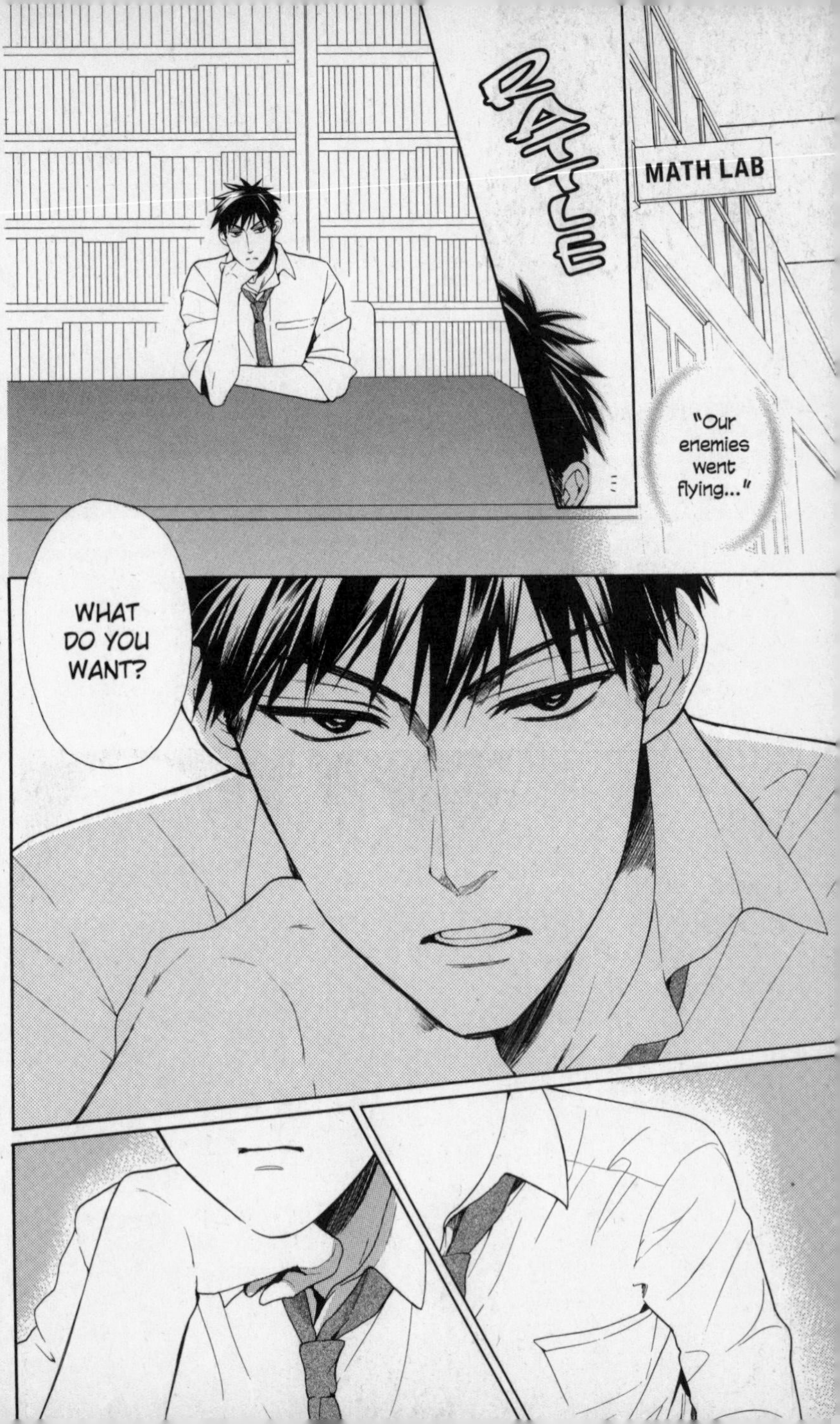
MATH LAB
RATTLE
"Our enemies went flying..."
WHAT DO YOU WANT?

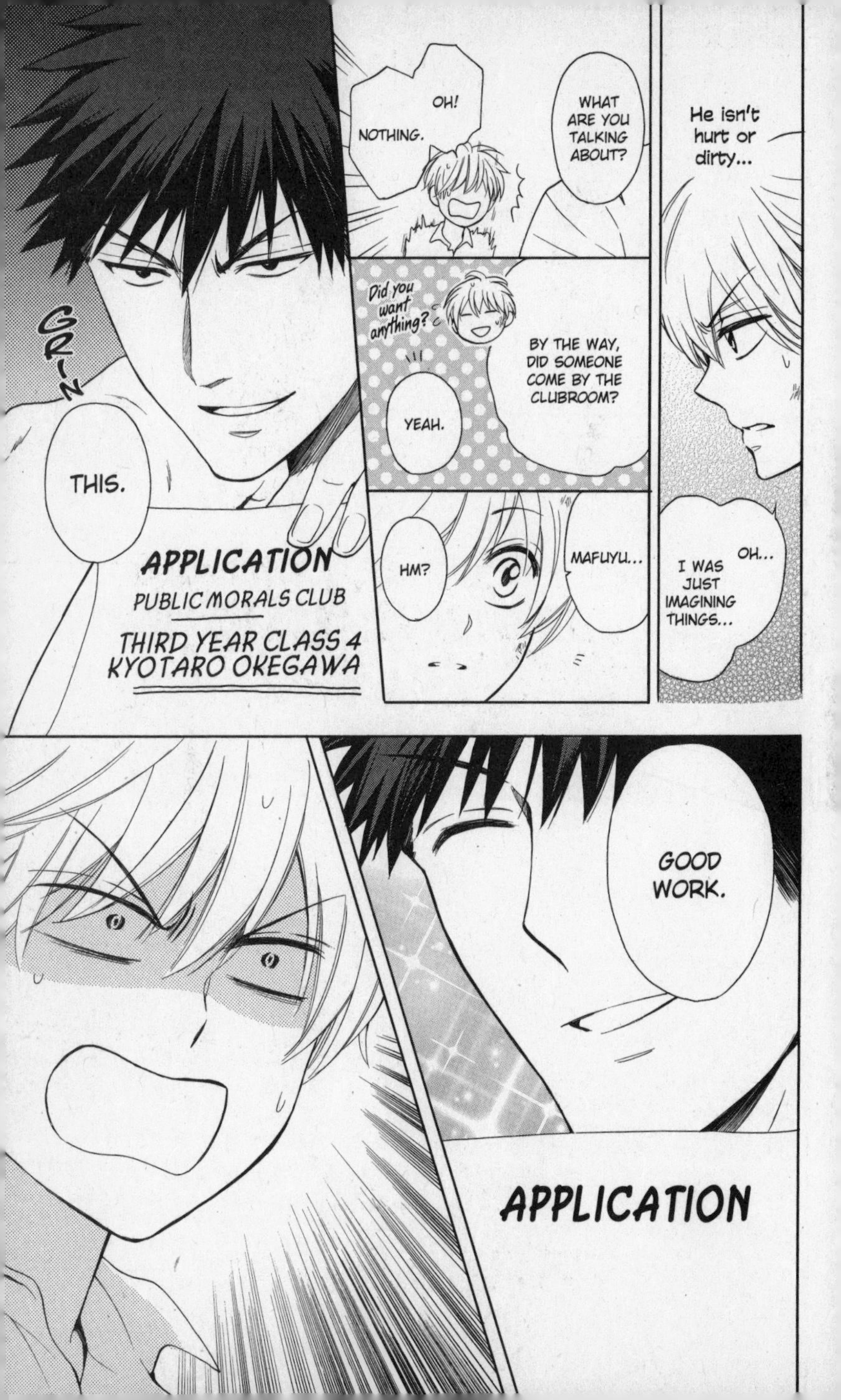
He isn't hurt or dirty...
OH... I WAS JUST IMAGINING THINGS...
WHAT ARE YOU TALKING ABOUT?
OH! NOTHING.
BY THE WAY, DID SOMEONE COME BY THE CLUBROOM?
Did you want anything?
YEAH.
MAFUYU...
HM?
GRIN
THIS.
APPLICATION
PUBLIC MORALS CLUB
THIRD YEAR CLASS 4
KYOTARO OKEGAWA
GOOD WORK.
APPLICATION

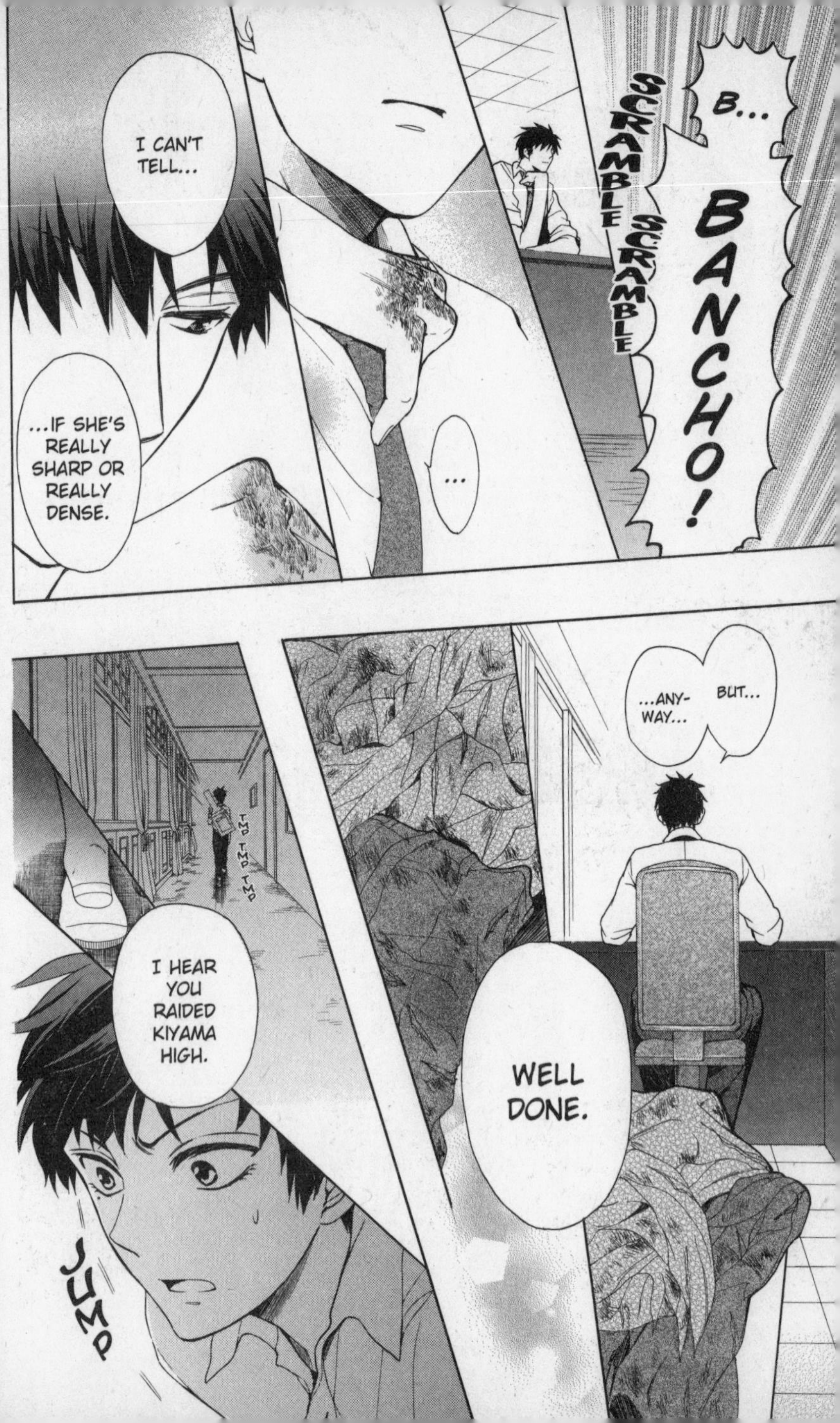
B...
BANCHO!
SCRAMBLE SCRAMBLE
...
I CAN'T TELL...
...IF SHE'S REALLY SHARP OR REALLY DENSE.
BUT...
...ANYWAY...
WELL DONE.
TMP TMP TMP
I HEAR YOU RAIDED KIYAMA HIGH.
JUMP

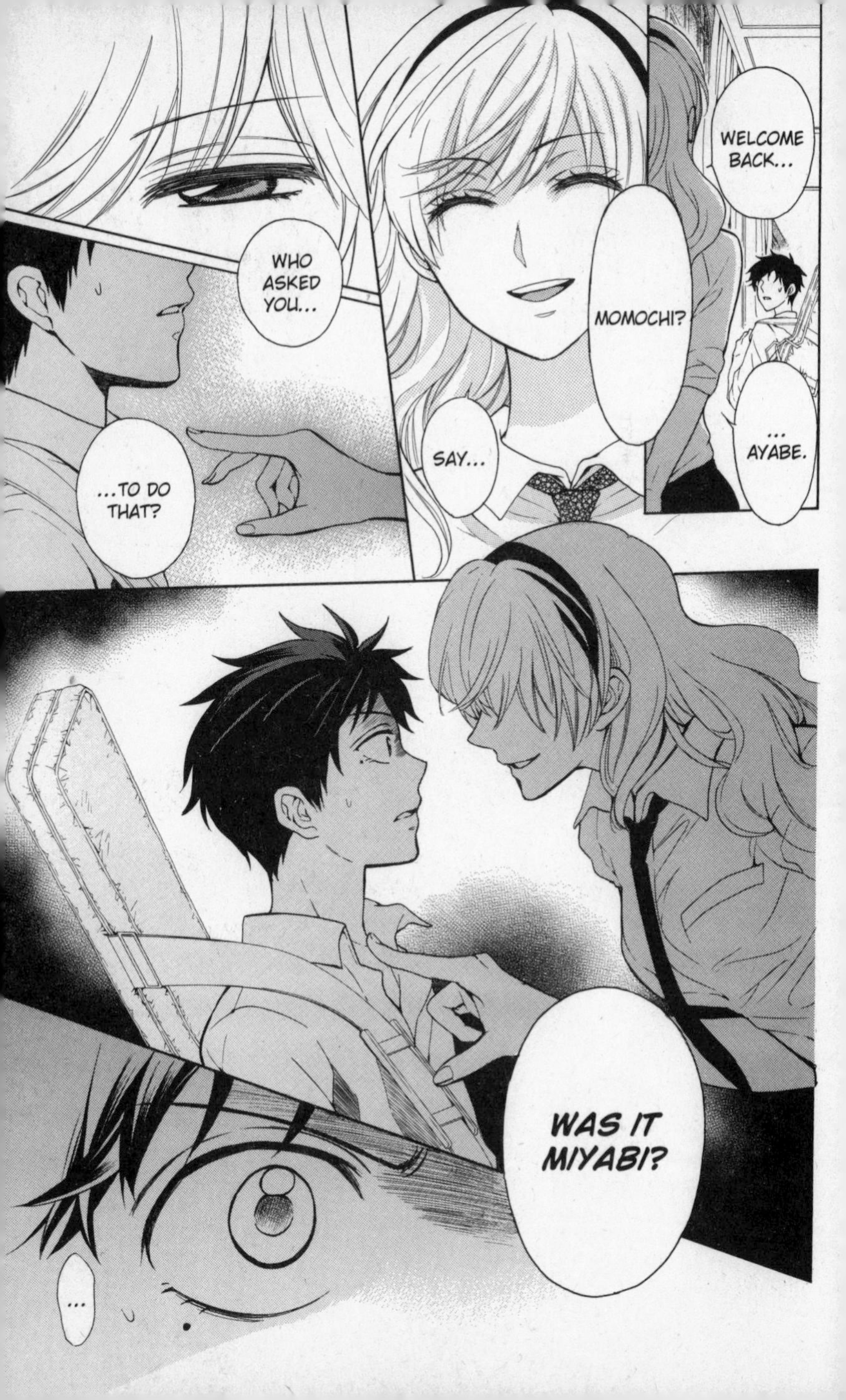
WELCOME BACK...
...AYABE.
MOMOCHI?
SAY...
WHO ASKED YOU...
...TO DO THAT?
WAS IT MIYABI?
...

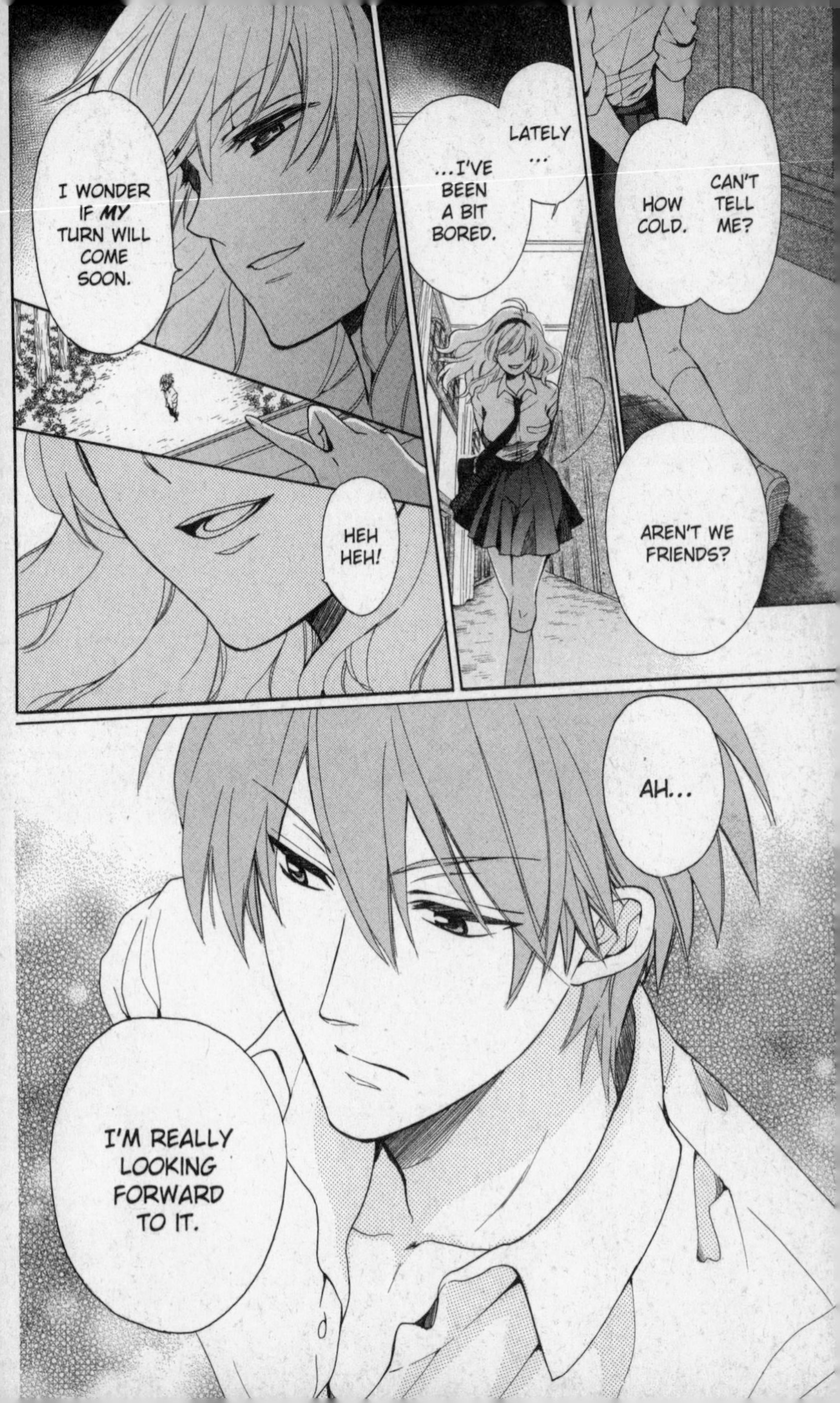
CAN'T TELL ME? HOW COLD.
AREN'T WE FRIENDS?
LATELY...
...I'VE BEEN A BIT BORED.
I WONDER IF *MY* TURN WILL COME SOON.
HEH HEH!
AH...
I'M REALLY LOOKING FORWARD TO IT.

NONOGUCHI & NOGAMI ARC

SUBTITLE: A COMPLICATED FIRST LOVE

THE MAIN STORY OPENED WITH KANON, SO NOGAMI DIDN'T GET MANY SCENES. BUT I ORIGINALLY PLANNED TO HAVE THE STORY UNFOLD FROM BOTH SIDES. I ACTUALLY CAME UP WITH A STORY ABOUT THE INCIDENT FROM KIYAMA HIGH'S POINT OF VIEW. I WAS THINKING ABOUT SWITCHING THE POINT OF VIEW AT SOME POINT, BUT KIYAMA TURNED INTO A COMPLETE JOKE, SO I KILLED THE IDEA. THEN I FIGURED I WOULD EXPLAIN WHAT HAPPENED FROM NOGAMI'S POINT OF VIEW INSTEAD.

"THE PERSON WHO WAS PICKING FIGHTS IN TOWN WAS MY FIRST LOVE, WHO I HURT IN THE PAST... I WASN'T ALLOWED TO ATONE FOR WHAT I DID, BUT I'M KIYAMA'S BANCHO NOW, SO I'M GOING TO USE MY SUBORDINATES TO PUT AN END TO THIS!"

THAT WAS NOGAMI'S MOTIVATION, BUT THINGS ESCALATED EACH TIME KANON DID SOMETHING. NOGAMI WAS TRYING TO HELP WHILE HIDING IN THE SHADOWS, BUT AS THE SITUATION BETWEEN THE TWO SCHOOLS GOT WORSE, HE HAD TO TAKE ON THE FIGHT AS KIYAMA'S REPRESENTATIVE. HE WAS BANCHO, SO HE WAS ABLE TO HELP, BUT HE ALSO WASN'T ABLE TO DO ANYTHING DIRECTLY. HE NEEDED TO SUBDUE THE CAUSE OF THE INCIDENT (KANON) EVEN JUST FOR SHOW. SHOULD HE LET SOMEONE ELSE BE BANCHO AND HANDLE THIS HIMSELF? BUT IF HE DID THAT, THE NEW BANCHO MIGHT MERCILESSLY ATTACK KANON. SO HE THOUGHT THAT HE SHOULD CAPTURE HER, GIVE HER A LECTURE, AND RELEASE HER. BUT HE WOULD MAKE A BIG SHOW OF HER CAPTURE TO SHOW THE STUDENTS OF KIYAMA THAT THE INCIDENT HAD BEEN PUT TO REST.

WHEN HE SEES KANON AGAIN, HE FINDS THAT SHE STILL HATES MEN, BUT THE PHONE HE PICKS UP IS FILLED WITH MEN'S NUMBERS. WHEN HE ASKED HER ABOUT IT, SHE SAYS THAT THEY'RE HER FRIENDS. HE HAS MIXED FEELINGS ABOUT THIS AND HE REALIZES THAT THESE ARE THE GUYS WHO ARE FIGHTING KIYAMA IN TOWN. (NOGAMI RECEIVED REPORTS THAT YUI AND HAYASAKA HAVE BEEN PATROLLING THE AREA, SO HE THOUGHT THAT THEY WERE ACTING AS KANON'S ALLIES.) HE DECIDED TO CALL THEM OUT TO SEE HOW CONFIDENT THEY WERE. IT WAS ALL A PERFORMANCE TO SEE THE MEN WHO HAD COME TO SAVE KANON. BUT NATSUO'S GROUP ADVANCED BETTER THAN EXPECTED AND NOGAMI LOST HIS CHANCE TO END THINGS SIMPLY. HE SOON REALIZED THEY WOULD PROBABLY COME TO THE TOP FLOOR. HE DELIBERATELY SAID THE WORD "PRINCE" TO MAKE KANON THINK ABOUT THE PAST. HAVING THE PRINCE (NATSUO) SAVE KANON FROM THE BAD GUY (NOGAMI) WAS A RECREATION OF PAST EVENTS THAT HE DEDICATED TO KANON, WHO NO LONGER BELIEVED IN PRINCES.

HE WASN'T PLANNING ON REVEALING HIS IDENTITY, BUT HE MENTIONED IT, AND ENDED UP BEING FORGIVEN. KANON WAS HELD CAPTIVE BY HER PAST, BUT NOGAMI WAS HAUNTED BY GUILT AND THE NEED TO ATONE TO HER. THIS ENDING IS A MIRACLE FOR NOGAMI BECAUSE ONLY ONE PERSON IN THE WORLD COULD HAVE SAVED HIM. MEANWHILE, KANON COULD BARELY REMEMBER NOGAMI'S FACE OR NAME! OR RATHER, SHE FORGOT ABOUT ALL THE BOYS FROM THAT TIME. SHE WAS ONLY IN SECOND GRADE, AFTER ALL. I TRIED TO INTRODUCE NOGAMI'S ABILITY TO LEARN THINGS EASILY HERE. OH, NOGAMI..

THE TWO OF THEM SPENT MOST OF THEIR YOUTH DRAGGING THE CHAINS OF THEIR PAST... NOW I THINK THEY'LL FINALLY HAVE THE CHANCE AT A NORMAL STUDENT LIFE. ISN'T THAT GREAT?

NOGAMI'S CONCERNS

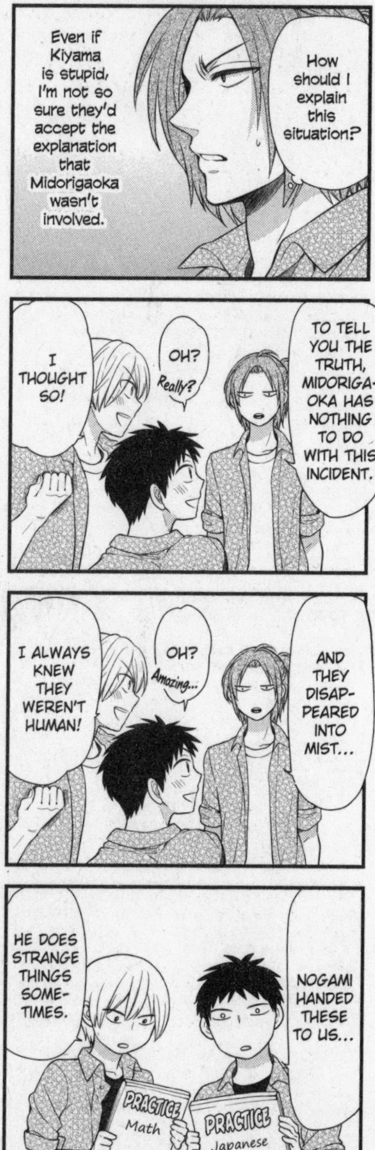
How should I explain this situation?
Even if Kiyama is stupid, I'm not so sure they'd accept the explanation that Midorigaoka wasn't involved.
TO TELL YOU THE TRUTH, MIDORIGAOKA HAS NOTHING TO DO WITH THIS INCIDENT.
OH?
Really?
I THOUGHT SO!
AND THEY DISAPPEARED INTO MIST...
OH?
Amazing...
I ALWAYS KNEW THEY WEREN'T HUMAN!
NOGAMI HANDED THESE TO US...
PRACTICE
Japanese
PRACTICE
Math
HE DOES STRANGE THINGS SOMETIMES.

THINGS HE WANTS TO DO: UNLEASHED

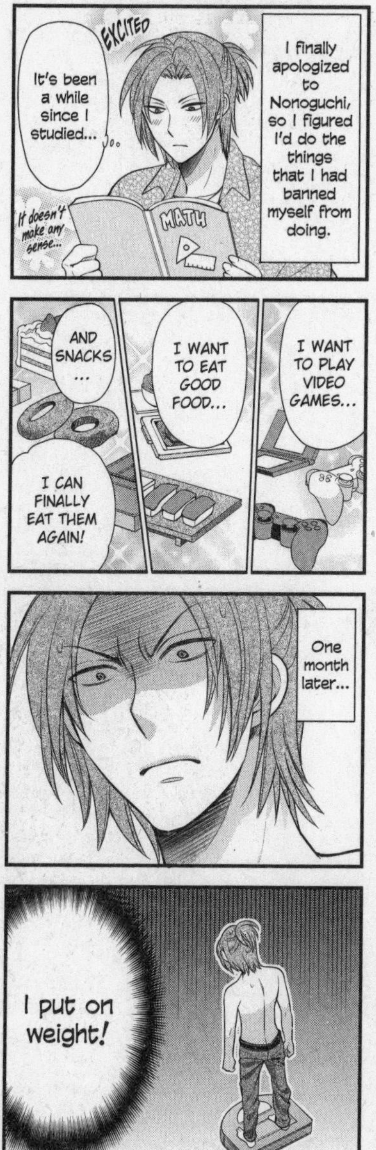
I finally apologized to Nonoguchi, so I figured I'd do the things that I had banned myself from doing.
EXCITED
It's been a while since I studied...
MATH
It doesn't make any sense...
I WANT TO PLAY VIDEO GAMES...
I WANT TO EAT GOOD FOOD...
AND SNACKS...
I CAN FINALLY EAT THEM AGAIN!
One month later...
I put on weight!

THAT TYPE

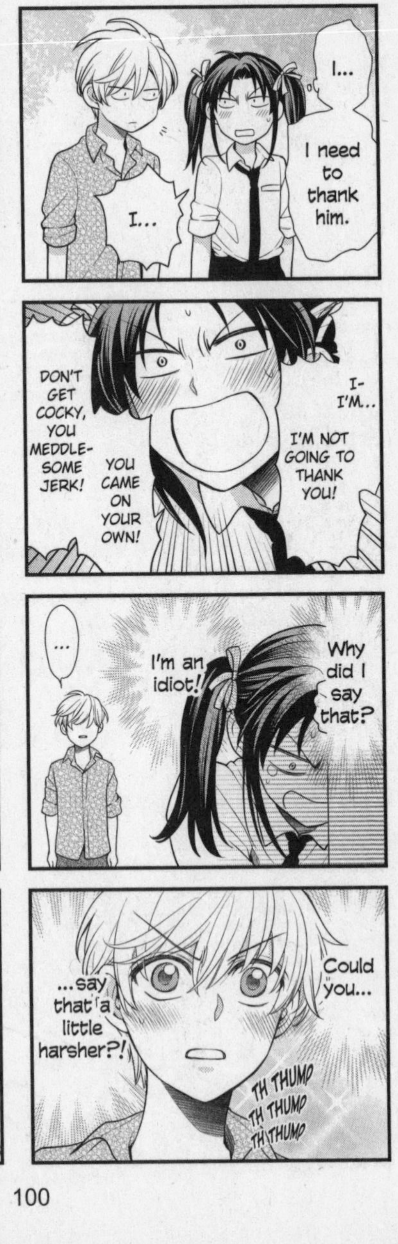
I...
I need to thank him.
I...
I- I'M...
I'M NOT GOING TO THANK YOU!
DON'T GET COCKY, YOU MEDDLESOME JERK!
YOU CAME ON YOUR OWN!
Why did I say that?
I'm an idiot!
...
Could you...
...say that a little harsher?!
TH THUMP
TH THUMP
TH THUMP

DOUBLE ☆ PRINCESS

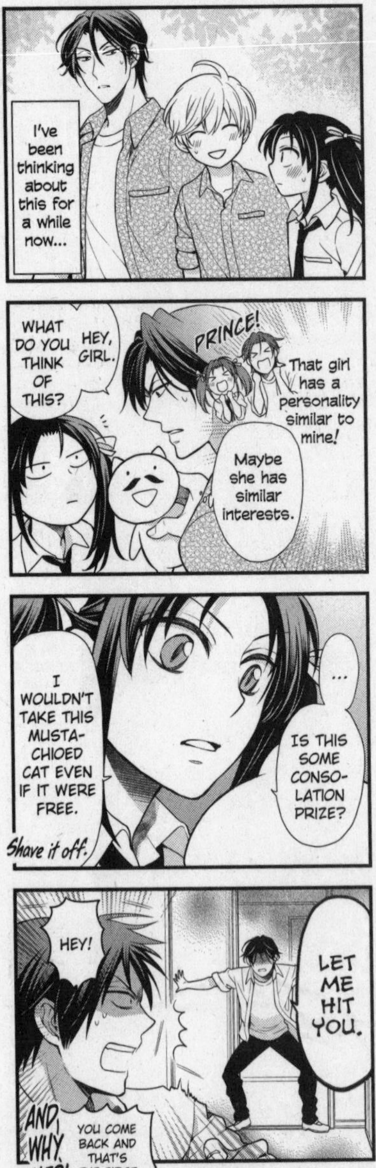
I've been thinking about this for a while now...
That girl has a personality similar to mine!
PRINCE!
HEY, GIRL.
WHAT DO YOU THINK OF THIS?
Maybe she has similar interests.
...
IS THIS SOME CONSOLATION PRIZE?
I WOULDN'T TAKE THIS MUSTACHIOED CAT EVEN IF IT WERE FREE.
Shave it off.
LET ME HIT YOU.
HEY!
YOU COME BACK AND THAT'S THE FIRST THING YOU SAY?!
AND, WHY ME?!

INVINCIBLE AT CERTAIN LOCATIONS

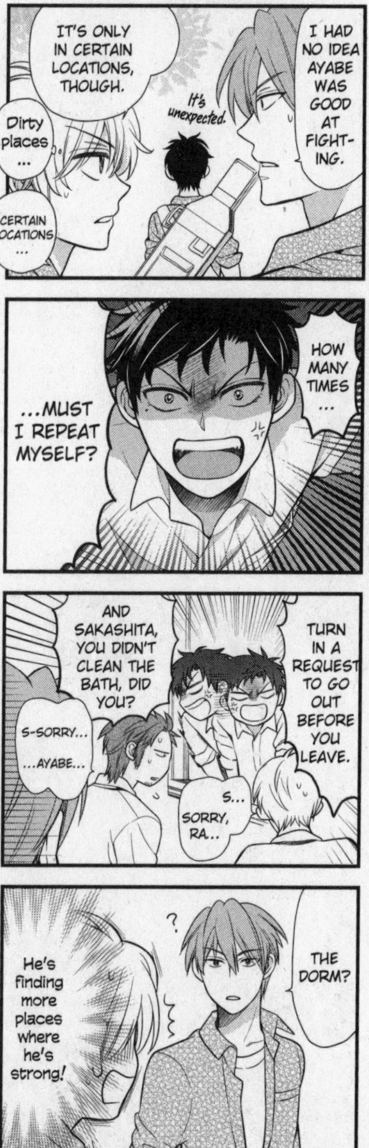
I HAD NO IDEA AYABE WAS GOOD AT FIGHT-ING.
It's unexpected.
IT'S ONLY IN CERTAIN LOCATIONS, THOUGH.
Dirty places...
CERTAIN LOCATIONS...
HOW MANY TIMES...
...MUST I REPEAT MYSELF?
TURN IN A REQUEST TO GO OUT BEFORE YOU LEAVE.
AND SAKASHITA, YOU DIDN'T CLEAN THE BATH, DID YOU?
S... SORRY, RA...
S-SORRY... ...AYABE...
THE DORM?
?
He's finding more places where he's strong!

DON'T KEEP CALLING ME

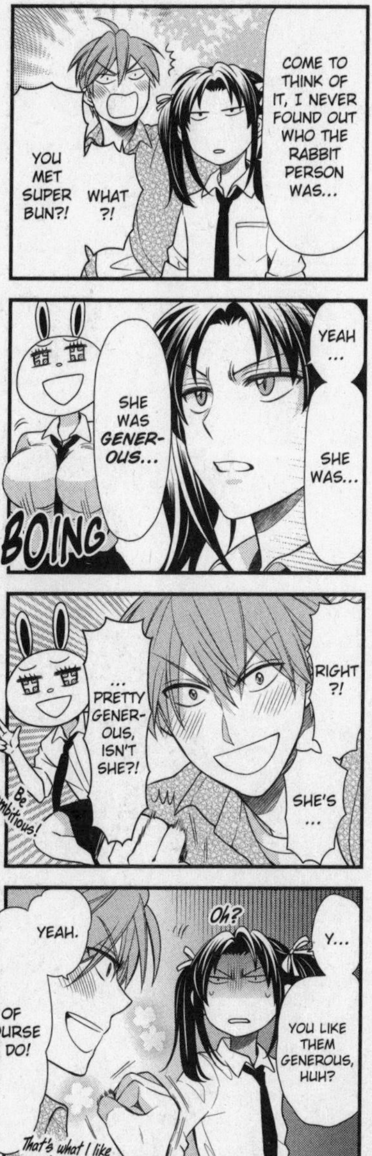
COME TO THINK OF IT, I NEVER FOUND OUT WHO THE RABBIT PERSON WAS...
WHAT?!
YOU MET SUPER BUN?!
YEAH...
SHE WAS...
SHE WAS GENER-OUS...
BOING
RIGHT?!
SHE'S...
...PRETTY GENER-OUS, ISN'T SHE?!
Be ambitious!
Y...
Oh?
YOU LIKE THEM GENEROUS, HUH?
YEAH.
OF COURSE I DO!
That's what I like most about her!

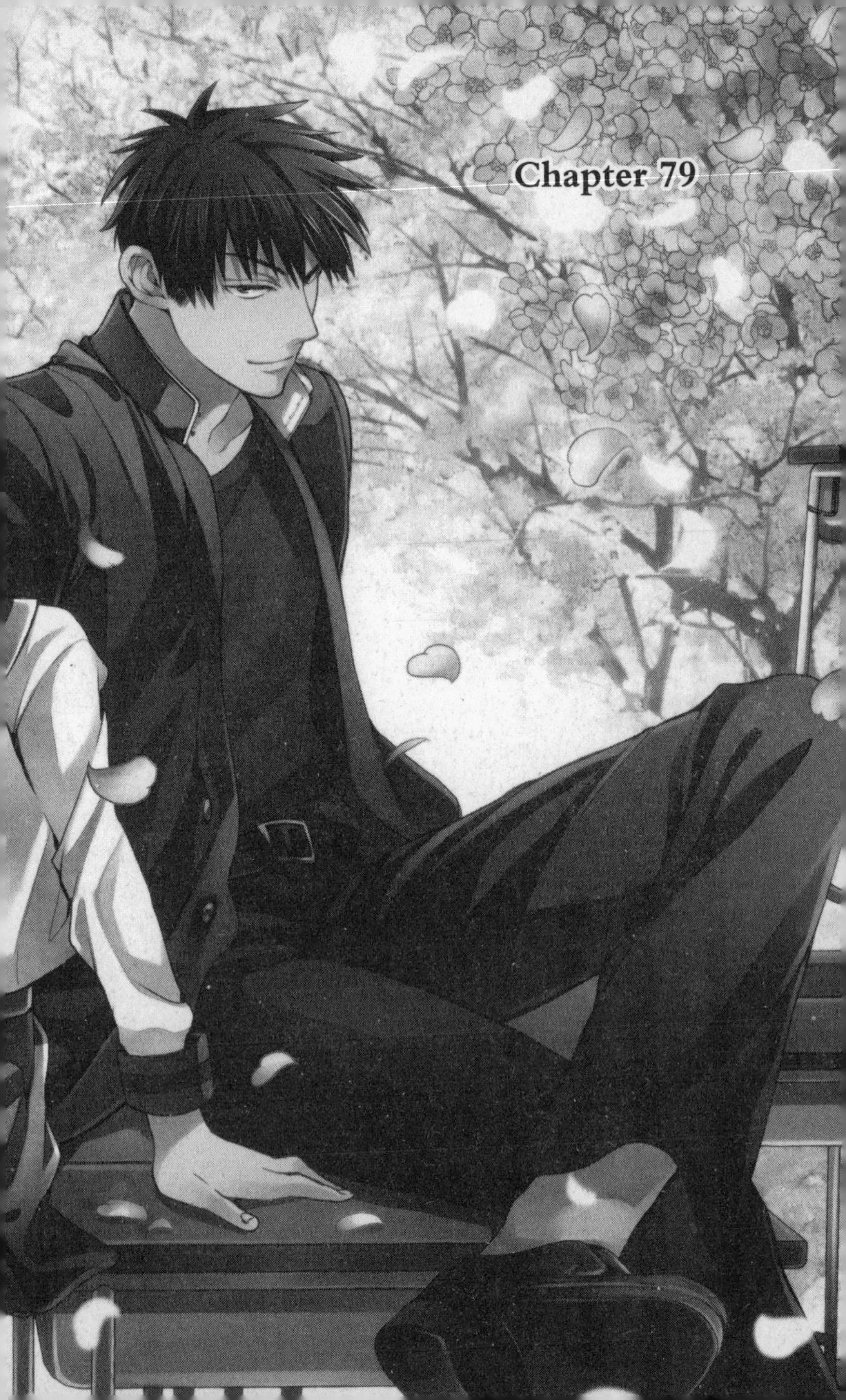
Chapter 79

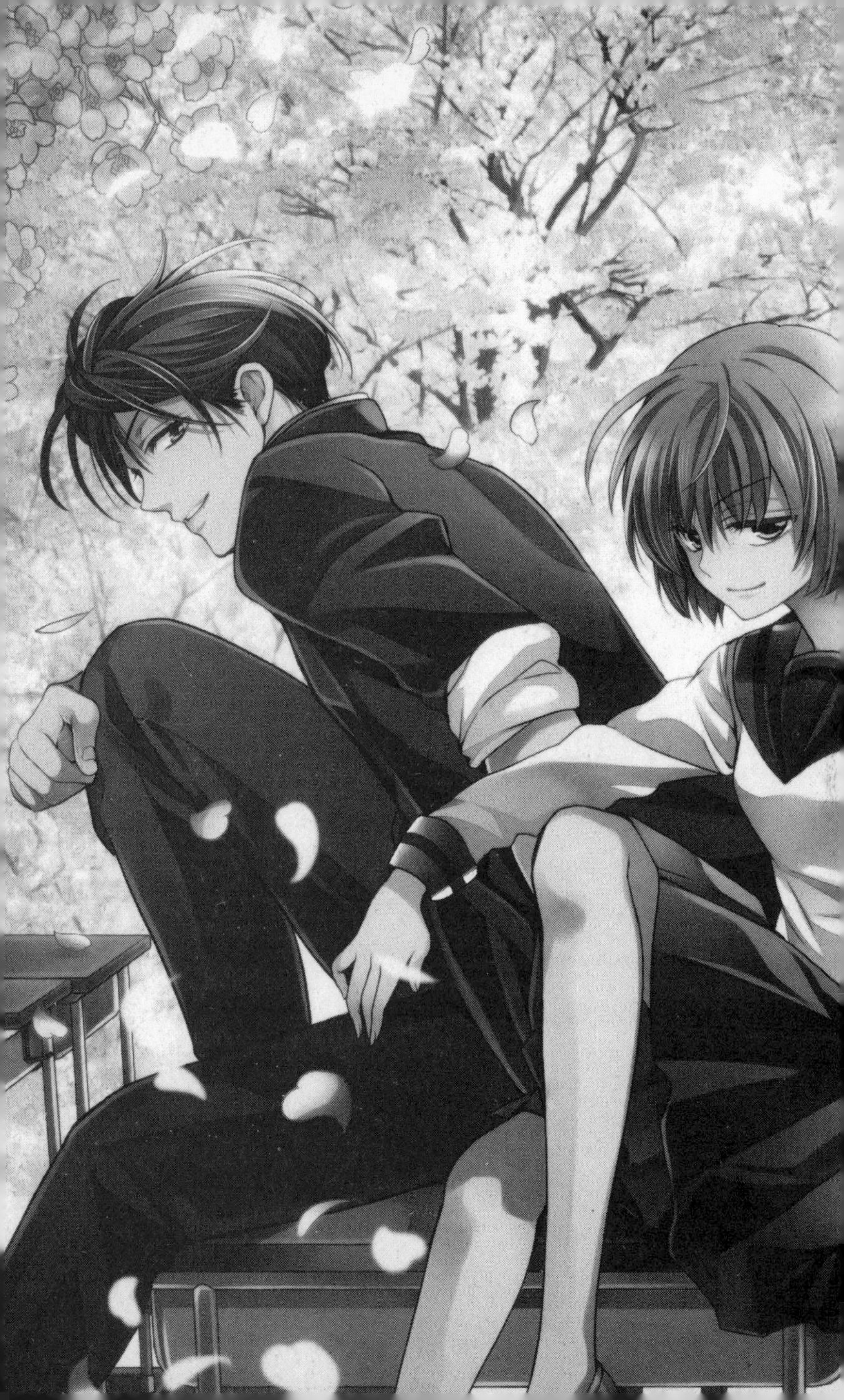

AN EXCITING INFILTRATION ☆

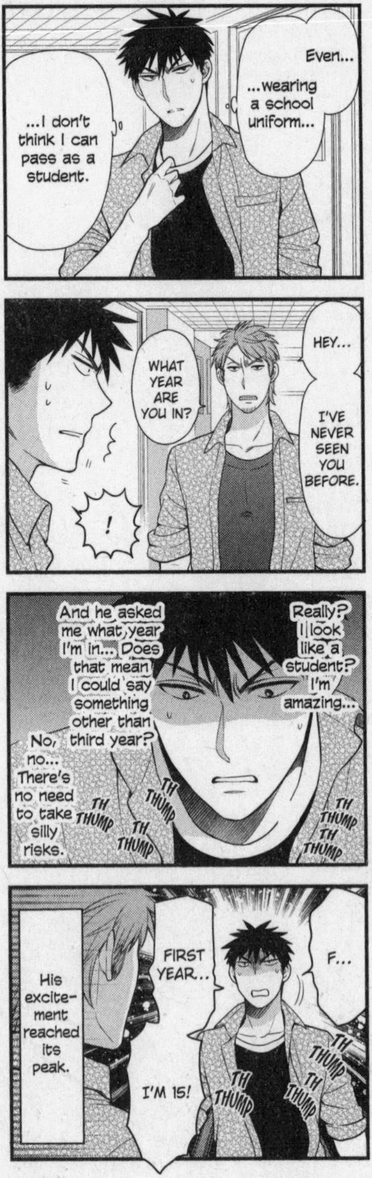
Even...
...wearing a school uniform...
...I don't think I can pass as a student.
HEY...
I'VE NEVER SEEN YOU BEFORE.
WHAT YEAR ARE YOU IN?
!
Really? I look like a student? I'm amazing...
TH THUMP TH THUMP
And he asked me what year I'm in... Does that mean I could say something other than third year?
TH THUMP
TH THUMP
No, no... There's no need to take silly risks.
TH THUMP
F...
TH THUMP
TH THUMP
FIRST YEAR...
I'M 15!
TH THUMP
His excitement reached its peak.

FULL OF CONFIDENCE

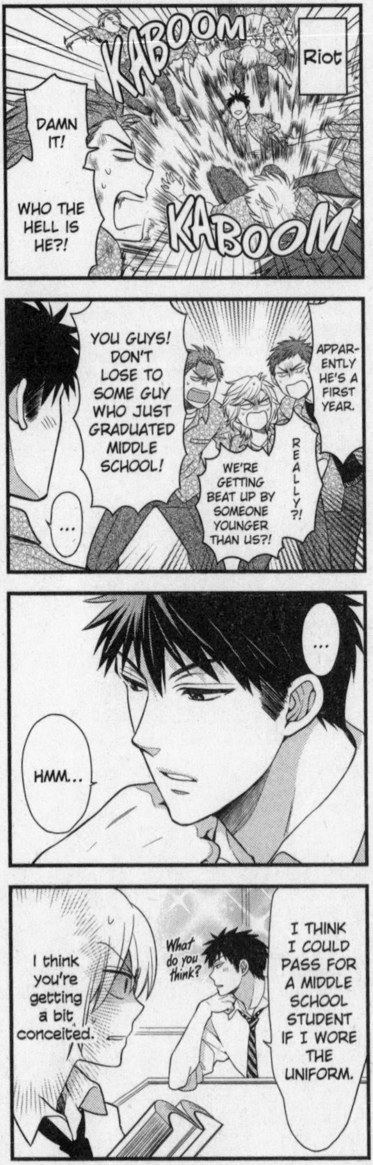
Riot
KABOOM
DAMN IT!
WHO THE HELL IS HE?!
KABOOM
APPARENTLY HE'S A FIRST YEAR.
REALLY?!
YOU GUYS! DON'T LOSE TO SOME GUY WHO JUST GRADUATED MIDDLE SCHOOL!
WE'RE GETTING BEAT UP BY SOMEONE YOUNGER THAN US?!
...
...
HMM...
I THINK I COULD PASS FOR A MIDDLE SCHOOL STUDENT IF I WORE THE UNIFORM.
What do you think?
I think you're getting a bit conceited.

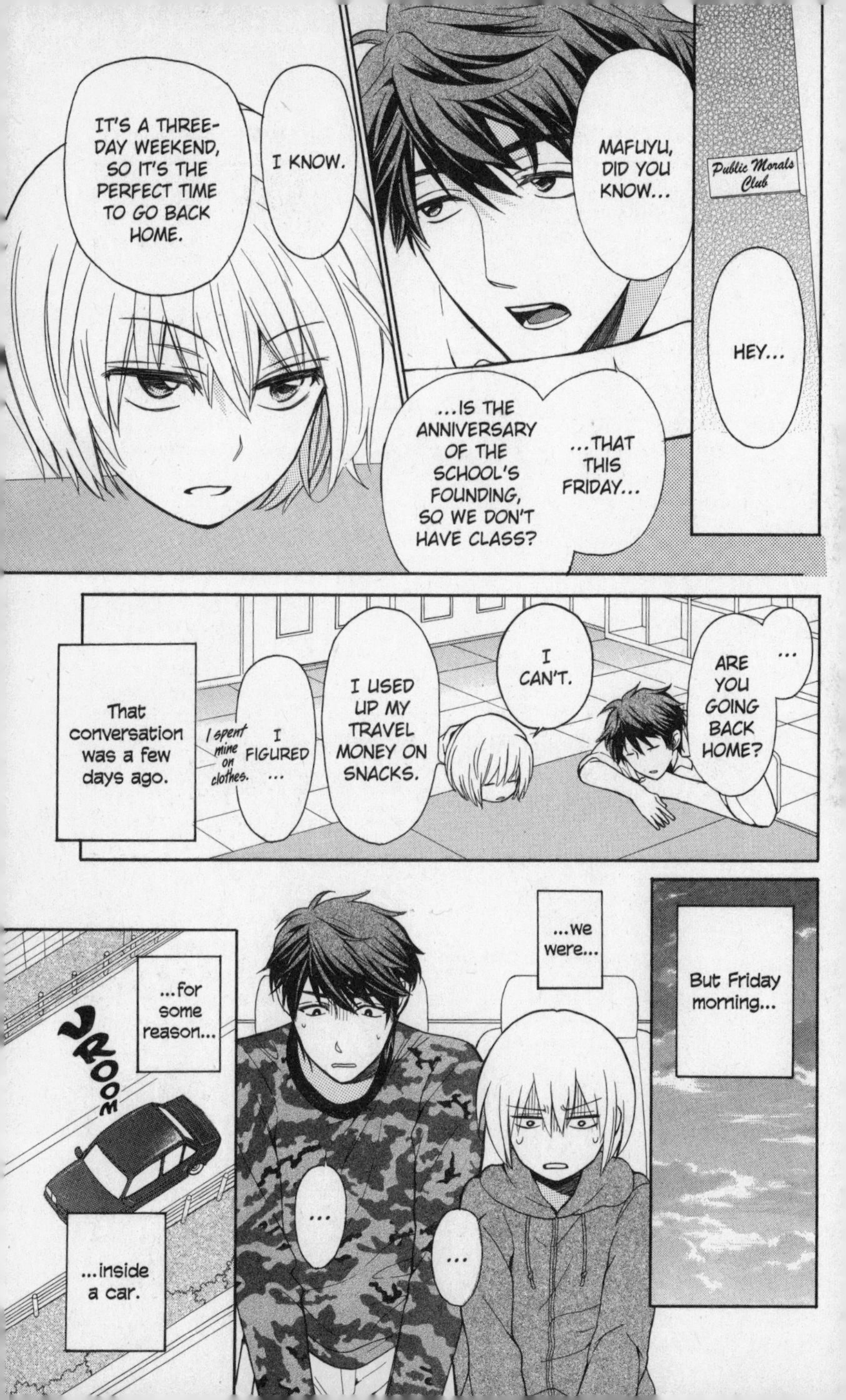
Public Morals Club
HEY...
MAFUYU, DID YOU KNOW...
...THAT THIS FRIDAY...
...IS THE ANNIVERSARY OF THE SCHOOL'S FOUNDING, SO WE DON'T HAVE CLASS?
I KNOW.
IT'S A THREE-DAY WEEKEND, SO IT'S THE PERFECT TIME TO GO BACK HOME.
...
ARE YOU GOING BACK HOME?
I CAN'T.
I USED UP MY TRAVEL MONEY ON SNACKS.
I FIGURED ...
I spent mine on clothes.
That conversation was a few days ago.
But Friday morning...
...we were...
...for some reason...
...
...
VROOM
...inside a car.

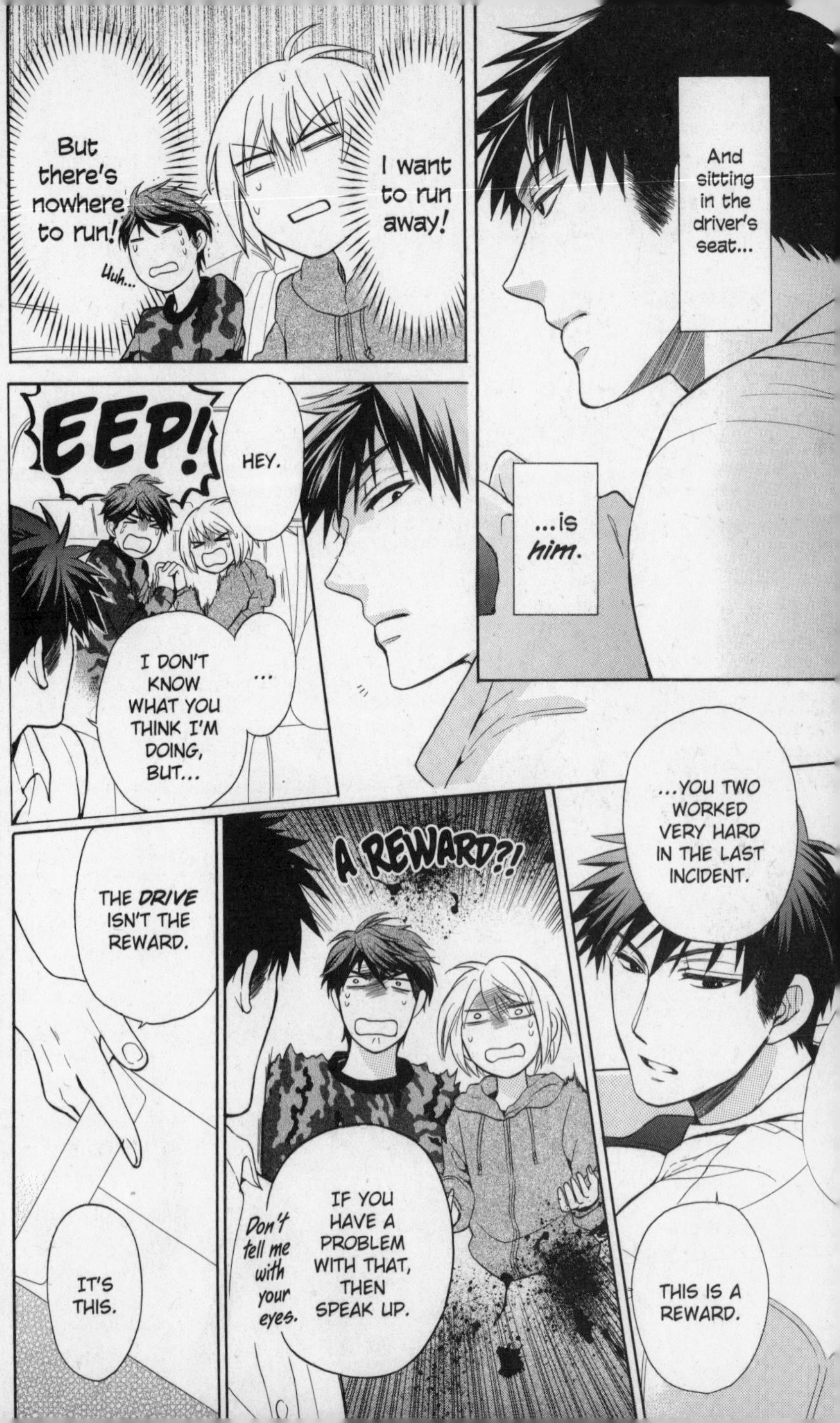
And sitting in the driver's seat...
...is him.
I want to run away!
But there's nowhere to run!
Uuh...
HEY.
EEP!
...
I DON'T KNOW WHAT YOU THINK I'M DOING, BUT...
...YOU TWO WORKED VERY HARD IN THE LAST INCIDENT.
THIS IS A REWARD.
A REWARD?!
IF YOU HAVE A PROBLEM WITH THAT, THEN SPEAK UP.
Don't tell me with your eyes.
THE *DRIVE* ISN'T THE REWARD.
IT'S THIS.

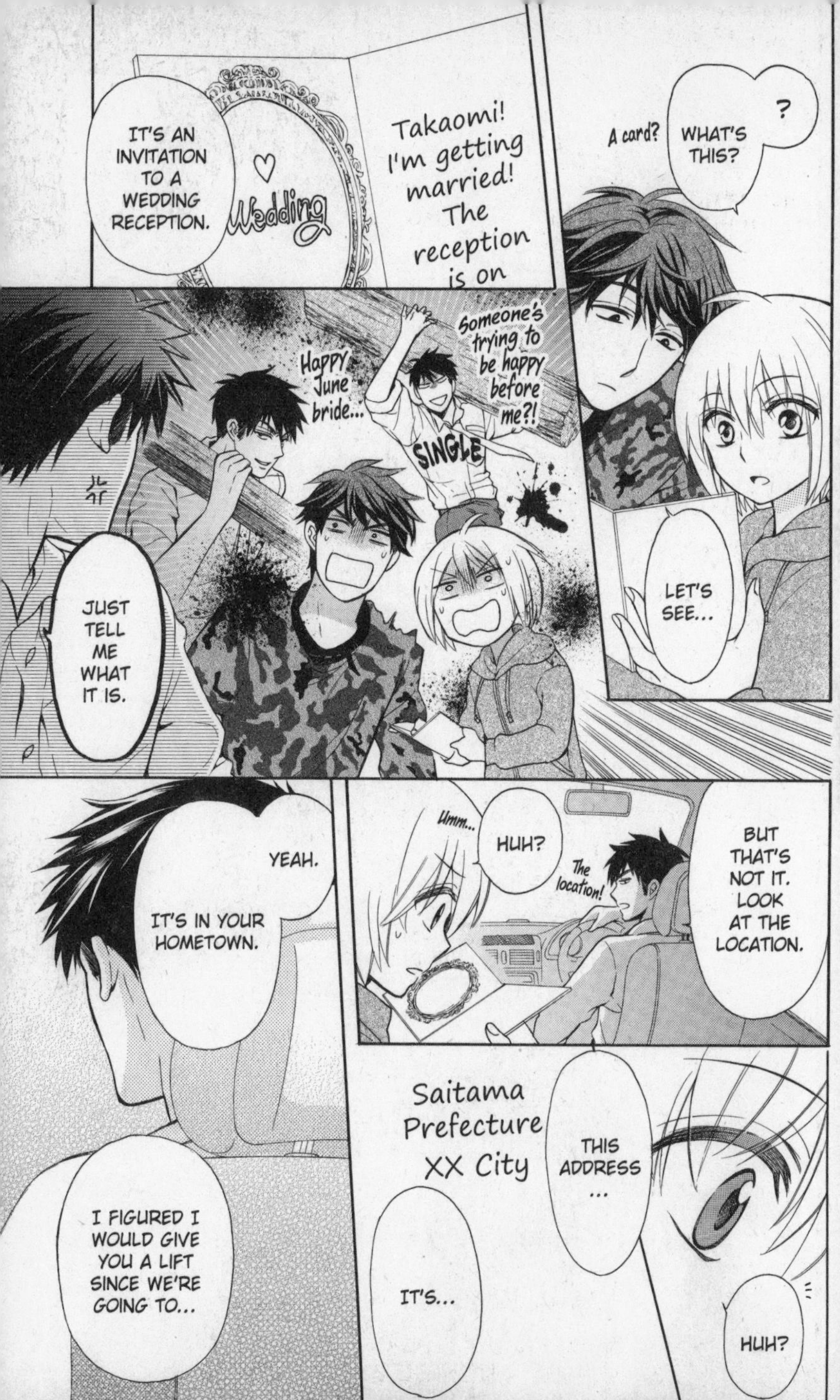
?
WHAT'S THIS?
A card?
LET'S SEE...
Takaomi! I'm getting married! The reception is on
IT'S AN INVITATION TO A WEDDING RECEPTION.
Wedding
Someone's trying to be happy before me?!
Happy June bride...
SINGLE
JUST TELL ME WHAT IT IS.
BUT THAT'S NOT IT. LOOK AT THE LOCATION.
The location!
HUH?
Umm...
THIS ADDRESS...
Saitama Prefecture XX City
IT'S...
HUH?
YEAH.
IT'S IN YOUR HOMETOWN.
I FIGURED I WOULD GIVE YOU A LIFT SINCE WE'RE GOING TO...

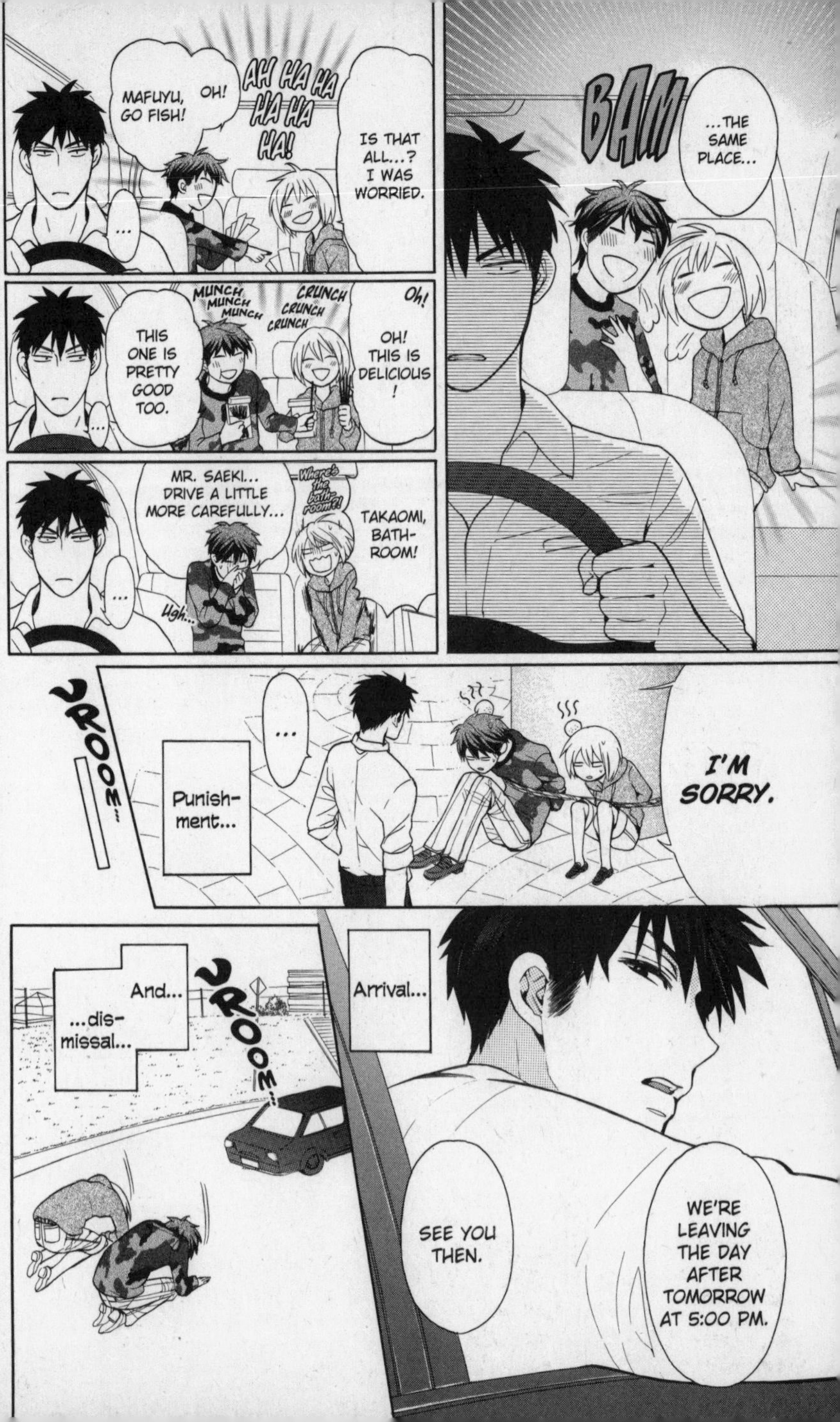
BAM
...THE SAME PLACE...
IS THAT ALL...? I WAS WORRIED.
AH HA HA HA HA HA!
OH!
MAFUYU, GO FISH!
...
Oh!
OH! THIS IS DELICIOUS!
CRUNCH CRUNCH CRUNCH
MUNCH MUNCH MUNCH
THIS ONE IS PRETTY GOOD TOO.
...
Where's the bathroom?!
TAKAOMI, BATHROOM!
MR. SAEKI... DRIVE A LITTLE MORE CAREFULLY...
Ugh...
...
I'M SORRY.
...
Punishment...
VROOOM...
Arrival...
WE'RE LEAVING THE DAY AFTER TOMORROW AT 5:00 PM.
SEE YOU THEN.
VROOOM...
And... ...dismissal...

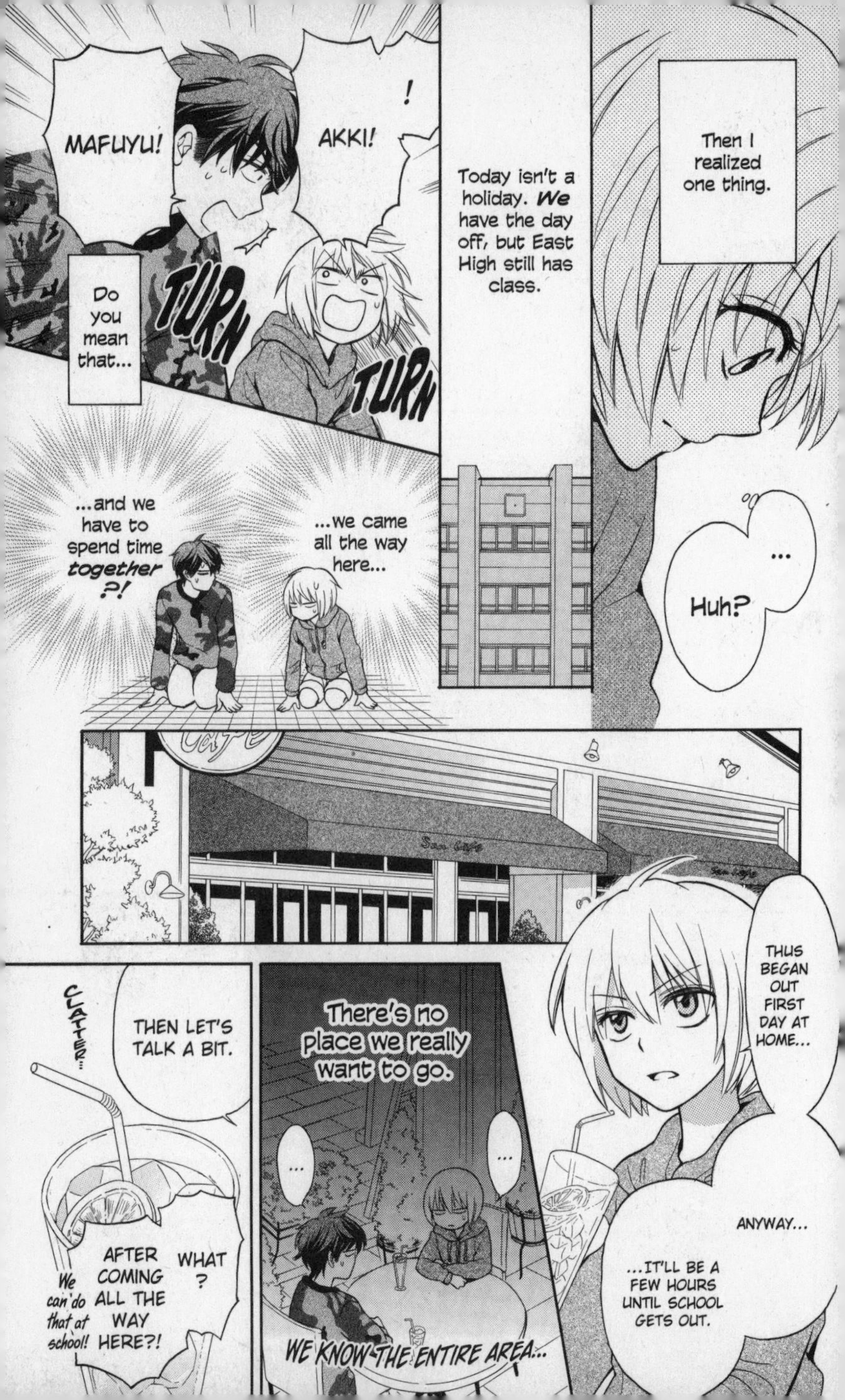
Then I realized one thing.
...
Huh?
Today isn't a holiday. ***We*** have the day off, but East High still has class.
!
AKKI!
MAFUYU!
TURN
TURN
Do you mean that...
...we came all the way here...
...and we have to spend time ***together***?!
THUS BEGAN OUT FIRST DAY AT HOME...
ANYWAY...
...IT'LL BE A FEW HOURS UNTIL SCHOOL GETS OUT.
There's no place we really want to go.
...
...
WE KNOW THE ENTIRE AREA...
THEN LET'S TALK A BIT.
CLATTER...
WHAT?
AFTER COMING ALL THE WAY HERE?!
We can't do that at school!

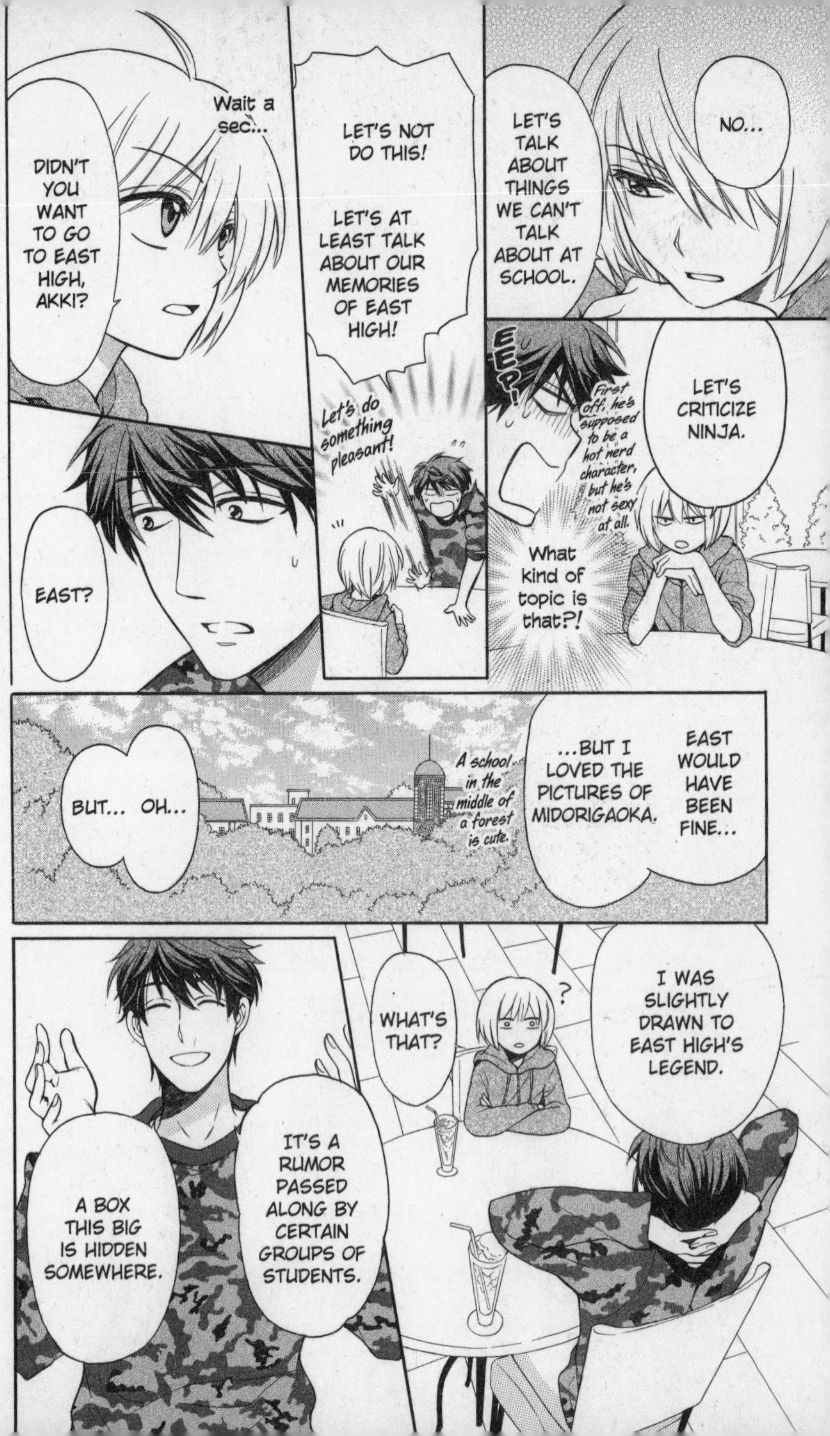
NO...
LET'S TALK ABOUT THINGS WE CAN'T TALK ABOUT AT SCHOOL.
LET'S CRITICIZE NINJA.
EEP!
First off, he's supposed to be a hot nerd character, but he's not sexy at all.
What kind of topic is that?!
LET'S NOT DO THIS!
LET'S AT LEAST TALK ABOUT OUR MEMORIES OF EAST HIGH!
Let's do something pleasant!
Wait a sec...
DIDN'T YOU WANT TO GO TO EAST HIGH, AKKI?
EAST?
EAST WOULD HAVE BEEN FINE...
...BUT I LOVED THE PICTURES OF MIDORIGAOKA.
A school in the middle of a forest is cute.
BUT... OH...
I WAS SLIGHTLY DRAWN TO EAST HIGH'S LEGEND.
?
WHAT'S THAT?
IT'S A RUMOR PASSED ALONG BY CERTAIN GROUPS OF STUDENTS.
A BOX THIS BIG IS HIDDEN SOMEWHERE.

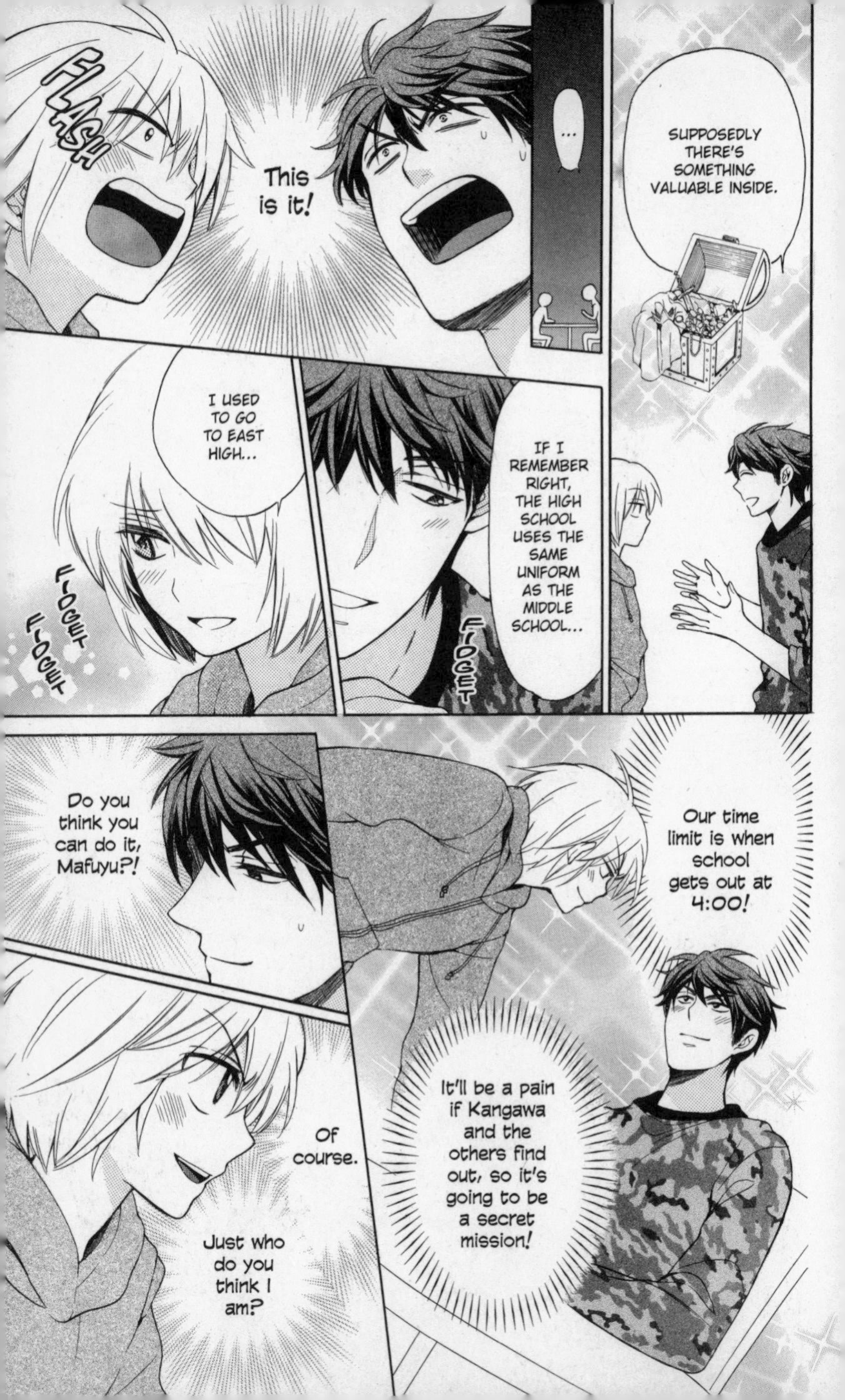
SUPPOSEDLY THERE'S SOMETHING VALUABLE INSIDE.
...
This is it!
FLASH
IF I REMEMBER RIGHT, THE HIGH SCHOOL USES THE SAME UNIFORM AS THE MIDDLE SCHOOL...
FIDGET
I USED TO GO TO EAST HIGH...
FIDGET FIDGET
Our time limit is when school gets out at 4:00!
It'll be a pain if Kangawa and the others find out, so it's going to be a secret mission!
Do you think you can do it, Mafuyu?!
Of course.
Just who do you think I am?

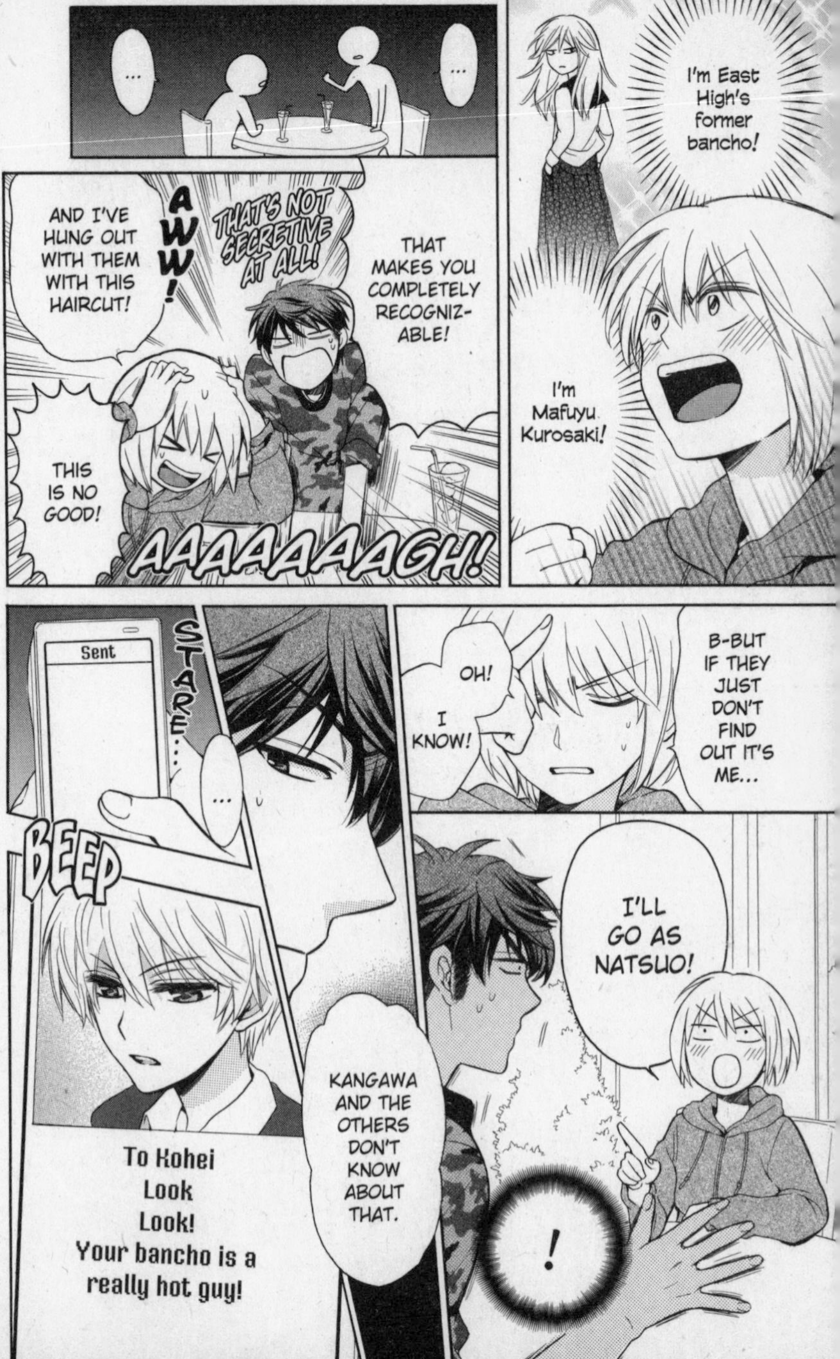
I'm East High's former bancho!
I'm Mafuyu Kurosaki!
...
...
THAT MAKES YOU COMPLETELY RECOGNIZ-ABLE!
THAT'S NOT SECRETIVE AT ALL!
AWW!
AND I'VE HUNG OUT WITH THEM WITH THIS HAIRCUT!
THIS IS NO GOOD!
AAAAAAAAGH!
B-BUT IF THEY JUST DON'T FIND OUT IT'S ME...
OH!
I KNOW!
I'LL GO AS NATSUO!
KANGAWA AND THE OTHERS DON'T KNOW ABOUT THAT.
!
STARE...
...
Sent
BEEP
To Kohei
Look
Look!
Your bancho is a really hot guy!

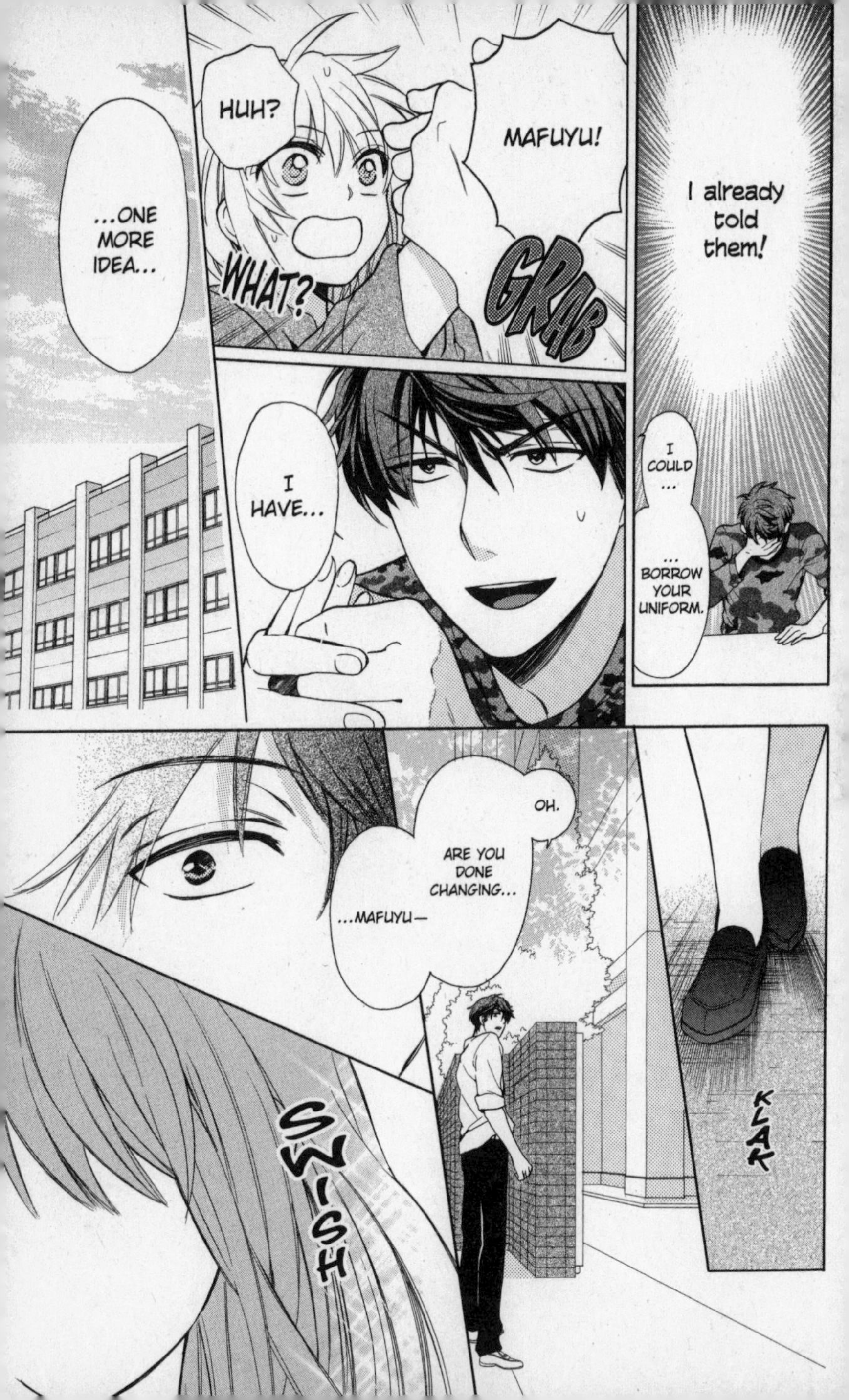
I already told them!
I COULD ...
... BORROW YOUR UNIFORM.
MAFUYU!
GRAB
HUH?
WHAT?
I HAVE...
...ONE MORE IDEA...
KLAK
OH.
ARE YOU DONE CHANGING...
...MAFUYU—
SWISH

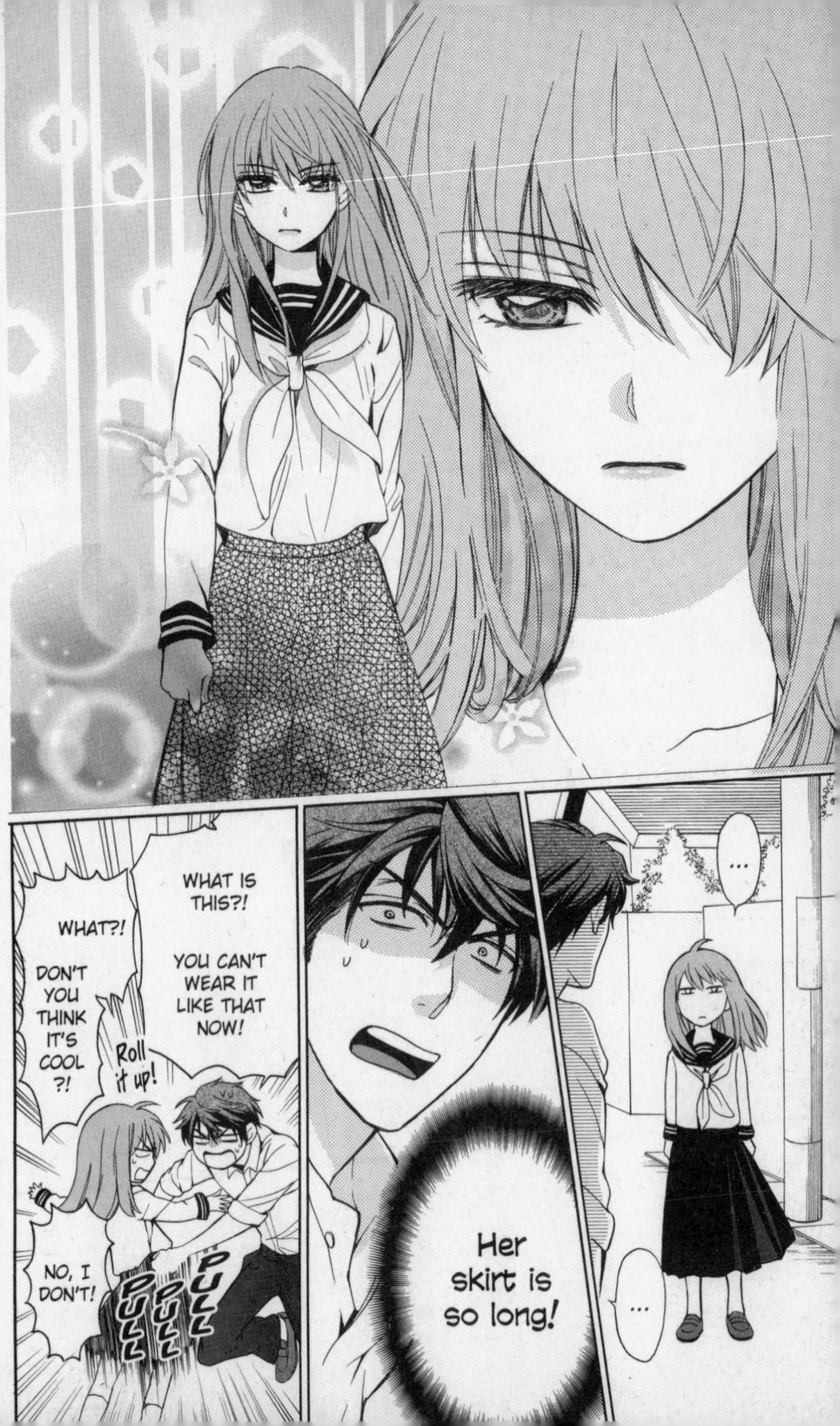
...
...
Her skirt is so long!
WHAT IS THIS?! YOU CAN'T WEAR IT LIKE THAT NOW!
WHAT?! DON'T YOU THINK IT'S COOL?!
Roll it up!
NO, I DON'T!
PULL PULL PULL

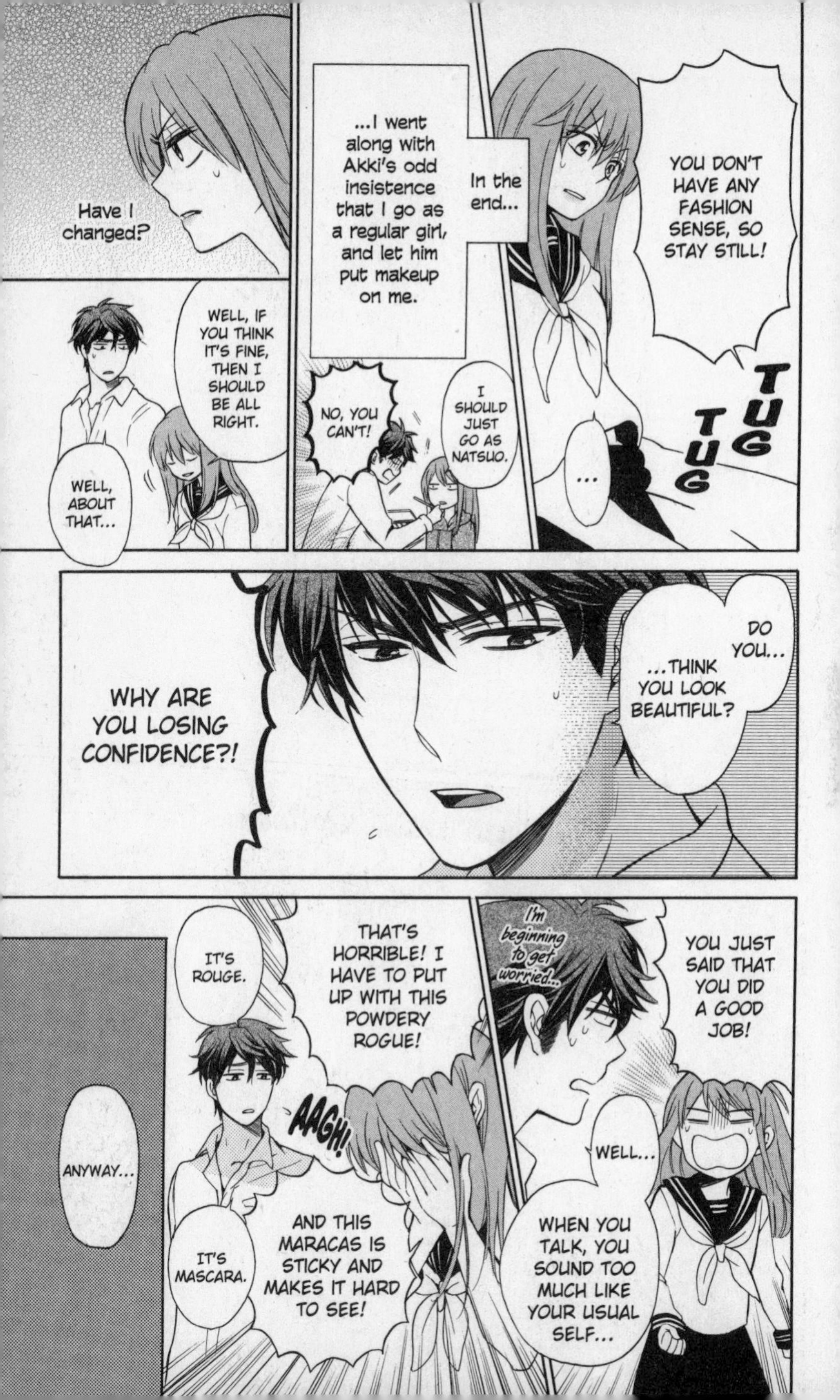
YOU DON'T HAVE ANY FASHION SENSE, SO STAY STILL!
TUG TUG
...
In the end...
...I went along with Akki's odd insistence that I go as a regular girl, and let him put makeup on me.
I SHOULD JUST GO AS NATSUO.
NO, YOU CAN'T!
Have I changed?
WELL, IF YOU THINK IT'S FINE, THEN I SHOULD BE ALL RIGHT.
WELL, ABOUT THAT...
DO YOU...
...THINK YOU LOOK BEAUTIFUL?
WHY ARE YOU LOSING CONFIDENCE?!
YOU JUST SAID THAT YOU DID A GOOD JOB!
I'm beginning to get worried...
WELL...
WHEN YOU TALK, YOU SOUND TOO MUCH LIKE YOUR USUAL SELF...
THAT'S HORRIBLE! I HAVE TO PUT UP WITH THIS POWDERY ROGUE!
IT'S ROUGE.
AAGH!
AND THIS MARACAS IS STICKY AND MAKES IT HARD TO SEE!
IT'S MASCARA.
ANYWAY...

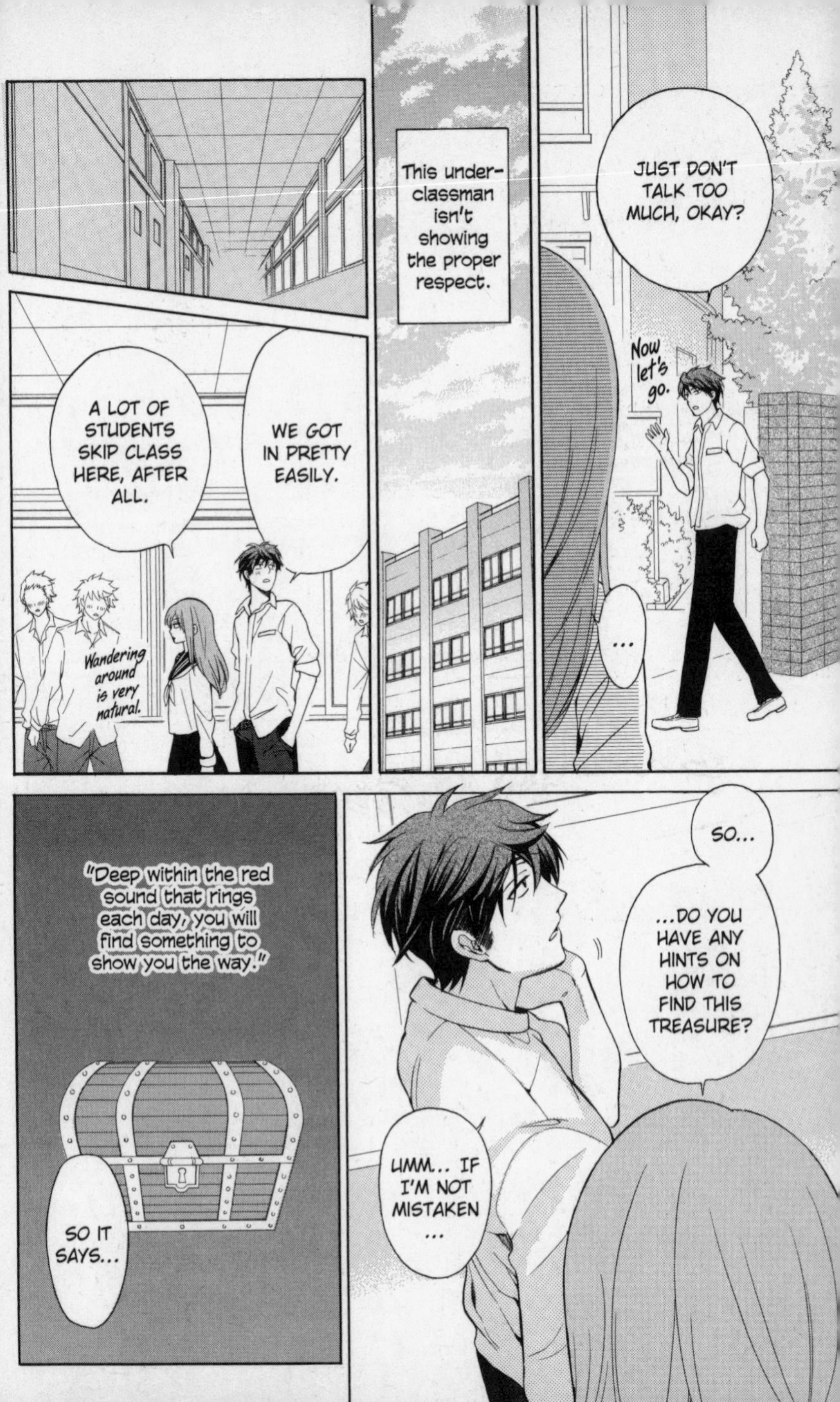
JUST DON'T TALK TOO MUCH, OKAY?
Now let's go.
...
This under-classman isn't showing the proper respect.
WE GOT IN PRETTY EASILY.
A LOT OF STUDENTS SKIP CLASS HERE, AFTER ALL.
Wandering around is very natural.
SO...
...DO YOU HAVE ANY HINTS ON HOW TO FIND THIS TREASURE?
UMM... IF I'M NOT MISTAKEN ...
"Deep within the red sound that rings each day, you will find something to show you the way."
SO IT SAYS...

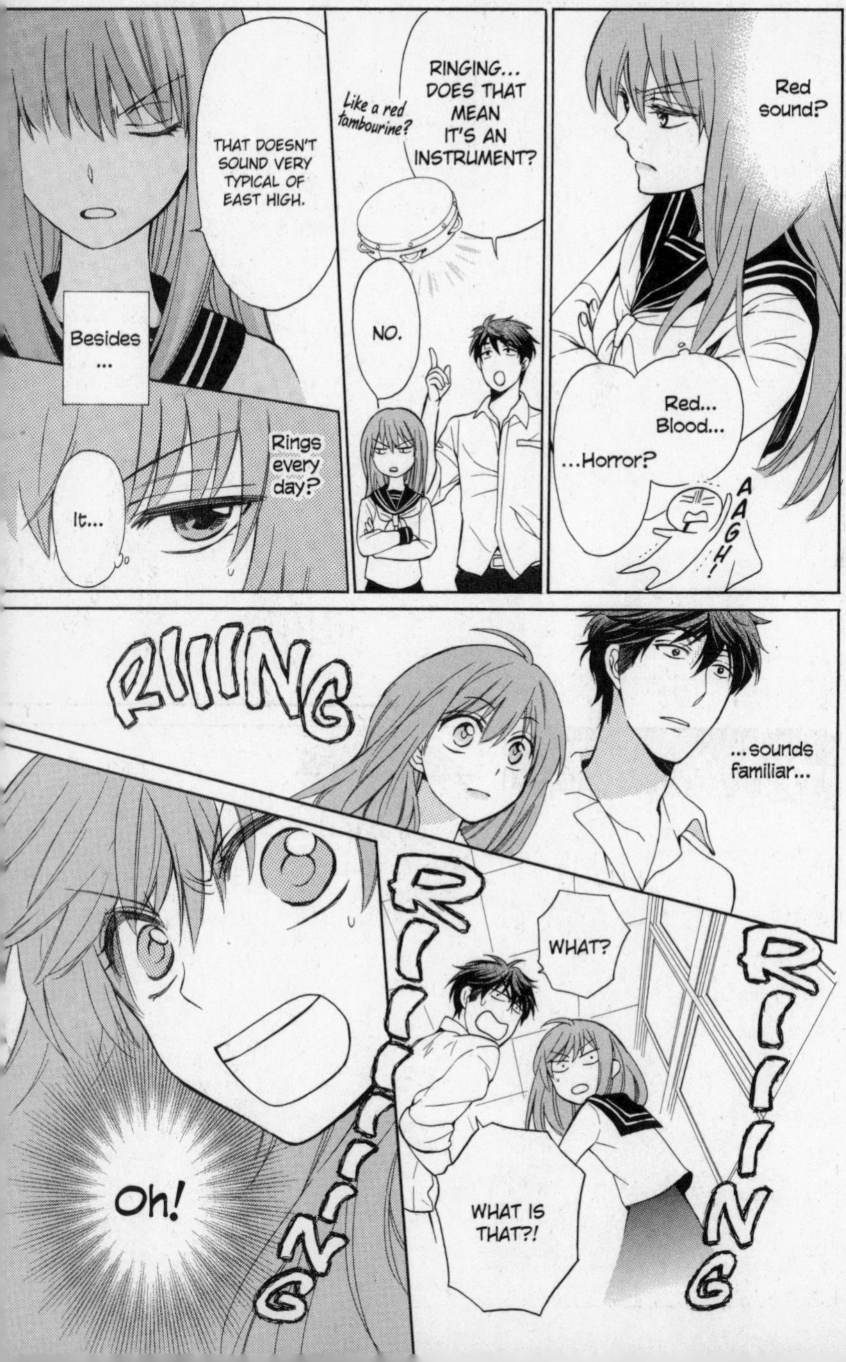
Red sound?
Red... Blood...
...Horror?
AAGH!
RINGING... DOES THAT MEAN IT'S AN INSTRUMENT?
Like a red tambourine?
NO.
THAT DOESN'T SOUND VERY TYPICAL OF EAST HIGH.
Besides...
Rings every day?
It...
RIIING
...sounds familiar...
RIIING
WHAT?
WHAT IS THAT?!
RIIING
Oh!

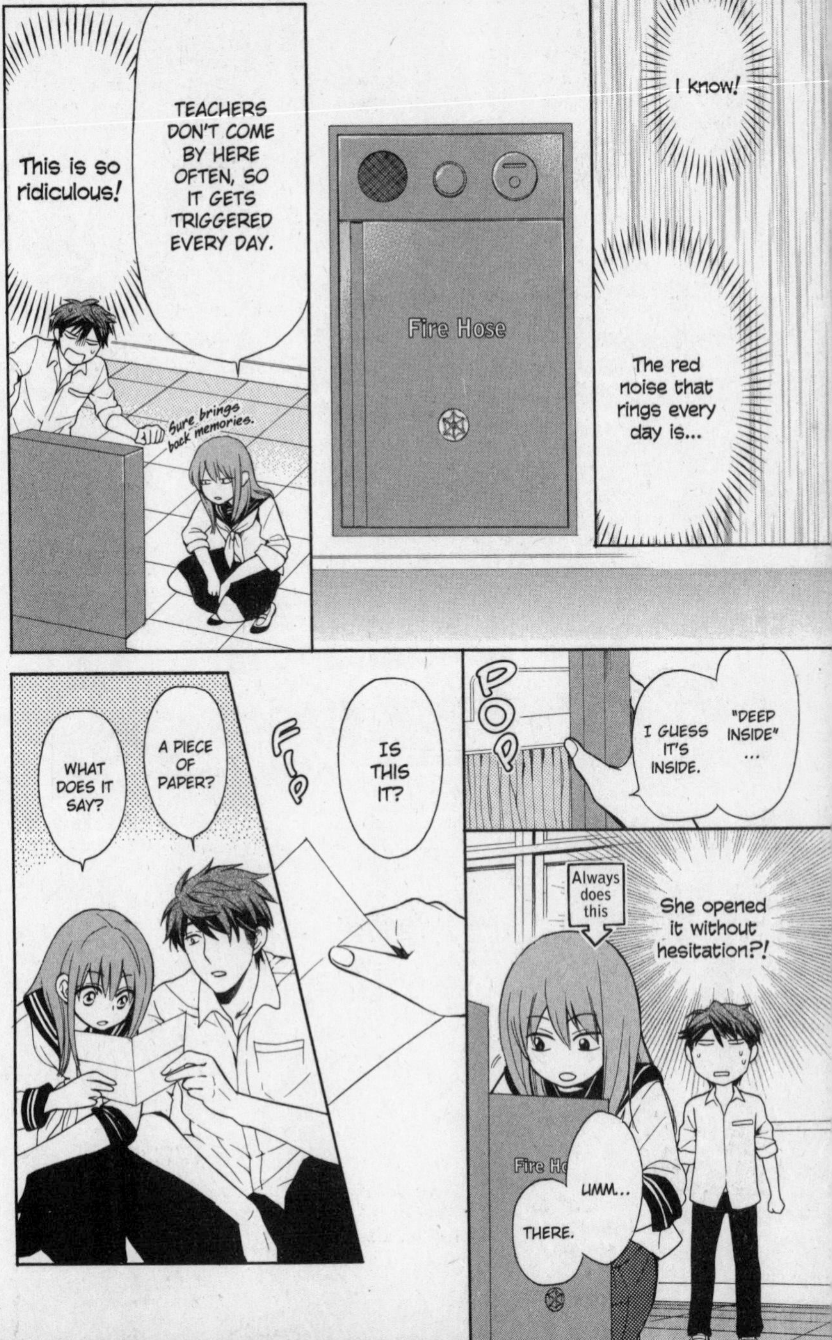
I know!
The red noise that rings every day is...
Fire Hose
TEACHERS DON'T COME BY HERE OFTEN, SO IT GETS TRIGGERED EVERY DAY.
This is so ridiculous!
Sure brings back memories.
"DEEP INSIDE" ...
I GUESS IT'S INSIDE.
POP
She opened it without hesitation?!
Always does this
Fire Ho
UMM...
THERE.
FLIP
IS THIS IT?
A PIECE OF PAPER?
WHAT DOES IT SAY?

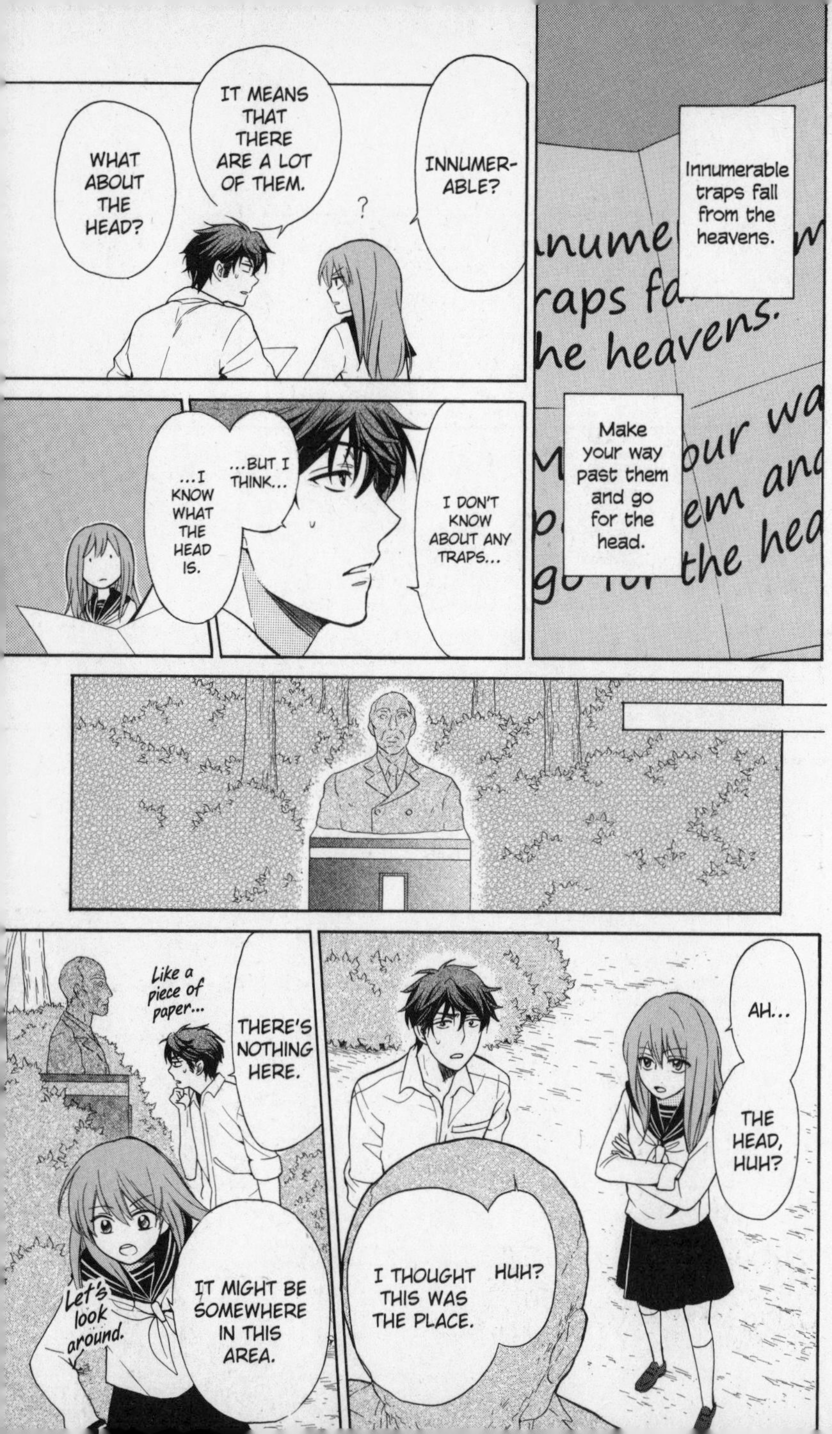
Innumerable traps fall from the heavens.
Make your way past them and go for the head.
INNUMERABLE?
?
IT MEANS THAT THERE ARE A LOT OF THEM.
WHAT ABOUT THE HEAD?
I DON'T KNOW ABOUT ANY TRAPS...
...BUT I THINK...
...I KNOW WHAT THE HEAD IS.
AH...
THE HEAD, HUH?
HUH?
I THOUGHT THIS WAS THE PLACE.
THERE'S NOTHING HERE.
Like a piece of paper...
IT MIGHT BE SOMEWHERE IN THIS AREA.
Let's look around.

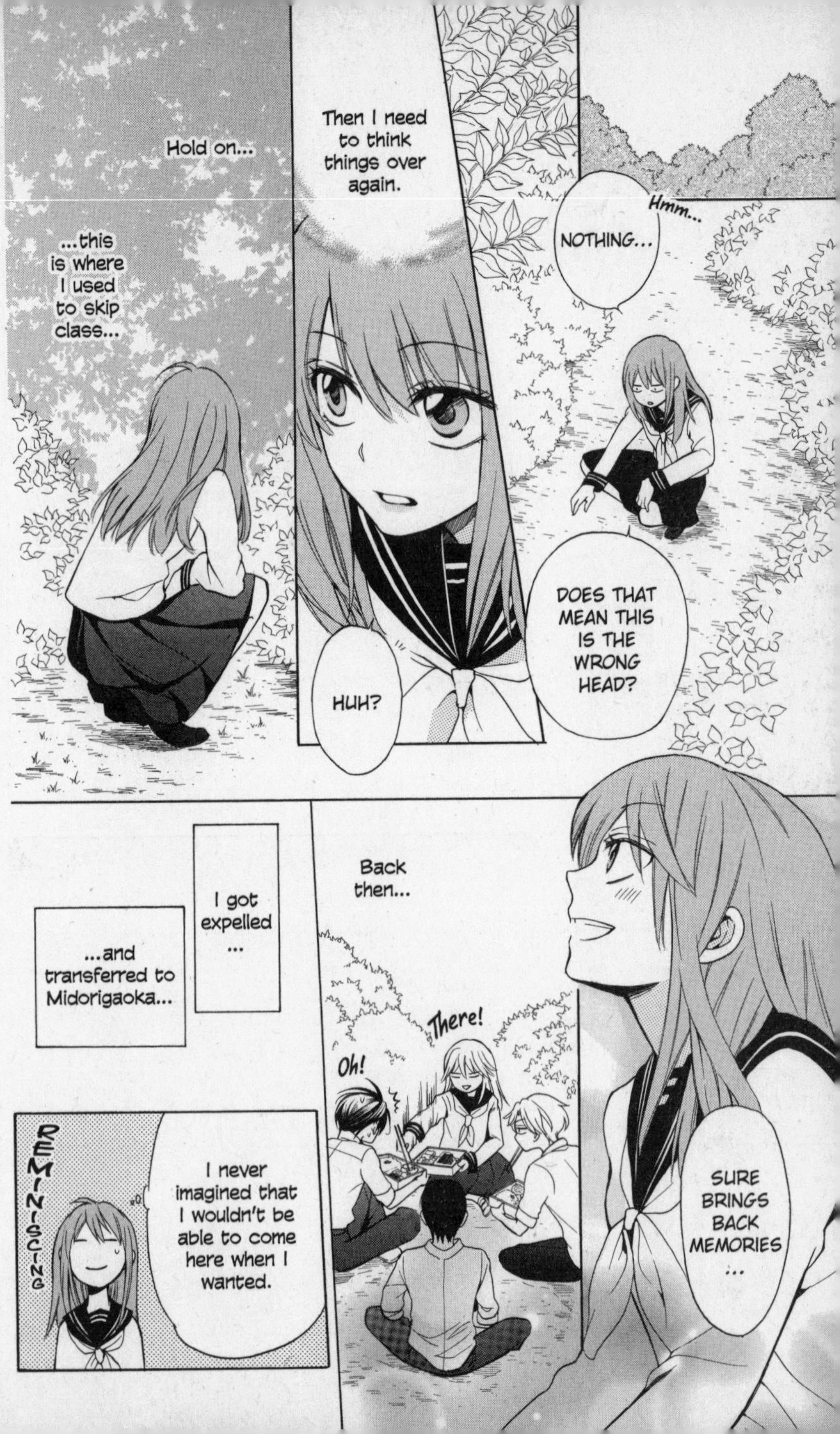
Hmm...
NOTHING...
DOES THAT MEAN THIS IS THE WRONG HEAD?
Then I need to think things over again.
HUH?
Hold on...
...this is where I used to skip class...
SURE BRINGS BACK MEMORIES...
Back then...
There!
Oh!
I got expelled...
...and transferred to Midorigaoka...
I never imagined that I wouldn't be able to come here when I wanted.
REMINISCING

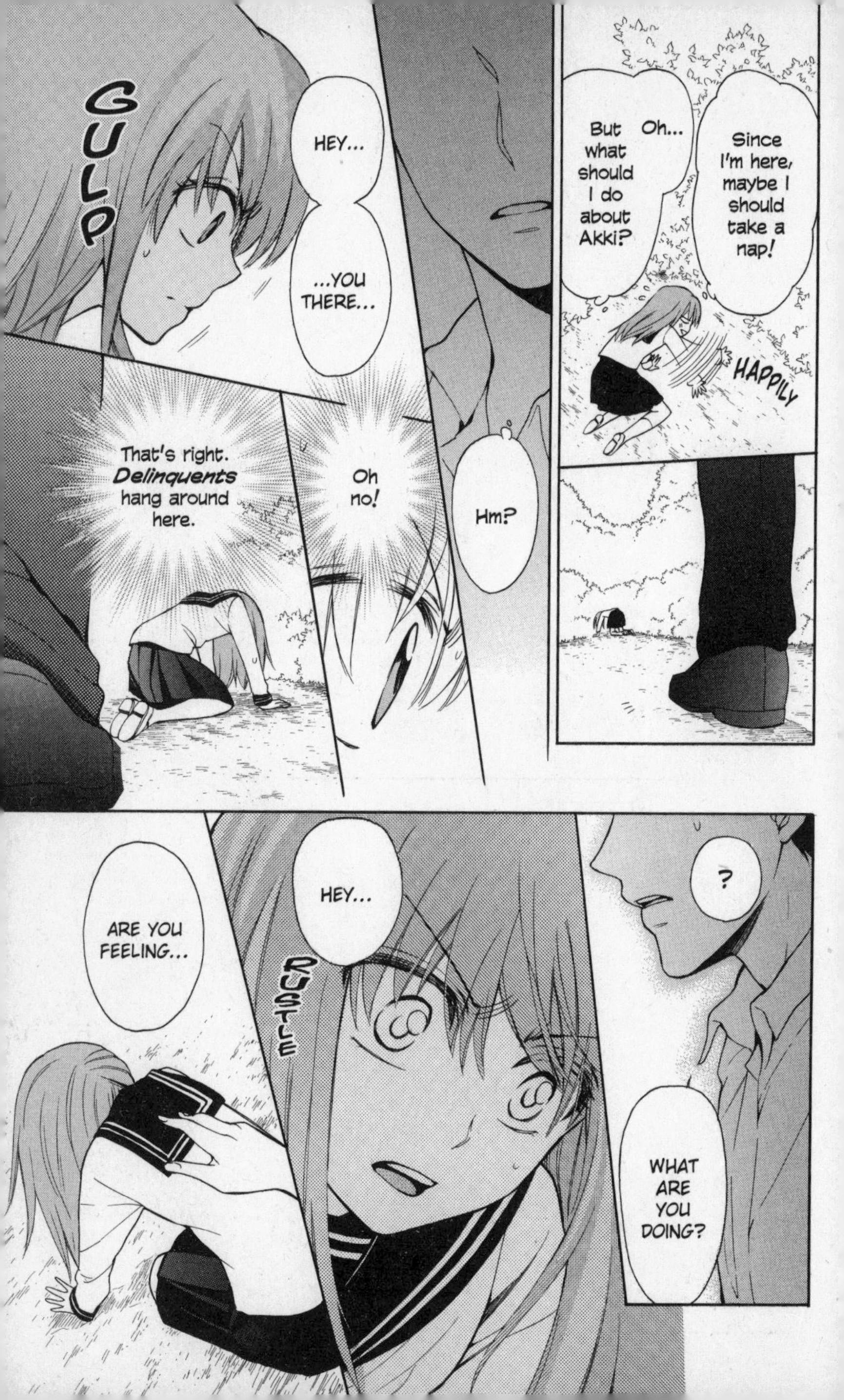
Since I'm here, maybe I should take a nap!
Oh...
But what should I do about Akki?
HAPPILY
HEY...
...YOU THERE...
Hm?
GULP
Oh no!
That's right. *Delinquents* hang around here.
?
WHAT ARE YOU DOING?
HEY...
RUSTLE
ARE YOU FEELING...

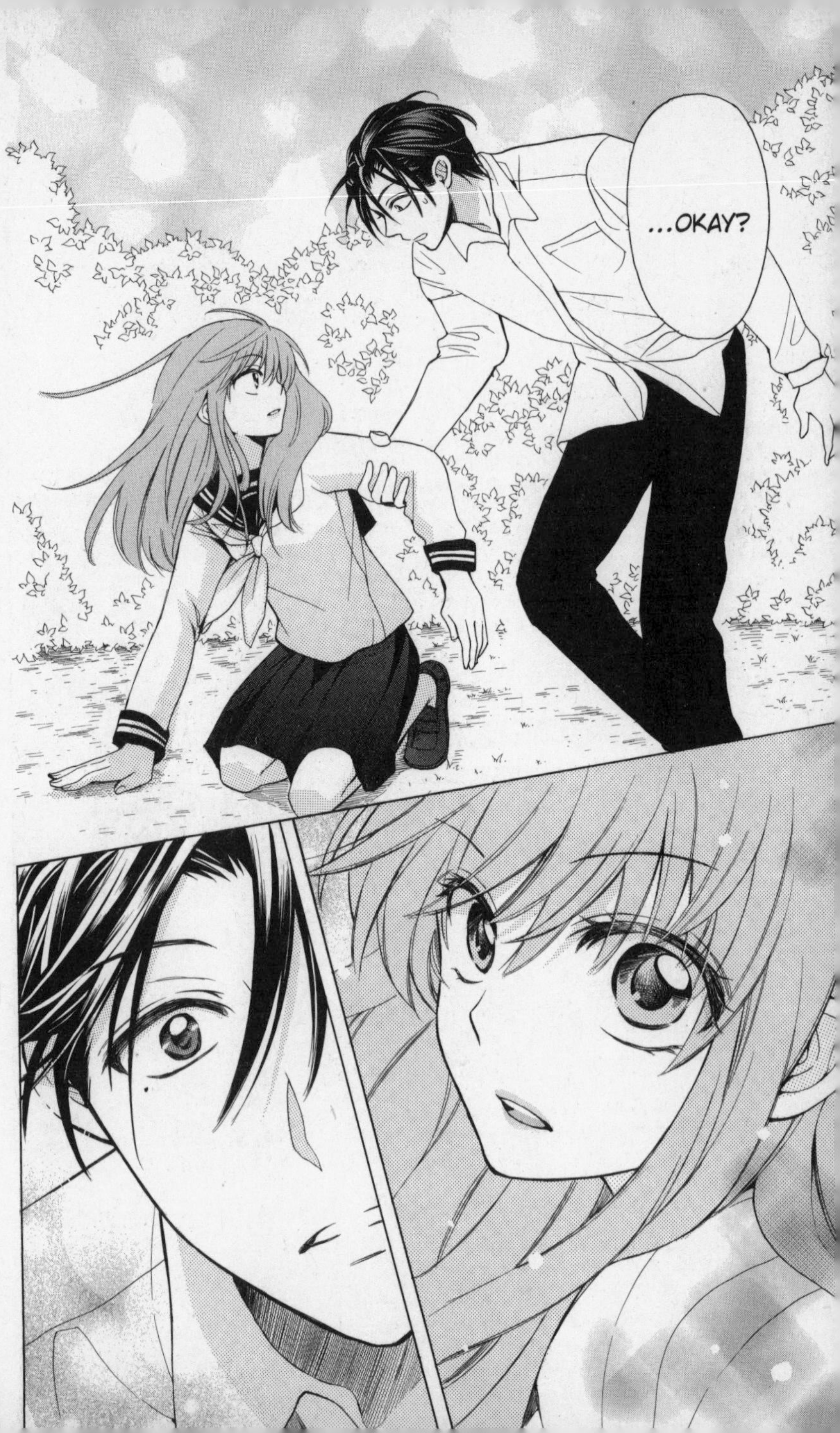
...OKAY?

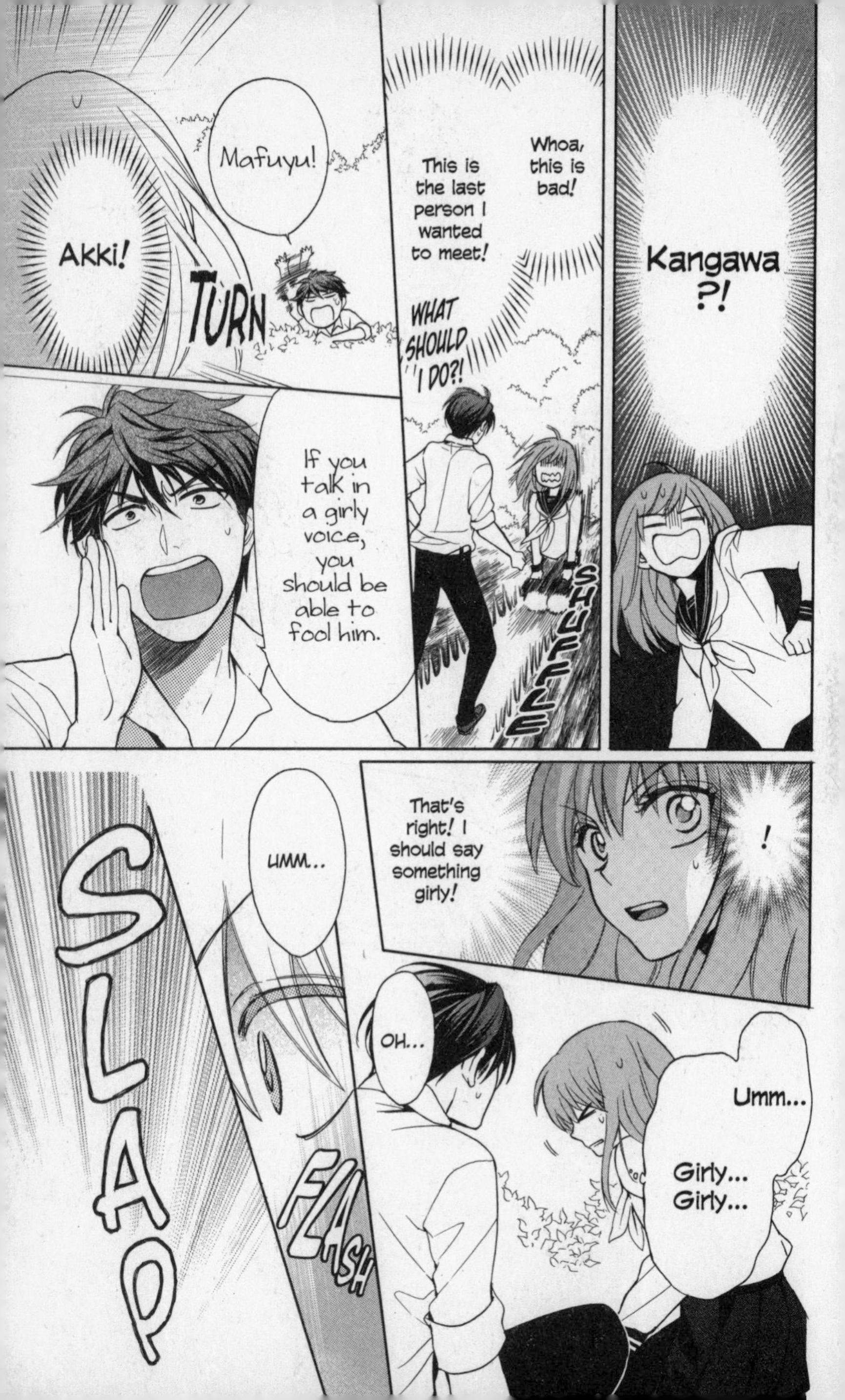
Kangawa?!
Whoa, this is bad!
This is the last person I wanted to meet!
WHAT SHOULD I DO?!
SHUFFLE
Mafuyu!
TURN
Akki!
If you talk in a girly voice, you should be able to fool him.
!
That's right! I should say something girly!
Umm...
Girly... Girly...
OH...
UMM...
FLASH
SLAP

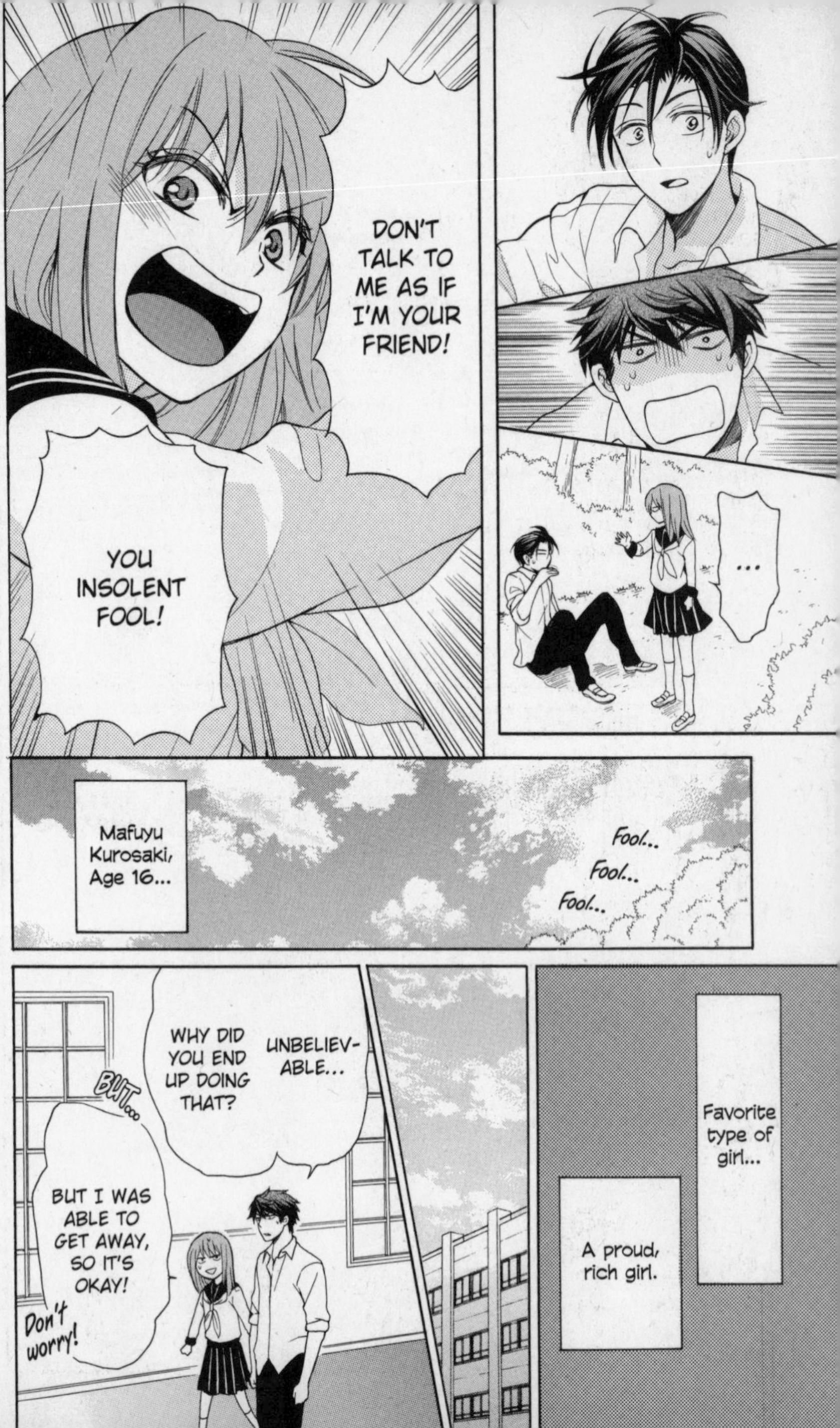
...
DON'T TALK TO ME AS IF I'M YOUR FRIEND!
YOU INSOLENT FOOL!
Fool... Fool... Fool...
Mafuyu Kurosaki, Age 16...
Favorite type of girl...
A proud, rich girl.
UNBELIEV-ABLE...
WHY DID YOU END UP DOING THAT?
BUT...
BUT I WAS ABLE TO GET AWAY, SO IT'S OKAY!
Don't worry!

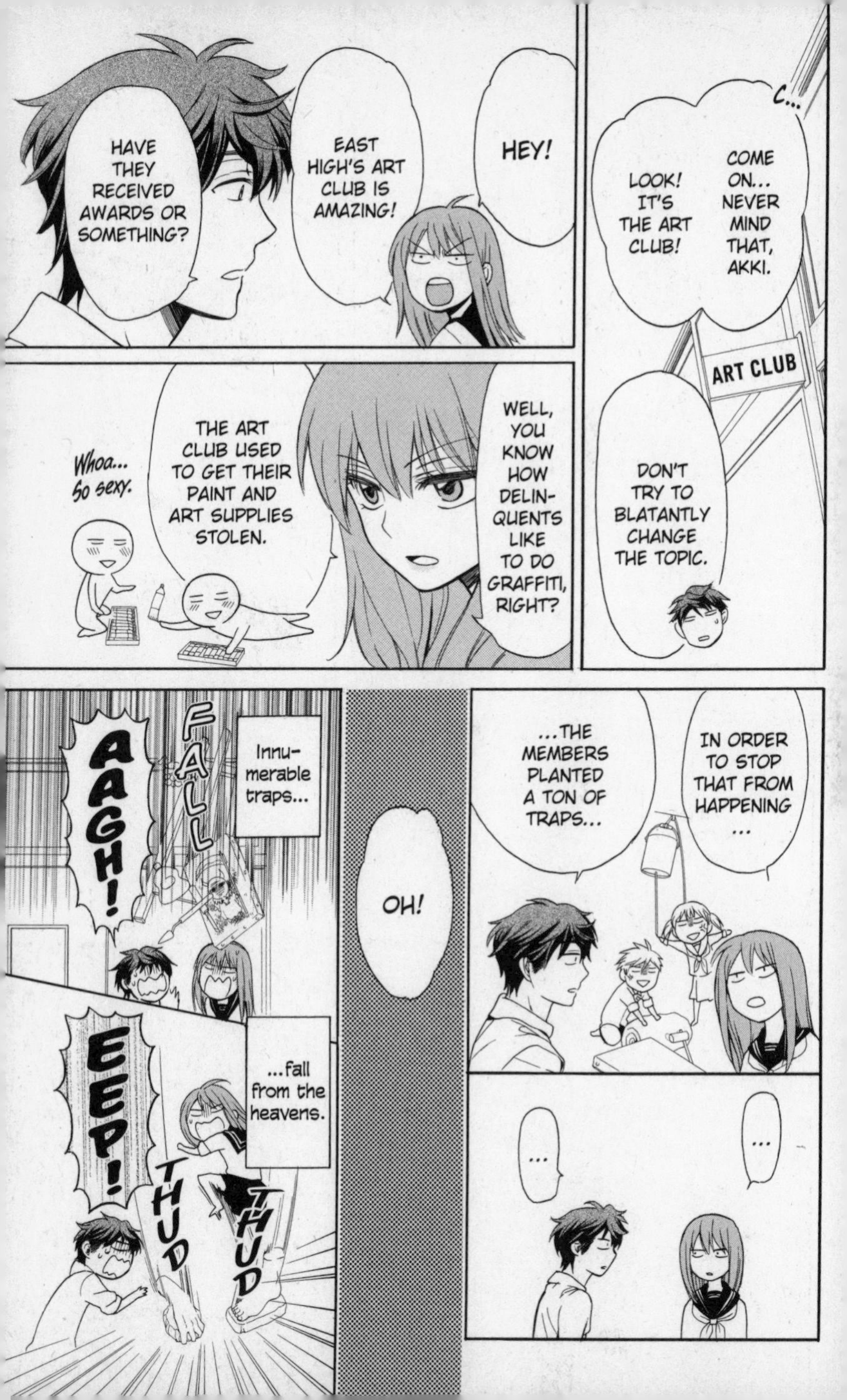
C...
COME ON... NEVER MIND THAT, AKKI.
LOOK! IT'S THE ART CLUB!
ART CLUB
DON'T TRY TO BLATANTLY CHANGE THE TOPIC.
HEY!
EAST HIGH'S ART CLUB IS AMAZING!
HAVE THEY RECEIVED AWARDS OR SOMETHING?
WELL, YOU KNOW HOW DELIN-QUENTS LIKE TO DO GRAFFITI, RIGHT?
THE ART CLUB USED TO GET THEIR PAINT AND ART SUPPLIES STOLEN.
Whoa... So sexy.
IN ORDER TO STOP THAT FROM HAPPENING...
...THE MEMBERS PLANTED A TON OF TRAPS...
...
...
OH!
Innu-merable traps...
FALL
AAGH!
...fall from the heavens.
EEP!
THUD
THUD

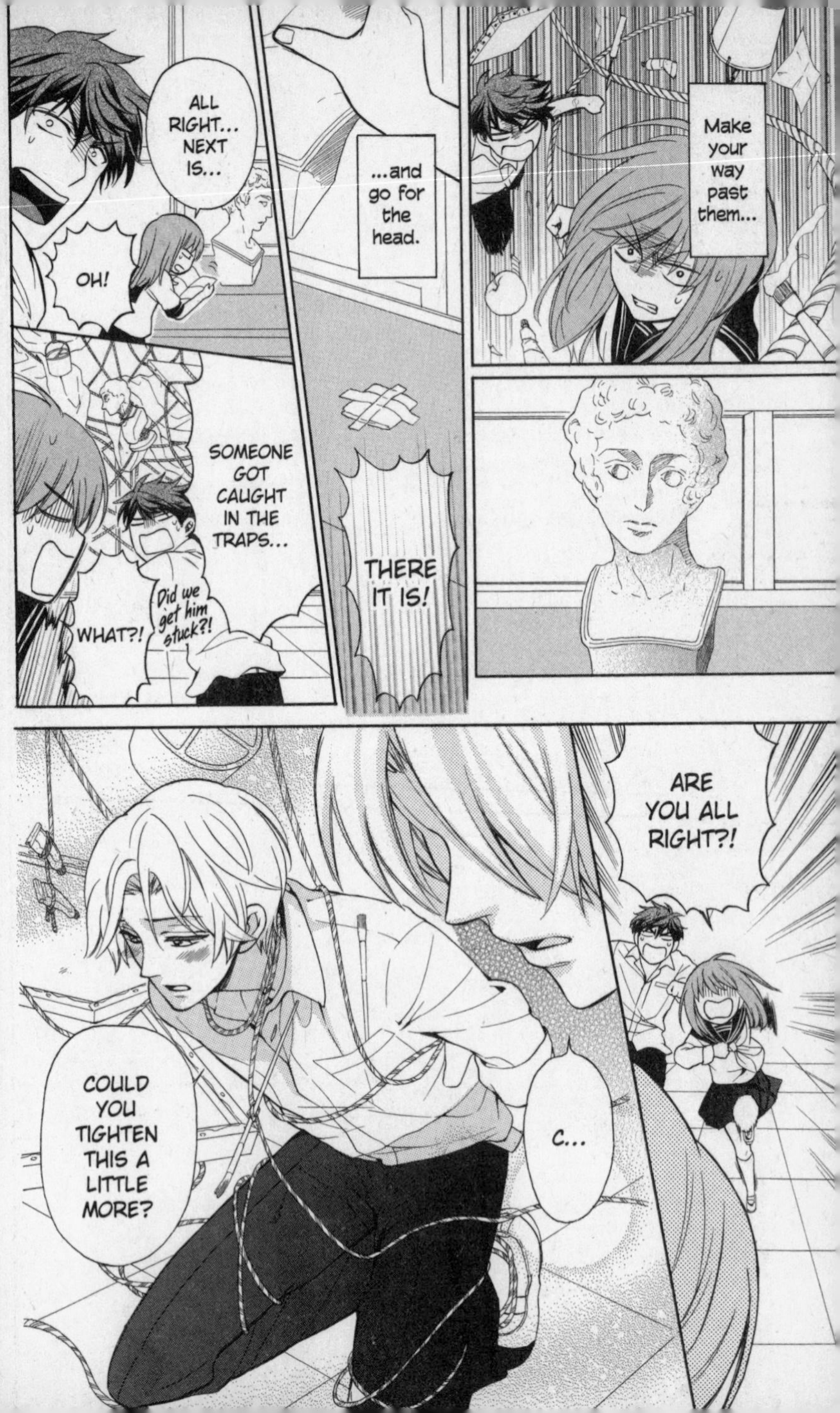
Make your way past them...
...and go for the head.
ALL RIGHT... NEXT IS...
OH!
THERE IT IS!
SOMEONE GOT CAUGHT IN THE TRAPS...
Did we get him stuck?!
WHAT?!
ARE YOU ALL RIGHT?!
C...
COULD YOU TIGHTEN THIS A LITTLE MORE?

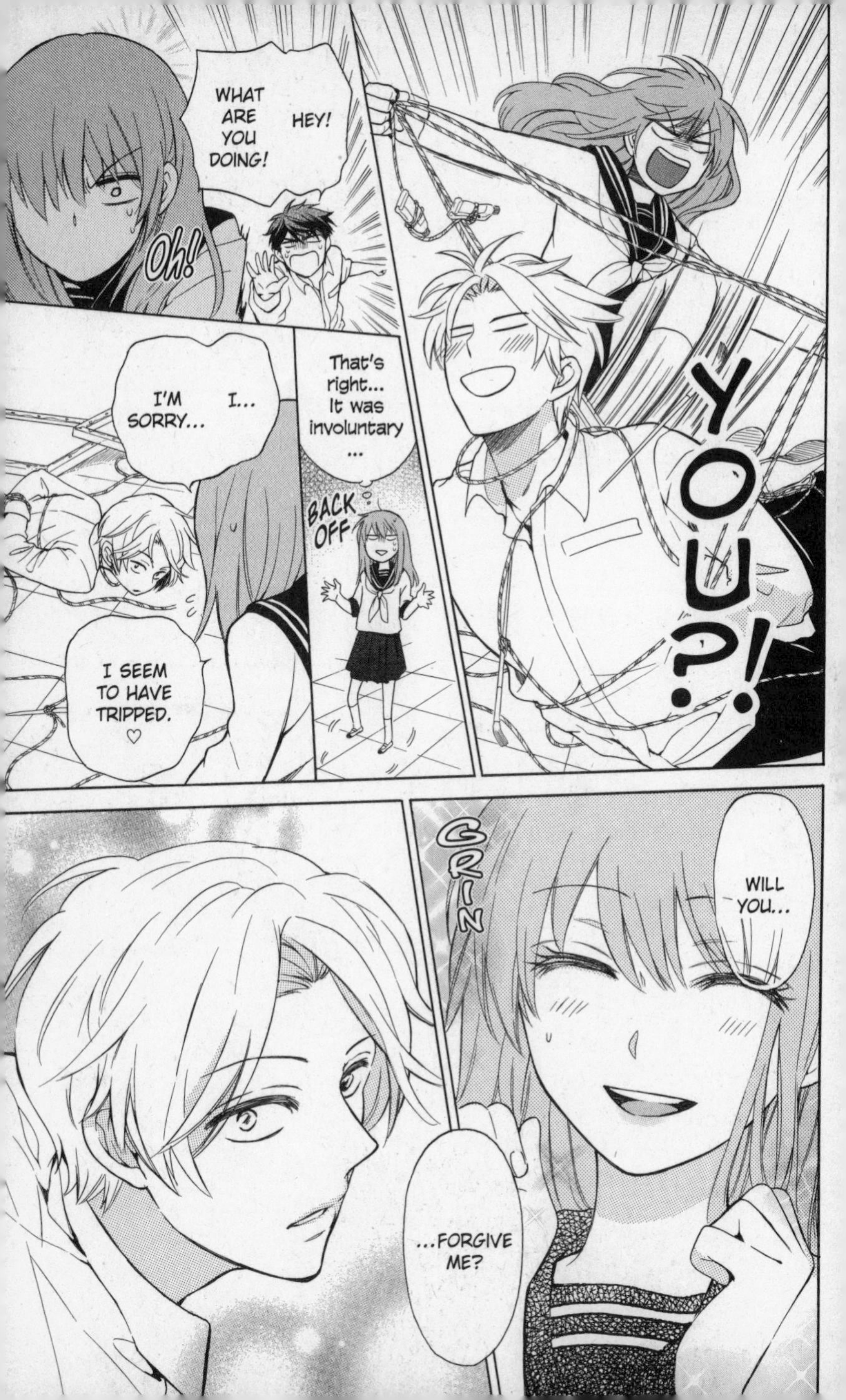
YOU?!
HEY!
WHAT ARE YOU DOING!
Oh!
That's right... It was involuntary...
BACK OFF
I...
I'M SORRY...
I SEEM TO HAVE TRIPPED. ♡
GRIN
WILL YOU...
...FORGIVE ME?

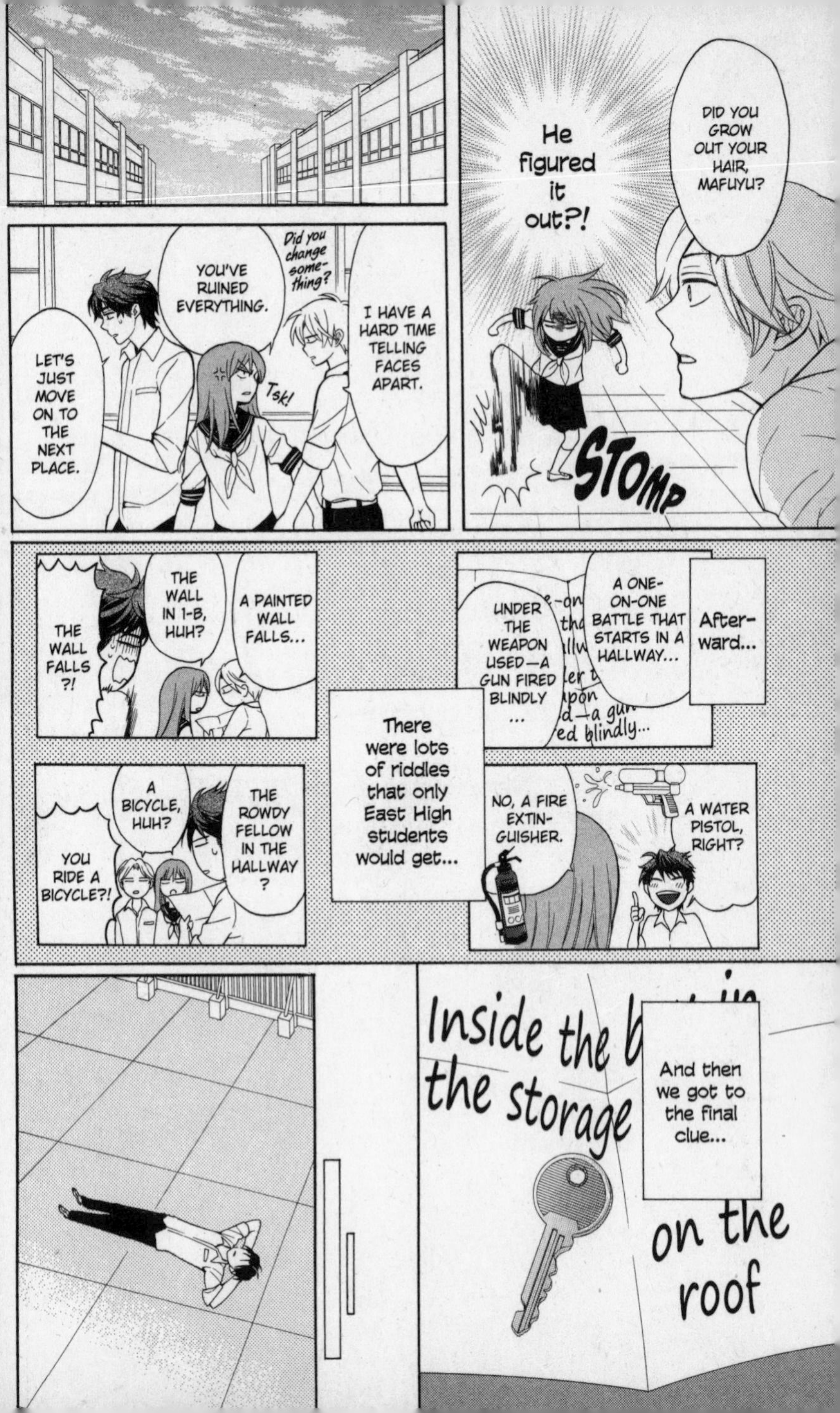
DID YOU GROW OUT YOUR HAIR, MAFUYU?
He figured it out?!
STOMP
I HAVE A HARD TIME TELLING FACES APART.
Did you change something?
YOU'VE RUINED EVERYTHING.
Tsk!
LET'S JUST MOVE ON TO THE NEXT PLACE.
After-ward...
A ONE-ON-ONE BATTLE THAT STARTS IN A HALLWAY...
UNDER THE WEAPON USED—A GUN FIRED BLINDLY...
A WATER PISTOL, RIGHT?
NO, A FIRE EXTINGUISHER.
There were lots of riddles that only East High students would get...
A PAINTED WALL FALLS...
THE WALL IN 1-B, HUH?
THE WALL FALLS?!
THE ROWDY FELLOW IN THE HALLWAY?
A BICYCLE, HUH?
YOU RIDE A BICYCLE?!
Inside the b
the storage
on the roof
And then we got to the final clue...

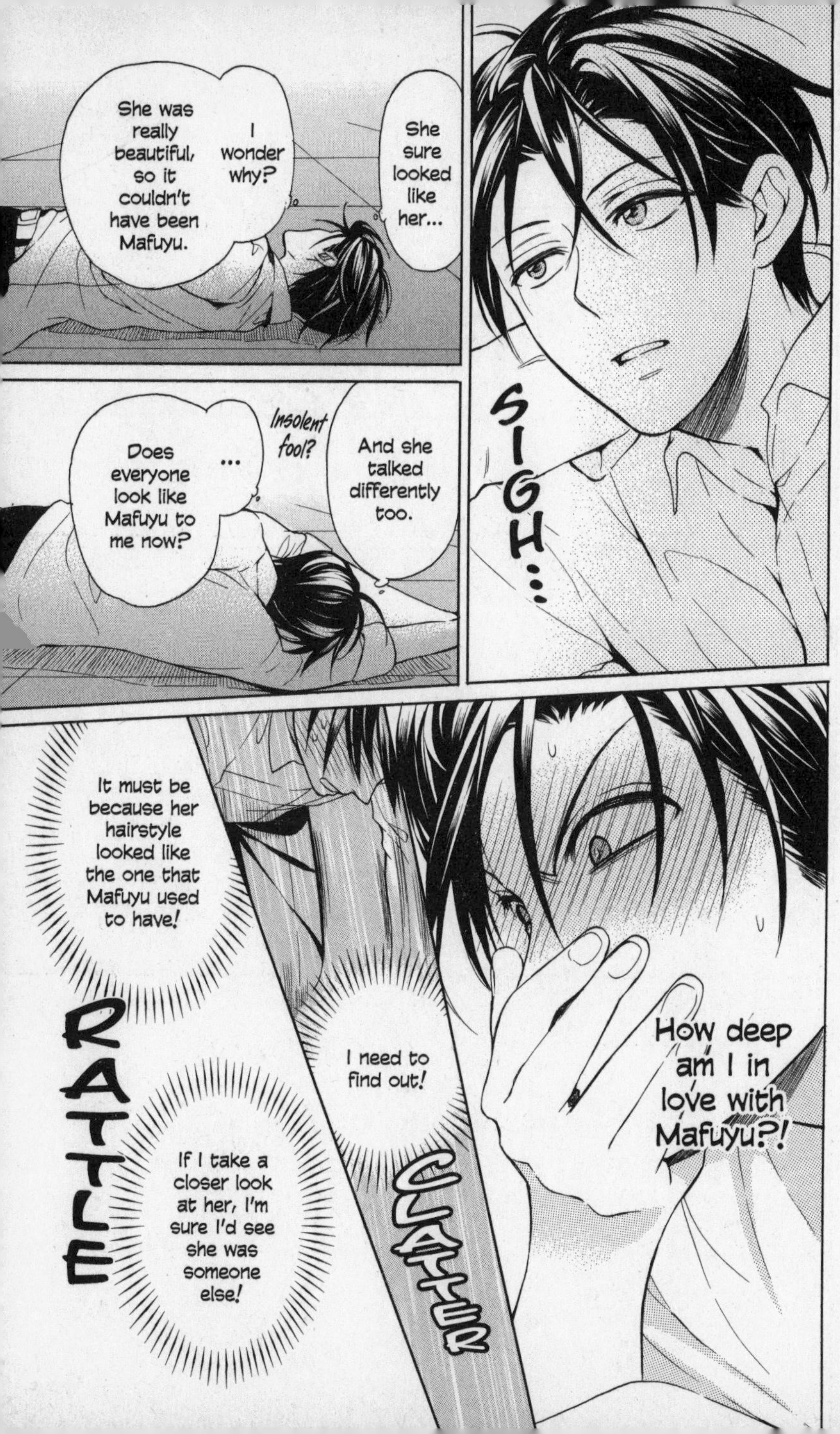
SIGH...
She sure looked like her...
I wonder why?
She was really beautiful, so it couldn't have been Mafuyu.
And she talked differently too.
Insolent fool?
...
Does everyone look like Mafuyu to me now?
How deep am I in love with Mafuyu?!
CLATTER
I need to find out!
It must be because her hairstyle looked like the one that Mafuyu used to have!
If I take a closer look at her, I'm sure I'd see she was someone else!
RATTLE

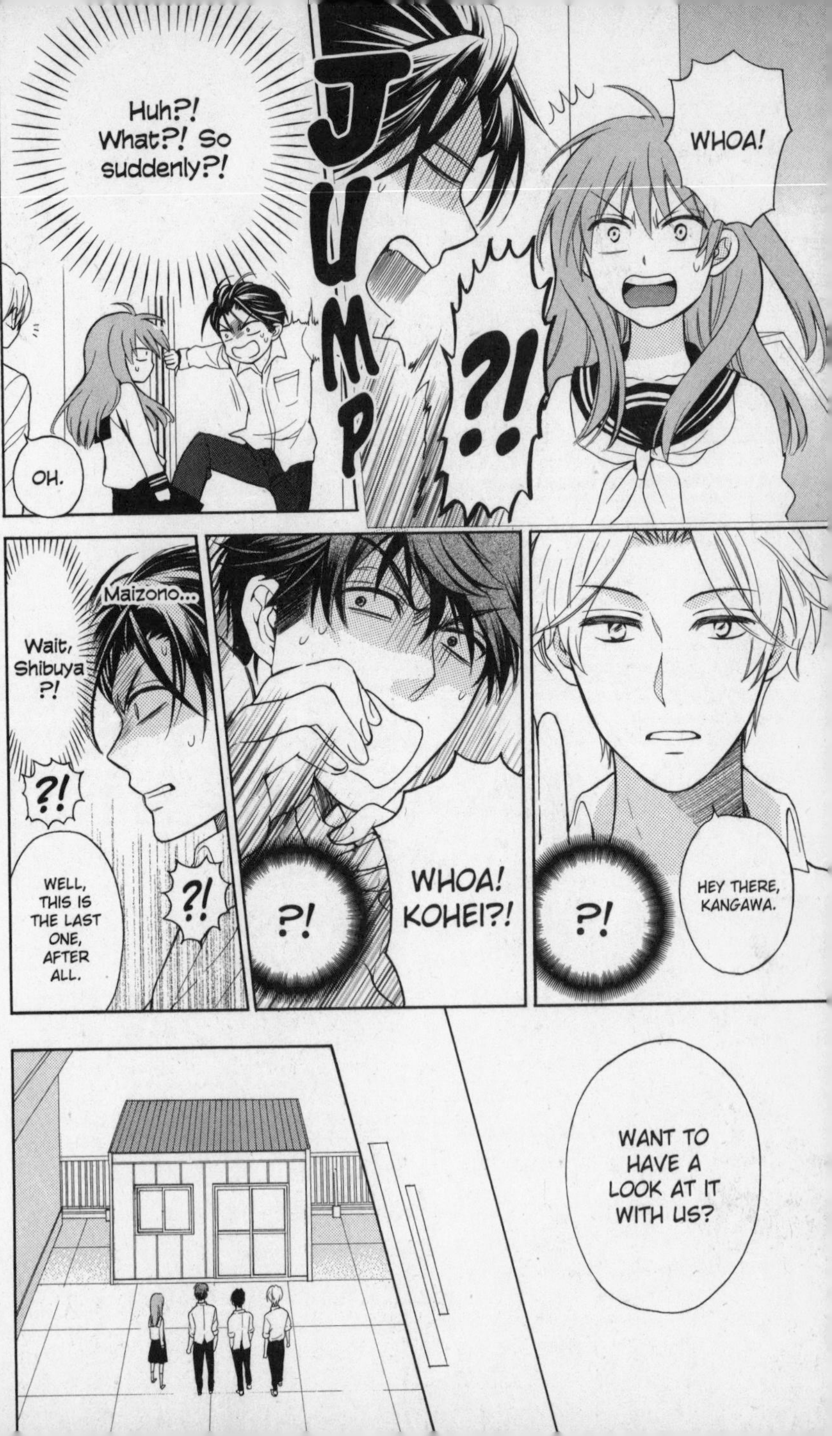
WHOA!
JUMP
?!!
Huh?! What?! So suddenly?!
OH.
HEY THERE, KANGAWA.
?!
WHOA! KOHEI?!
?!
Maizono...
Wait, Shibuya?!
?!
WELL, THIS IS THE LAST ONE, AFTER ALL.
?!
WANT TO HAVE A LOOK AT IT WITH US?

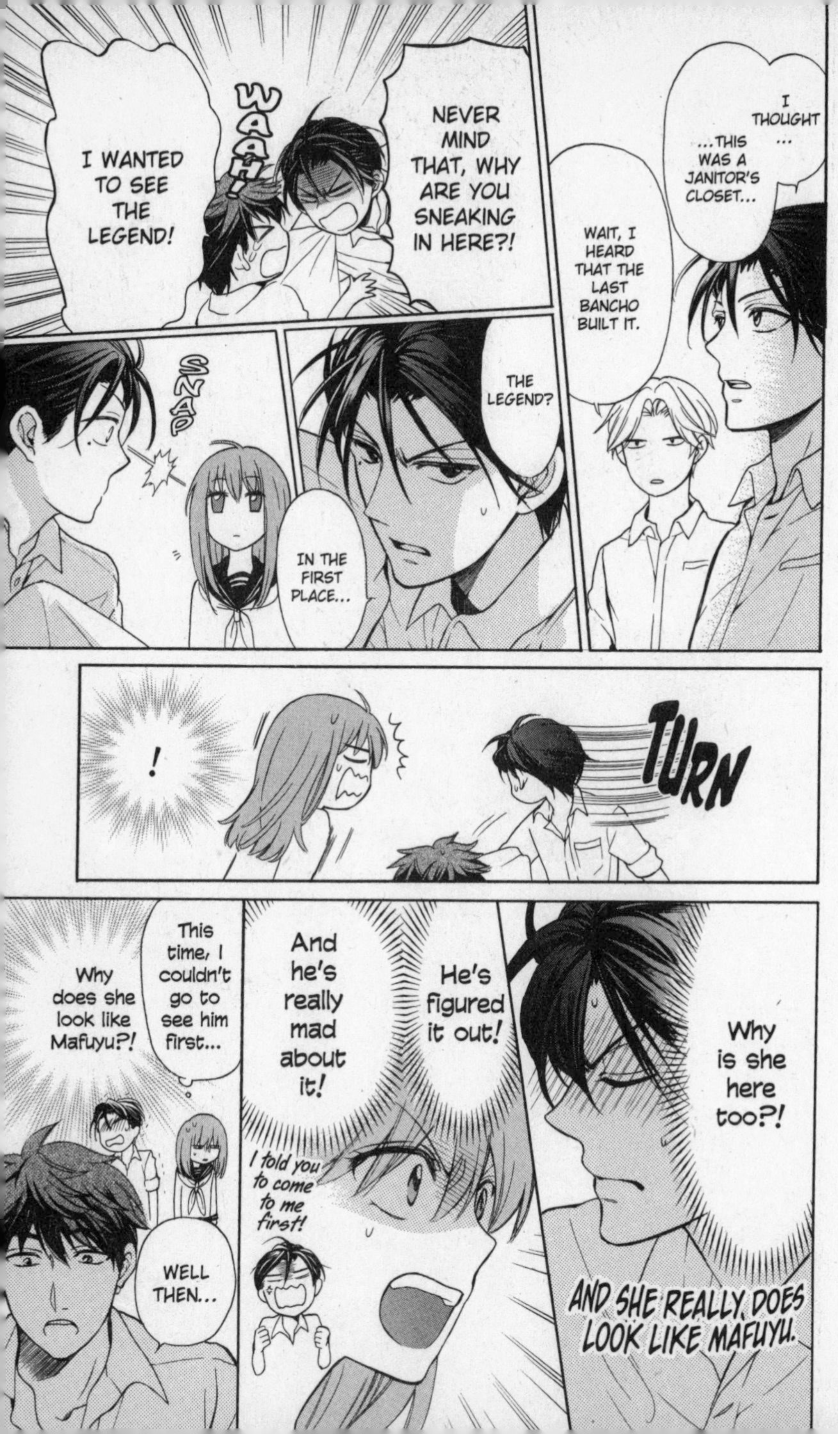
I THOUGHT...
...THIS WAS A JANITOR'S CLOSET...
WAIT, I HEARD THAT THE LAST BANCHO BUILT IT.
NEVER MIND THAT, WHY ARE YOU SNEAKING IN HERE?!
WAAH!
I WANTED TO SEE THE LEGEND!
THE LEGEND?
IN THE FIRST PLACE...
SNAP
TURN
!
Why is she here too?!
AND SHE REALLY DOES LOOK LIKE MAFUYU.
He's figured it out!
And he's really mad about it!
I told you to come to me first!
This time, I couldn't go to see him first...
Why does she look like Mafuyu?!
WELL THEN...

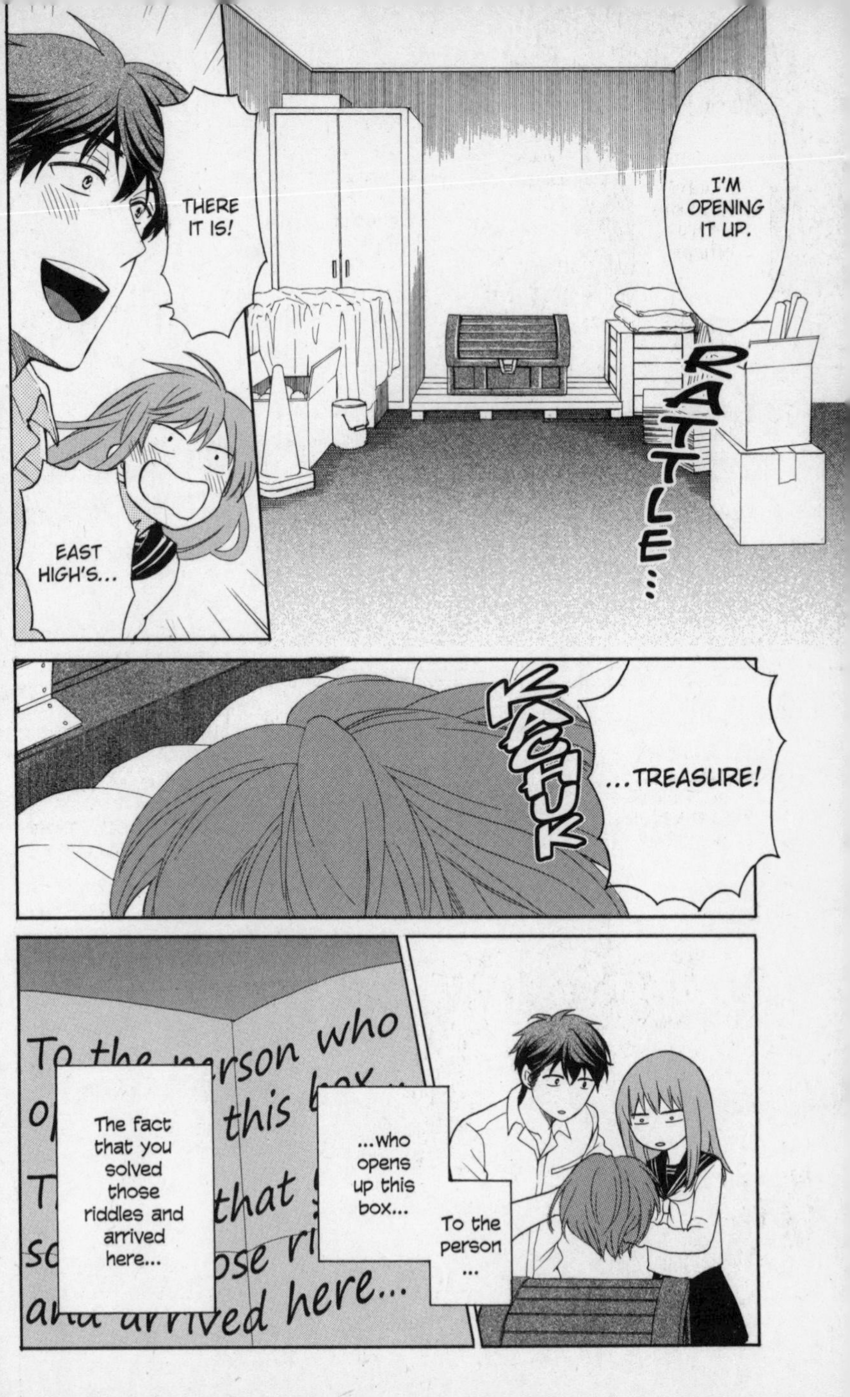
I'M OPENING IT UP.
RATTLE...
THERE IT IS!
EAST HIGH'S...
KACHUK
...TREASURE!
To the person ...
...who opens up this box...
The fact that you solved those riddles and arrived here...
To the person who
and arrived here...

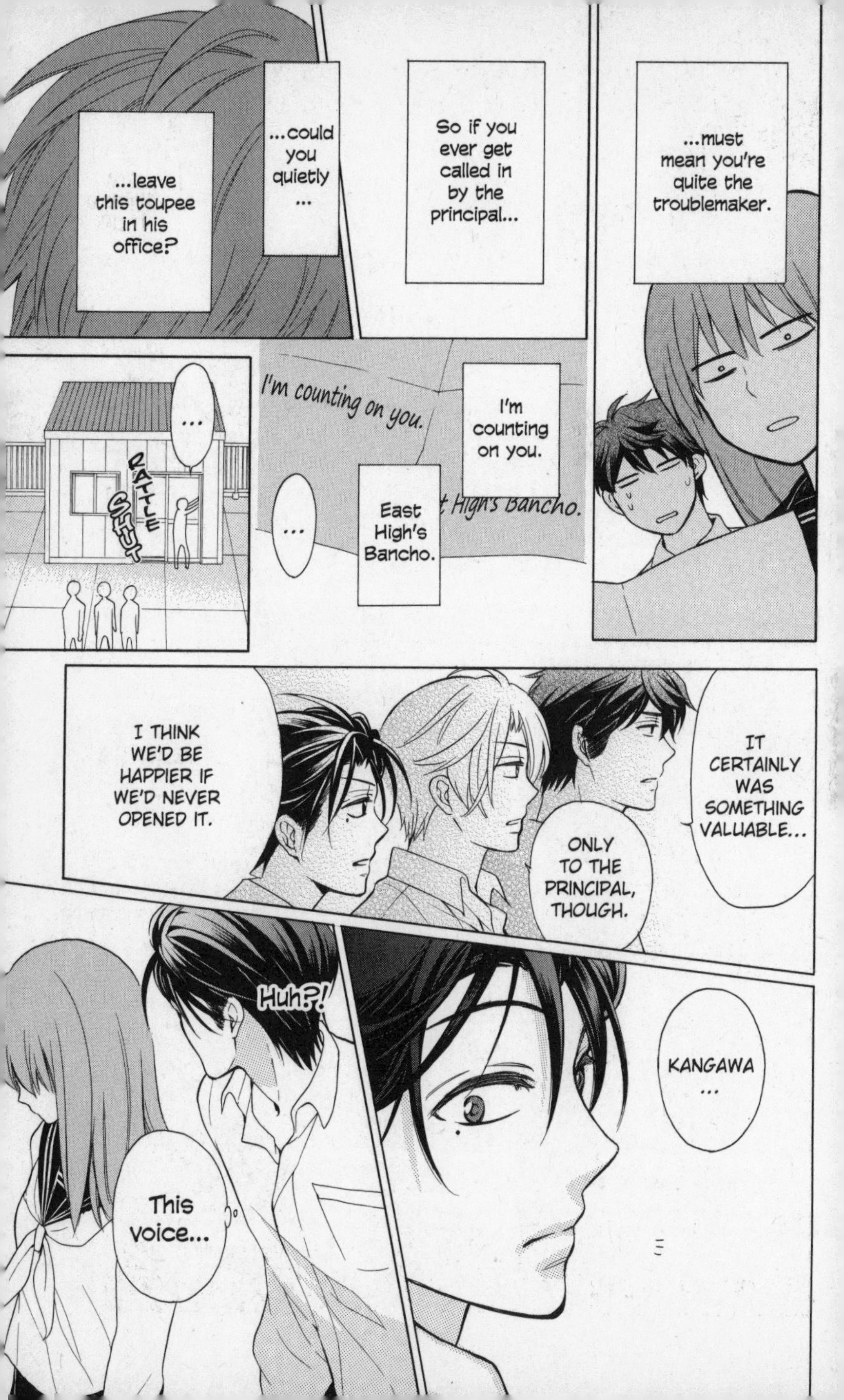
...must mean you're quite the troublemaker.
So if you ever get called in by the principal...
...could you quietly ...
...leave this toupee in his office?
I'm counting on you.
I'm counting on you.
East High's Bancho.
...
...
RATTLE
SHUT
IT CERTAINLY WAS SOMETHING VALUABLE...
ONLY TO THE PRINCIPAL, THOUGH.
I THINK WE'D BE HAPPIER IF WE'D NEVER OPENED IT.
KANGAWA ...
Huh?!
This voice...

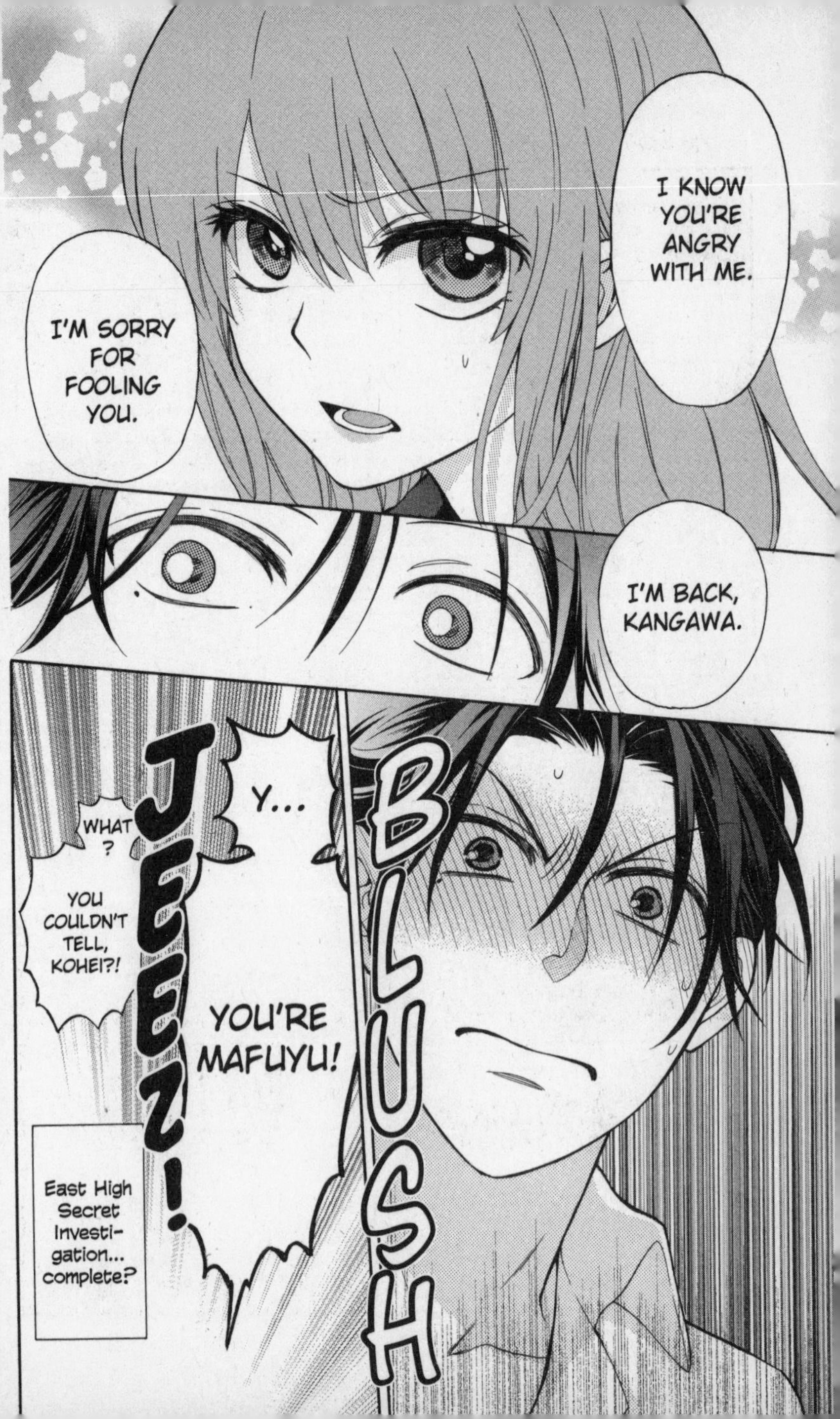
I KNOW YOU'RE ANGRY WITH ME.
I'M SORRY FOR FOOLING YOU.
I'M BACK, KANGAWA.
BLUSH
Y...
YOU'RE MAFUYU!
JEEZ!
WHAT? YOU COULDN'T TELL, KOHEI?!
East High Secret Investigation... complete?

THIS JOKE CAME UP A LOT

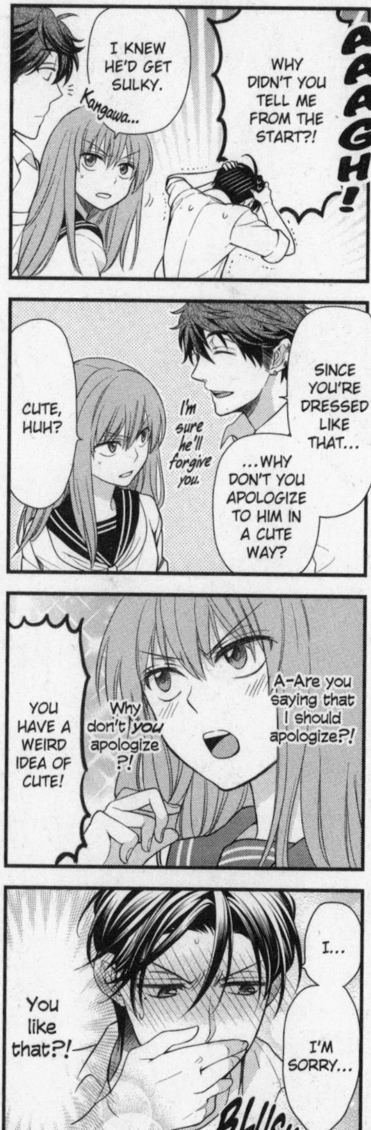
AAAGH!
WHY DIDN'T YOU TELL ME FROM THE START?!
I KNEW HE'D GET SULKY.
Kangawa...
SINCE YOU'RE DRESSED LIKE THAT...
...WHY DON'T YOU APOLOGIZE TO HIM IN A CUTE WAY?
I'm sure he'll forgive you.
CUTE, HUH?
A-Are you saying that I should apologize?!
Why don't you apologize?!
YOU HAVE A WEIRD IDEA OF CUTE!
I...
I'M SORRY...
BLUSH
You like that?!

I'M SORRY ♡ REQUEST

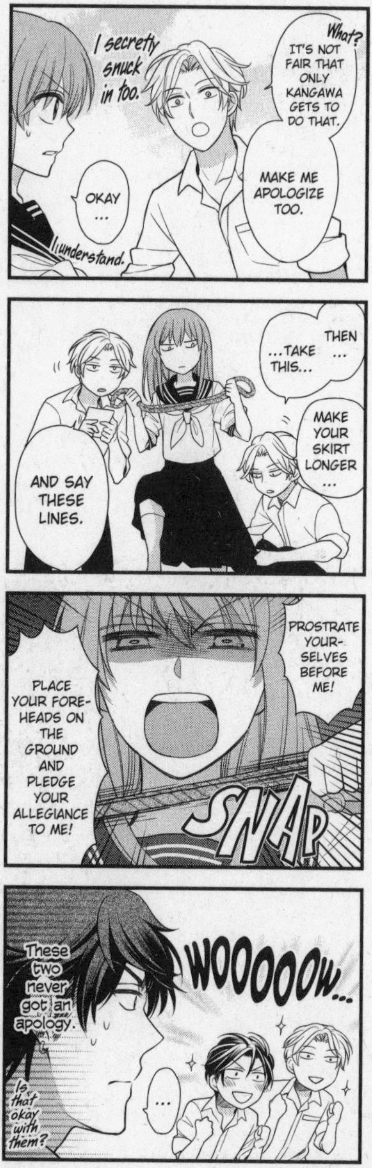
What?
IT'S NOT FAIR THAT ONLY KANGAWA GETS TO DO THAT.
MAKE ME APOLOGIZE TOO.
I secretly snuck in too.
OKAY...
I understand.
THEN...
...TAKE THIS...
MAKE YOUR SKIRT LONGER...
AND SAY THESE LINES.
PROSTRATE YOURSELVES BEFORE ME!
PLACE YOUR FOREHEADS ON THE GROUND AND PLEDGE YOUR ALLEGIANCE TO ME!
SNAP
WOOOOOW...
These two never got an apology.
...
Is that okay with them?

CONFIDENCE

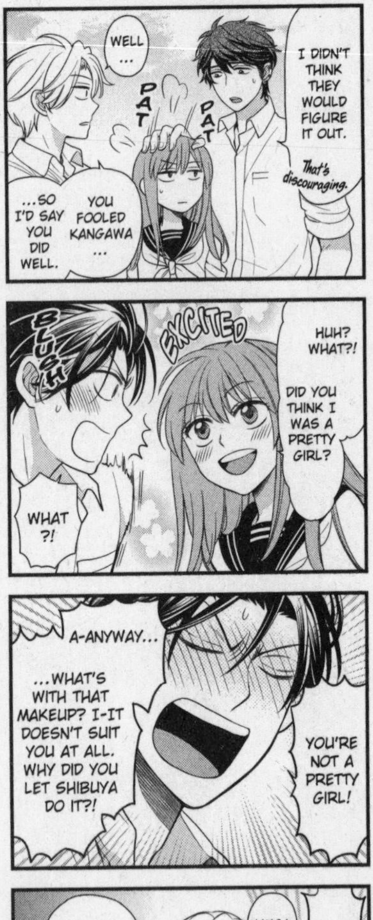
I DIDN'T THINK THEY WOULD FIGURE IT OUT.
That's discouraging.
WELL ...
PAT
PAT
YOU FOOLED KANGAWA ...
...SO I'D SAY YOU DID WELL.
HUH? WHAT?!
DID YOU THINK I WAS A PRETTY GIRL?
EXCITED
BLUSH
WHAT ?!
YOU'RE NOT A PRETTY GIRL!
A-ANYWAY...
...WHAT'S WITH THAT MAKEUP? I-IT DOESN'T SUIT YOU AT ALL. WHY DID YOU LET SHIBUYA DO IT?!
ALSO...
KANGA-WA...
STOP RIGHT THERE.
They look depressed.
KANGA-WA...
GLOOMY

BIG BROTHER IS CONCERNED

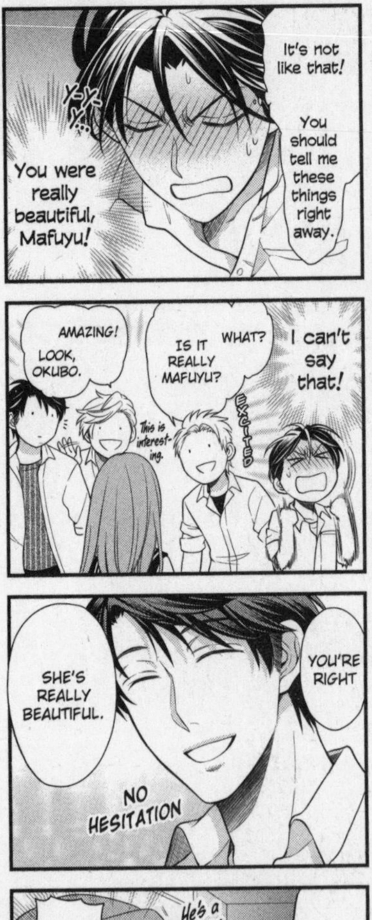
It's not like that!
You should tell me these things right away.
Y-Y-Y...
You were really beautiful, Mafuyu!
I can't say that!
WHAT?
IS IT REALLY MAFUYU?
EXCITED
AMAZING!
LOOK, OKUBO.
This is interesting.
YOU'RE RIGHT
SHE'S REALLY BEAUTIFUL.
NO HESITATION
I FORBID YOU TO SEE OKUBO ANYMORE.
He's a scary man.
HUH?!
WHAT ARE YOU TALKING ABOUT, KOHEI?!
I'm not doing that!

Chapter 80

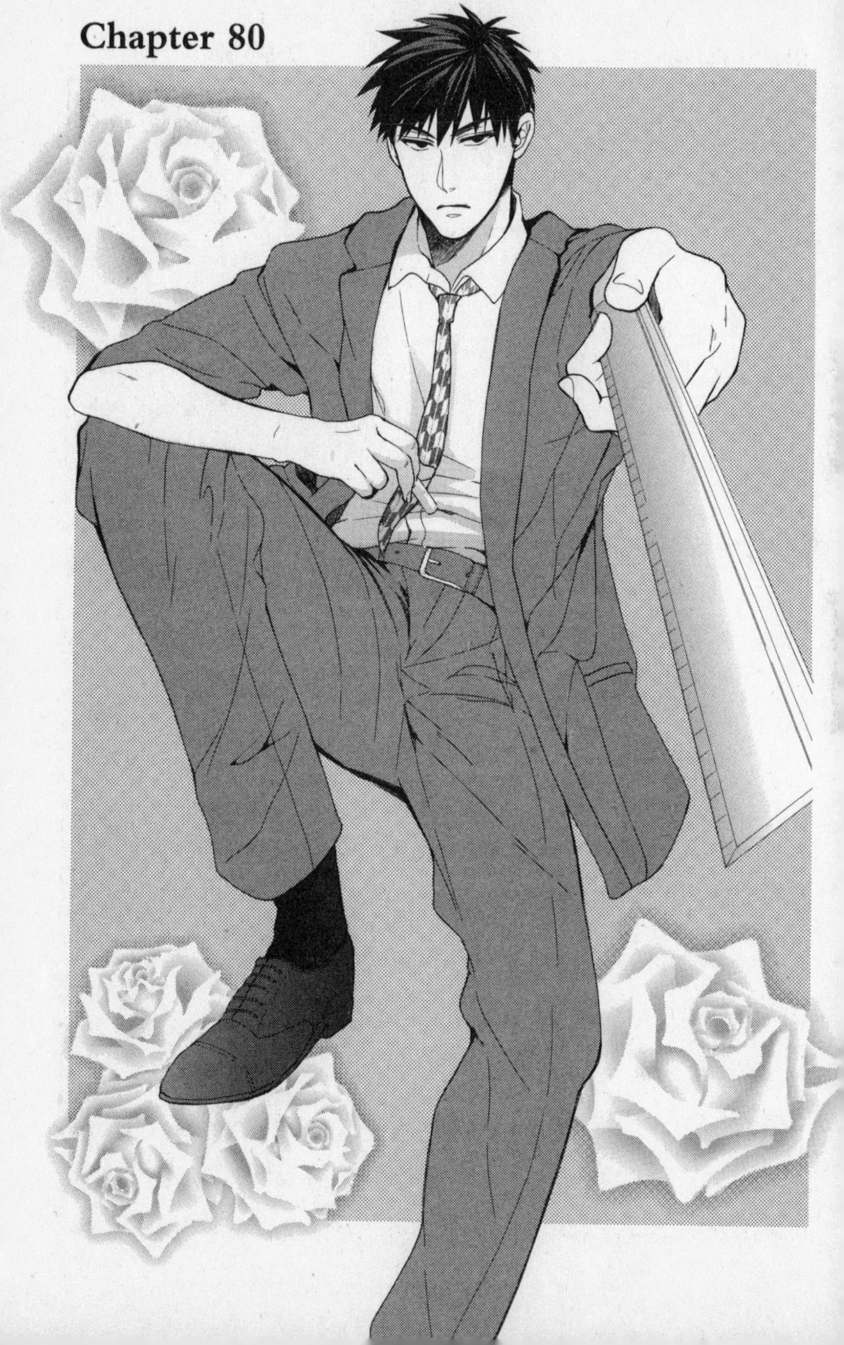

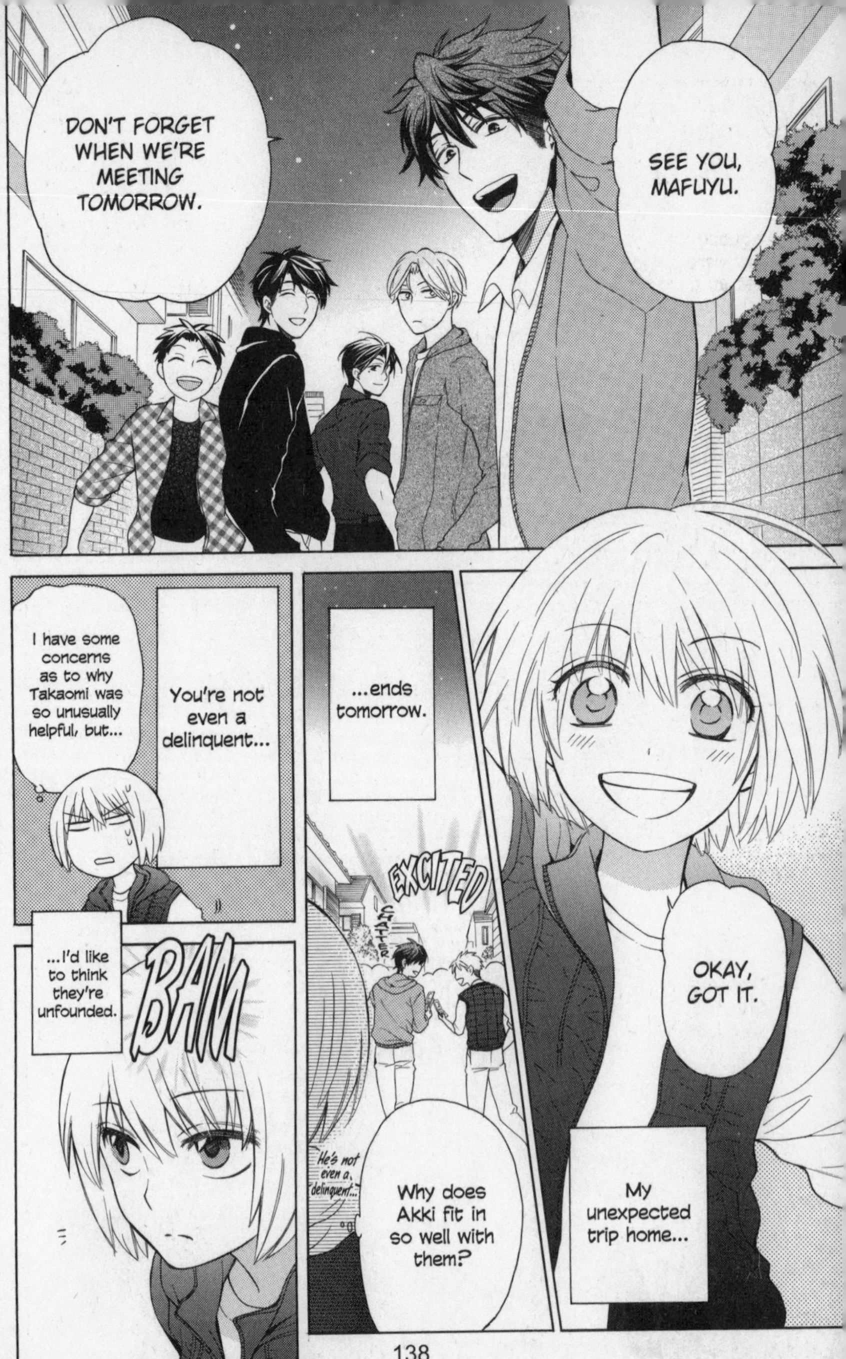
SEE YOU, MAFUYU.
DON'T FORGET WHEN WE'RE MEETING TOMORROW.
OKAY, GOT IT.
My unexpected trip home...
...ends tomorrow.
EXCITED
CHATTER
Why does Akki fit in so well with them?
He's not even a delinquent...
You're not even a delinquent...
I have some concerns as to why Takaomi was so unusually helpful, but...
...I'd like to think they're unfounded.
BAM

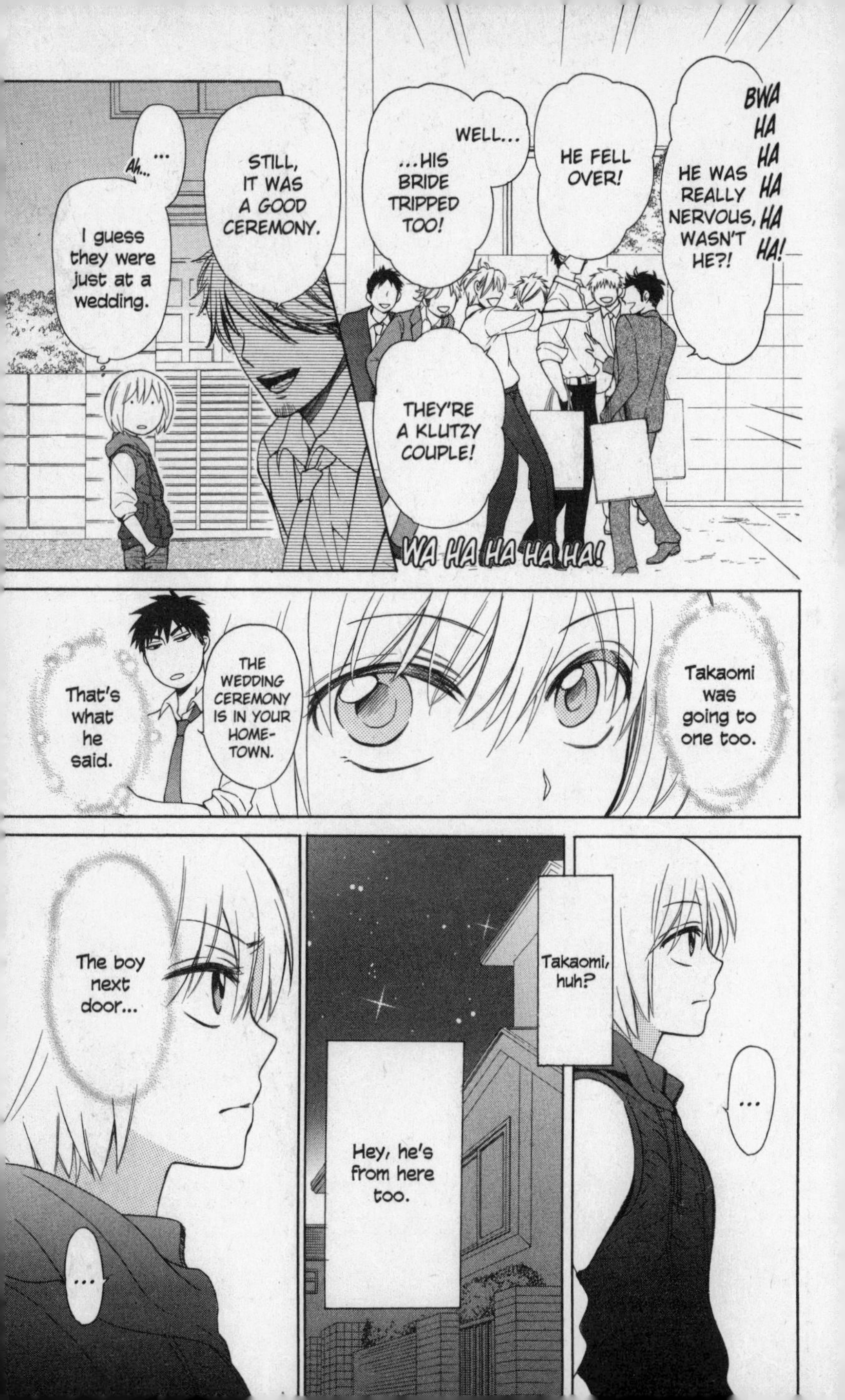
BWA HA HA HA HA HA!
HE WAS REALLY NERVOUS, WASN'T HE?!
HE FELL OVER!
WELL...
...HIS BRIDE TRIPPED TOO!
THEY'RE A KLUTZY COUPLE!
WA HA HA HA HA!
STILL, IT WAS A GOOD CEREMONY.
...
Ah...
I guess they were just at a wedding.
Takaomi was going to one too.
THE WEDDING CEREMONY IS IN YOUR HOME-TOWN.
That's what he said.
Takaomi, huh?
...
Hey, he's from here too.
The boy next door...
...

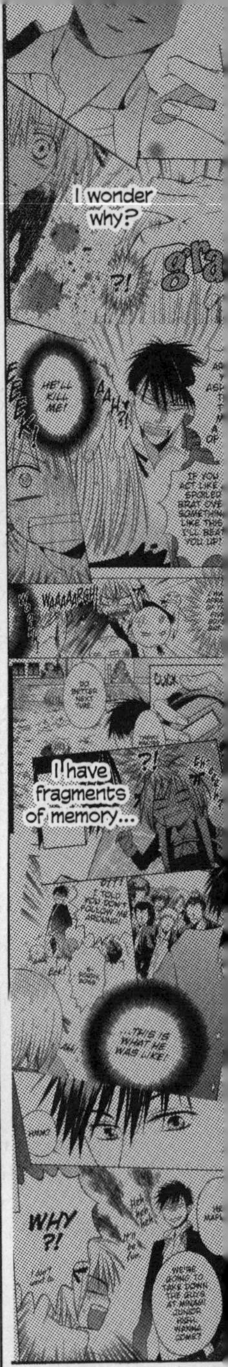
I wonder why?
?!
HE'LL KILL ME!
WAAAAARGH!!
DO BETTER NEXT TIME.
I have fragments of memory...
I TOLD YOU DON'T FOLLOW ME AROUND!
...THIS IS WHAT HE WAS LIKE!
WHY ?!

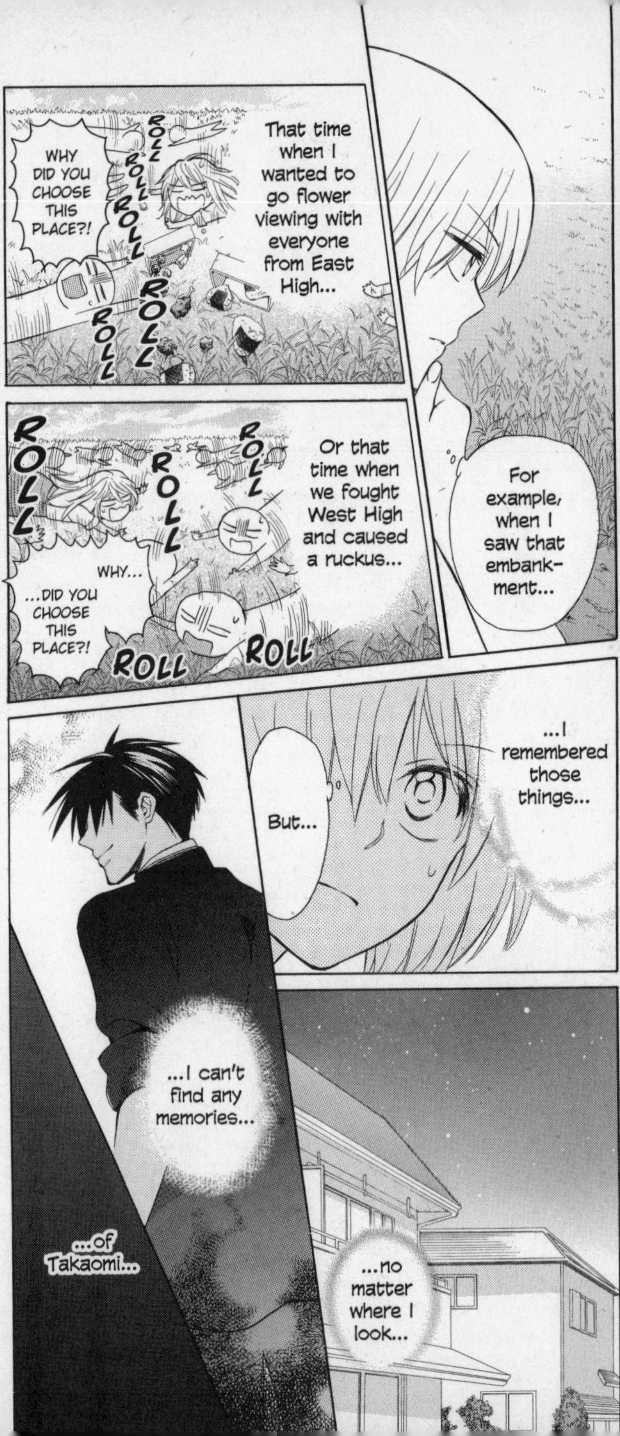
For example, when I saw that embankment...
That time when I wanted to go flower viewing with everyone from East High...
ROLL ROLL ROLL ROLL ROLL
WHY DID YOU CHOOSE THIS PLACE?!
Or that time when we fought West High and caused a ruckus...
ROLL ROLL ROLL ROLL ROLL
WHY...
...DID YOU CHOOSE THIS PLACE?!
...I remembered those things...
But...
...no matter where I look...
...I can't find any memories...
...of Takaomi...

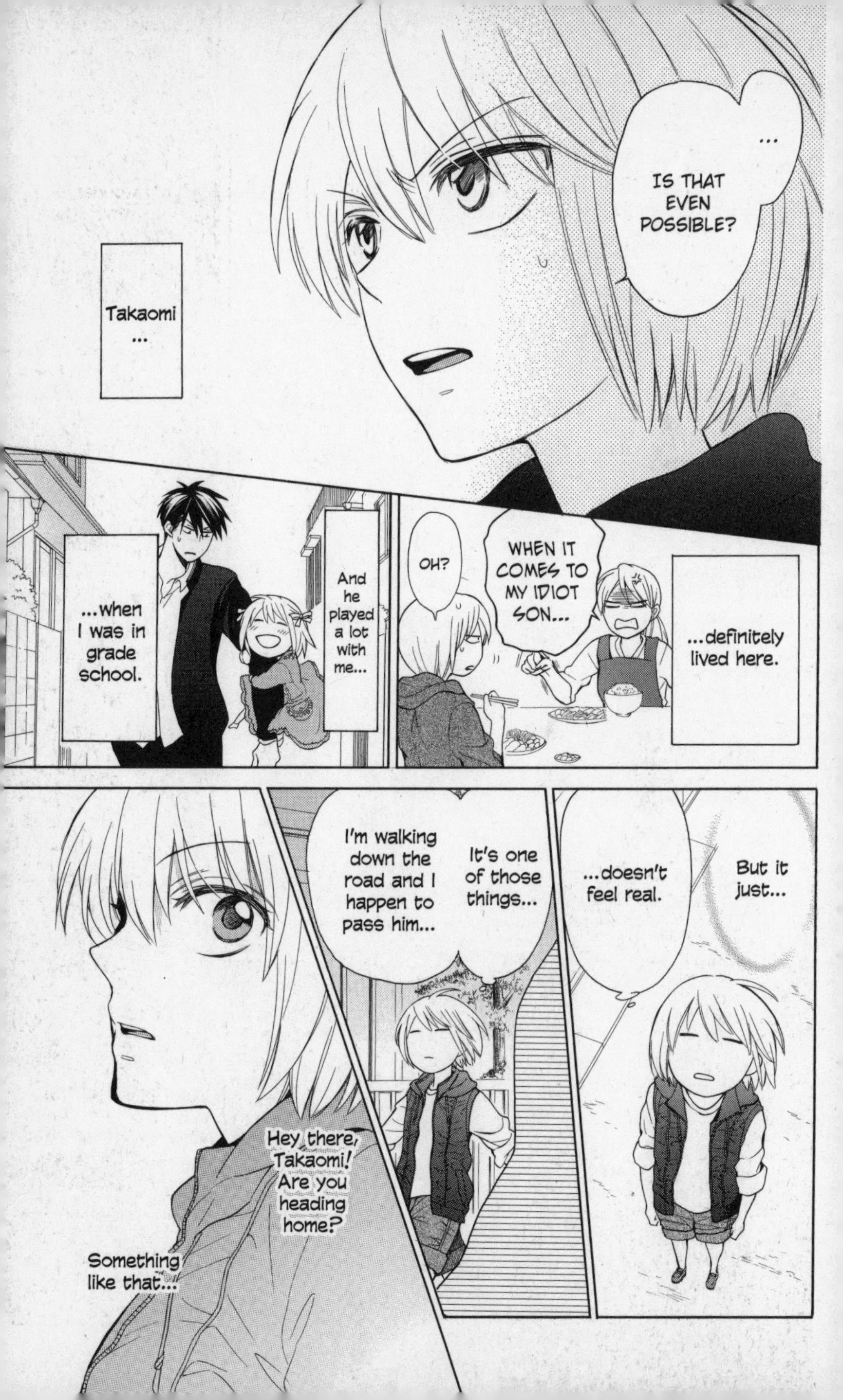
...
IS THAT EVEN POSSIBLE?
Takaomi ...
...definitely lived here.
WHEN IT COMES TO MY IDIOT SON...
OH?
And he played a lot with me...
...when I was in grade school.
But it just...
...doesn't feel real.
It's one of those things...
I'm walking down the road and I happen to pass him...
Hey there, Takaomi! Are you heading home?
Something like that...

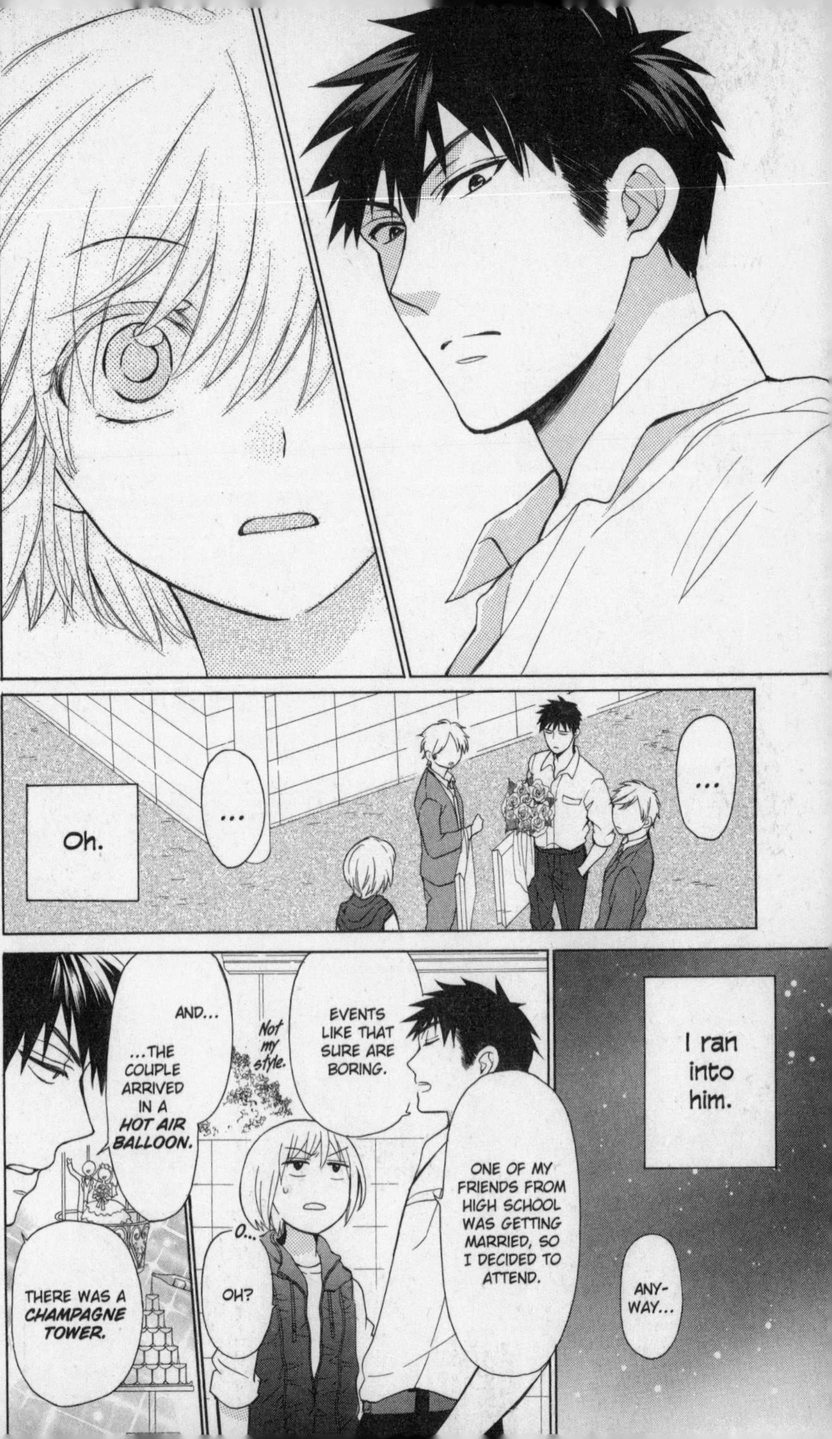
...
...
Oh.
I ran into him.
ANY-WAY...
ONE OF MY FRIENDS FROM HIGH SCHOOL WAS GETTING MARRIED, SO I DECIDED TO ATTEND.
O... OH?
AND... ...THE COUPLE ARRIVED IN A HOT AIR BALLOON.
THERE WAS A CHAMPAGNE TOWER.
EVENTS LIKE THAT SURE ARE BORING.
Not my style.

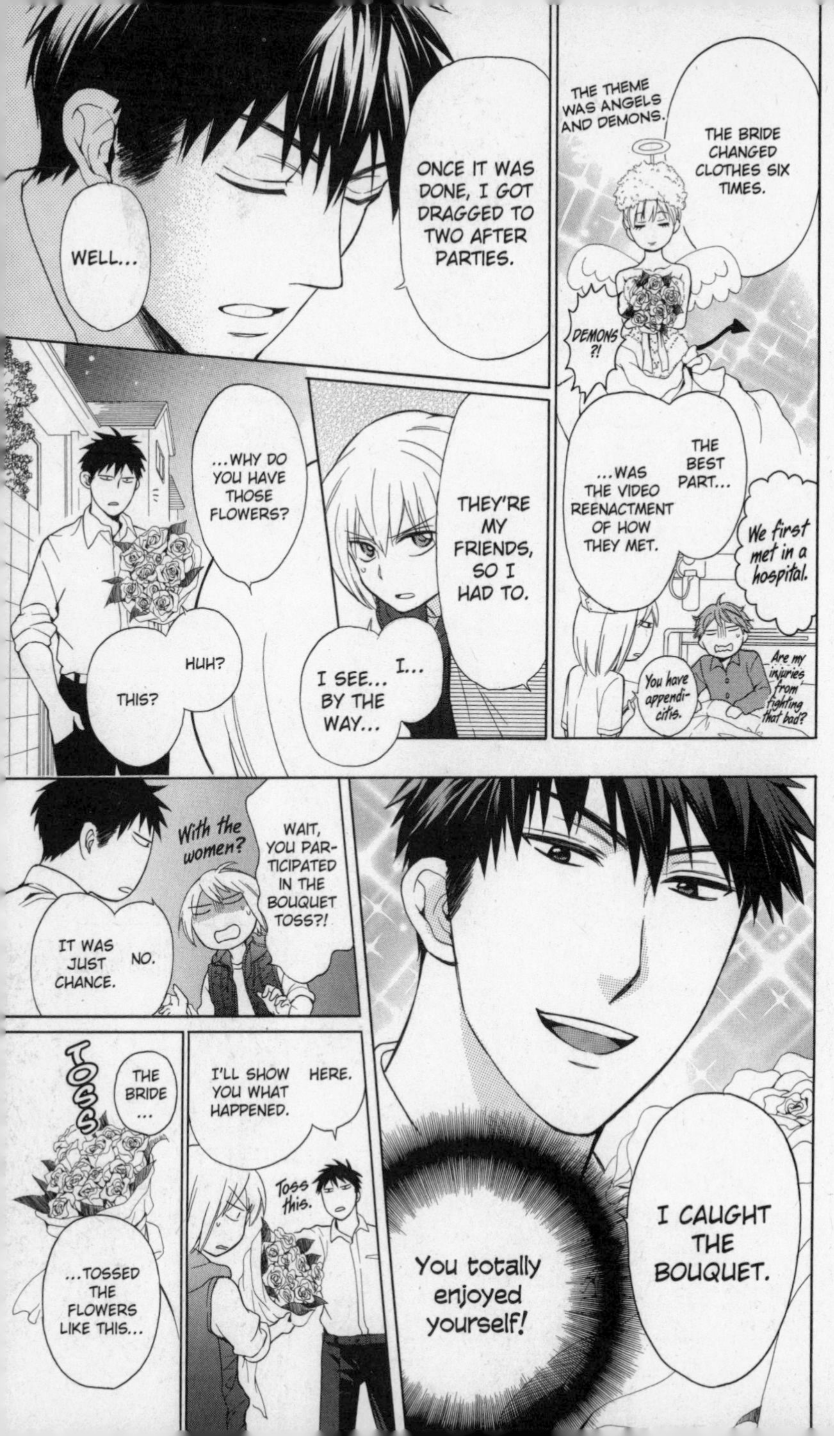
THE BRIDE CHANGED CLOTHES SIX TIMES.
THE THEME WAS ANGELS AND DEMONS.
DEMONS ?!
WELL...
ONCE IT WAS DONE, I GOT DRAGGED TO TWO AFTER PARTIES.
THE BEST PART...
...WAS THE VIDEO REENACTMENT OF HOW THEY MET.
We first met in a hospital.
Are my injuries from fighting that bad?
You have appendicitis.
THEY'RE MY FRIENDS, SO I HAD TO.
I...
I SEE... BY THE WAY...
...WHY DO YOU HAVE THOSE FLOWERS?
HUH?
THIS?
I CAUGHT THE BOUQUET.
You totally enjoyed yourself!
WAIT, YOU PARTICIPATED IN THE BOUQUET TOSS?!
With the women?
NO.
IT WAS JUST CHANCE.
HERE.
I'LL SHOW YOU WHAT HAPPENED.
Toss this.
THE BRIDE...
TOSS
...TOSSED THE FLOWERS LIKE THIS...

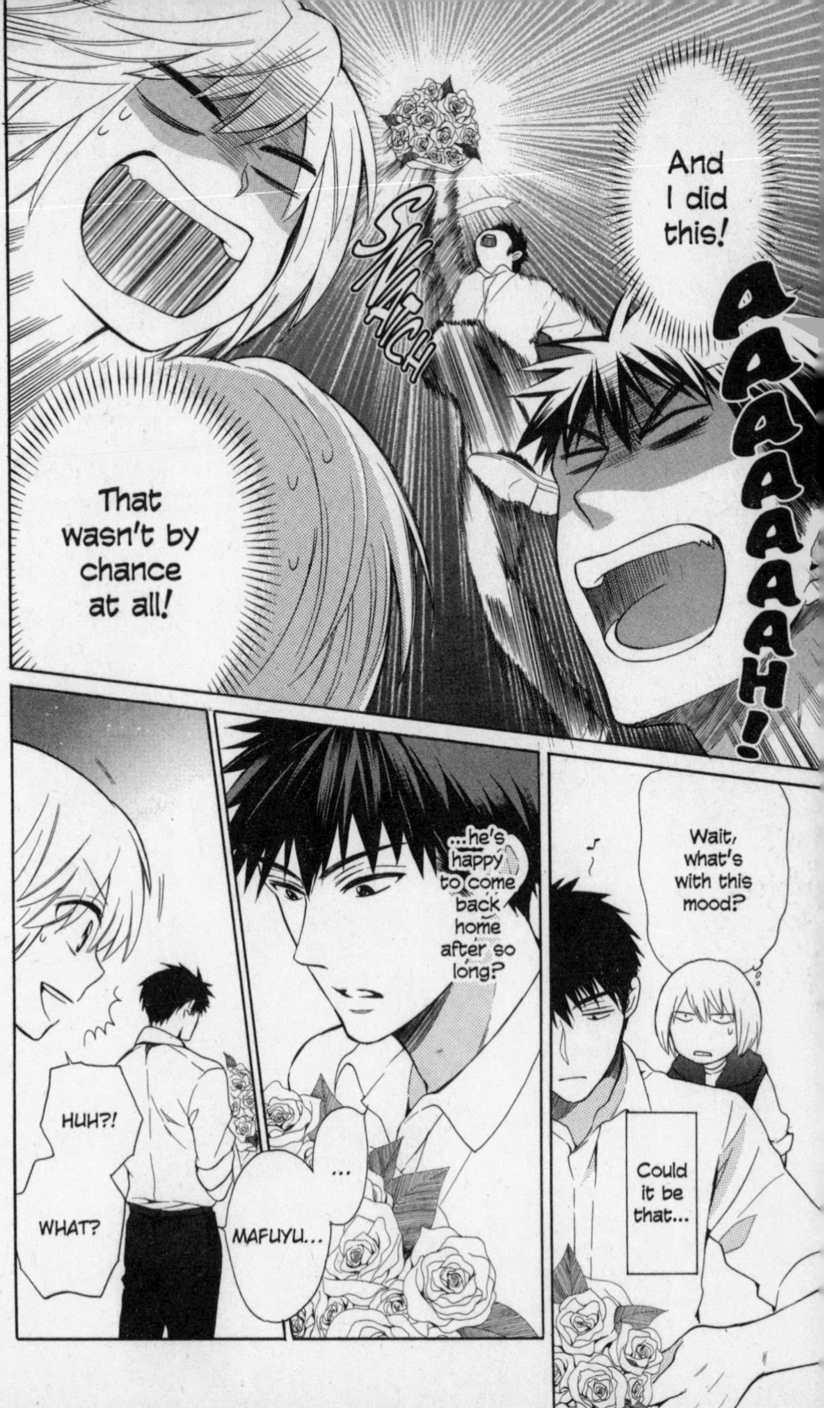
And I did this!
AAAAAAAH!
SNATCH
That wasn't by chance at all!
Wait, what's with this mood?
Could it be that...
...he's happy to come back home after so long?
...
MAFUYU...
HUH?!
WHAT?

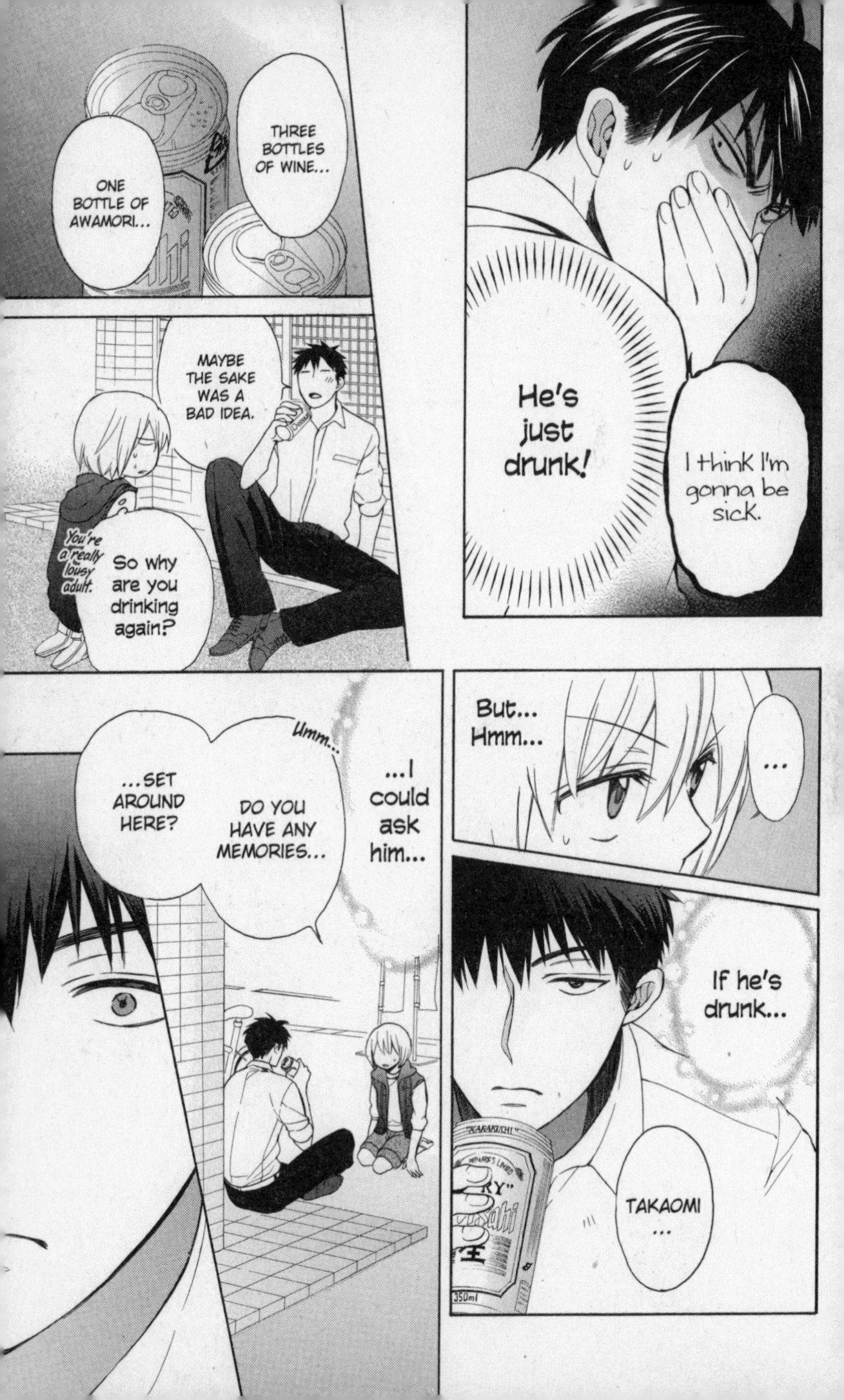
I think I'm gonna be sick.
He's just drunk!
THREE BOTTLES OF WINE...
ONE BOTTLE OF AWAMORI...
MAYBE THE SAKE WAS A BAD IDEA.
So why are you drinking again?
You're a really lousy adult.
...
But... Hmm...
If he's drunk...
TAKAOMI ...
...I could ask him...
Umm...
DO YOU HAVE ANY MEMORIES...
...SET AROUND HERE?

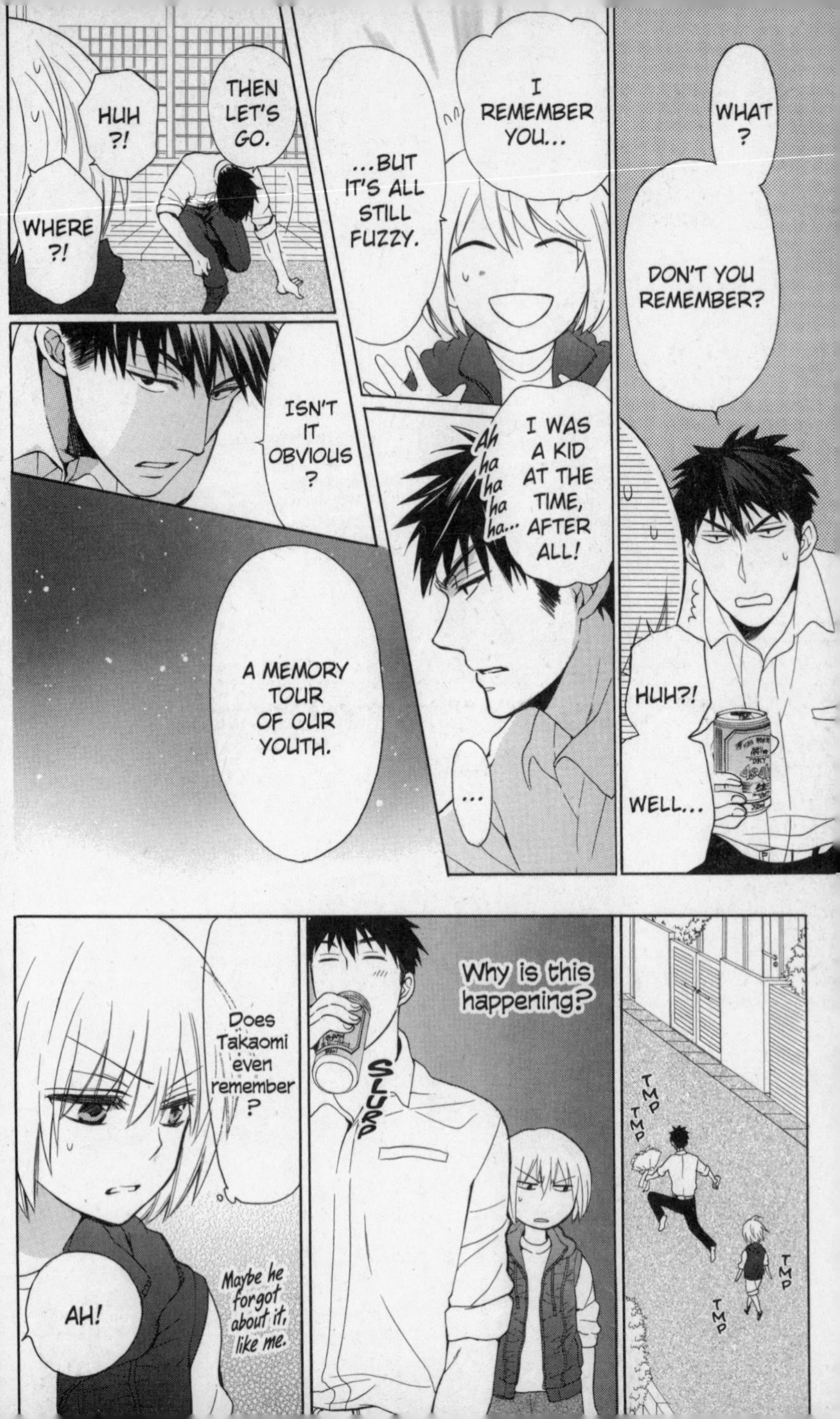
WHAT?
DON'T YOU REMEMBER?
HUH?!
WELL...
I REMEMBER YOU...
...BUT IT'S ALL STILL FUZZY.
I WAS A KID AT THE TIME, AFTER ALL!
Ah ha ha ha ha...
...
THEN LET'S GO.
HUH?!
WHERE?!
ISN'T IT OBVIOUS?
A MEMORY TOUR OF OUR YOUTH.
TMP TMP
TMP TMP
Why is this happening?
SLURP
Does Takaomi even remember?
Maybe he forgot about it, like me.
AH!

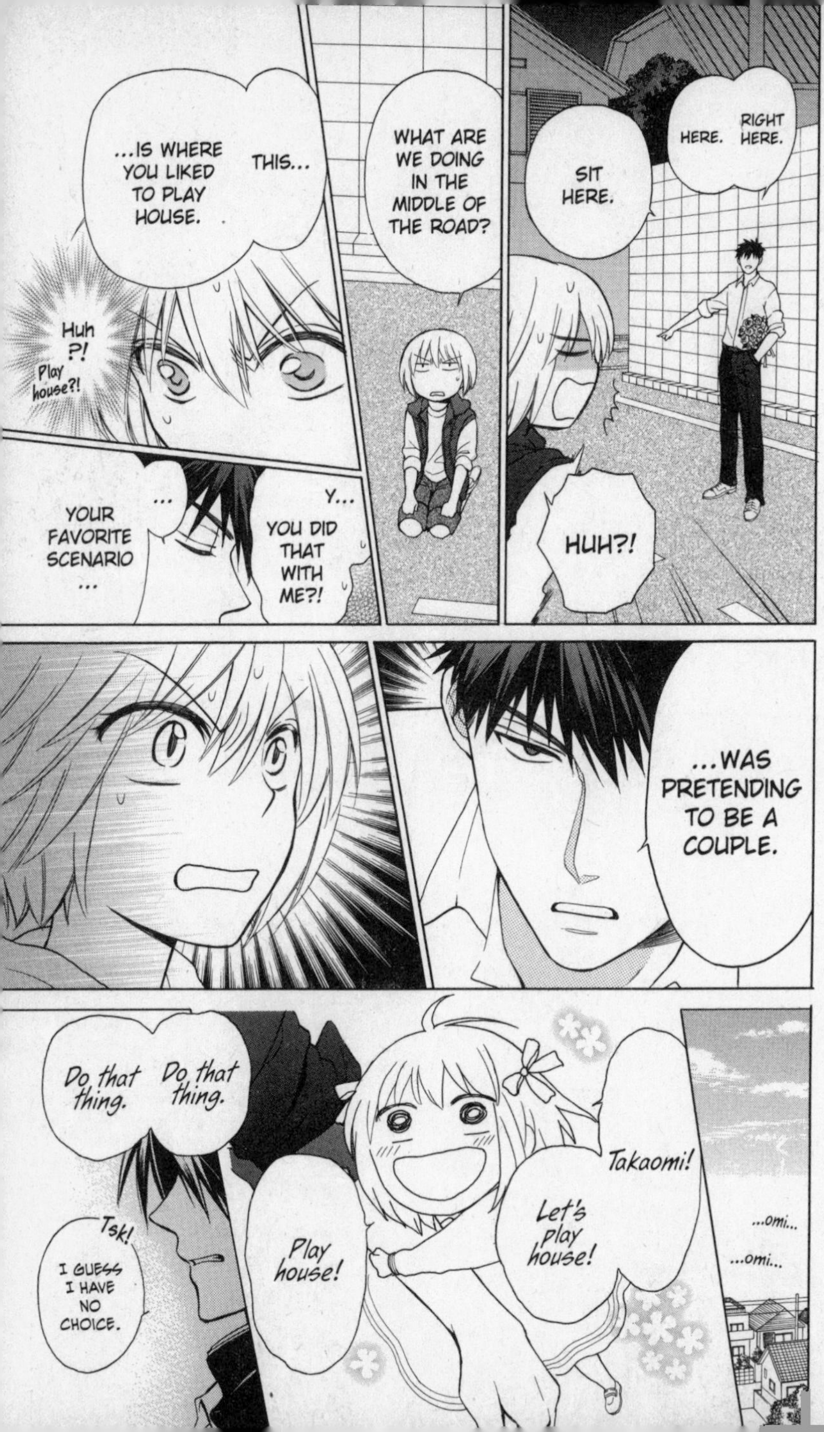
RIGHT HERE.
HERE.
SIT HERE.
HUH?!
WHAT ARE WE DOING IN THE MIDDLE OF THE ROAD?
THIS...
...IS WHERE YOU LIKED TO PLAY HOUSE.
Huh?! Play house?!
Y... YOU DID THAT WITH ME?!
... YOUR FAVORITE SCENARIO ...
...WAS PRETENDING TO BE A COUPLE.
...omi...
...omi...
Takaomi!
Let's play house!
Play house!
Do that thing.
Do that thing.
Tsk!
I GUESS I HAVE NO CHOICE.

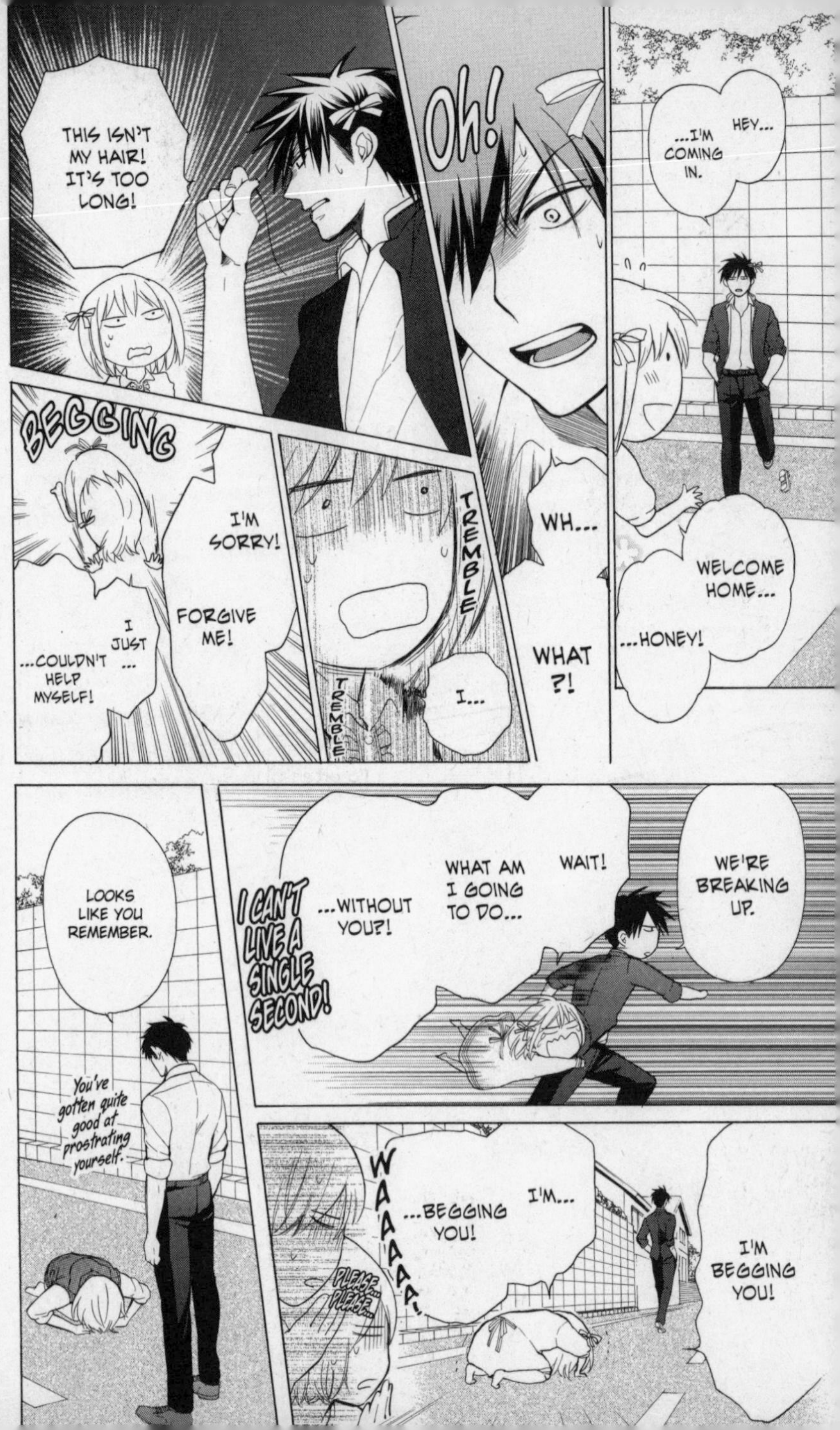
HEY...
...I'M COMING IN.
WELCOME HOME...
...HONEY!
Oh!
WH...
WHAT?!
THIS ISN'T MY HAIR! IT'S TOO LONG!
TREMBLE
TREMBLE
I...
BEGGING
I'M SORRY!
FORGIVE ME!
I JUST...
...COULDN'T HELP MYSELF!
WE'RE BREAKING UP.
WAIT!
WHAT AM I GOING TO DO...
...WITHOUT YOU?!
I CAN'T LIVE A SINGLE SECOND!
I'M BEGGING YOU!
I'M...
...BEGGING YOU!
WAAAAA!
PLEASE... PLEASE...
LOOKS LIKE YOU REMEMBER.
You've gotten quite good at prostrating yourself.

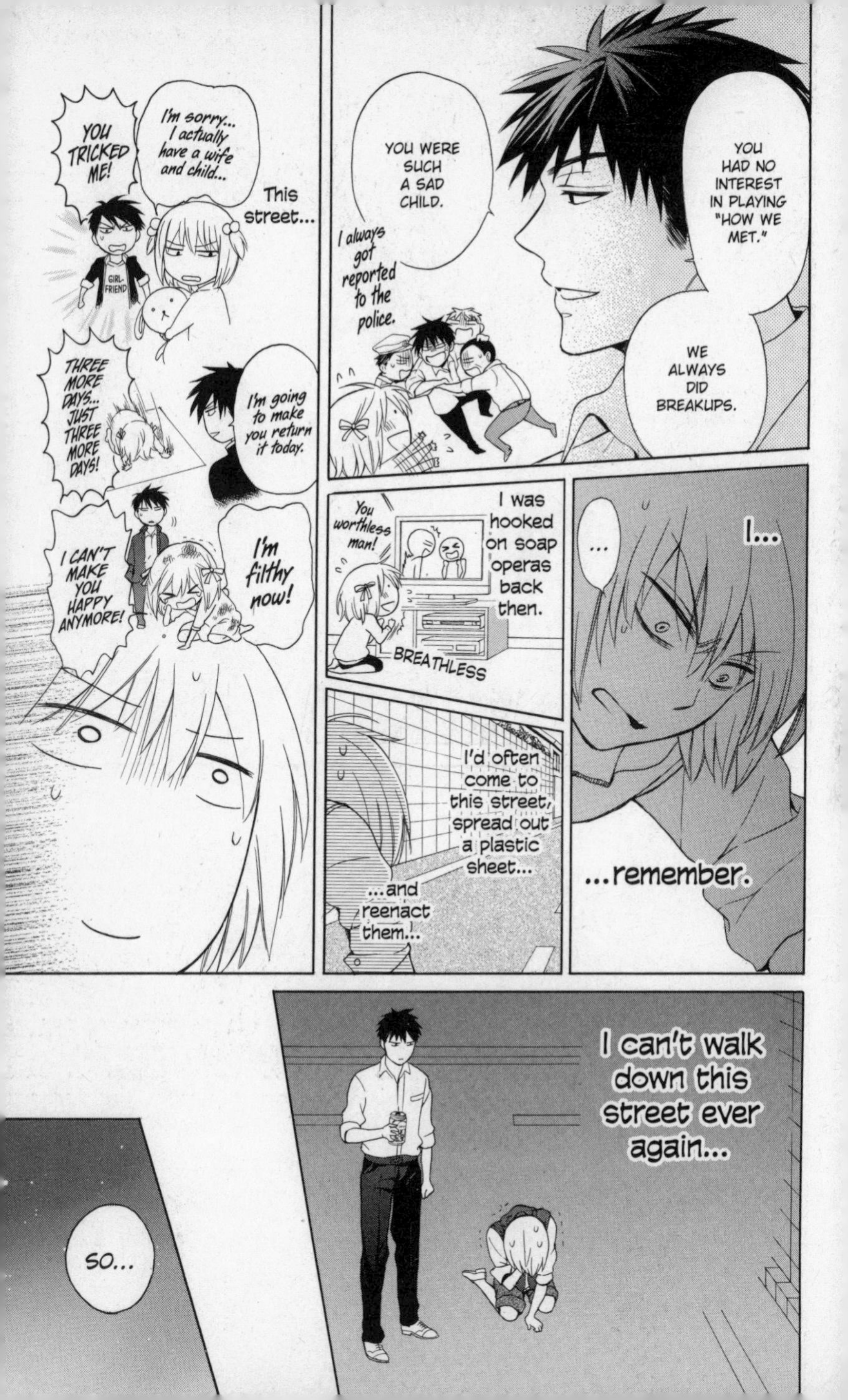

YOU HAD NO INTEREST IN PLAYING "HOW WE MET."
WE ALWAYS DID BREAKUPS.
YOU WERE SUCH A SAD CHILD.
I always got reported to the police.
...
I...
...remember.
I was hooked on soap operas back then.
You worthless man!
BREATHLESS
I'd often come to this street, spread out a plastic sheet...
...and reenact them...
This street...
I'm sorry... I actually have a wife and child...
YOU TRICKED ME!
GIRL-FRIEND
I'm going to make you return it today.
THREE MORE DAYS... JUST THREE MORE DAYS!
I'm filthy now!
I CAN'T MAKE YOU HAPPY ANYMORE!
I can't walk down this street ever again...
SO...

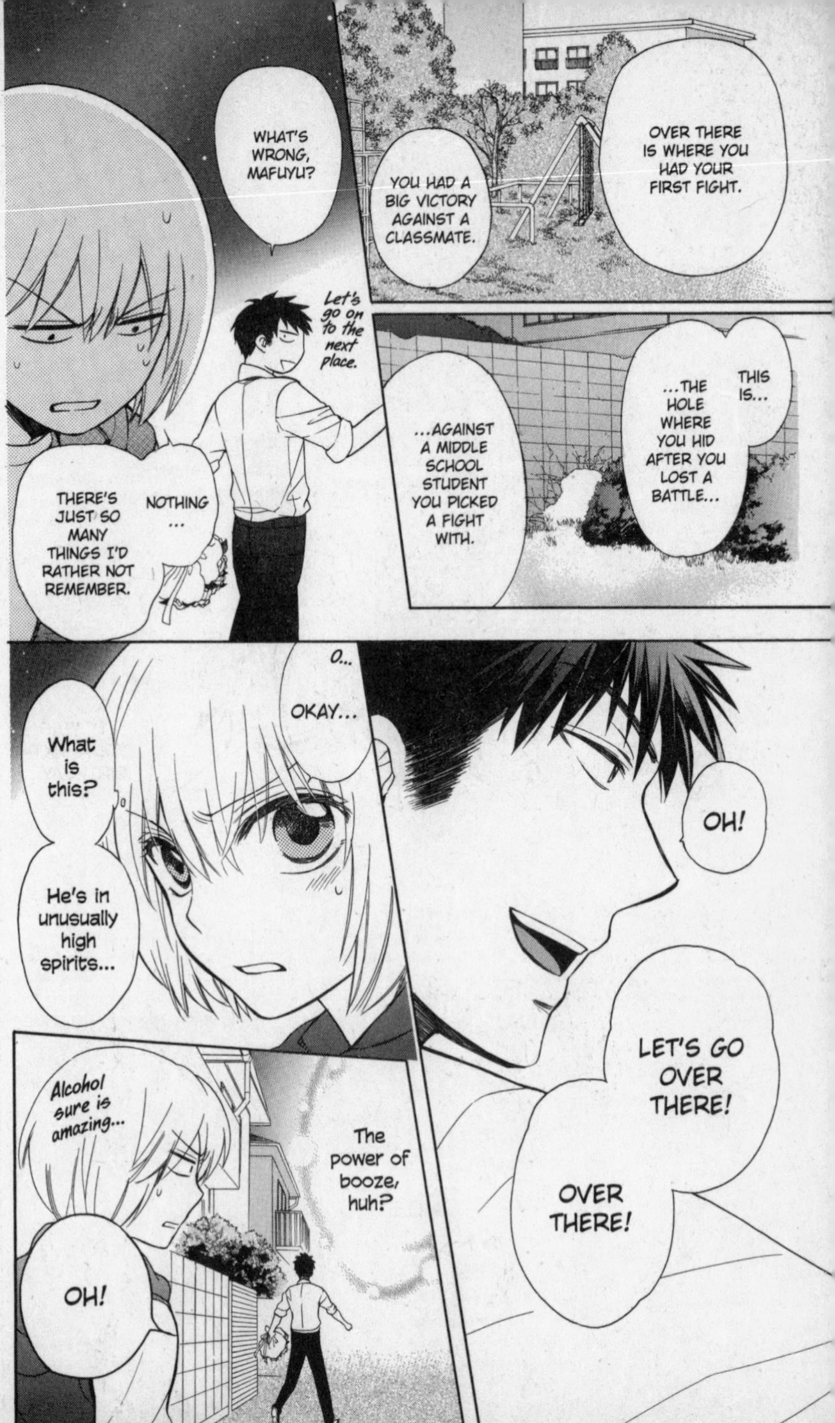

OVER THERE IS WHERE YOU HAD YOUR FIRST FIGHT.
YOU HAD A BIG VICTORY AGAINST A CLASSMATE.
THIS IS...
...THE HOLE WHERE YOU HID AFTER YOU LOST A BATTLE...
...AGAINST A MIDDLE SCHOOL STUDENT YOU PICKED A FIGHT WITH.
WHAT'S WRONG, MAFUYU?
Let's go on to the next place.
NOTHING...
THERE'S JUST SO MANY THINGS I'D RATHER NOT REMEMBER.
OH!
LET'S GO OVER THERE!
OVER THERE!
O...
OKAY...
What is this?
He's in unusually high spirits...
The power of booze, huh?
Alcohol sure is amazing...
OH!

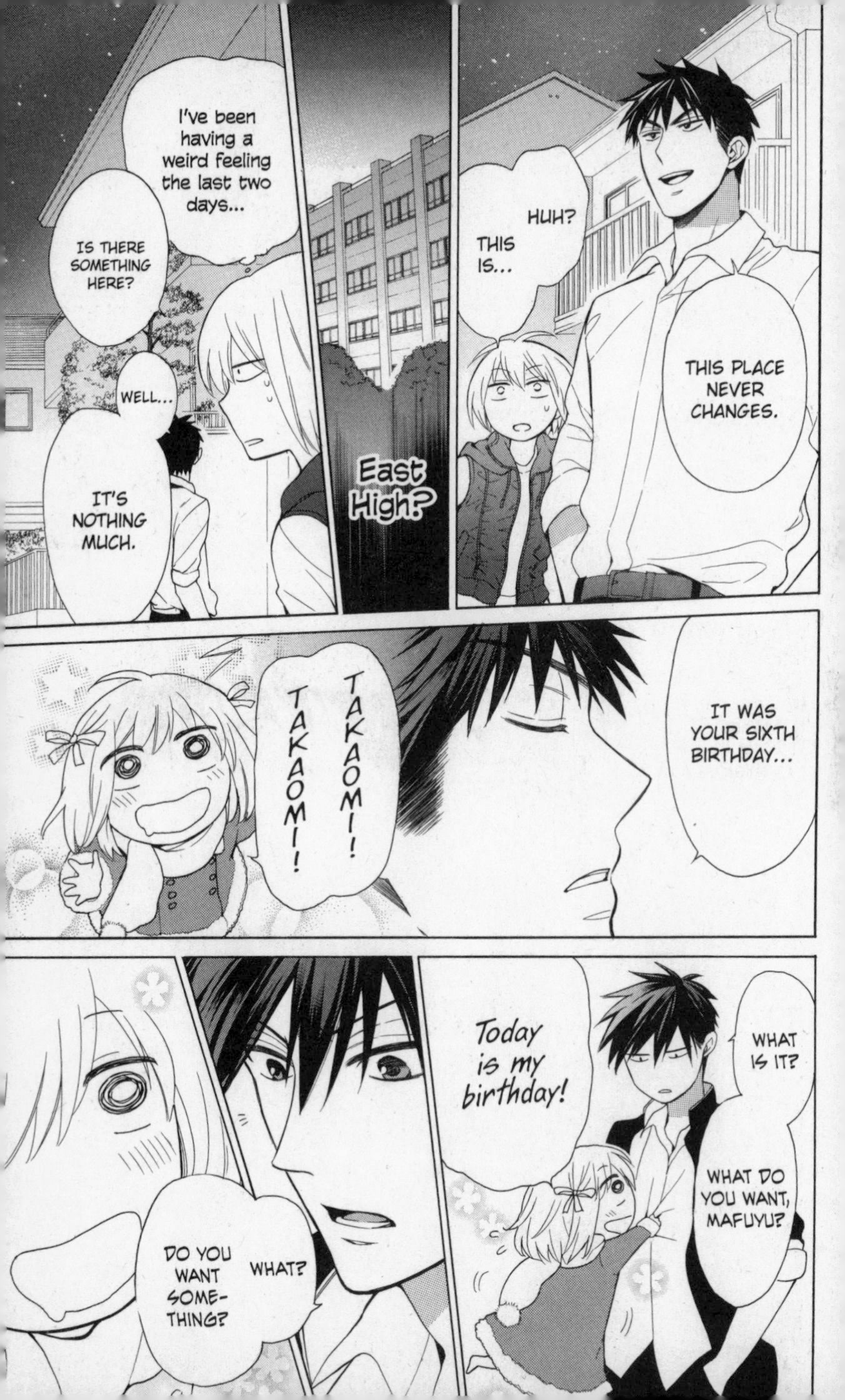
HUH?
THIS IS...
THIS PLACE NEVER CHANGES.
East High?
I've been having a weird feeling the last two days...
IS THERE SOMETHING HERE?
WELL...
IT'S NOTHING MUCH.
IT WAS YOUR SIXTH BIRTHDAY...
TAKAOMI!
TAKAOMI!
WHAT IS IT?
WHAT DO YOU WANT, MAFUYU?
Today is my birthday!
WHAT?
DO YOU WANT SOMETHING?

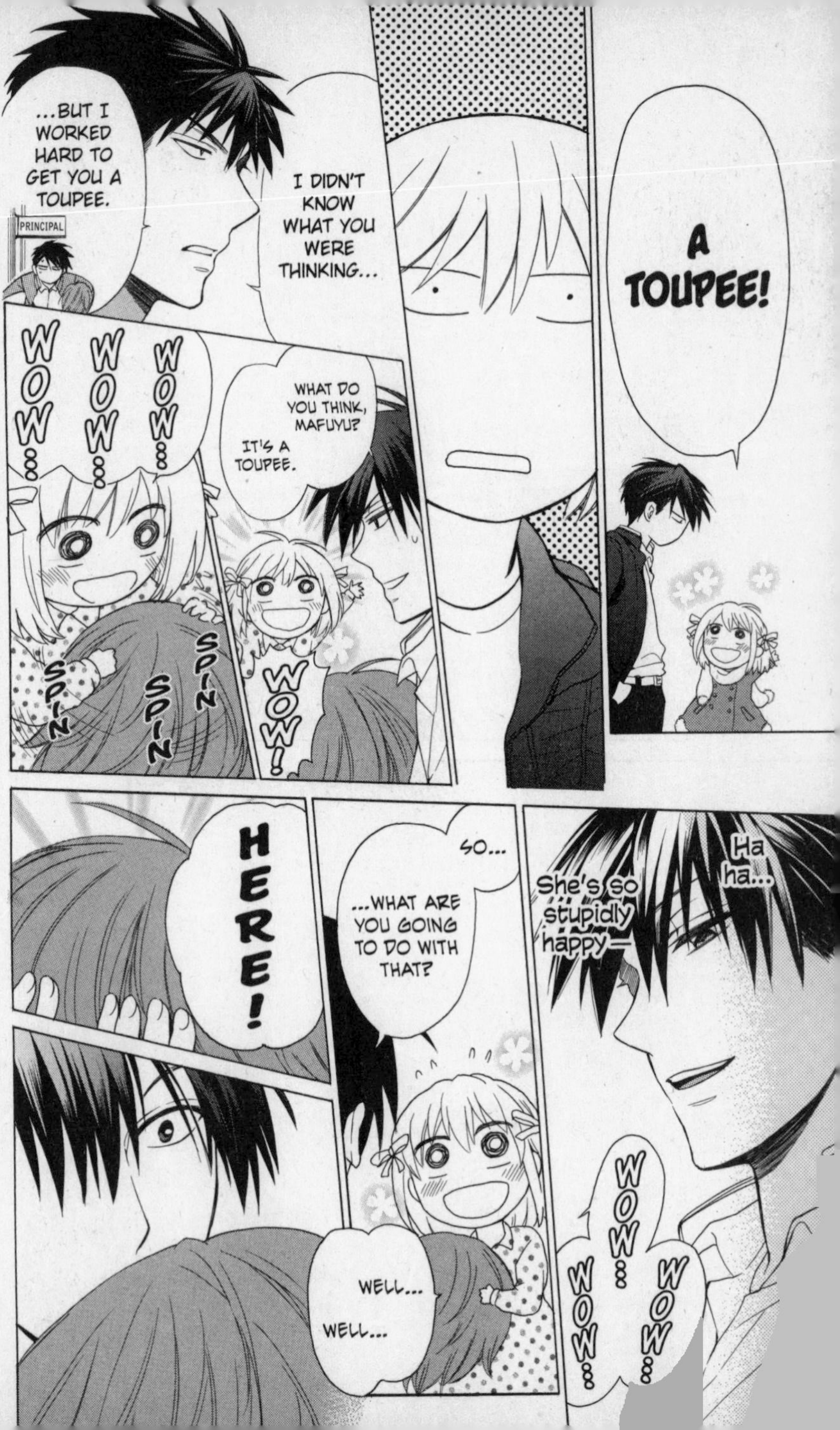
A TOUPEE!
I DIDN'T KNOW WHAT YOU WERE THINKING...
...BUT I WORKED HARD TO GET YOU A TOUPEE.
PRINCIPAL
WHAT DO YOU THINK, MAFUYU?
IT'S A TOUPEE.
WOW!
WOW...
WOW...
WOW...
SPIN
SPIN
SPIN
Ha ha...
She's so stupidly happy—
WOW...
WOW...
WOW...
SO...
...WHAT ARE YOU GOING TO DO WITH THAT?
HERE!
WELL...
WELL...

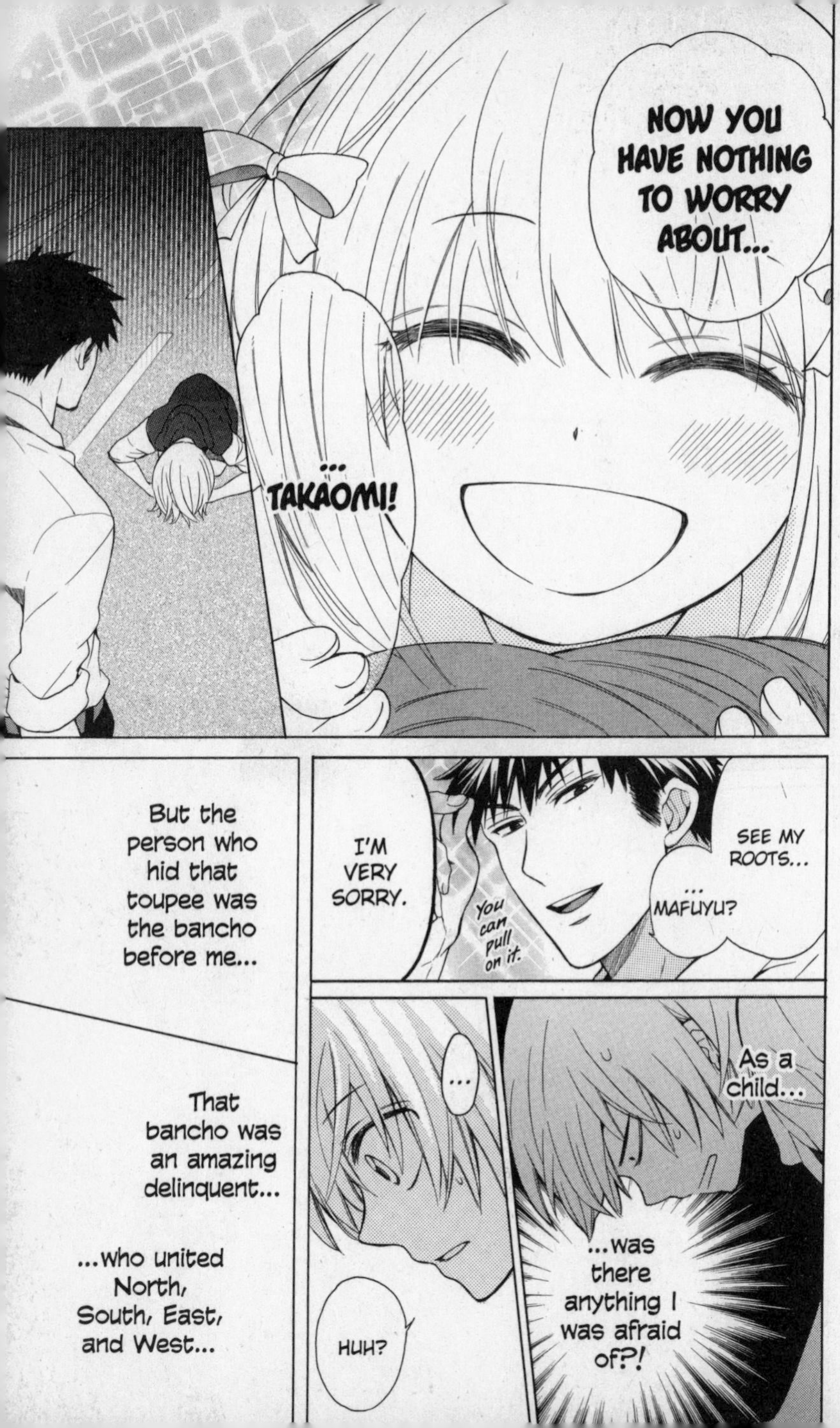
NOW YOU HAVE NOTHING TO WORRY ABOUT...
...TAKAOMI!
SEE MY ROOTS...
...MAFUYU?
You can pull on it.
I'M VERY SORRY.
But the person who hid that toupee was the bancho before me...
As a child...
...was there anything I was afraid of?!
...
HUH?
That bancho was an amazing delinquent...
...who united North, South, East, and West...

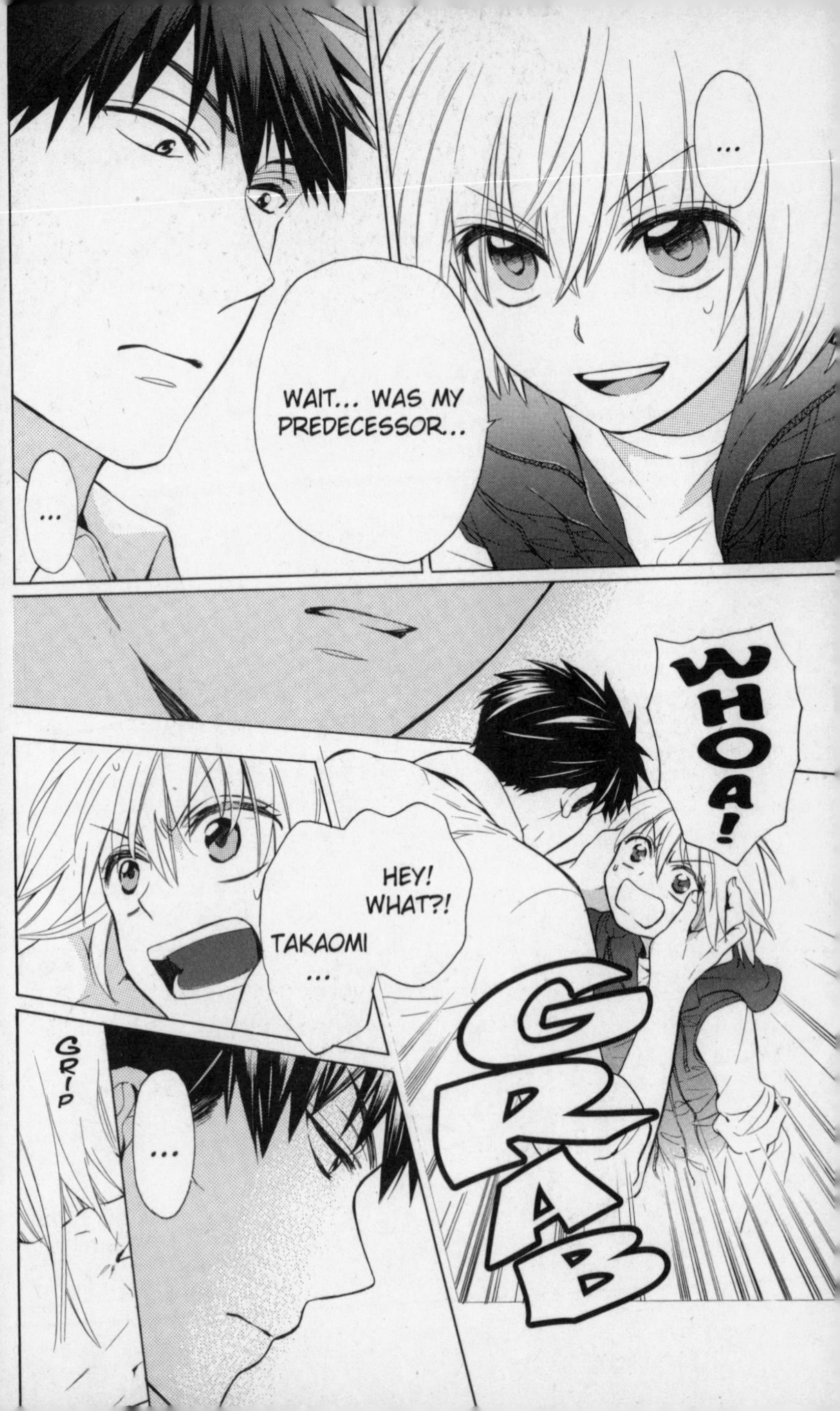
...
WAIT... WAS MY PREDECESSOR...
...
WHOA!
GRAB
HEY! WHAT?!
TAKAOMI ...
GRIP
...

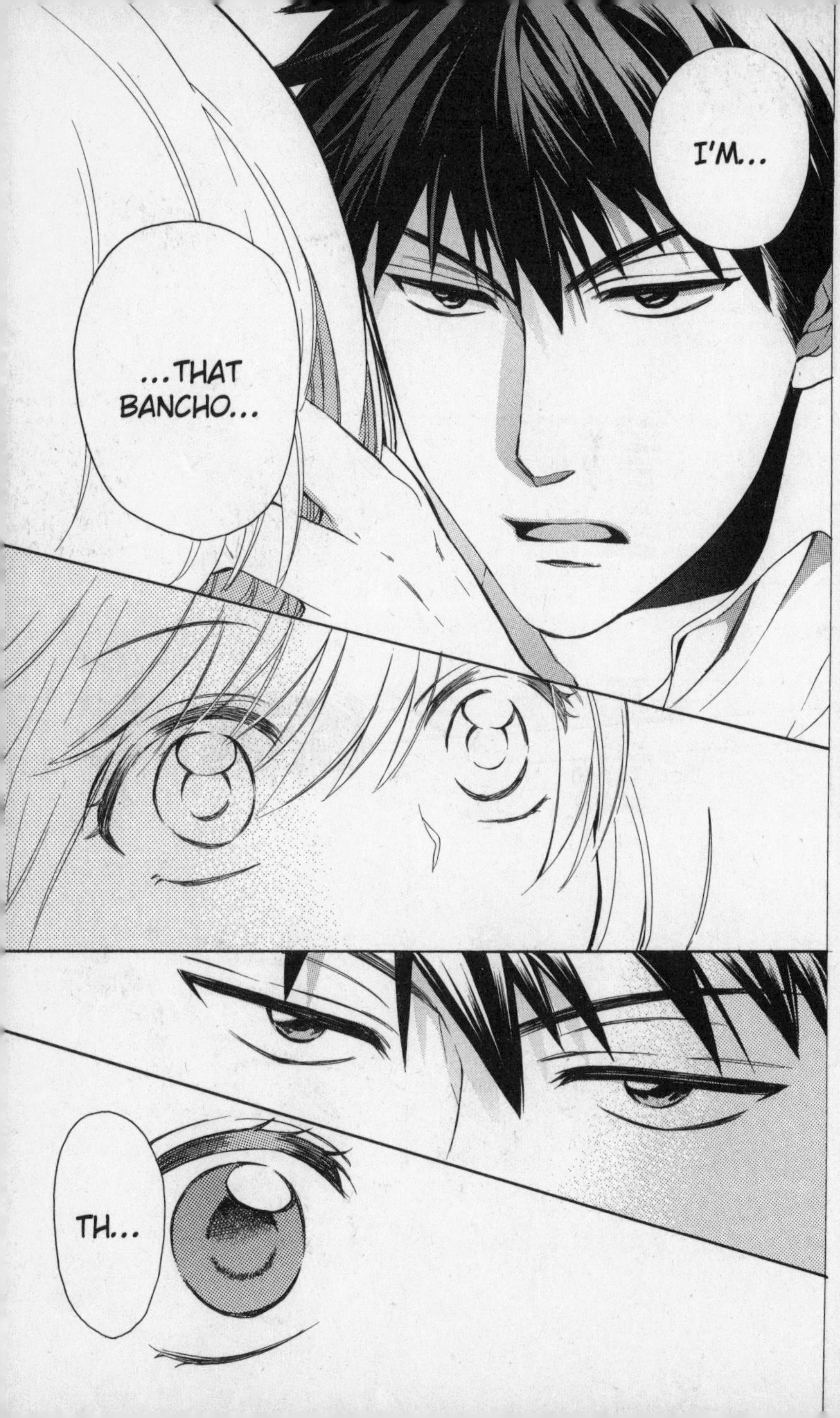
I'M...
...THAT BANCHO...
TH...

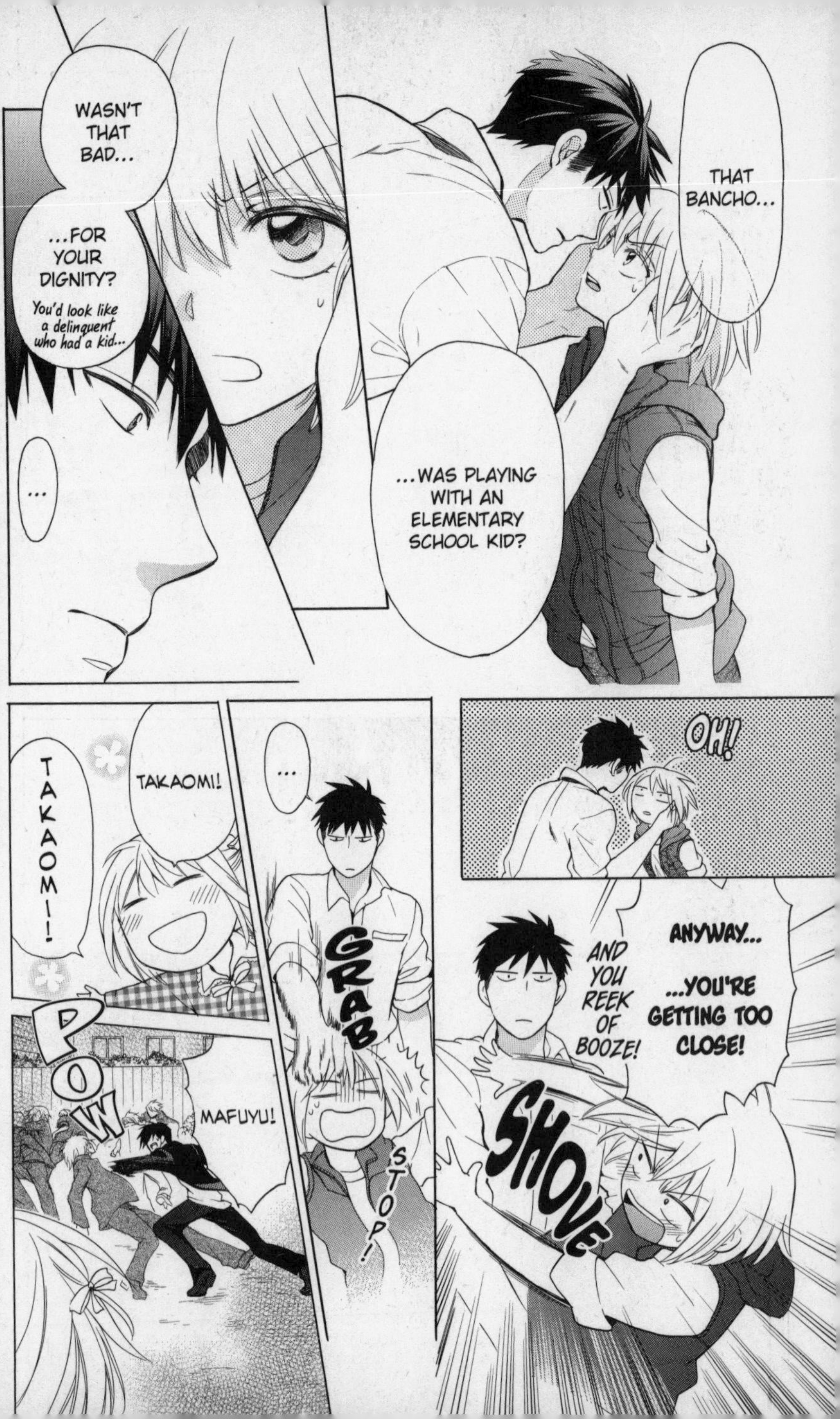
THAT BANCHO...
...WAS PLAYING WITH AN ELEMENTARY SCHOOL KID?
WASN'T THAT BAD...
...FOR YOUR DIGNITY?
You'd look like a delinquent who had a kid...
...
OH!
ANYWAY...
...YOU'RE GETTING TOO CLOSE!
AND YOU REEK OF BOOZE!
SHOVE
...
GRAB
STOP!
TAKAOMI!
TAKAOMI!
POW
MAFUYU!

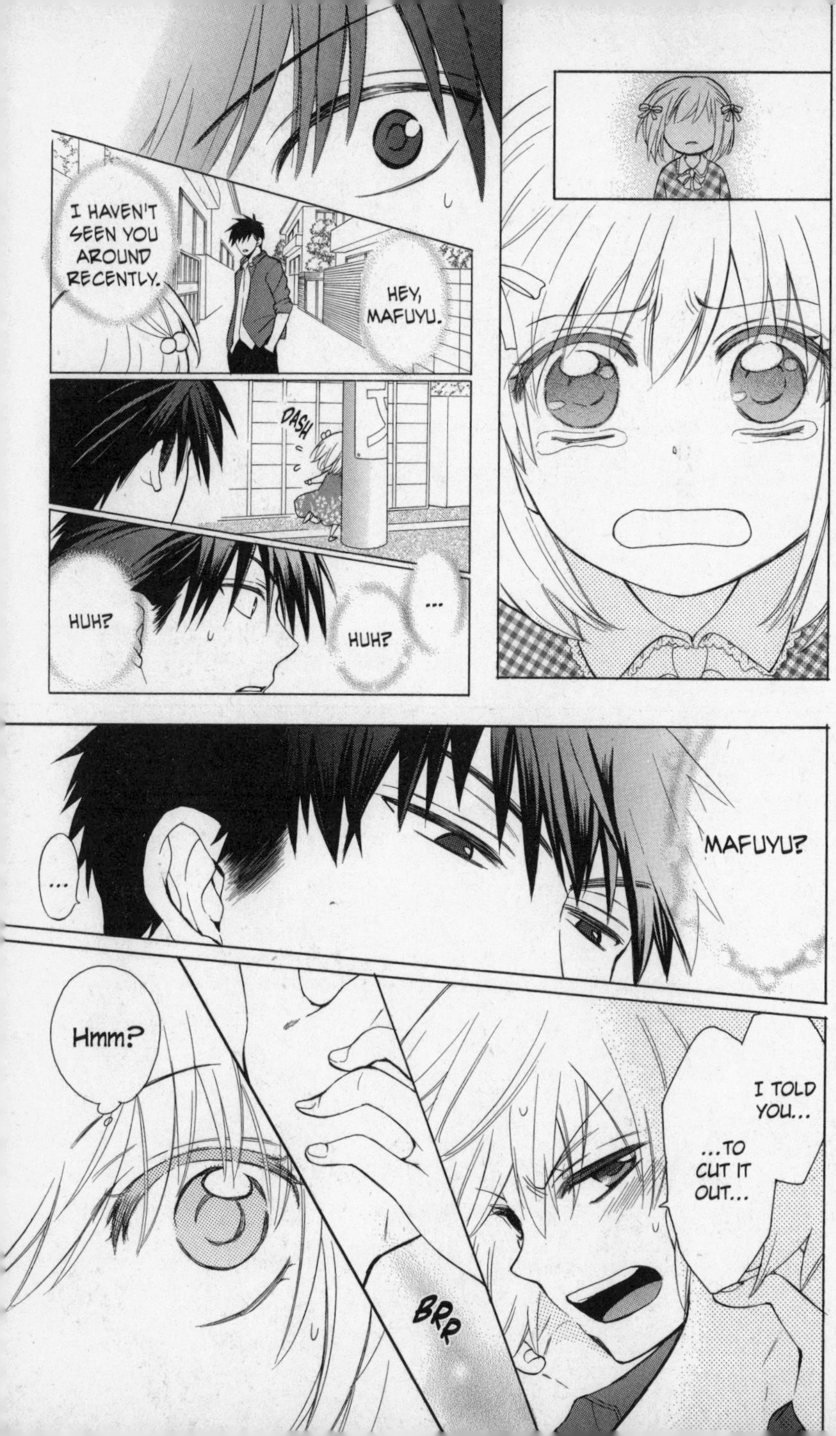
HEY, MAFUYU.
I HAVEN'T SEEN YOU AROUND RECENTLY.
DASH
...
HUH?
HUH?
MAFUYU?
...
I TOLD YOU...
...TO CUT IT OUT...
BRR
Hmm?

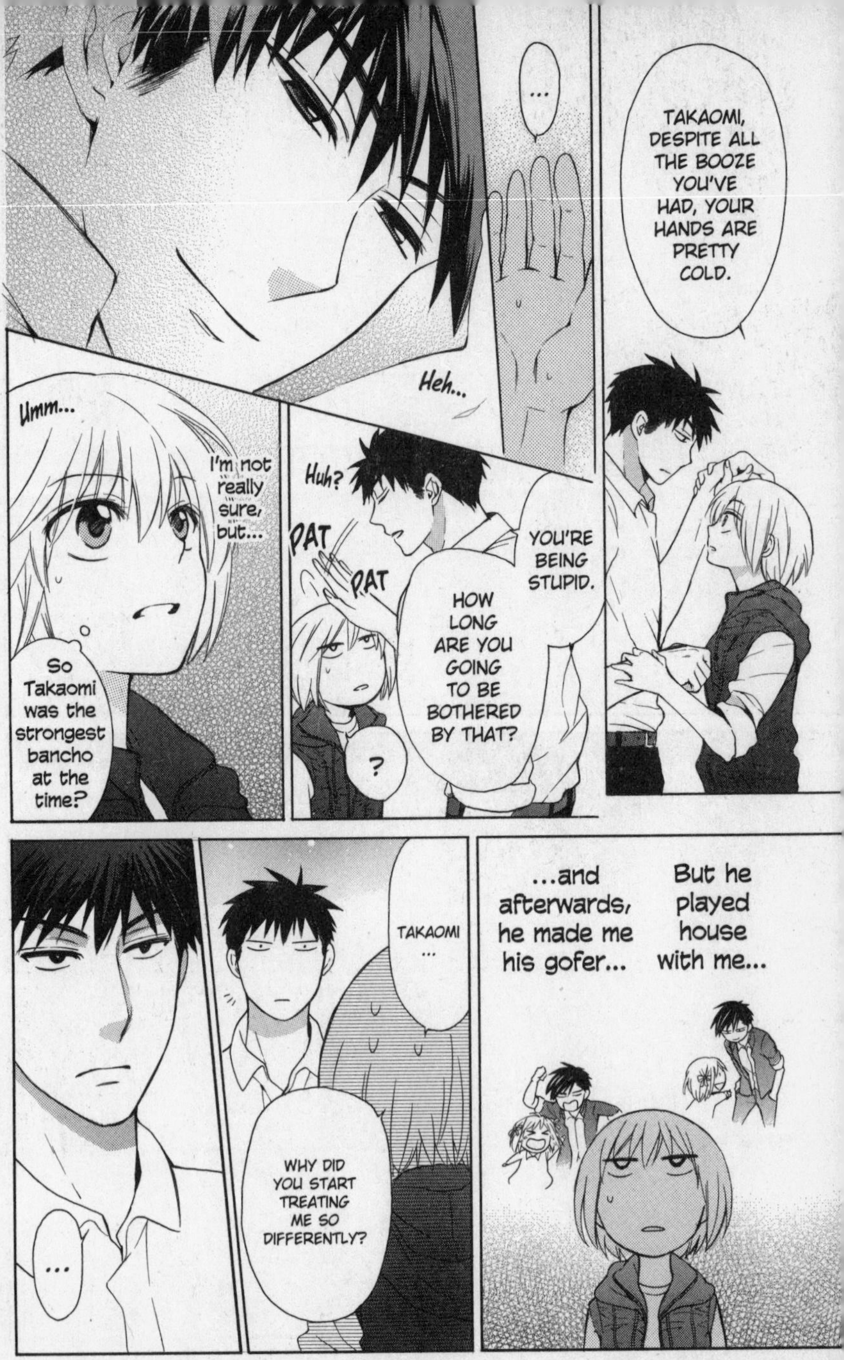
TAKAOMI, DESPITE ALL THE BOOZE YOU'VE HAD, YOUR HANDS ARE PRETTY COLD.
...
Heh...
Huh?
PAT
PAT
YOU'RE BEING STUPID.
HOW LONG ARE YOU GOING TO BE BOTHERED BY THAT?
?
Umm...
I'm not really sure, but...
So Takaomi was the strongest bancho at the time?
But he played house with me...
...and afterwards, he made me his gofer...
TAKAOMI ...
WHY DID YOU START TREATING ME SO DIFFERENTLY?
...

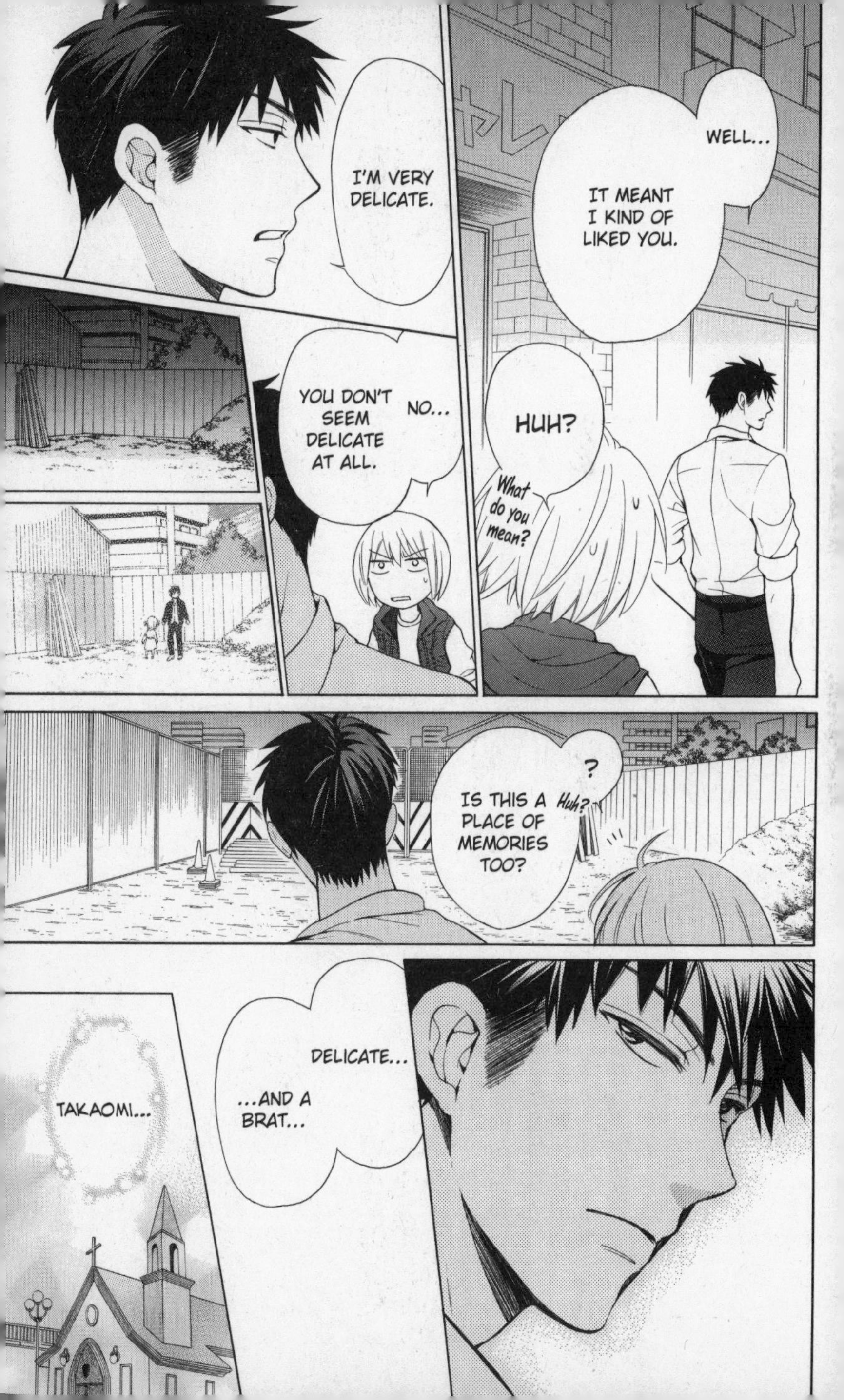

WELL...
IT MEANT I KIND OF LIKED YOU.
HUH?
What do you mean?
I'M VERY DELICATE.
NO...
YOU DON'T SEEM DELICATE AT ALL.
IS THIS A PLACE OF MEMORIES TOO?
?
Huh?
DELICATE...
...AND A BRAT...
TAKAOMI...

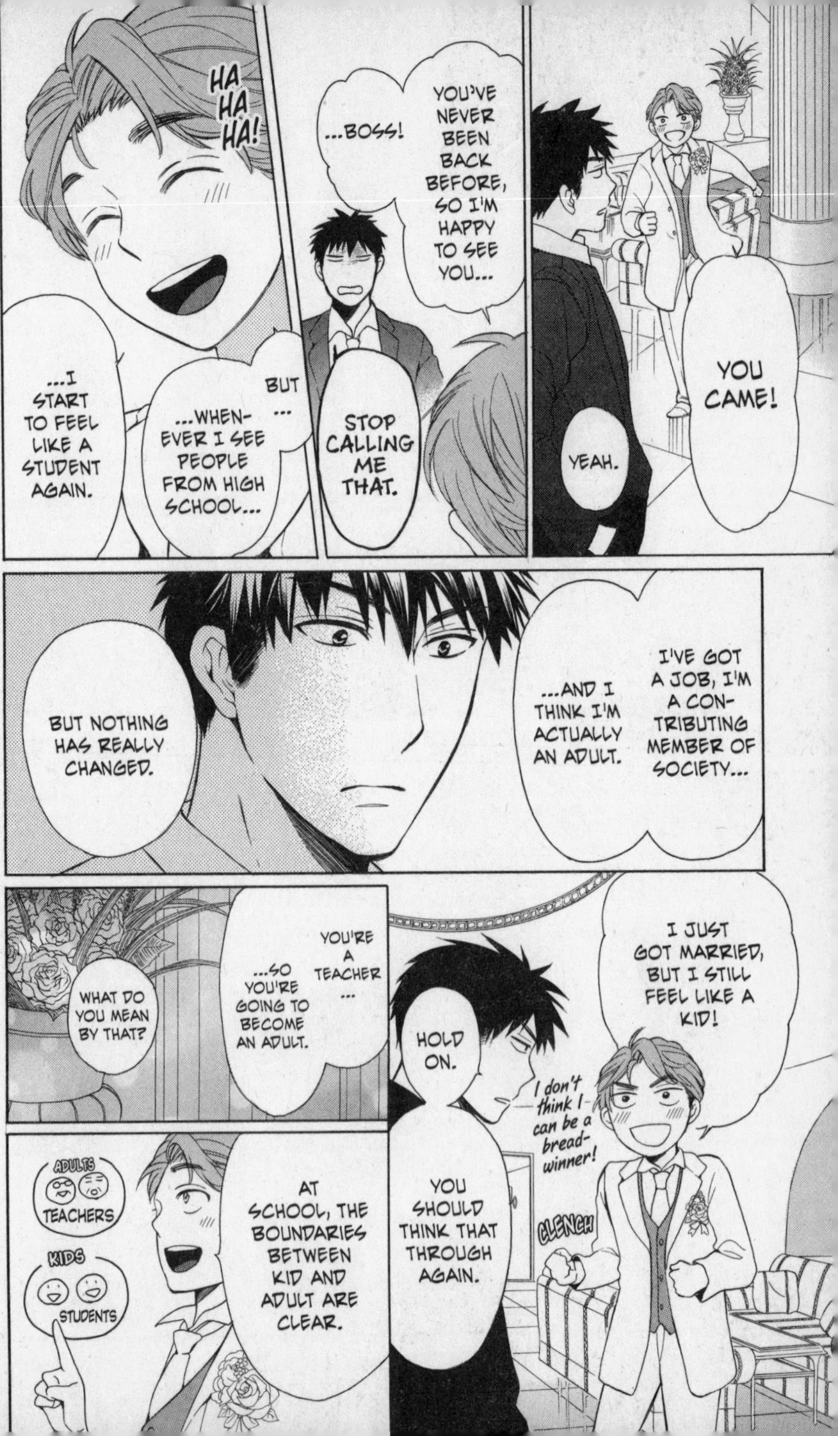
YOU CAME!
YEAH.
YOU'VE NEVER BEEN BACK BEFORE, SO I'M HAPPY TO SEE YOU...
...BOSS!
STOP CALLING ME THAT.
HA HA HA!
BUT...
...WHENEVER I SEE PEOPLE FROM HIGH SCHOOL...
...I START TO FEEL LIKE A STUDENT AGAIN.
I'VE GOT A JOB, I'M A CONTRIBUTING MEMBER OF SOCIETY...
...AND I THINK I'M ACTUALLY AN ADULT.
BUT NOTHING HAS REALLY CHANGED.
I JUST GOT MARRIED, BUT I STILL FEEL LIKE A KID!
I don't think I can be a breadwinner!
CLENCH
HOLD ON.
YOU SHOULD THINK THAT THROUGH AGAIN.
YOU'RE A TEACHER...
...SO YOU'RE GOING TO BECOME AN ADULT.
WHAT DO YOU MEAN BY THAT?
AT SCHOOL, THE BOUNDARIES BETWEEN KID AND ADULT ARE CLEAR.
ADULTS
TEACHERS
KIDS
STUDENTS

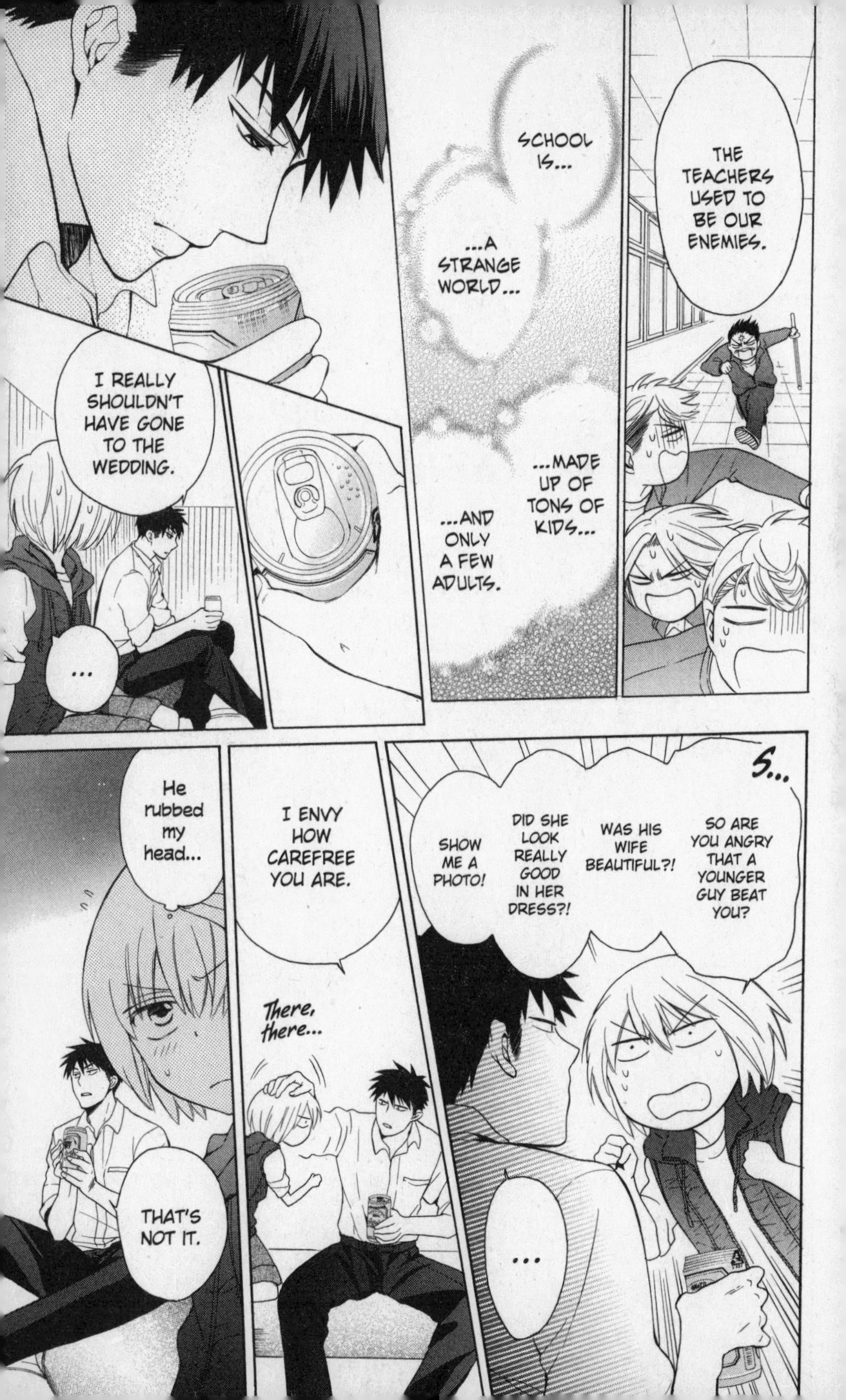
THE TEACHERS USED TO BE OUR ENEMIES.
SCHOOL IS...
...A STRANGE WORLD...
...MADE UP OF TONS OF KIDS...
...AND ONLY A FEW ADULTS.
I REALLY SHOULDN'T HAVE GONE TO THE WEDDING.
...
S...
SO ARE YOU ANGRY THAT A YOUNGER GUY BEAT YOU?
WAS HIS WIFE BEAUTIFUL?!
DID SHE LOOK REALLY GOOD IN HER DRESS?!
SHOW ME A PHOTO!
...
I ENVY HOW CAREFREE YOU ARE.
There, there...
He rubbed my head...
THAT'S NOT IT.

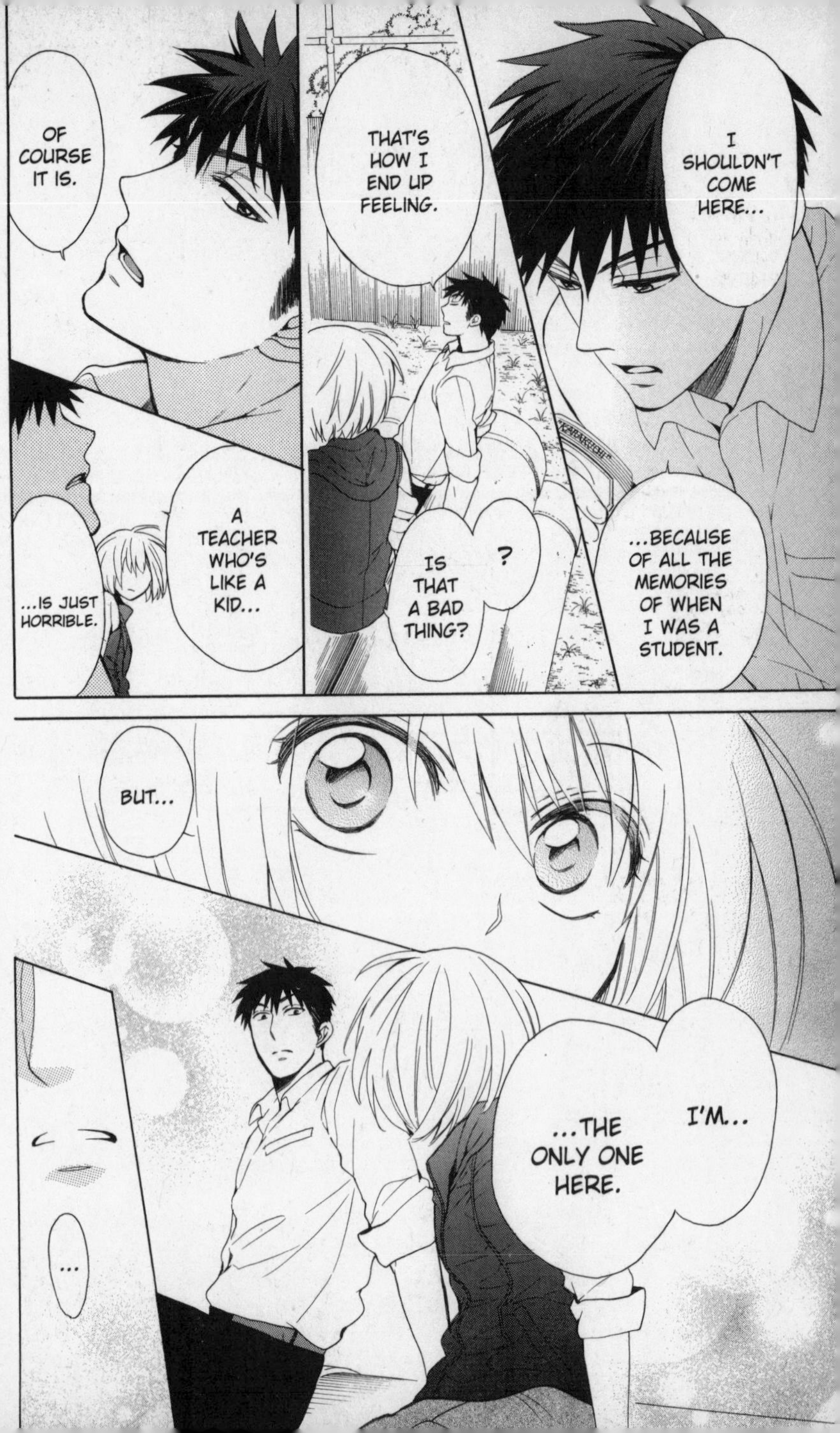
I SHOULDN'T COME HERE...
...BECAUSE OF ALL THE MEMORIES OF WHEN I WAS A STUDENT.
THAT'S HOW I END UP FEELING.
?
IS THAT A BAD THING?
OF COURSE IT IS.
A TEACHER WHO'S LIKE A KID...
...IS JUST HORRIBLE.
BUT...
I'M...
...THE ONLY ONE HERE.
...

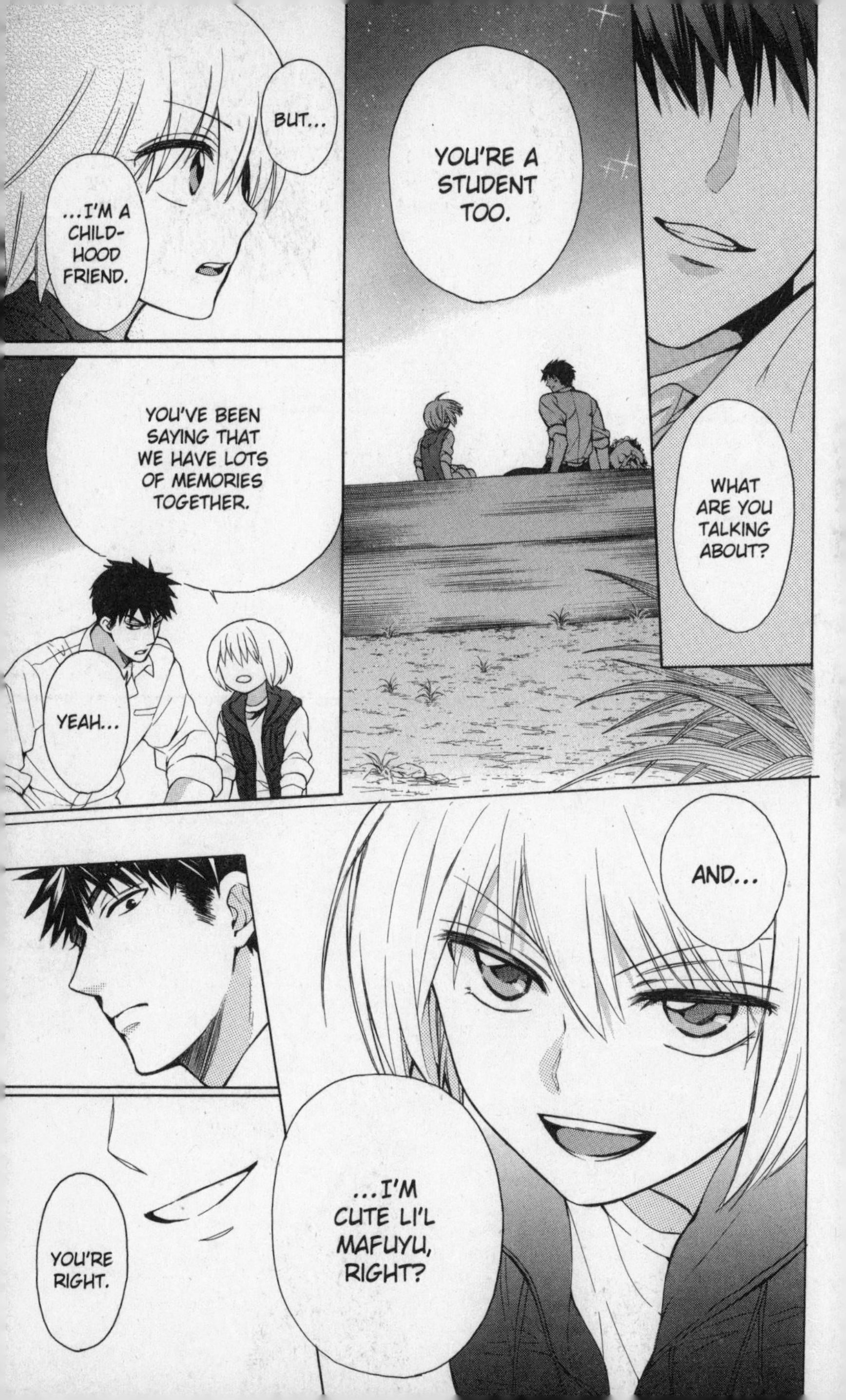
WHAT ARE YOU TALKING ABOUT?
YOU'RE A STUDENT TOO.
BUT...
...I'M A CHILD-HOOD FRIEND.
YOU'VE BEEN SAYING THAT WE HAVE LOTS OF MEMORIES TOGETHER.
YEAH...
AND...
...I'M CUTE LI'L MAFUYU, RIGHT?
YOU'RE RIGHT.

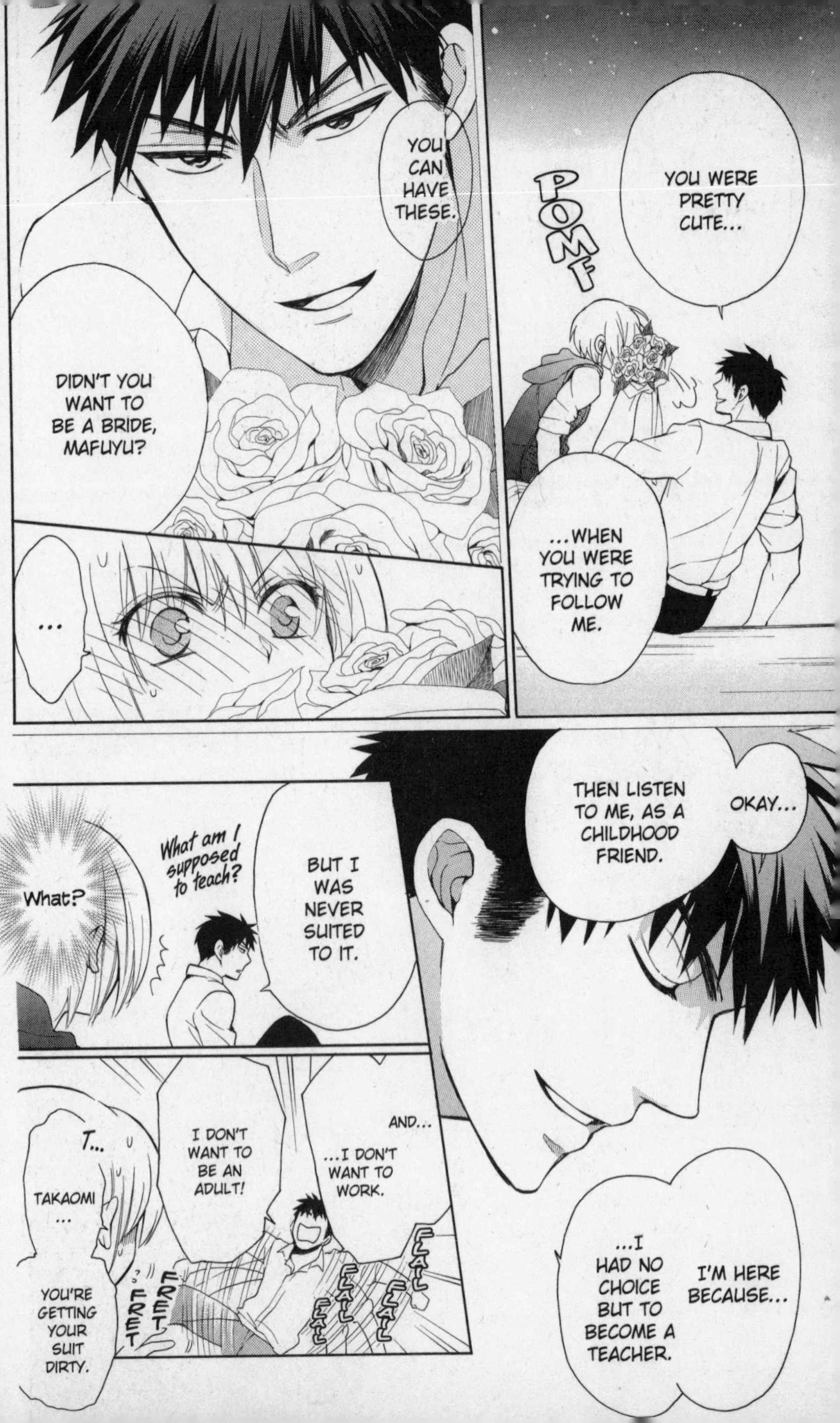
YOU WERE PRETTY CUTE...
POMF
...WHEN YOU WERE TRYING TO FOLLOW ME.
YOU CAN HAVE THESE.
DIDN'T YOU WANT TO BE A BRIDE, MAFUYU?
...
OKAY...
THEN LISTEN TO ME, AS A CHILDHOOD FRIEND.
I'M HERE BECAUSE...
...I HAD NO CHOICE BUT TO BECOME A TEACHER.
BUT I WAS NEVER SUITED TO IT.
What am I supposed to teach?
What?
AND...
...I DON'T WANT TO WORK.
I DON'T WANT TO BE AN ADULT!
FLAIL FLAIL FLAIL FLAIL
FRET FRET
T...
TAKAOMI ...
YOU'RE GETTING YOUR SUIT DIRTY.

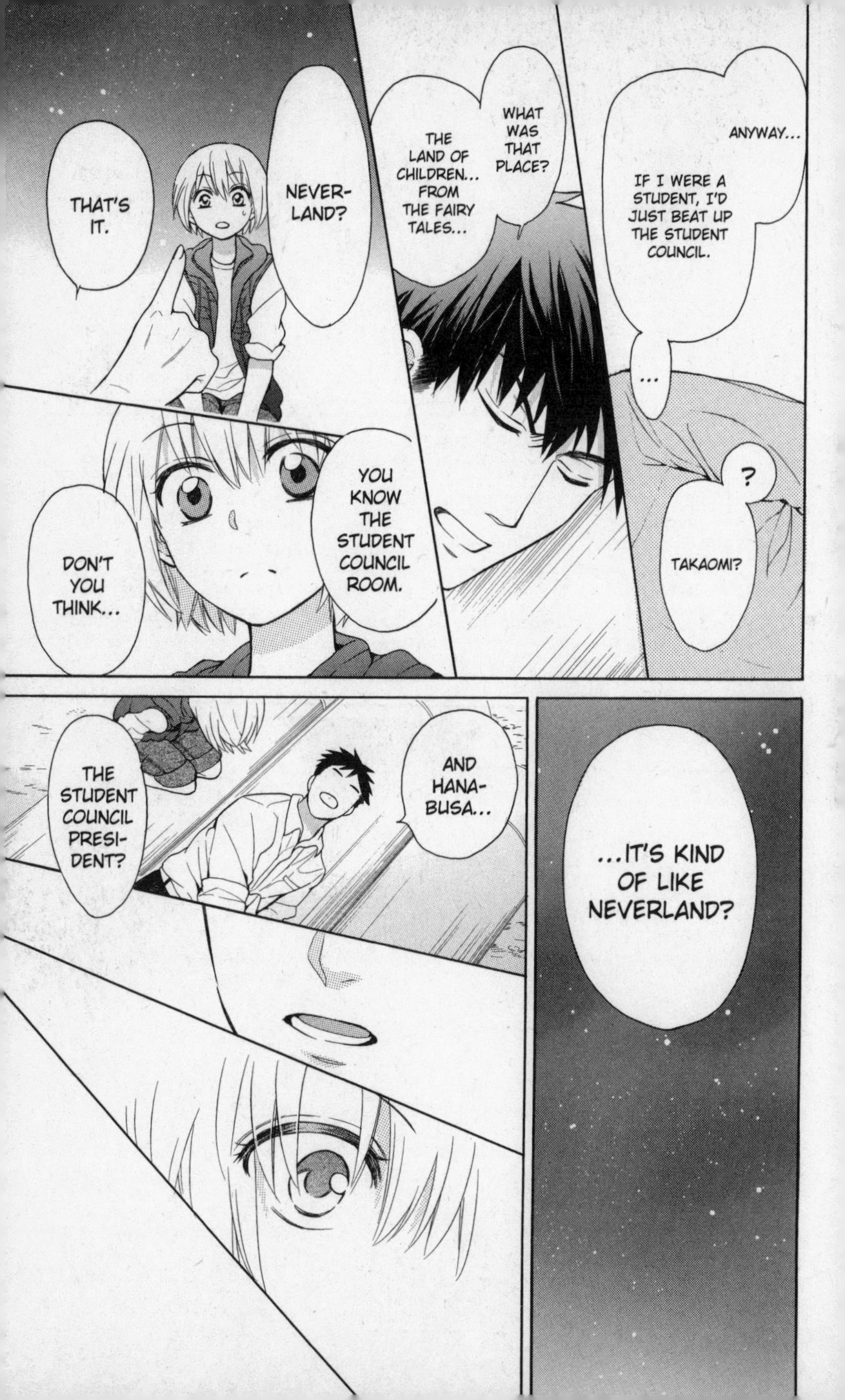
ANYWAY...
IF I WERE A STUDENT, I'D JUST BEAT UP THE STUDENT COUNCIL.
...
?
TAKAOMI?
WHAT WAS THAT PLACE?
THE LAND OF CHILDREN... FROM THE FAIRY TALES...
NEVER-LAND?
THAT'S IT.
YOU KNOW THE STUDENT COUNCIL ROOM.
DON'T YOU THINK...
AND HANA-BUSA...
THE STUDENT COUNCIL PRESI-DENT?
...IT'S KIND OF LIKE NEVERLAND?

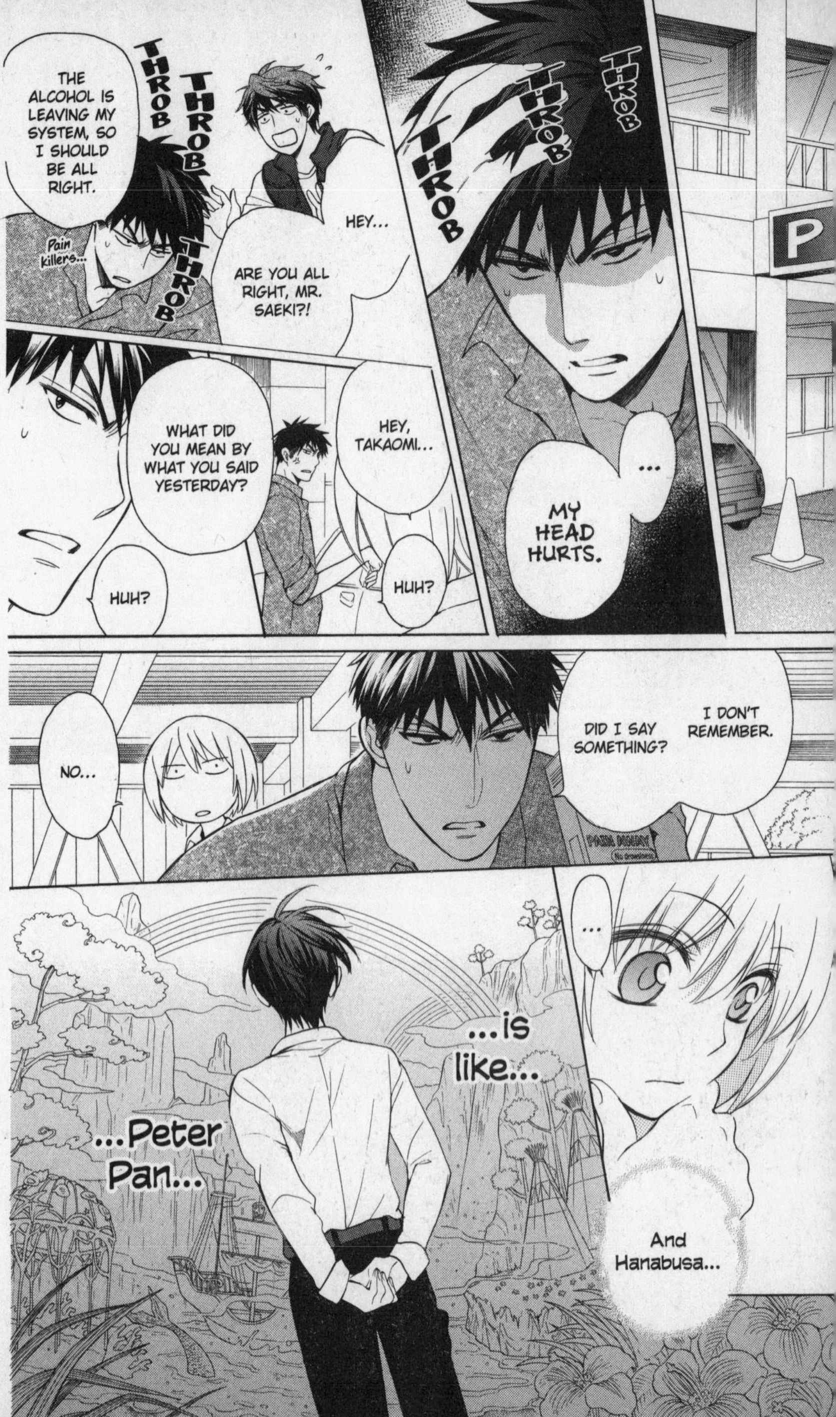
THROB
THROB
THROB
...
MY HEAD HURTS.
HEY...
ARE YOU ALL RIGHT, MR. SAEKI?!
THROB THROB
THE ALCOHOL IS LEAVING MY SYSTEM, SO I SHOULD BE ALL RIGHT.
Pain killers...
THROB
HEY, TAKAOMI...
WHAT DID YOU MEAN BY WHAT YOU SAID YESTERDAY?
HUH?
HUH?
I DON'T REMEMBER.
DID I SAY SOMETHING?
NO...
...
And Hanabusa...
...is like...
...Peter Pan...

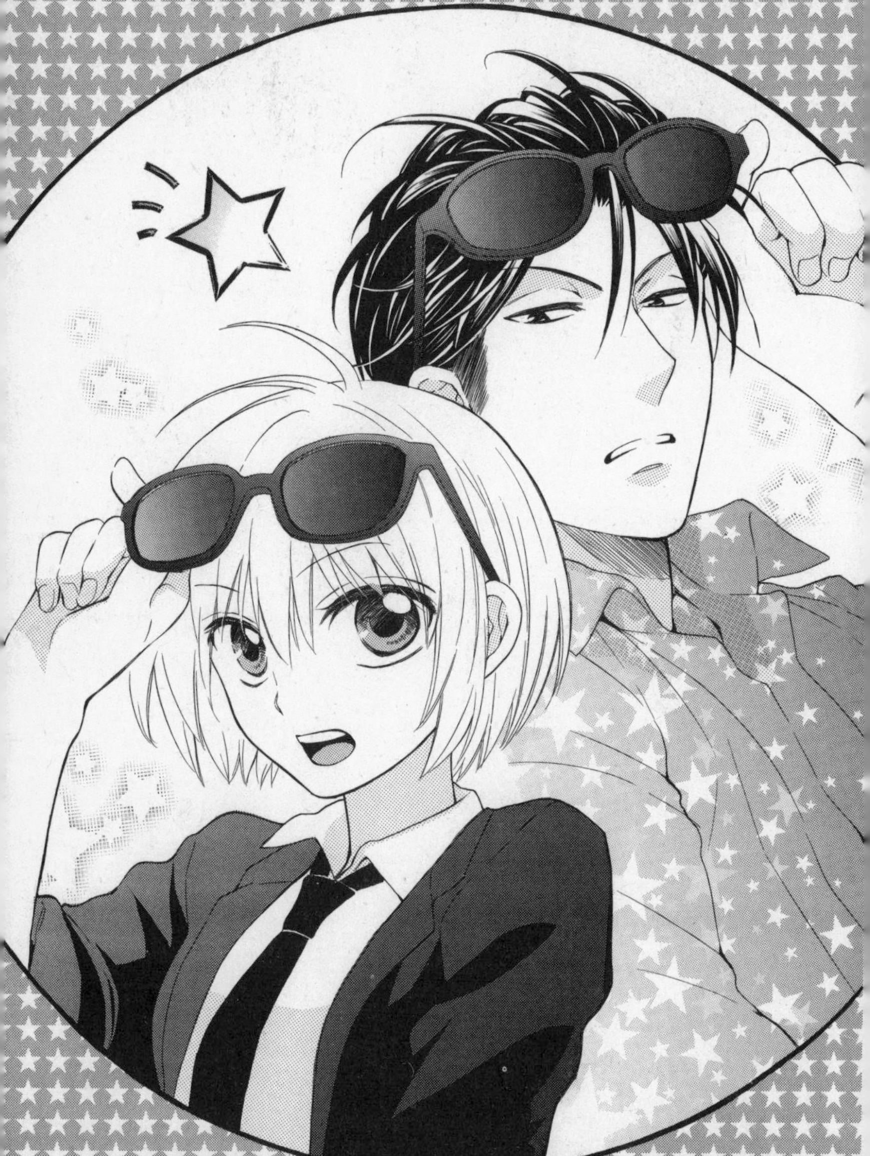

Chapter 81

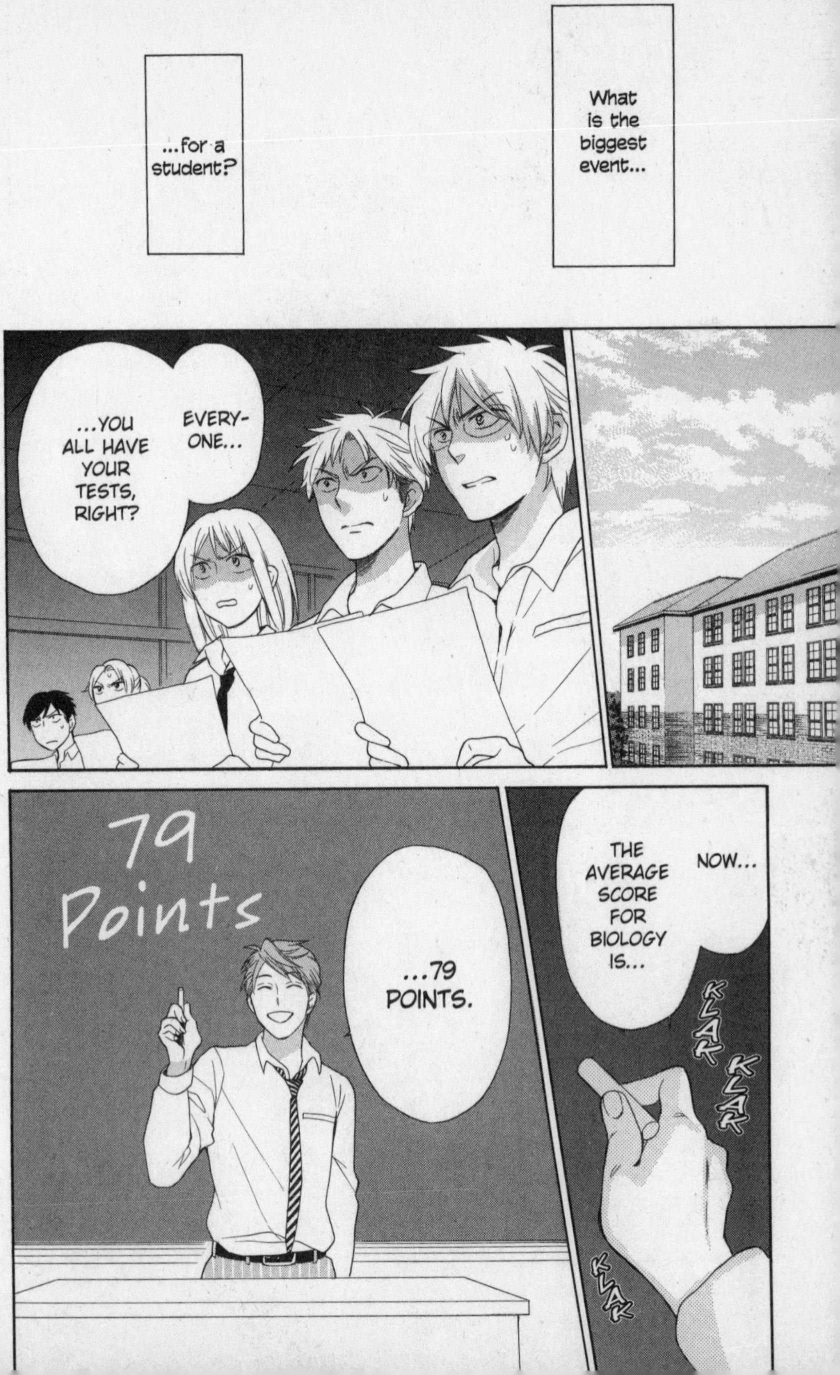
What is the biggest event...
...for a student?
EVERY-ONE...
...YOU ALL HAVE YOUR TESTS, RIGHT?
NOW...
THE AVERAGE SCORE FOR BIOLOGY IS...
KLAK KLAK
KLAK
79 Points
...79 POINTS.

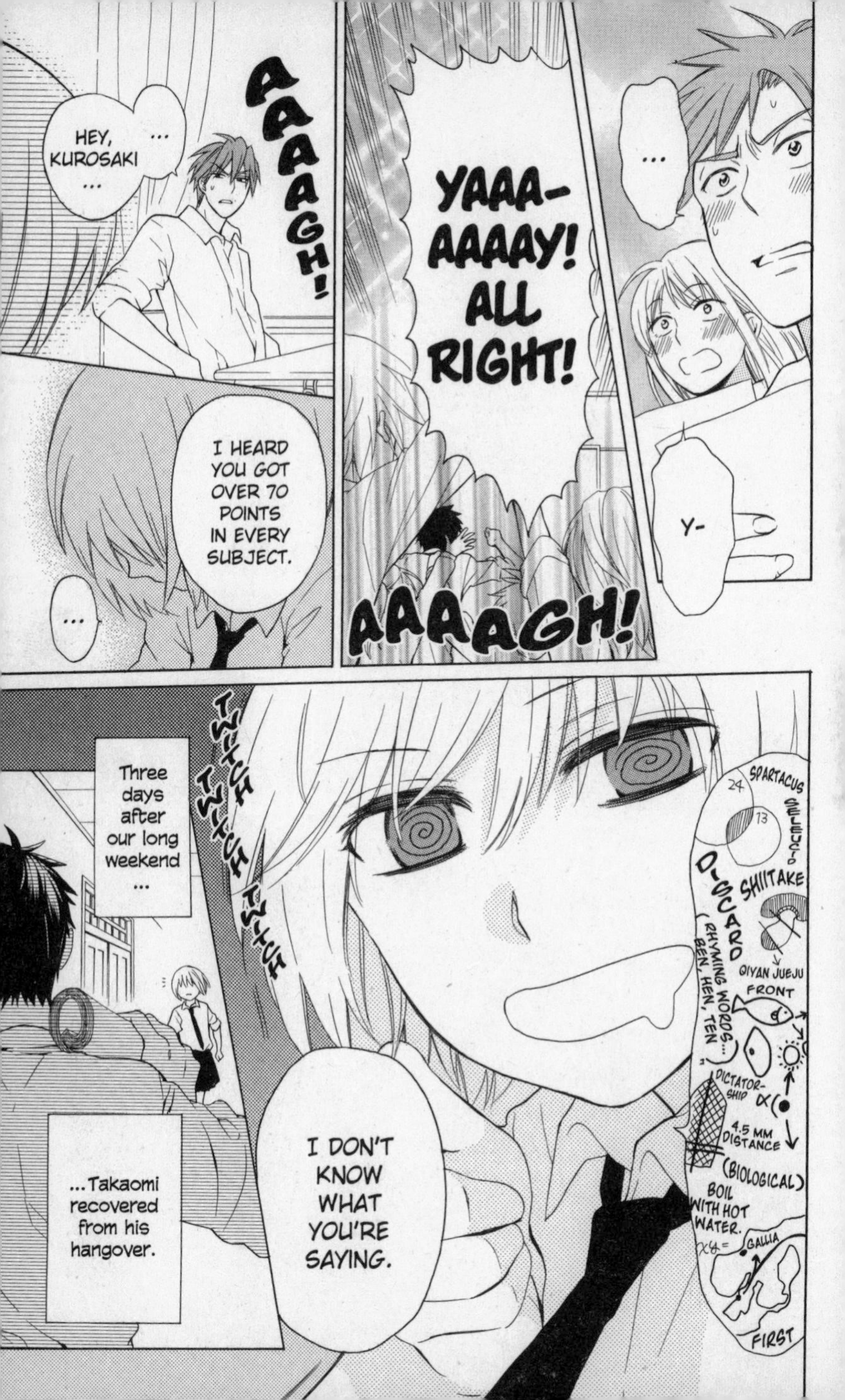
...
Y-
YAAAA-AAAAY! ALL RIGHT!
AAAAAGH!
AAAAGH!
HEY, KUROSAKI ...
...
I HEARD YOU GOT OVER 70 POINTS IN EVERY SUBJECT.
...
SPARTACUS
24
13
SELEUCID
SHIITAKE
DISCARD
(RHYMING WORDS... BEN, HEN, TEN)
QIYAN JUEJU
FRONT
DICTATORSHIP
4.5 MM DISTANCE
(BIOLOGICAL)
BOIL WITH HOT WATER.
GALLIA
FIRST
TWITCH TWITCH TWITCH
I DON'T KNOW WHAT YOU'RE SAYING.
Three days after our long weekend ...
...Takaomi recovered from his hangover.

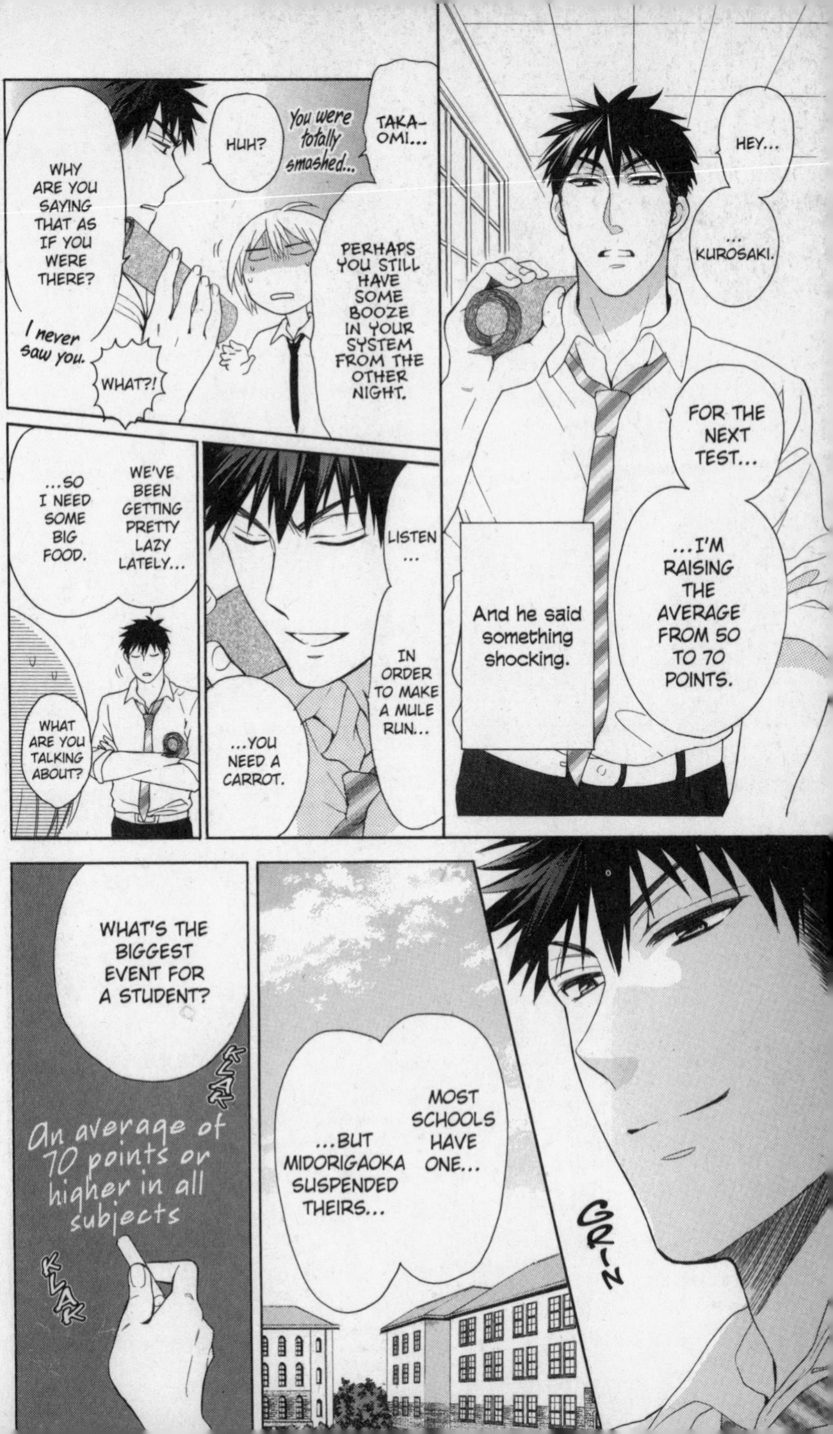
HEY...
...KUROSAKI.
FOR THE NEXT TEST...
...I'M RAISING THE AVERAGE FROM 50 TO 70 POINTS.
And he said something shocking.
TAKA-OMI...
You were totally smashed...
HUH?
PERHAPS YOU STILL HAVE SOME BOOZE IN YOUR SYSTEM FROM THE OTHER NIGHT.
WHY ARE YOU SAYING THAT AS IF YOU WERE THERE?
I never saw you.
WHAT?!
LISTEN...
IN ORDER TO MAKE A MULE RUN...
...YOU NEED A CARROT.
WE'VE BEEN GETTING PRETTY LAZY LATELY...
...SO I NEED SOME BIG FOOD.
WHAT ARE YOU TALKING ABOUT?
GRIN
MOST SCHOOLS HAVE ONE...
...BUT MIDORIGAOKA SUSPENDED THEIRS...
WHAT'S THE BIGGEST EVENT FOR A STUDENT?
KLAK
An average of 70 points or higher in all subjects
KLAK

The School Trip Returns

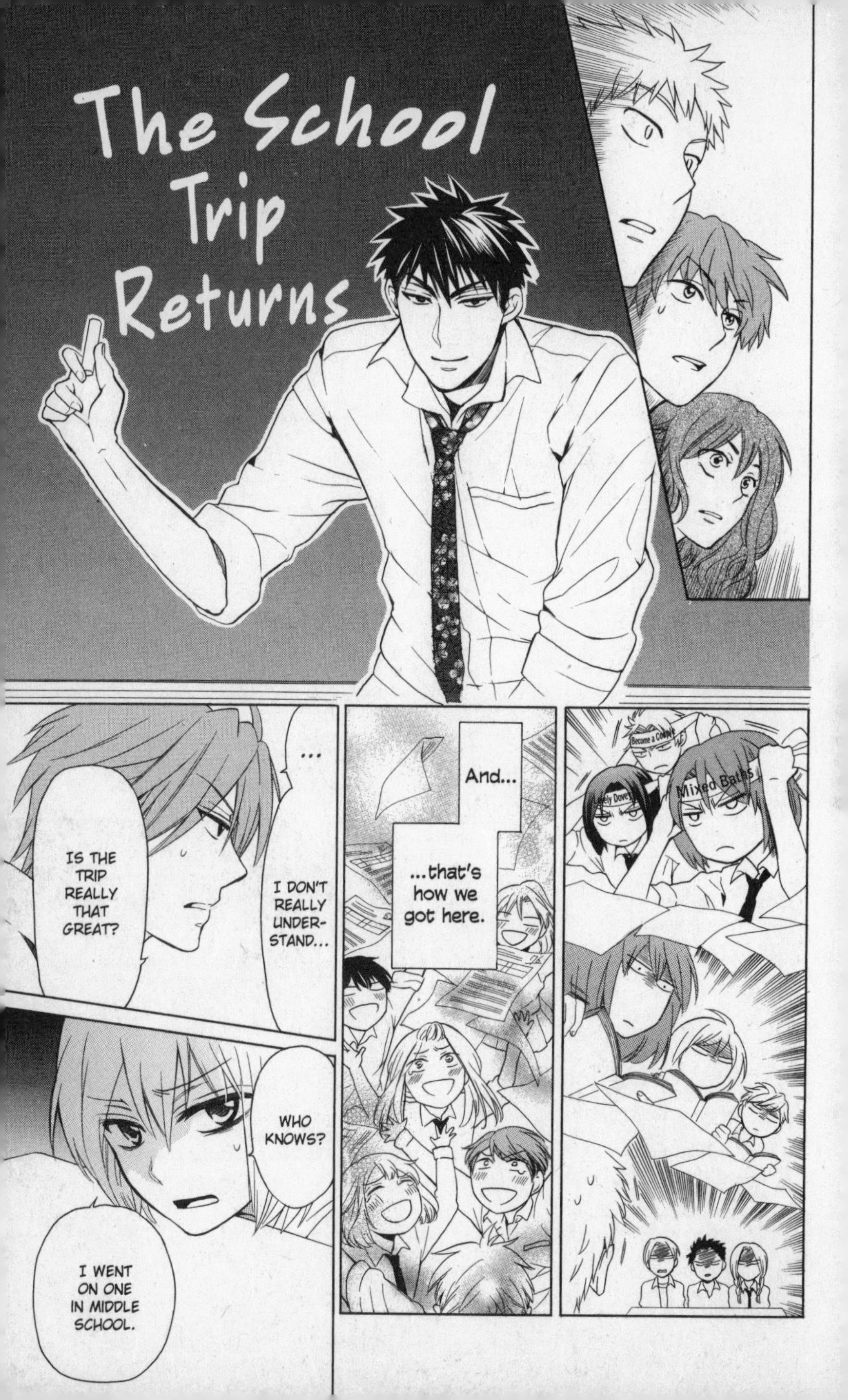

Become a Couple
Mixed Baths
Lovely Dove
And...
...that's how we got here.
...
I DON'T REALLY UNDERSTAND...
IS THE TRIP REALLY THAT GREAT?
WHO KNOWS?
I WENT ON ONE IN MIDDLE SCHOOL.

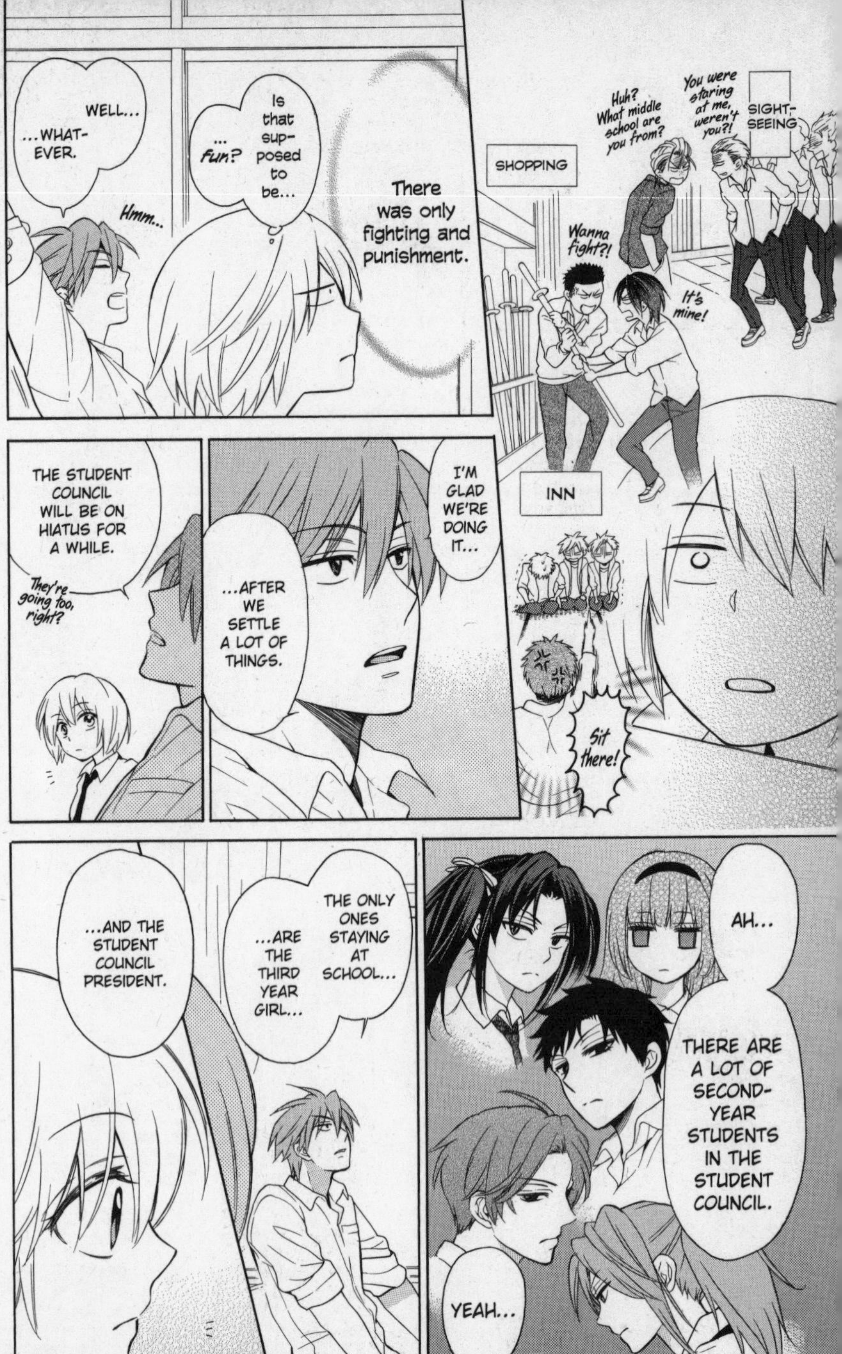
SIGHT-SEEING
You were staring at me, weren't you?!
Huh? What middle school are you from?
SHOPPING
Wanna fight?!
It's mine!
INN
Sit there!
There was only fighting and punishment.
Is that sup-posed to be...
...fun?
WELL...
...WHAT-EVER.
Hmm...
I'M GLAD WE'RE DOING IT...
...AFTER WE SETTLE A LOT OF THINGS.
THE STUDENT COUNCIL WILL BE ON HIATUS FOR A WHILE.
They're going too, right?
AH...
THERE ARE A LOT OF SECOND-YEAR STUDENTS IN THE STUDENT COUNCIL.
YEAH...
THE ONLY ONES STAYING AT SCHOOL...
...ARE THE THIRD YEAR GIRL...
...AND THE STUDENT COUNCIL PRESIDENT.

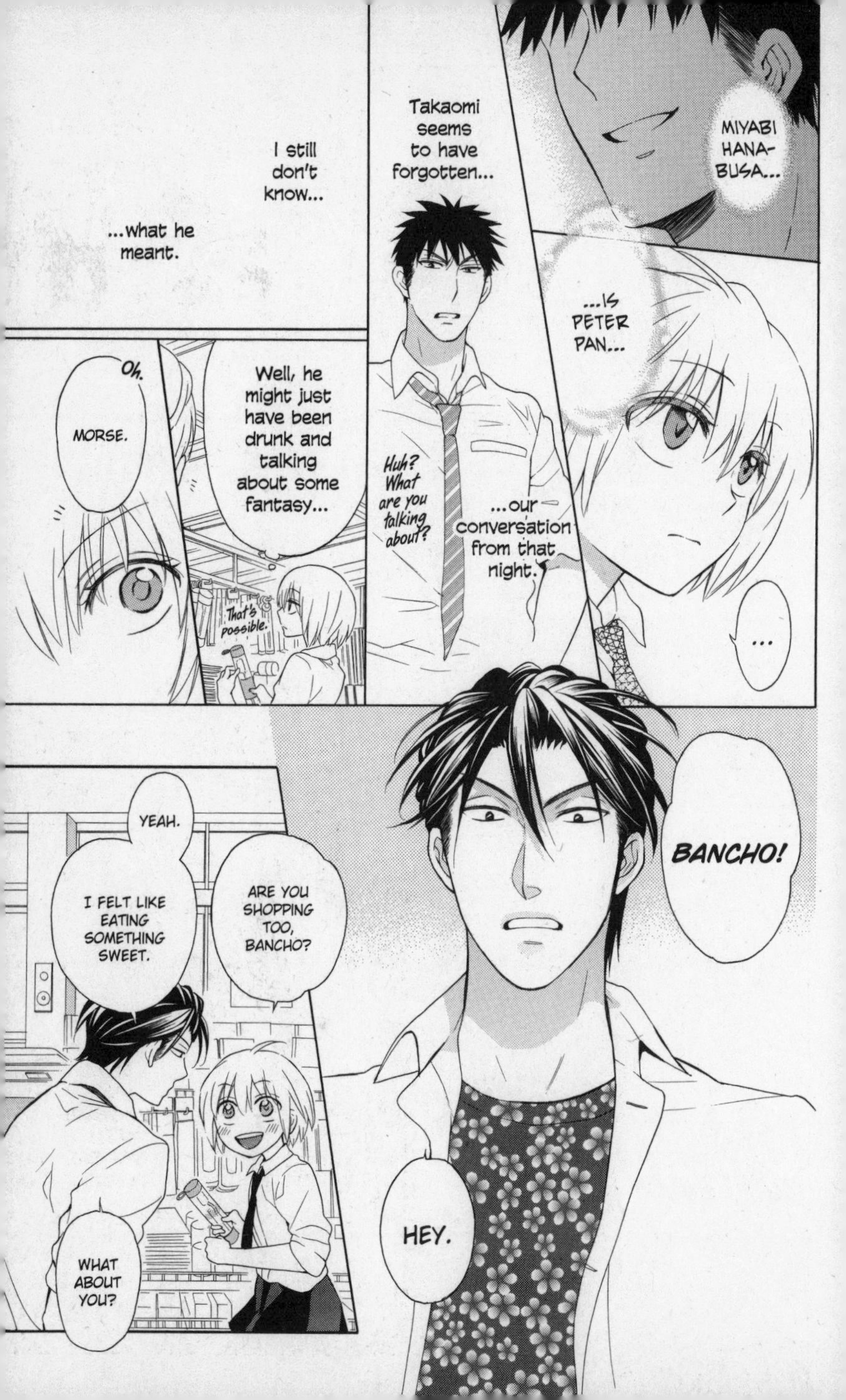
MIYABI HANA-BUSA...
...IS PETER PAN...
...
Takaomi seems to have forgotten...
...our conversation from that night.
Huh? What are you talking about?
I still don't know...
...what he meant.
Well, he might just have been drunk and talking about some fantasy...
That's possible.
Oh.
MORSE.
BANCHO!
HEY.
ARE YOU SHOPPING TOO, BANCHO?
YEAH.
I FELT LIKE EATING SOMETHING SWEET.
WHAT ABOUT YOU?

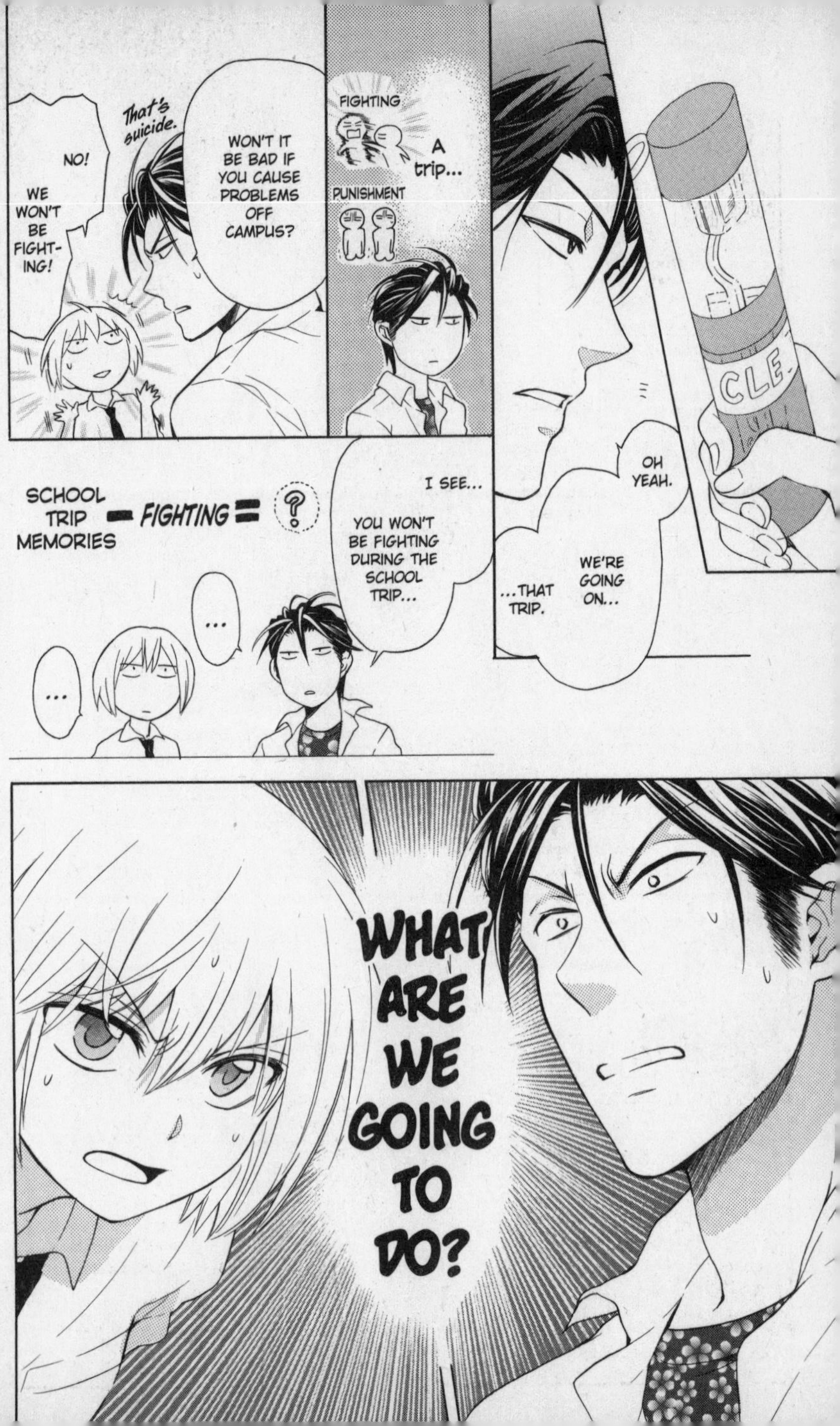

CLE
OH YEAH.
WE'RE GOING ON...
...THAT TRIP.
A trip...
FIGHTING
PUNISHMENT
WON'T IT BE BAD IF YOU CAUSE PROBLEMS OFF CAMPUS?
That's suicide.
NO!
WE WON'T BE FIGHT-ING!
I SEE...
YOU WON'T BE FIGHTING DURING THE SCHOOL TRIP...
...
...
SCHOOL TRIP MEMORIES - FIGHTING = ?
WHAT ARE WE GOING TO DO?

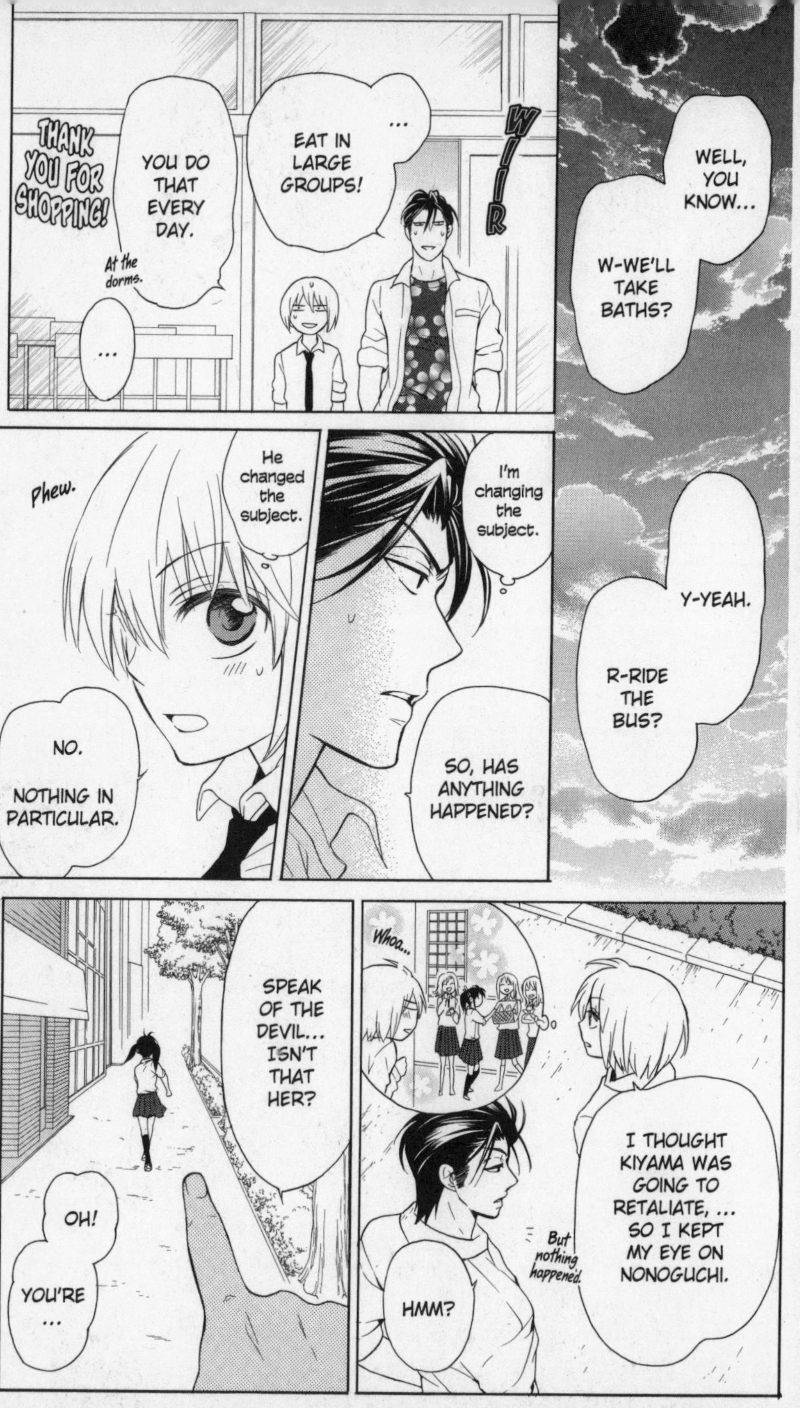
WELL, YOU KNOW...
W-WE'LL TAKE BATHS?
Y-YEAH.
R-RIDE THE BUS?
...
EAT IN LARGE GROUPS!
WIIR
YOU DO THAT EVERY DAY.
At the dorms.
THANK YOU FOR SHOPPING!
...
I'm changing the subject.
SO, HAS ANYTHING HAPPENED?
He changed the subject.
Phew.
NO.
NOTHING IN PARTICULAR.
Whoa...
I THOUGHT KIYAMA WAS GOING TO RETALIATE, ... SO I KEPT MY EYE ON NONOGUCHI.
But nothing happened.
HMM?
SPEAK OF THE DEVIL... ISN'T THAT HER?
OH!
YOU'RE ...

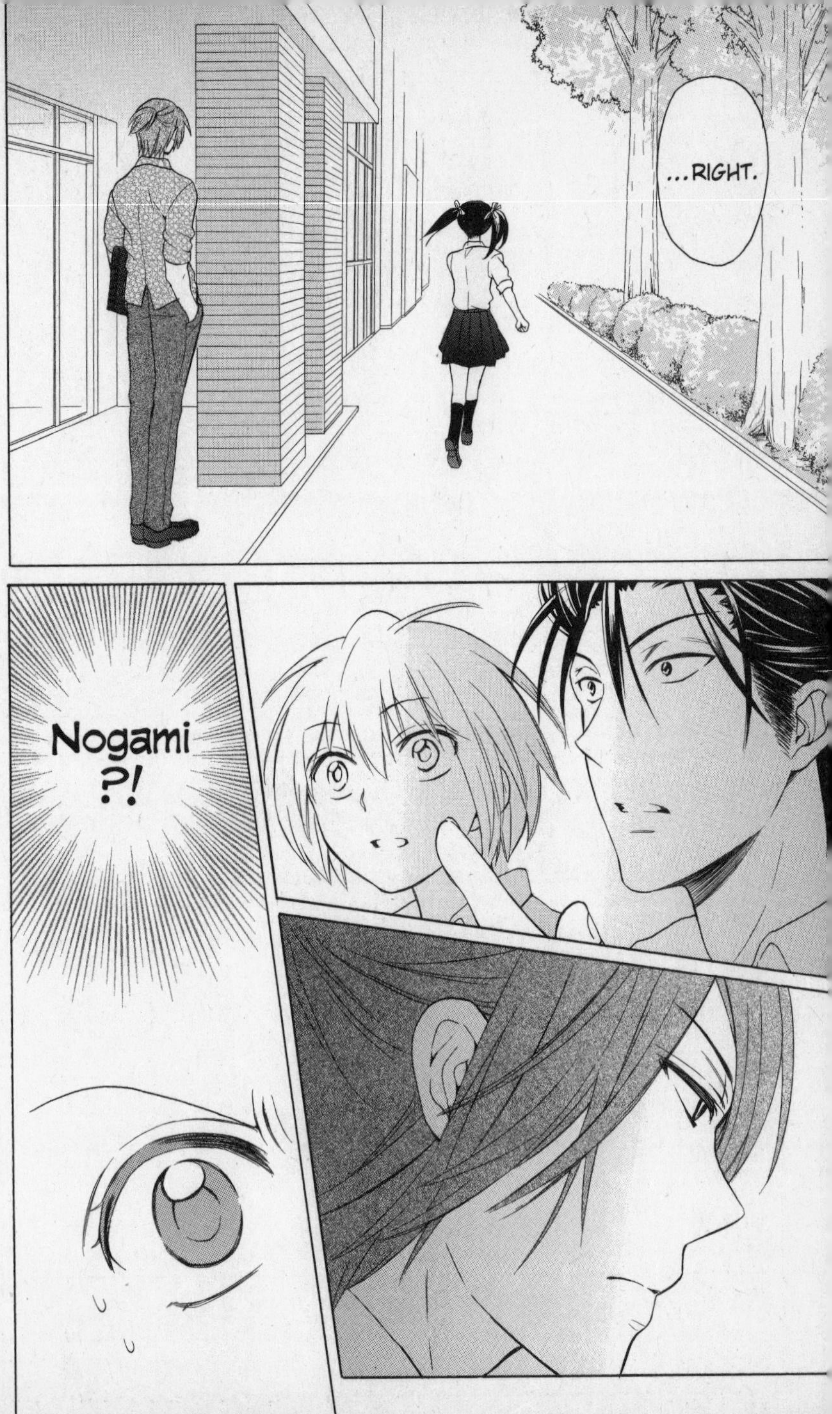
...RIGHT.
Nogami ?!

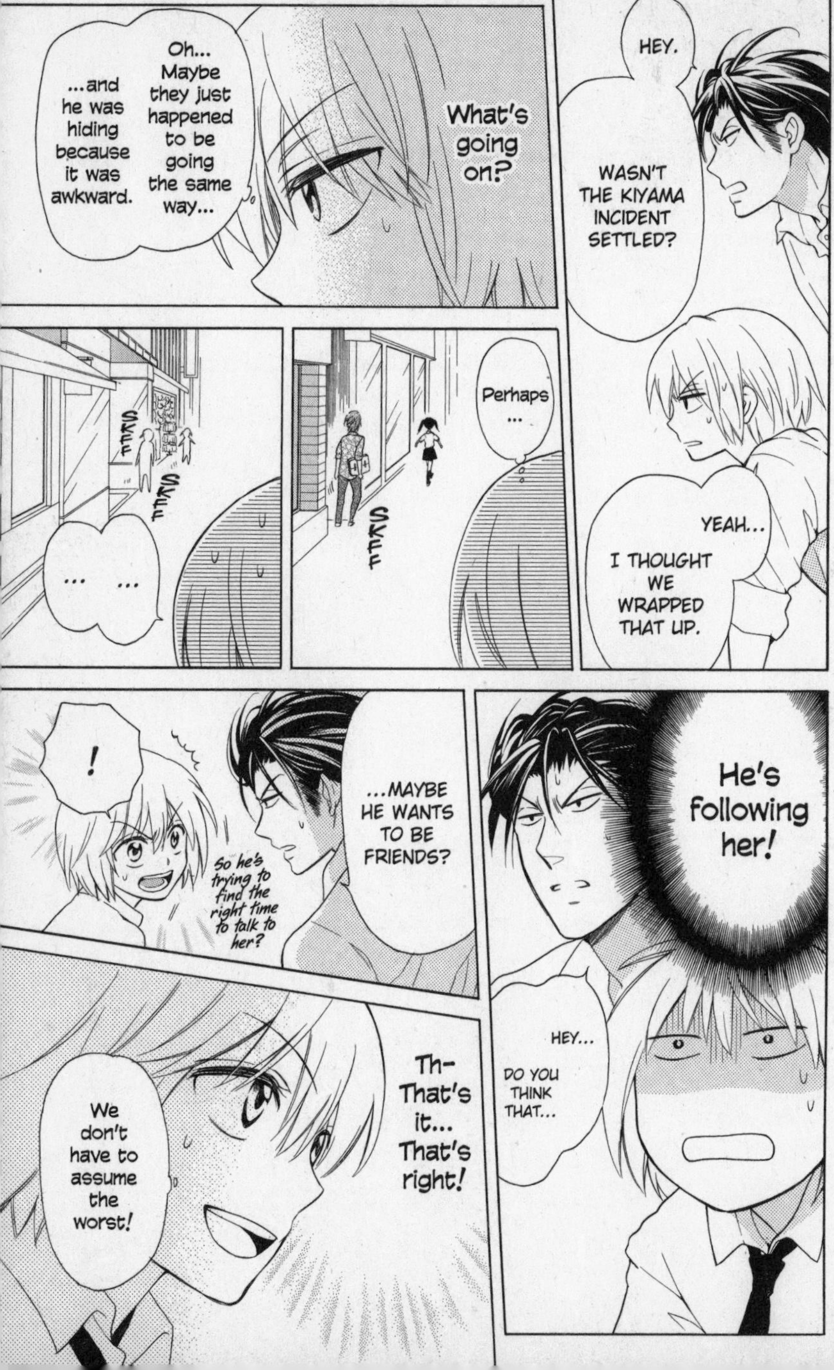
HEY.
WASN'T THE KIYAMA INCIDENT SETTLED?
YEAH... I THOUGHT WE WRAPPED THAT UP.
What's going on?
Oh... Maybe they just happened to be going the same way...
...and he was hiding because it was awkward.
Perhaps...
SKFF
SKFF
SKFF
... ...
He's following her!
HEY... DO YOU THINK THAT...
...MAYBE HE WANTS TO BE FRIENDS?
So he's trying to find the right time to talk to her?
!
Th- That's it... That's right!
We don't have to assume the worst!

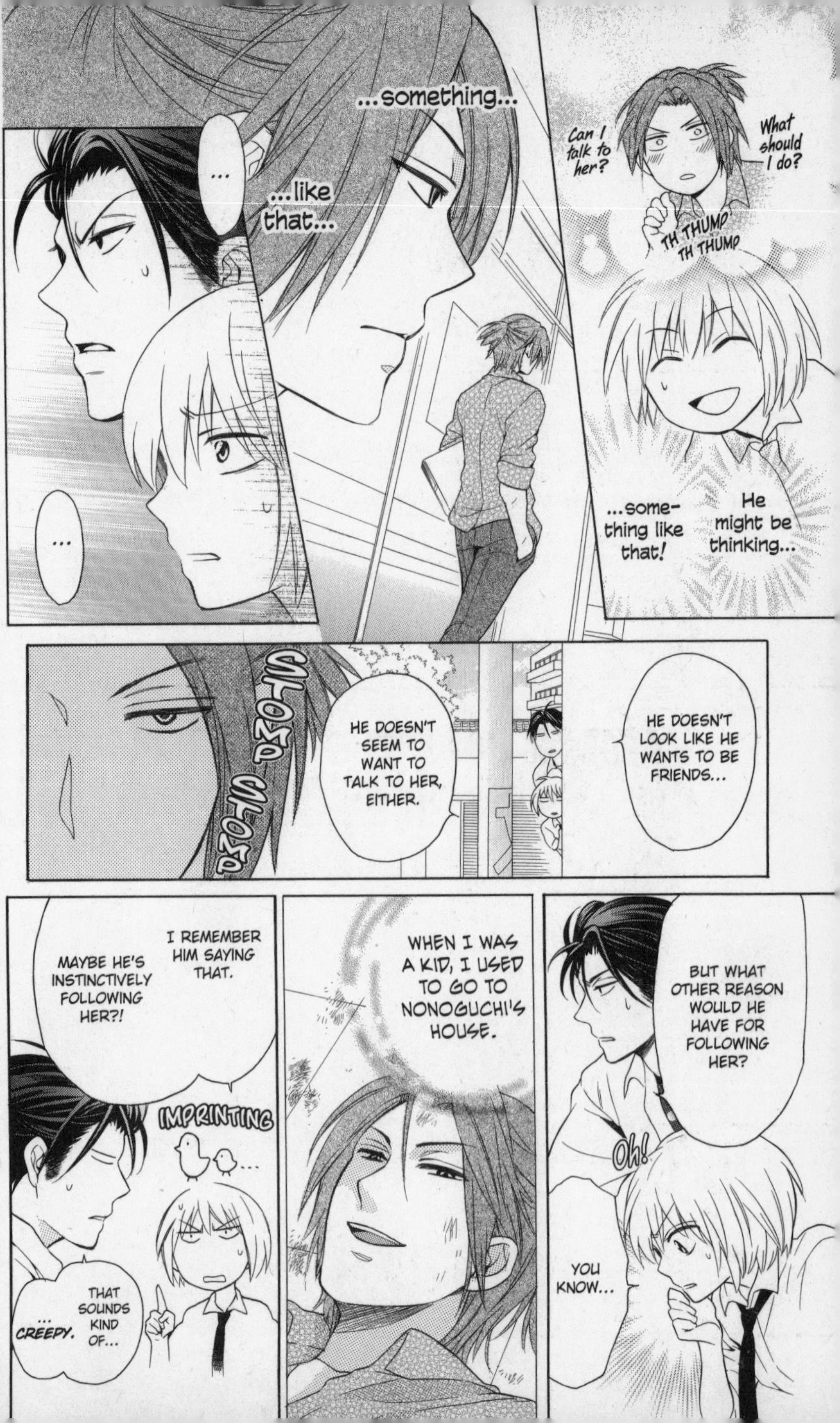
What should I do?
Can I talk to her?
TH THUMP TH THUMP
He might be thinking...
...something like that!
...something...
...like that...
...
...
HE DOESN'T LOOK LIKE HE WANTS TO BE FRIENDS...
HE DOESN'T SEEM TO WANT TO TALK TO HER, EITHER.
STOMP STOMP
BUT WHAT OTHER REASON WOULD HE HAVE FOR FOLLOWING HER?
Oh!
YOU KNOW...
WHEN I WAS A KID, I USED TO GO TO NONOGUCHI'S HOUSE.
I REMEMBER HIM SAYING THAT.
MAYBE HE'S INSTINCTIVELY FOLLOWING HER?!
IMPRINTING
THAT SOUNDS KIND OF...
...CREEPY.

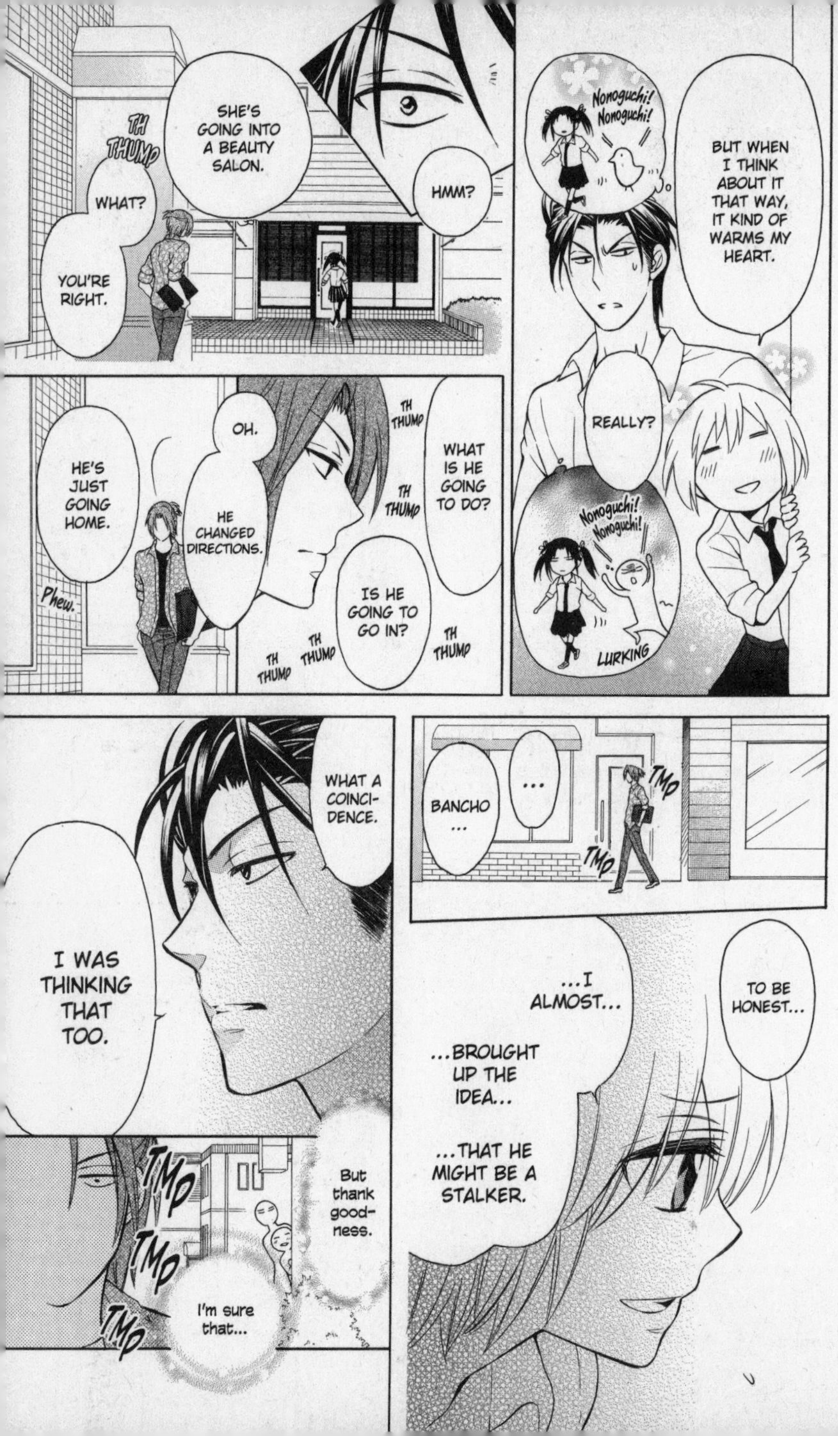
BUT WHEN I THINK ABOUT IT THAT WAY, IT KIND OF WARMS MY HEART.
Nonoguchi! Nonoguchi!
REALLY?
Nonoguchi! Nonoguchi!
LURKING
HMM?
SHE'S GOING INTO A BEAUTY SALON.
TH THUMP
WHAT?
YOU'RE RIGHT.
TH THUMP
WHAT IS HE GOING TO DO?
TH THUMP
IS HE GOING TO GO IN?
TH THUMP
TH THUMP
TH THUMP
OH.
HE CHANGED DIRECTIONS.
HE'S JUST GOING HOME.
Phew.
TMP
...
BANCHO ...
TMP
WHAT A COINCIDENCE.
I WAS THINKING THAT TOO.
TO BE HONEST...
...I ALMOST...
...BROUGHT UP THE IDEA...
...THAT HE MIGHT BE A STALKER.
But thank goodness.
TMP
TMP
TMP
I'm sure that...

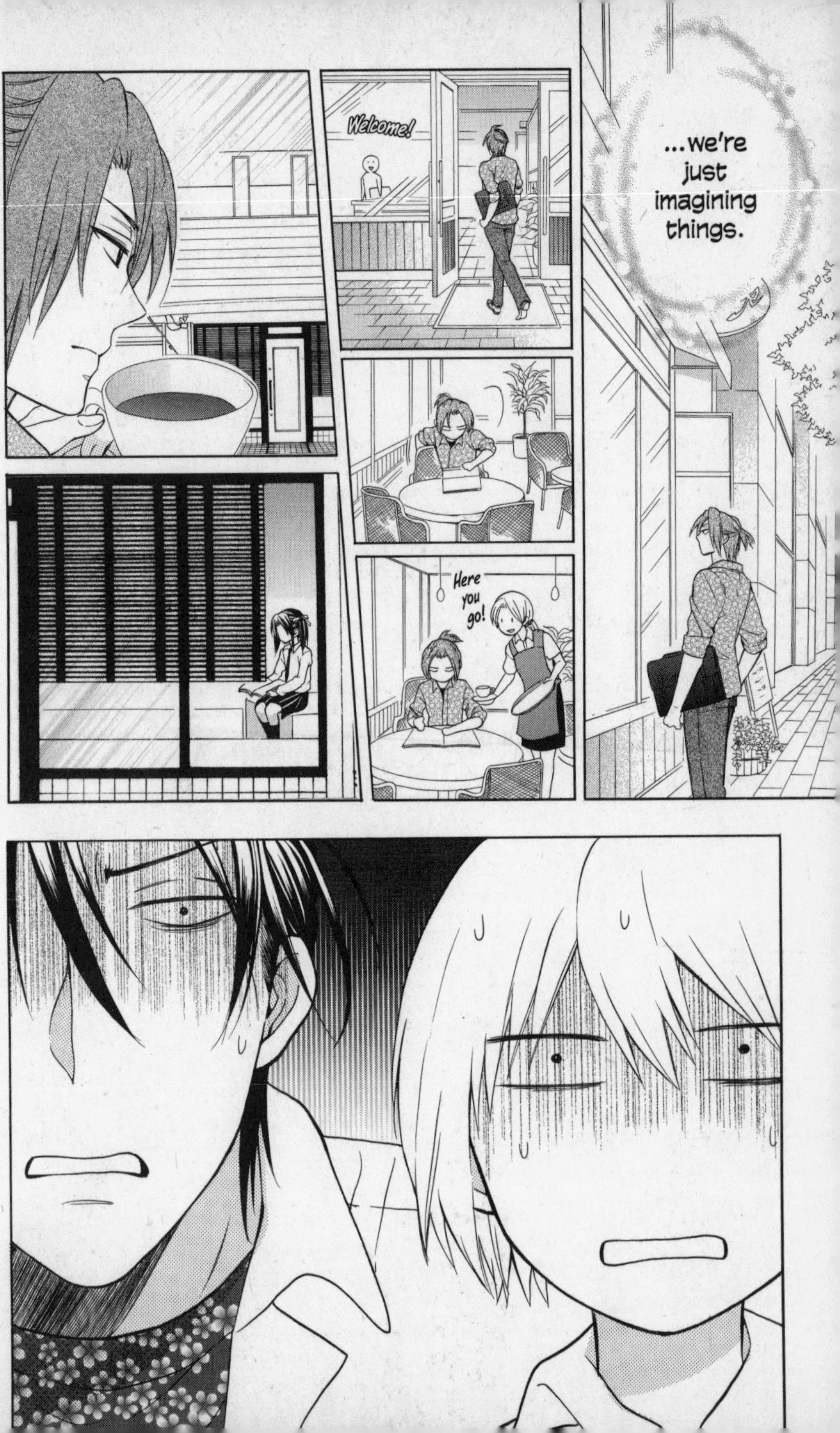
...we're just imagining things.
Welcome!
Here you go!

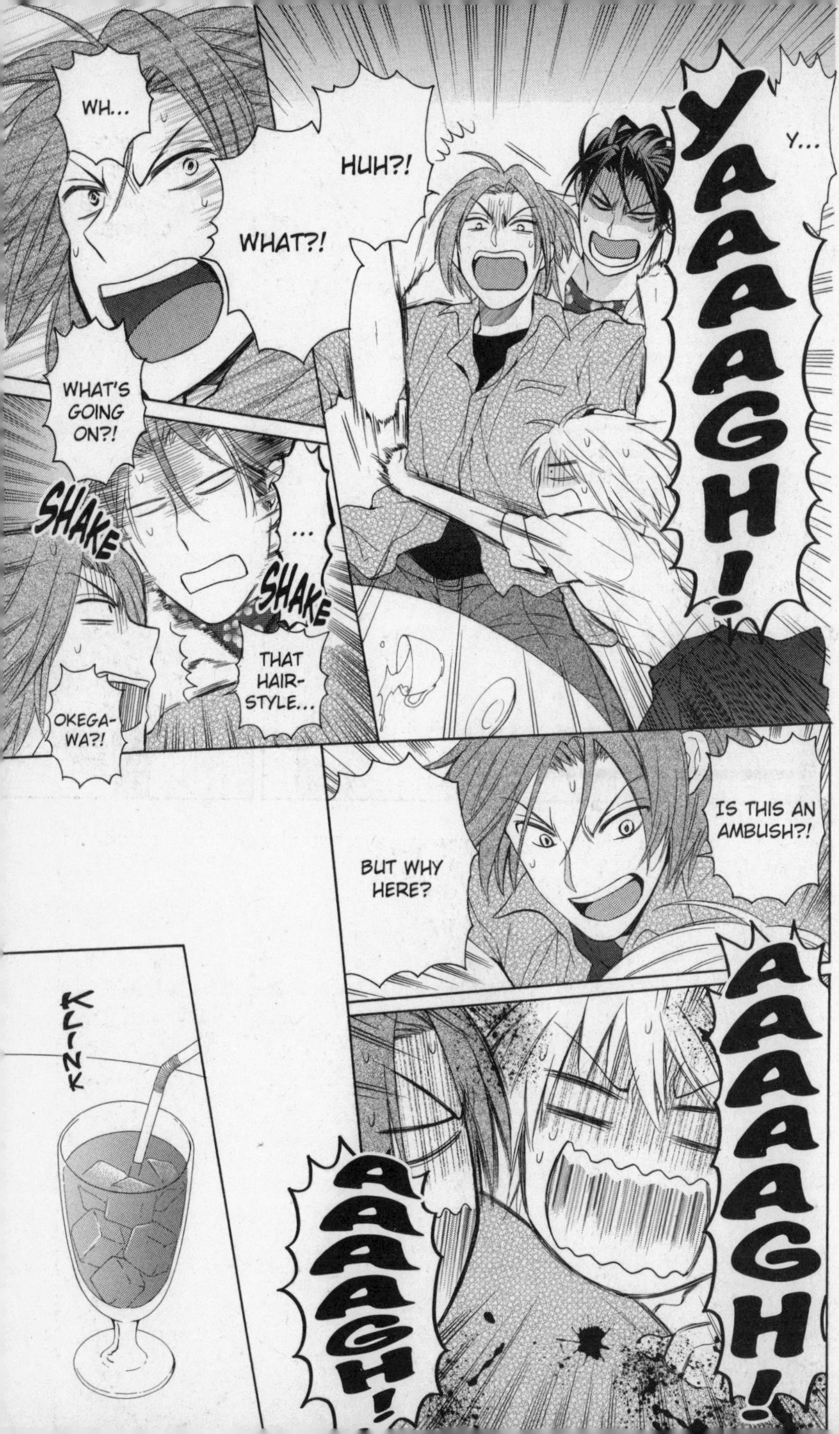

Y...
YAAAAGH!
HUH?!
WHAT?!
WH...
WHAT'S GOING ON?!
SHAKE
SHAKE
...
THAT HAIR-STYLE...
OKEGA-WA?!
IS THIS AN AMBUSH?!
BUT WHY HERE?
AAAAAGH!
AAAAAGH!
KLINK

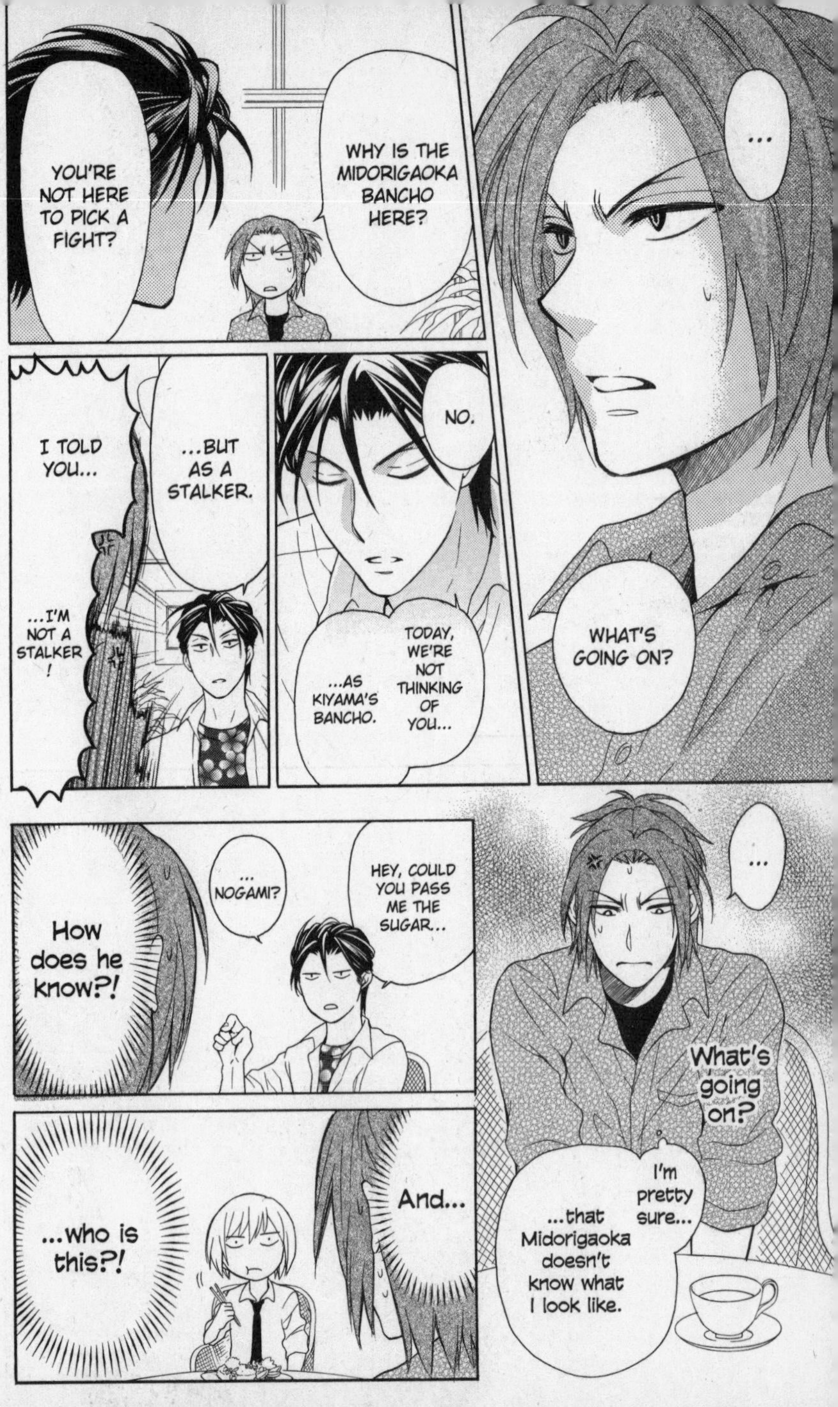
...
WHAT'S GOING ON?
WHY IS THE MIDORIGAOKA BANCHO HERE?
YOU'RE NOT HERE TO PICK A FIGHT?
NO.
TODAY, WE'RE NOT THINKING OF YOU...
...AS KIYAMA'S BANCHO.
...BUT AS A STALKER.
I TOLD YOU...
...I'M NOT A STALKER!
...
What's going on?
I'm pretty sure...
...that Midorigaoka doesn't know what I look like.
HEY, COULD YOU PASS ME THE SUGAR...
... NOGAMI?
How does he know?!
And...
...who is this?!

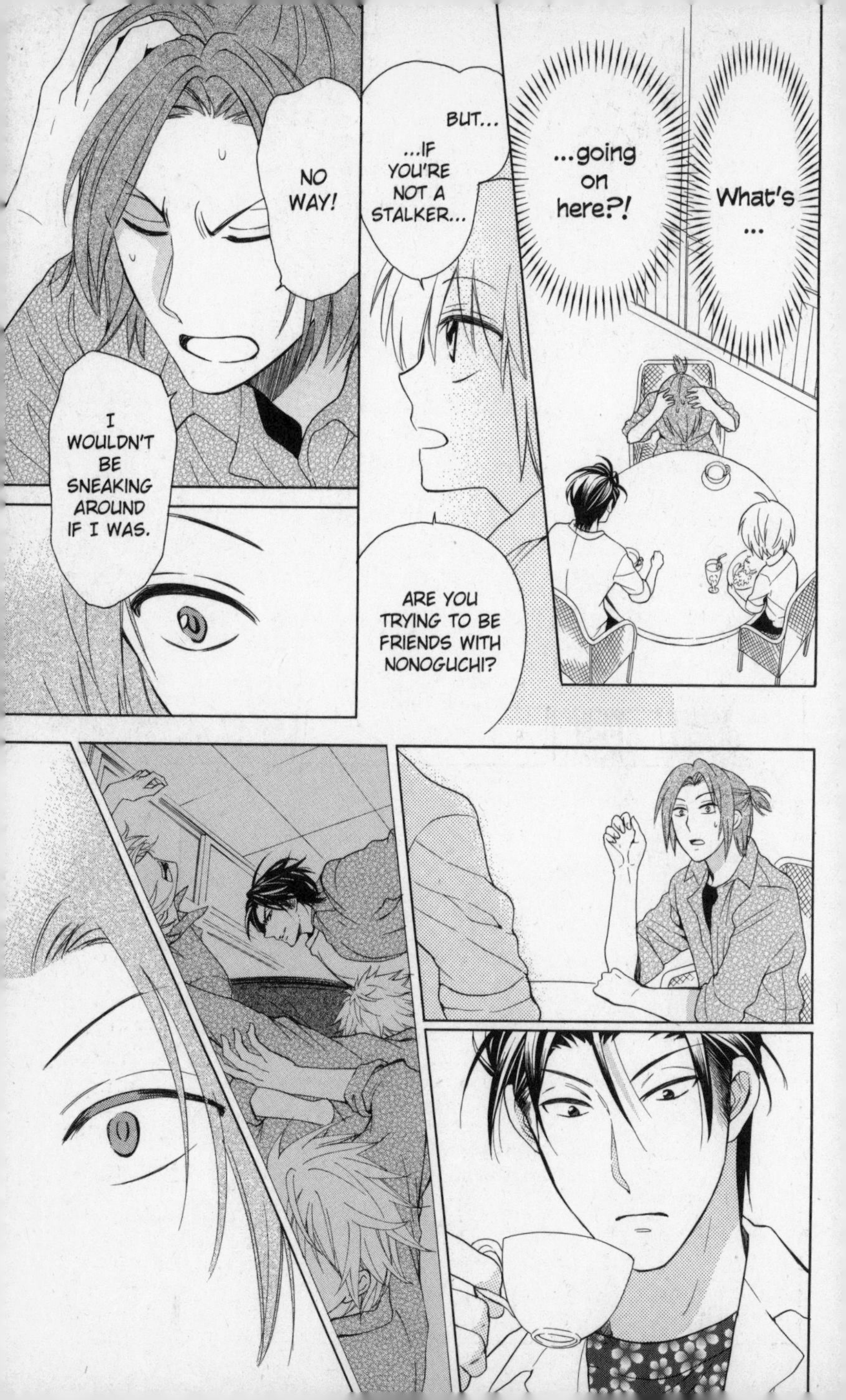
What's ...
...going on here?!
BUT...
...IF YOU'RE NOT A STALKER...
ARE YOU TRYING TO BE FRIENDS WITH NONOGUCHI?
NO WAY!
I WOULDN'T BE SNEAKING AROUND IF I WAS.

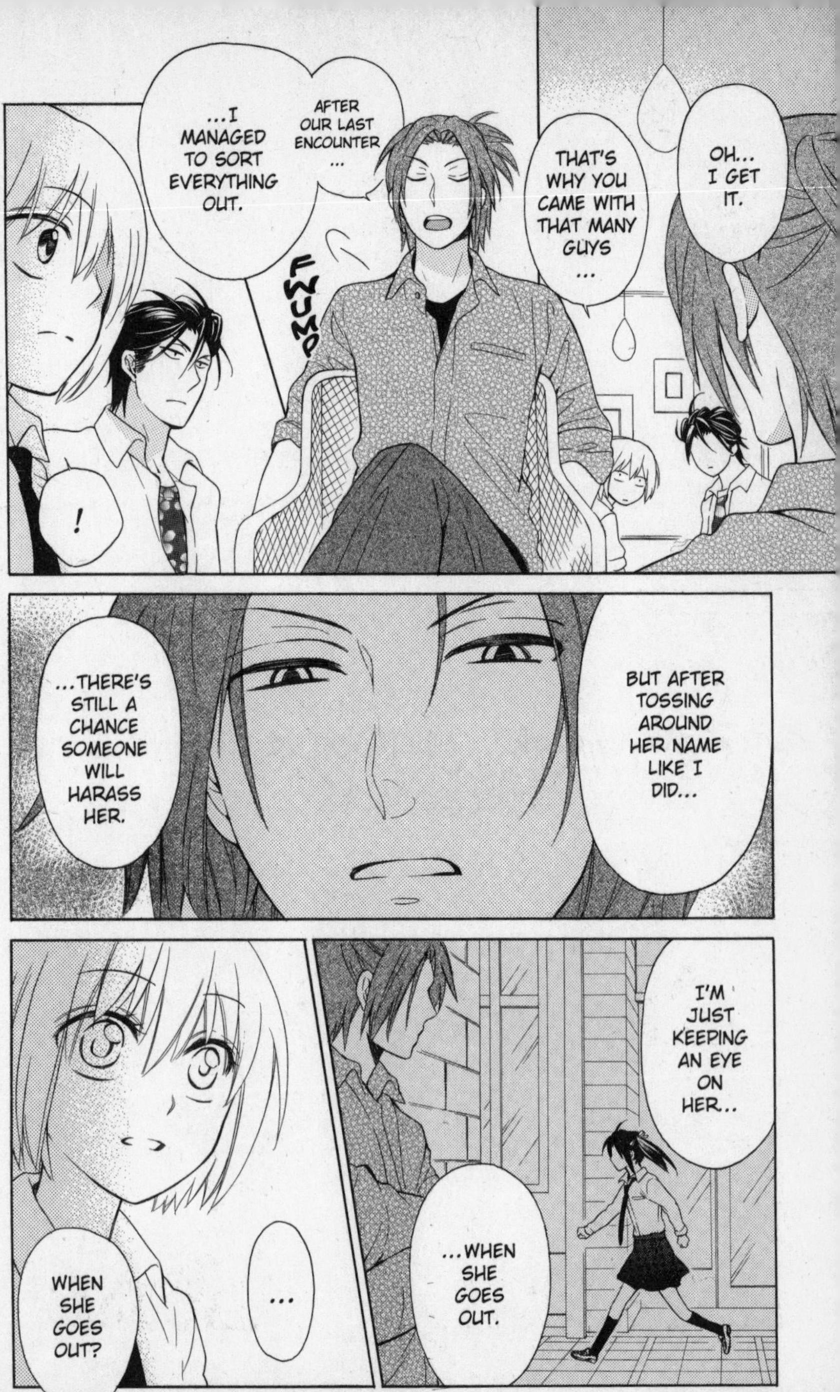
OH... I GET IT.
THAT'S WHY YOU CAME WITH THAT MANY GUYS ...
AFTER OUR LAST ENCOUNTER ...
...I MANAGED TO SORT EVERYTHING OUT.
FWUMP
!
BUT AFTER TOSSING AROUND HER NAME LIKE I DID...
...THERE'S STILL A CHANCE SOMEONE WILL HARASS HER.
I'M JUST KEEPING AN EYE ON HER...
...WHEN SHE GOES OUT.
...
WHEN SHE GOES OUT?

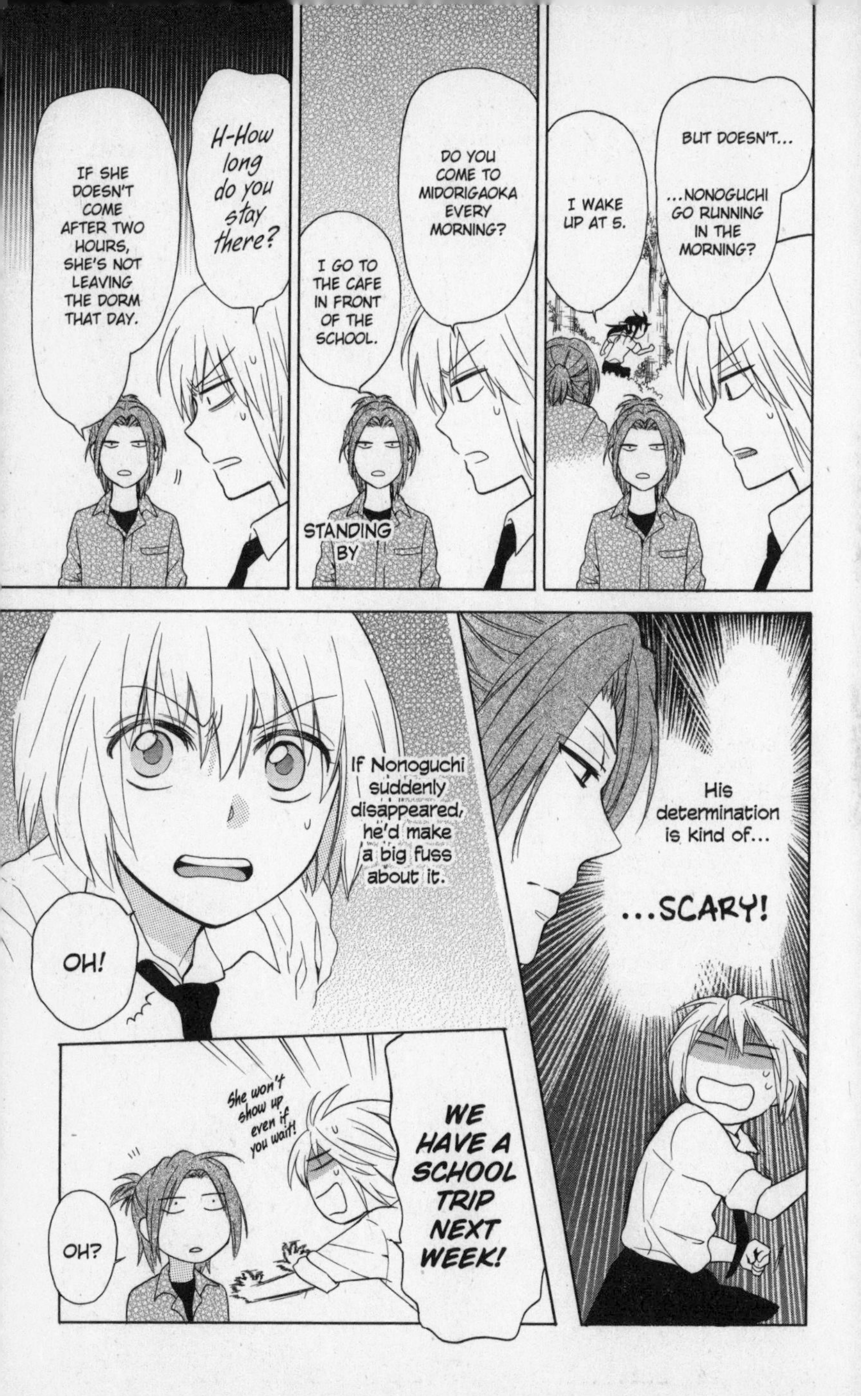
BUT DOESN'T...
...NONOGUCHI GO RUNNING IN THE MORNING?
I WAKE UP AT 5.
DO YOU COME TO MIDORIGAOKA EVERY MORNING?
I GO TO THE CAFE IN FRONT OF THE SCHOOL.
STANDING BY
H-How long do you stay there?
IF SHE DOESN'T COME AFTER TWO HOURS, SHE'S NOT LEAVING THE DORM THAT DAY.
His determination is kind of...
...SCARY!
If Nonoguchi suddenly disappeared, he'd make a big fuss about it.
OH!
WE HAVE A SCHOOL TRIP NEXT WEEK!
She won't show up even if you wait!
OH?

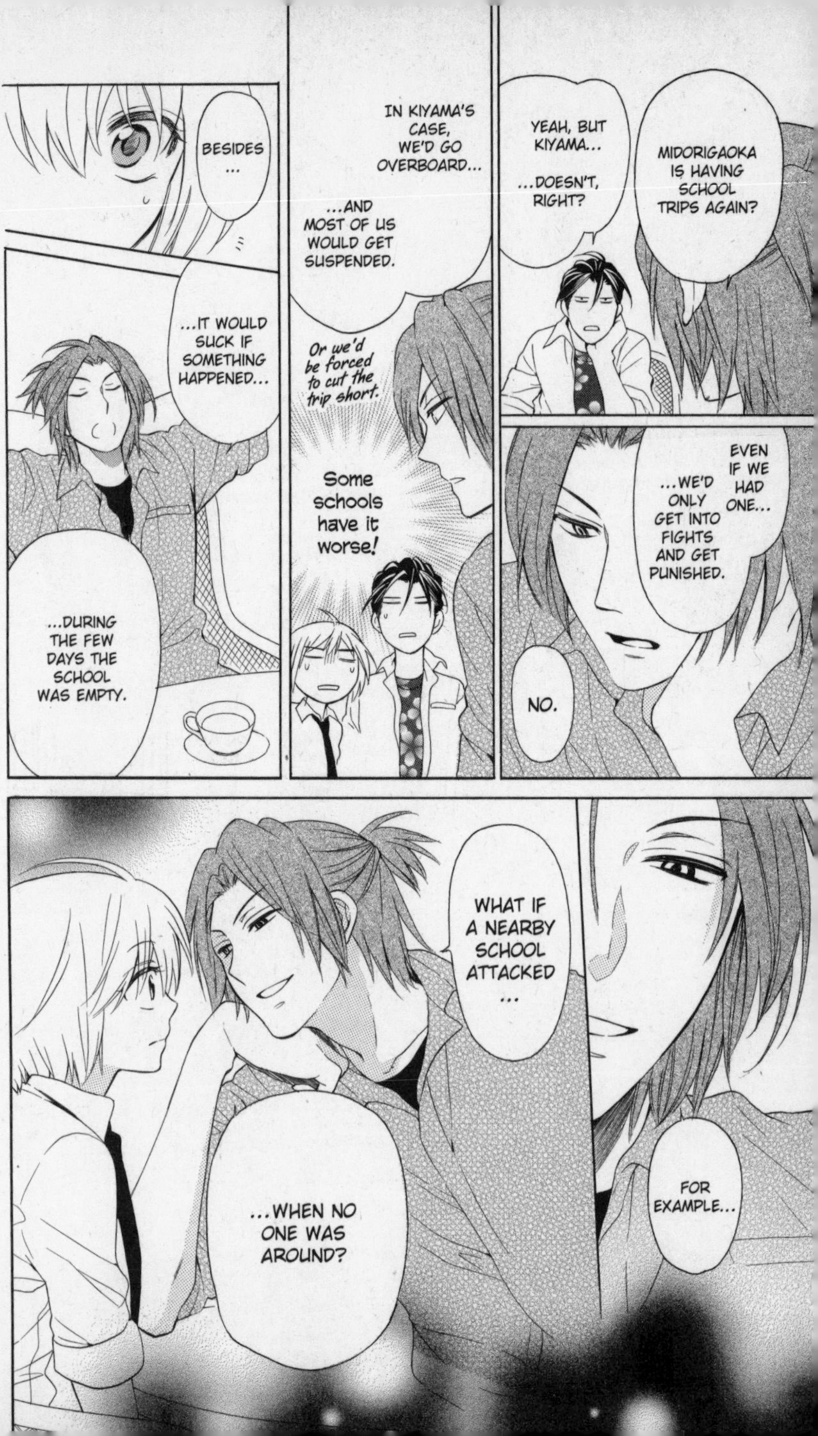
MIDORIGAOKA IS HAVING SCHOOL TRIPS AGAIN?
YEAH, BUT KIYAMA...
...DOESN'T, RIGHT?
EVEN IF WE HAD ONE...
...WE'D ONLY GET INTO FIGHTS AND GET PUNISHED.
NO.
IN KIYAMA'S CASE, WE'D GO OVERBOARD...
...AND MOST OF US WOULD GET SUSPENDED.
Or we'd be forced to cut the trip short.
Some schools have it worse!
BESIDES...
...IT WOULD SUCK IF SOMETHING HAPPENED...
...DURING THE FEW DAYS THE SCHOOL WAS EMPTY.
FOR EXAMPLE...
WHAT IF A NEARBY SCHOOL ATTACKED...
...WHEN NO ONE WAS AROUND?

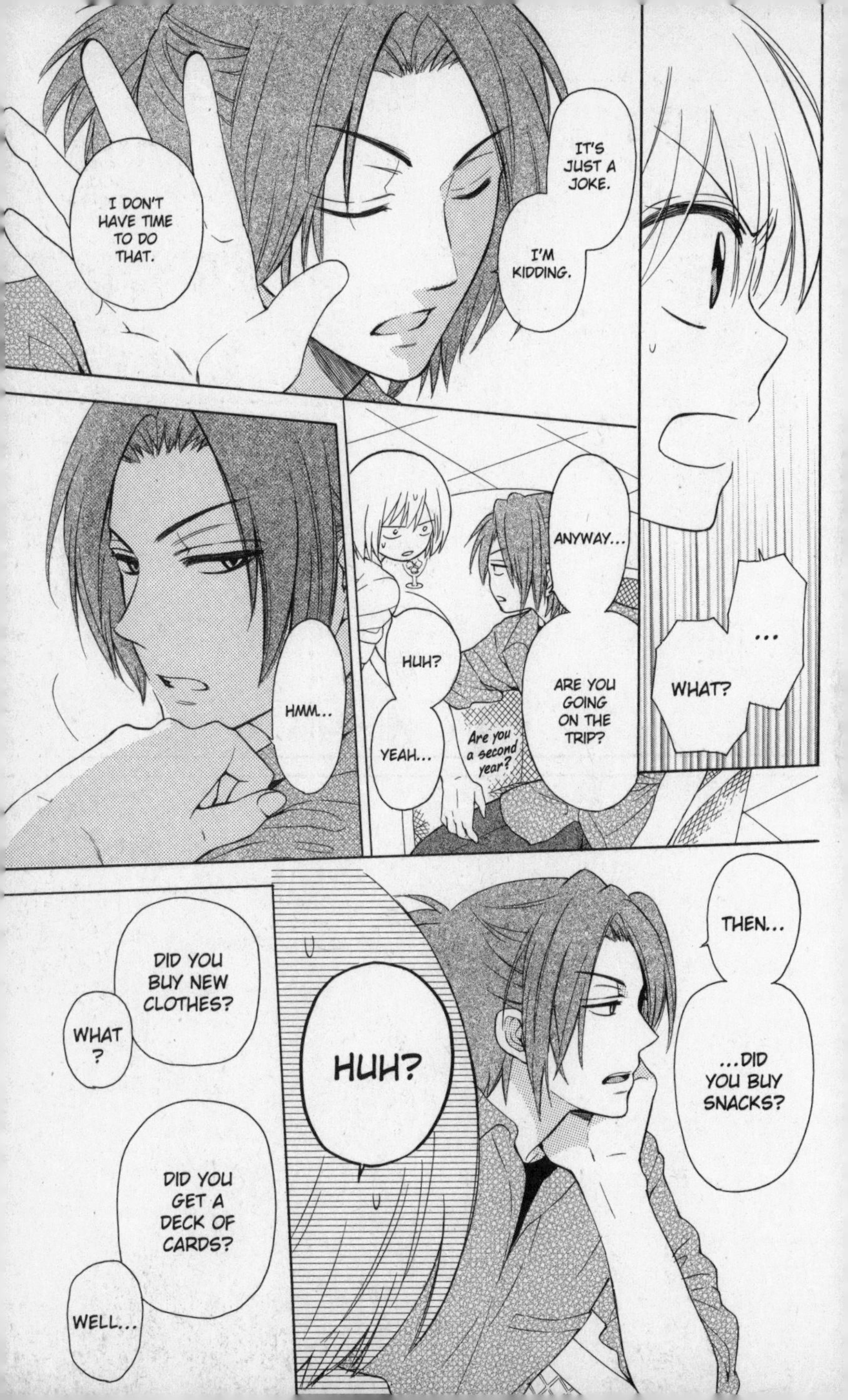
...
WHAT?
IT'S JUST A JOKE.
I'M KIDDING.
I DON'T HAVE TIME TO DO THAT.
ANYWAY...
ARE YOU GOING ON THE TRIP?
Are you a second year?
HUH?
YEAH...
HMM...
THEN...
...DID YOU BUY SNACKS?
HUH?
DID YOU BUY NEW CLOTHES?
WHAT?
DID YOU GET A DECK OF CARDS?
WELL...

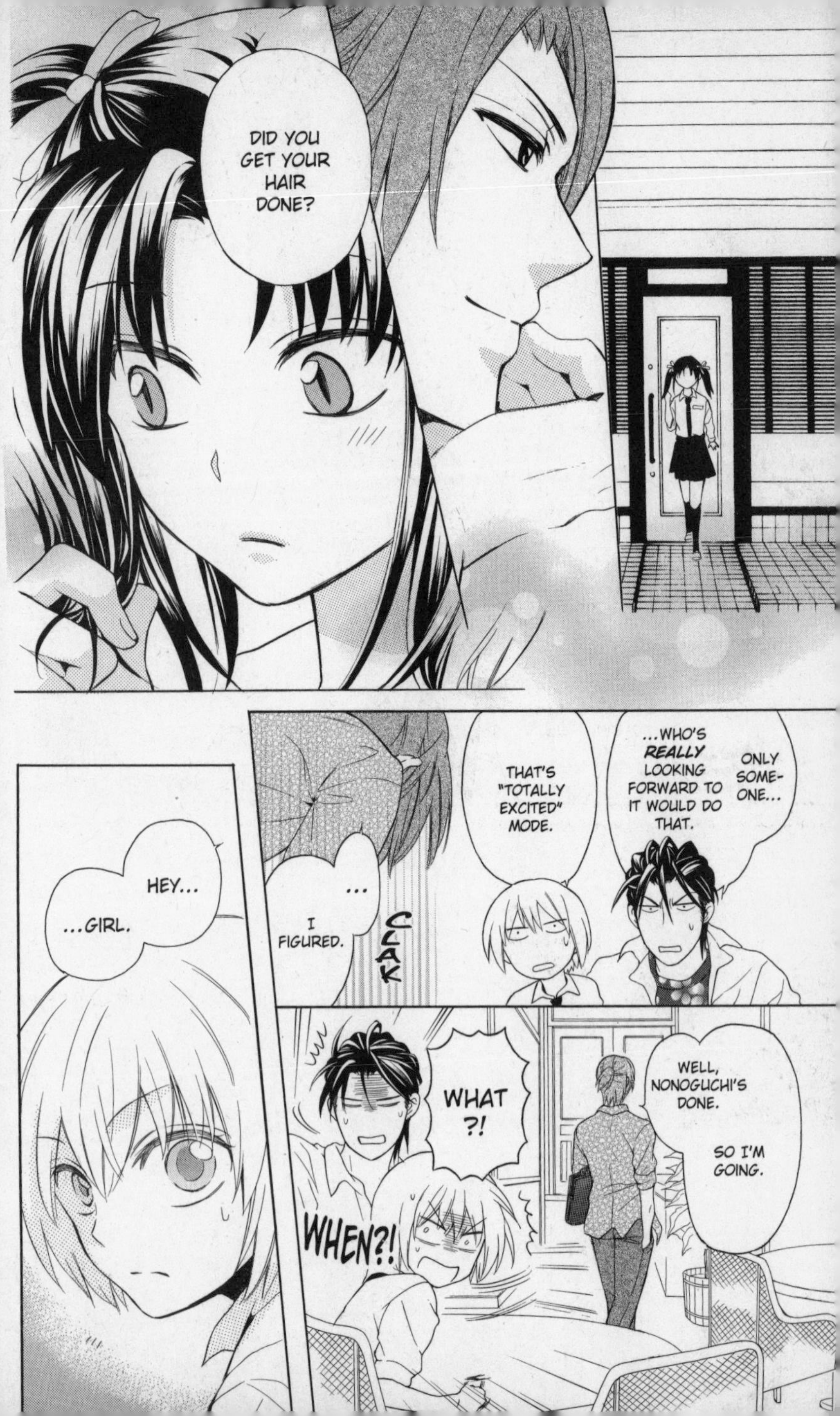
DID YOU GET YOUR HAIR DONE?
ONLY SOMEONE...
...WHO'S REALLY LOOKING FORWARD TO IT WOULD DO THAT.
THAT'S "TOTALLY EXCITED" MODE.
... I FIGURED.
CLAK
WELL, NONOGUCHI'S DONE.
SO I'M GOING.
WHAT?!
WHEN?!
HEY...
...GIRL.

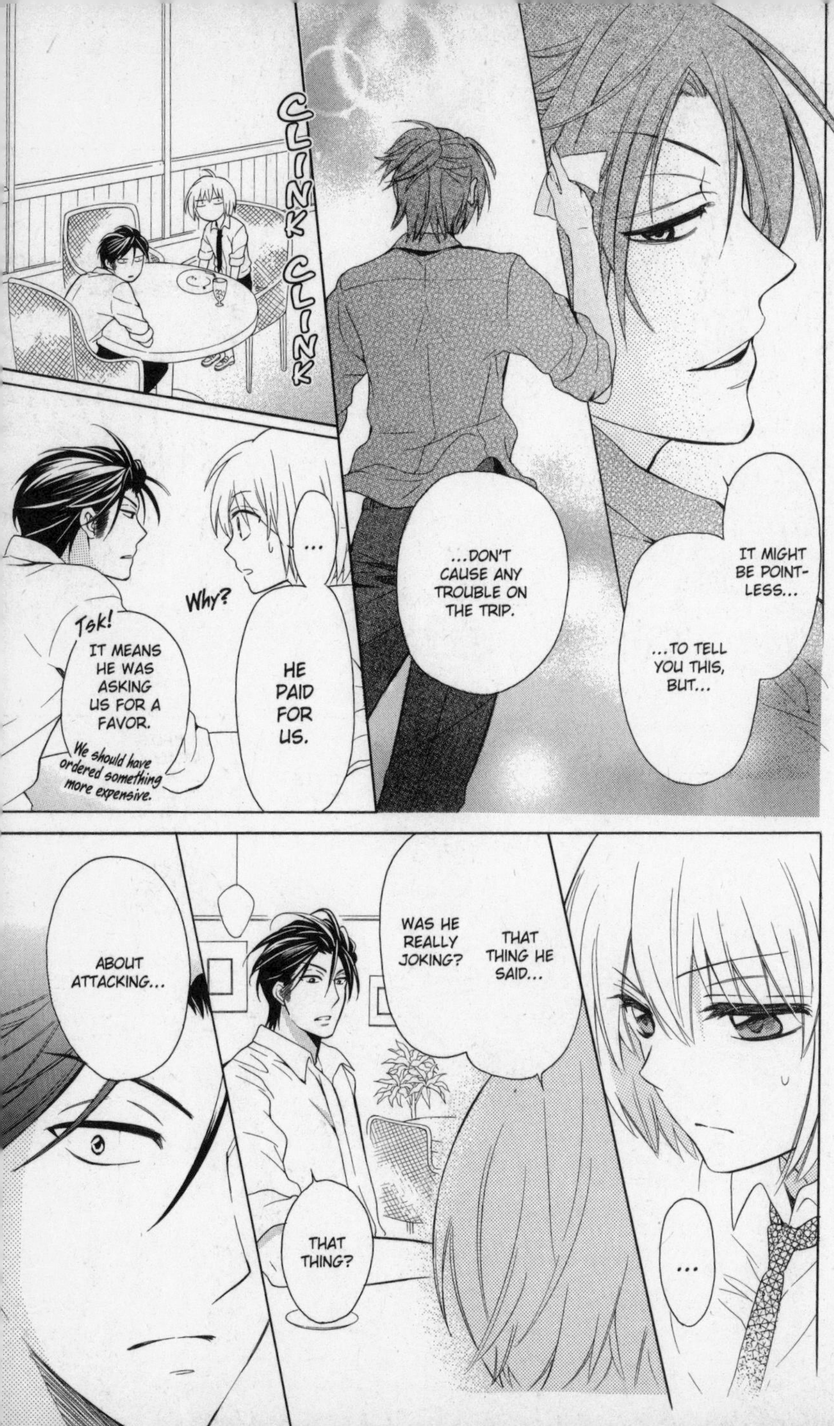
IT MIGHT BE POINT-LESS...
...TO TELL YOU THIS, BUT...
...DON'T CAUSE ANY TROUBLE ON THE TRIP.
CLINK CLINK
...
Why?
HE PAID FOR US.
Tsk!
IT MEANS HE WAS ASKING US FOR A FAVOR.
We should have ordered something more expensive.
...
THAT THING HE SAID...
WAS HE REALLY JOKING?
THAT THING?
ABOUT ATTACKING...

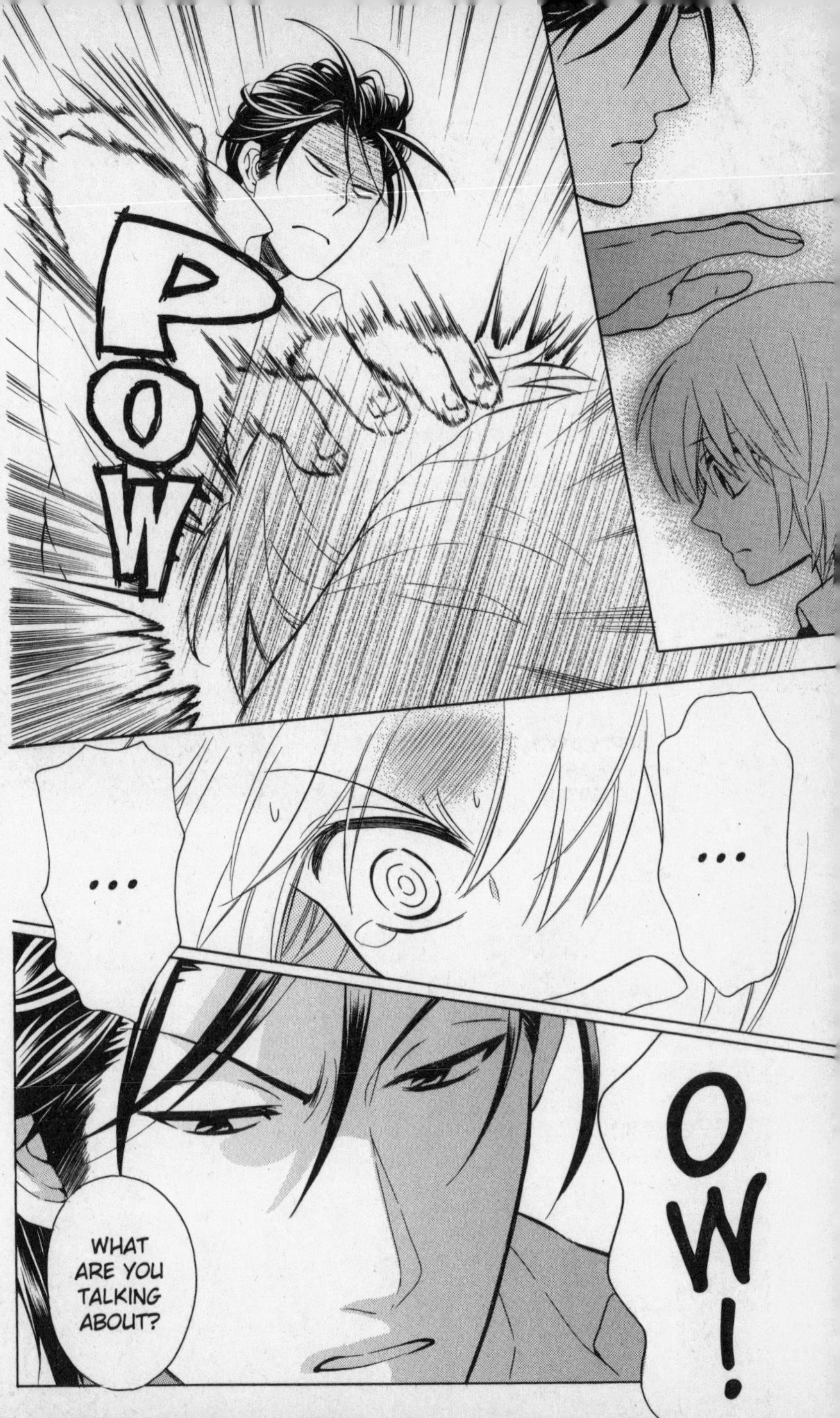
POW
...
...
OW!
WHAT ARE YOU TALKING ABOUT?

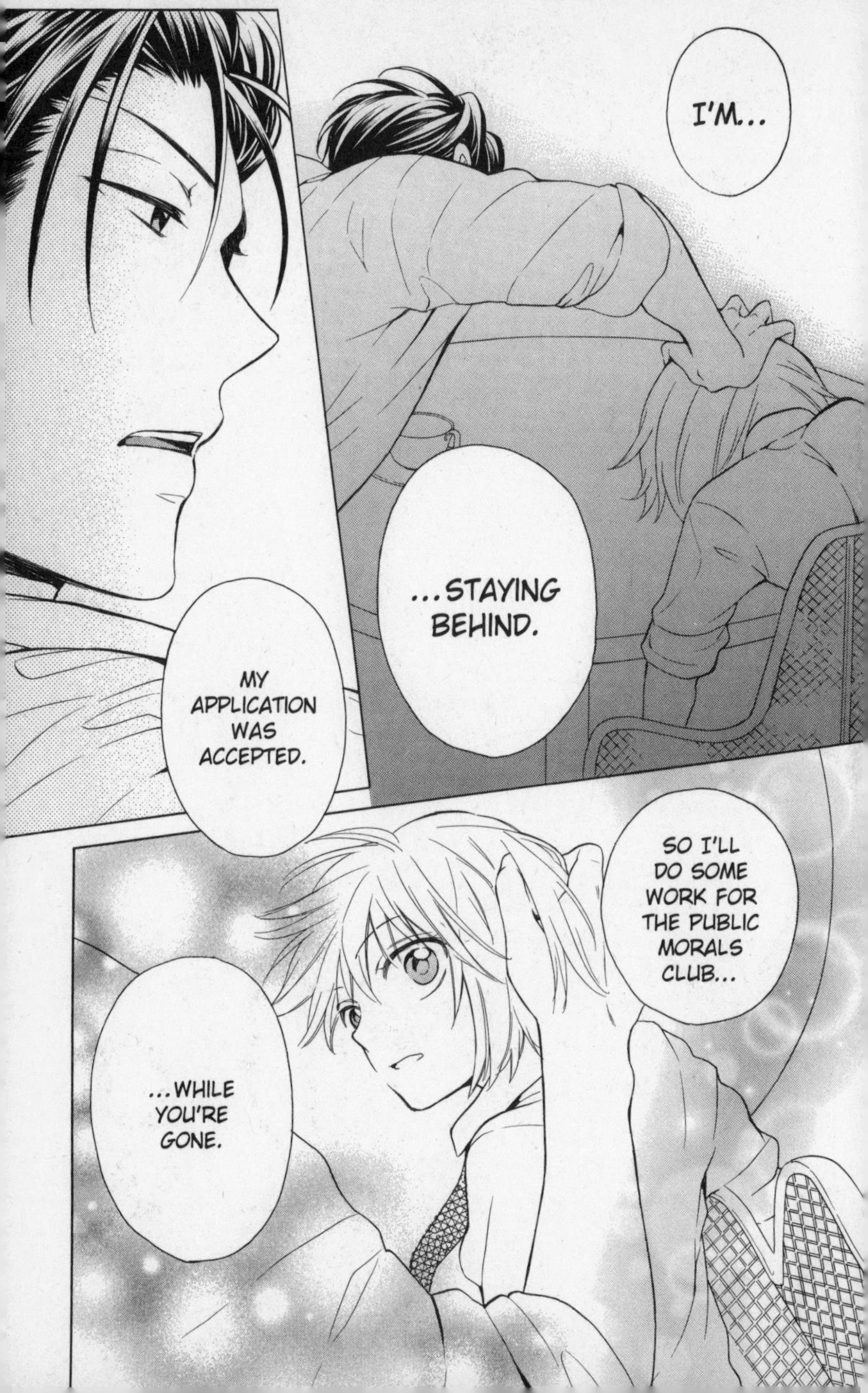
I'M...
...STAYING BEHIND.
MY APPLICATION WAS ACCEPTED.
SO I'LL DO SOME WORK FOR THE PUBLIC MORALS CLUB...
...WHILE YOU'RE GONE.

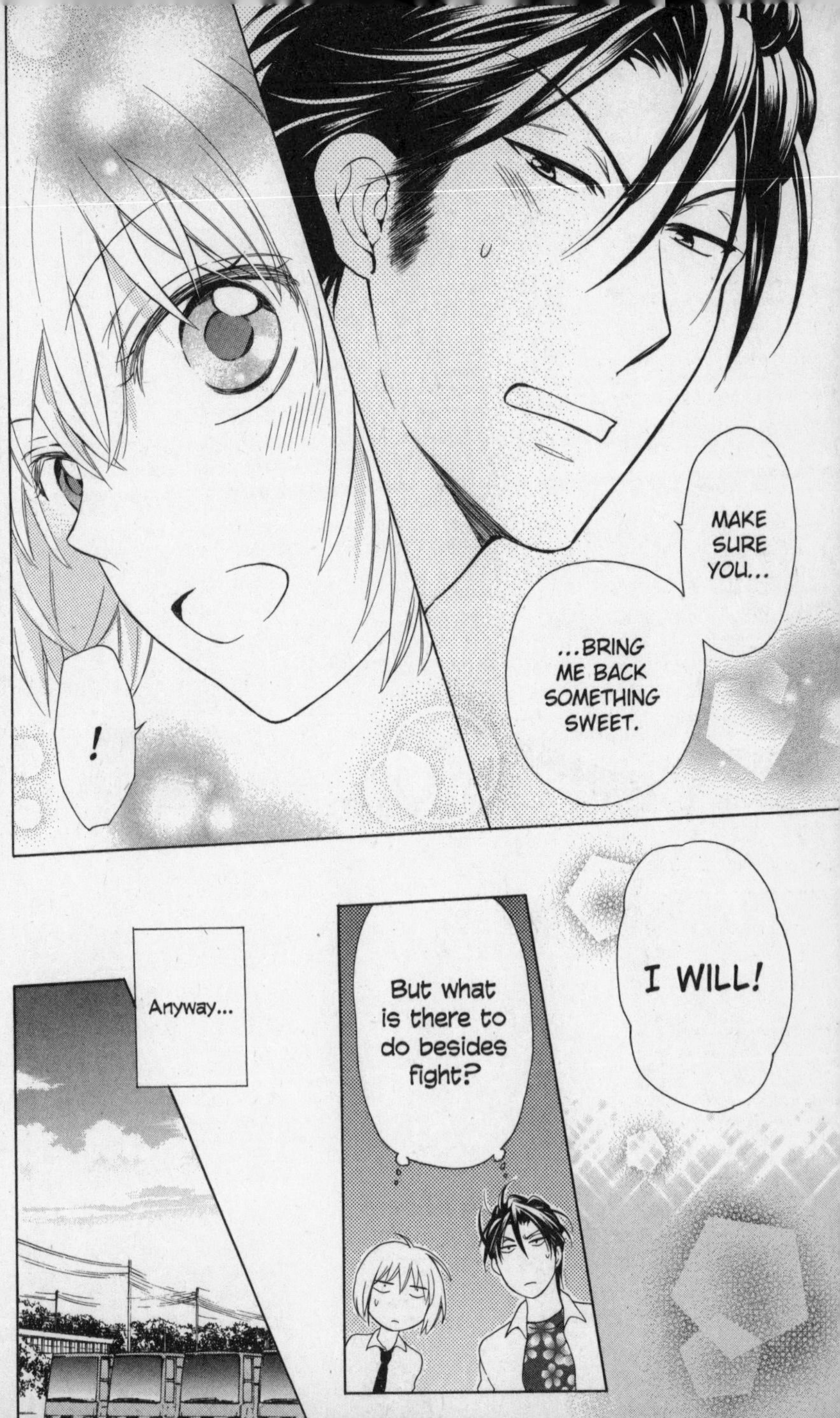
MAKE SURE YOU...
...BRING ME BACK SOMETHING SWEET.
!
I WILL!
But what is there to do besides fight?
Anyway...

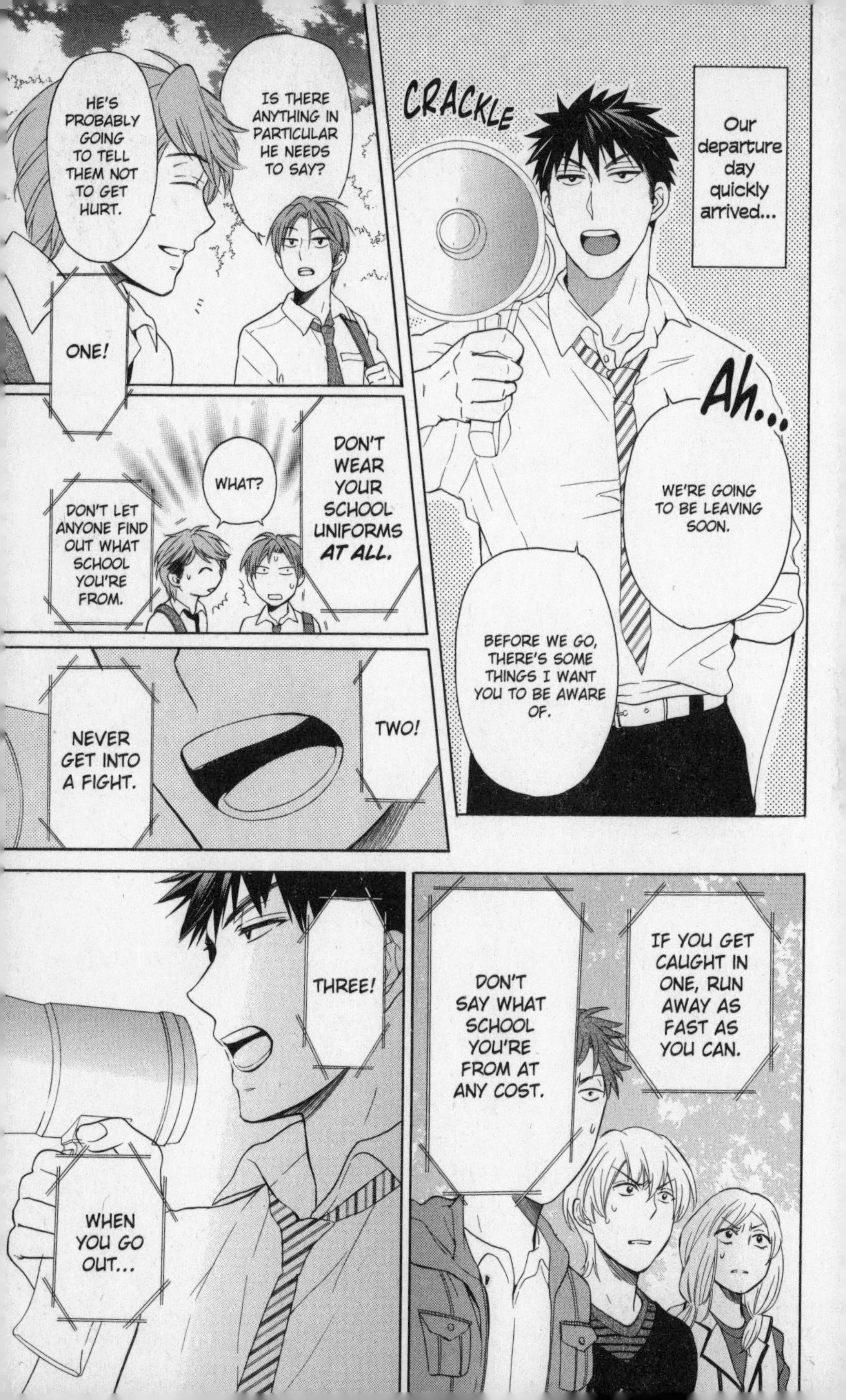

Our departure day quickly arrived...
CRACKLE
Ah...
WE'RE GOING TO BE LEAVING SOON.
BEFORE WE GO, THERE'S SOME THINGS I WANT YOU TO BE AWARE OF.
IS THERE ANYTHING IN PARTICULAR HE NEEDS TO SAY?
HE'S PROBABLY GOING TO TELL THEM NOT TO GET HURT.
ONE!
DON'T WEAR YOUR SCHOOL UNIFORMS AT ALL.
WHAT?
DON'T LET ANYONE FIND OUT WHAT SCHOOL YOU'RE FROM.
TWO!
NEVER GET INTO A FIGHT.
IF YOU GET CAUGHT IN ONE, RUN AWAY AS FAST AS YOU CAN.
DON'T SAY WHAT SCHOOL YOU'RE FROM AT ANY COST.
THREE!
WHEN YOU GO OUT...

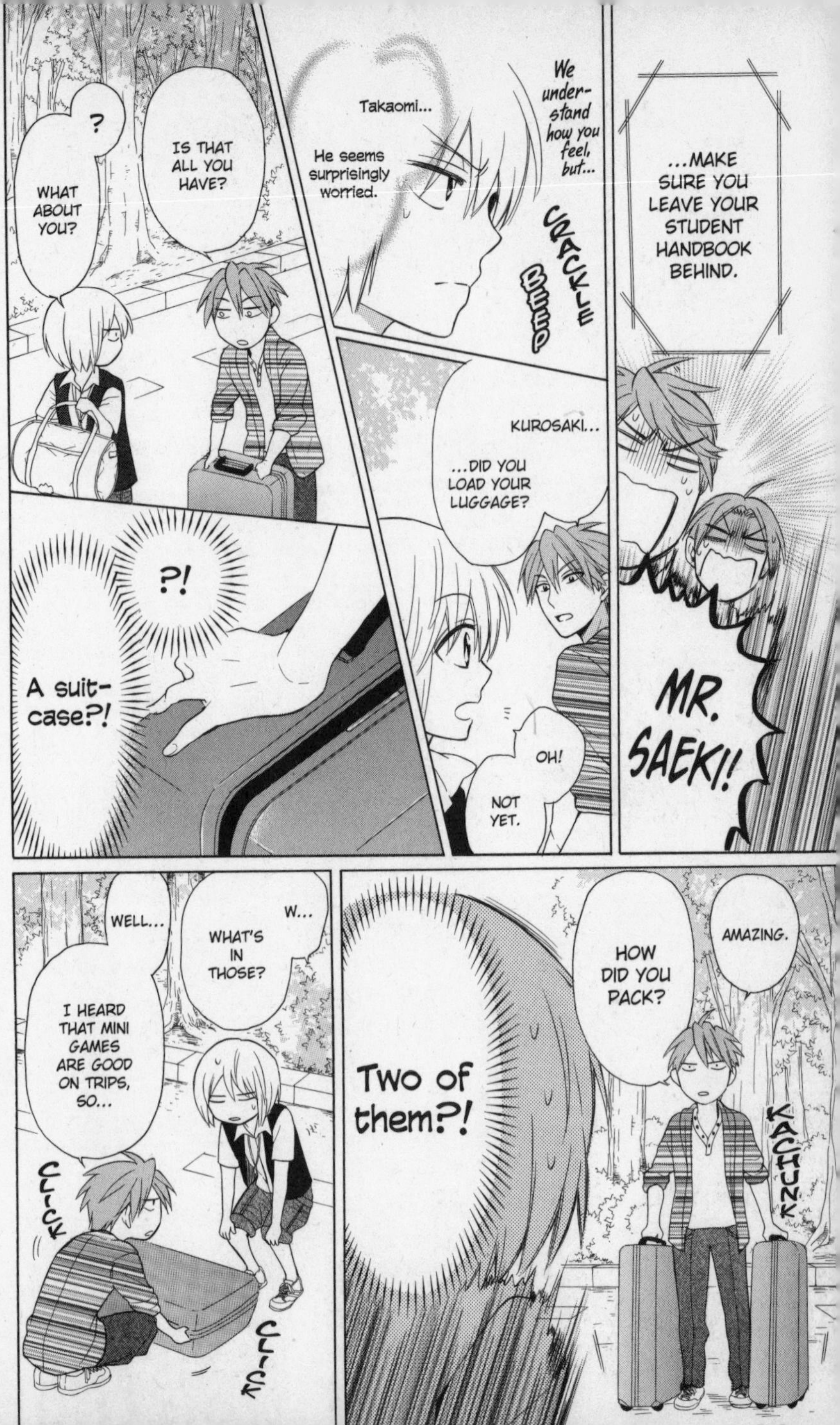
...MAKE SURE YOU LEAVE YOUR STUDENT HANDBOOK BEHIND.
MR. SAEKI!!
We understand how you feel, but...
CRACKLE
BEEP
Takaomi...
He seems surprisingly worried.
KUROSAKI...
...DID YOU LOAD YOUR LUGGAGE?
OH!
NOT YET.
IS THAT ALL YOU HAVE?
?
WHAT ABOUT YOU?
?!
A suit-case?!
AMAZING.
HOW DID YOU PACK?
KACHUNK
Two of them?!
W...
WHAT'S IN THOSE?
WELL...
I HEARD THAT MINI GAMES ARE GOOD ON TRIPS, SO...
CLICK
CLICK

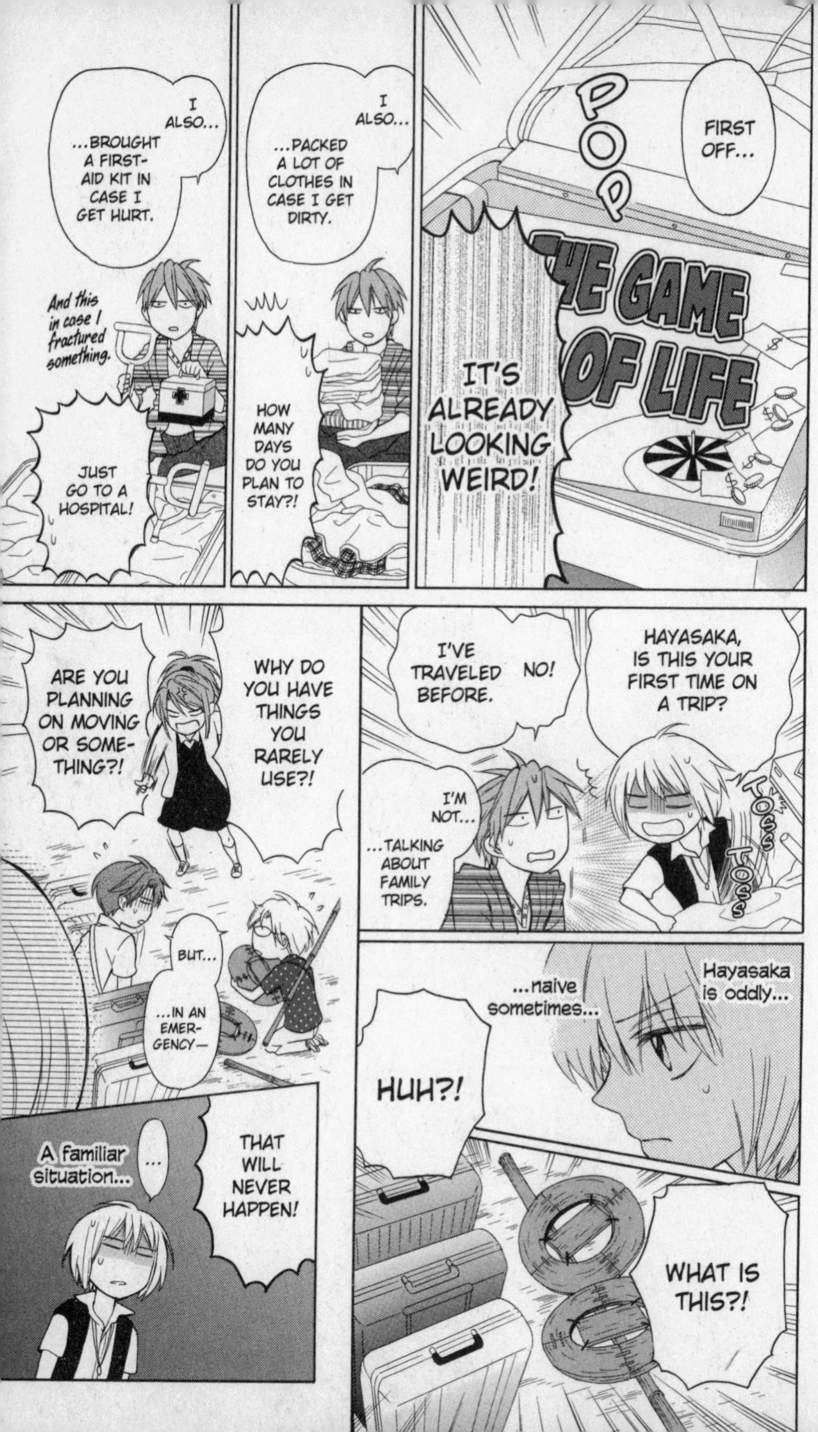
FIRST OFF...
POP
THE GAME OF LIFE
IT'S ALREADY LOOKING WEIRD!
I ALSO...
...PACKED A LOT OF CLOTHES IN CASE I GET DIRTY.
HOW MANY DAYS DO YOU PLAN TO STAY?!
I ALSO...
...BROUGHT A FIRST-AID KIT IN CASE I GET HURT.
And this in case I fractured something.
JUST GO TO A HOSPITAL!
HAYASAKA, IS THIS YOUR FIRST TIME ON A TRIP?
NO!
I'VE TRAVELED BEFORE.
TOSS TOSS
I'M NOT...
...TALKING ABOUT FAMILY TRIPS.
WHY DO YOU HAVE THINGS YOU RARELY USE?!
ARE YOU PLANNING ON MOVING OR SOME-THING?!
BUT...
...IN AN EMER-GENCY—
Hayasaka is oddly...
...naive sometimes...
HUH?!
WHAT IS THIS?!
THAT WILL NEVER HAPPEN!
...
A familiar situation...

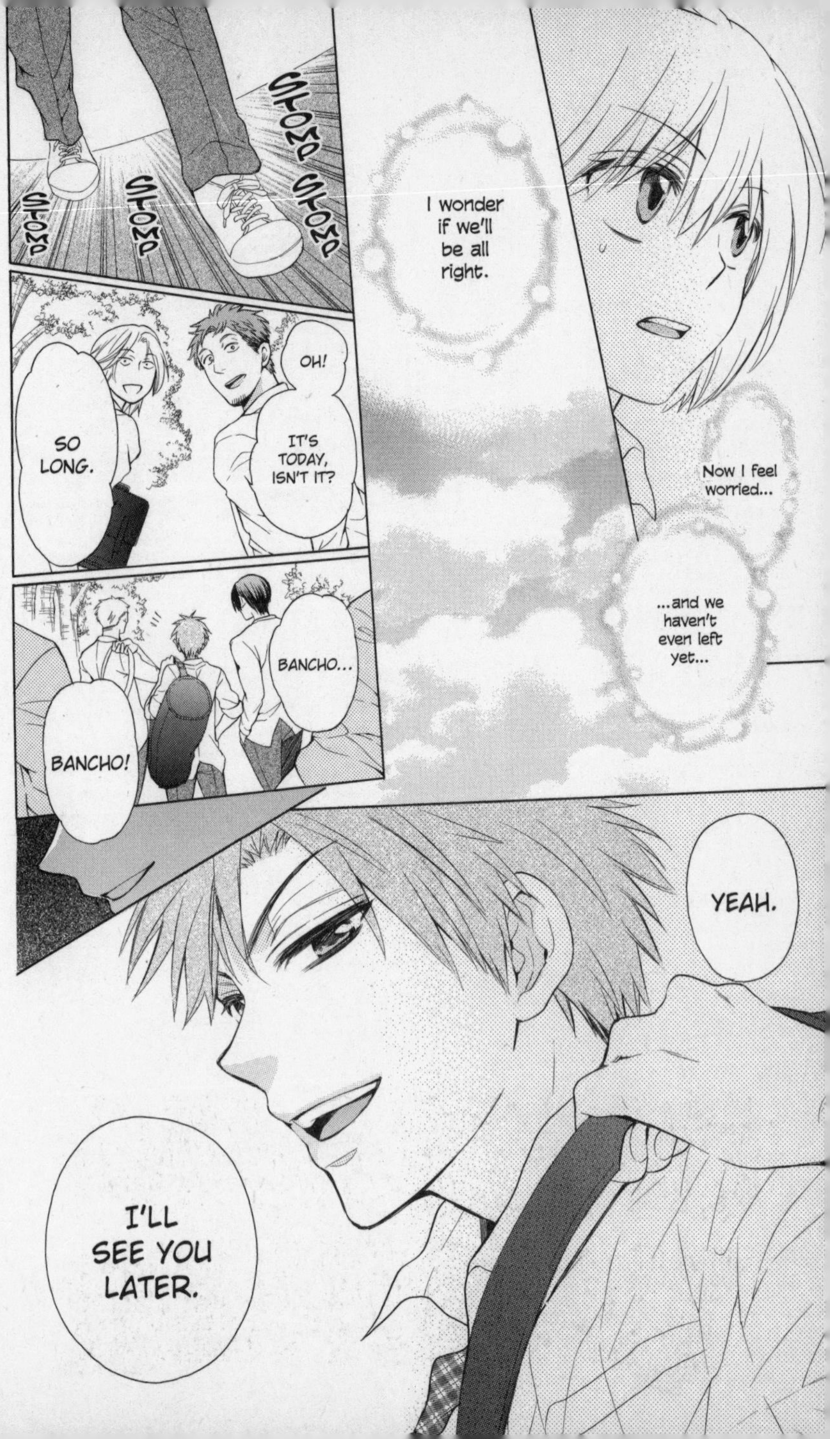
I wonder if we'll be all right.
Now I feel worried...
...and we haven't even left yet...
STOMP STOMP
STOMP
STOMP
OH!
IT'S TODAY, ISN'T IT?
SO LONG.
BANCHO...
BANCHO!
YEAH.
I'LL SEE YOU LATER.

ORESAMA TEACHER

CHARACTER RELATIONSHIPS

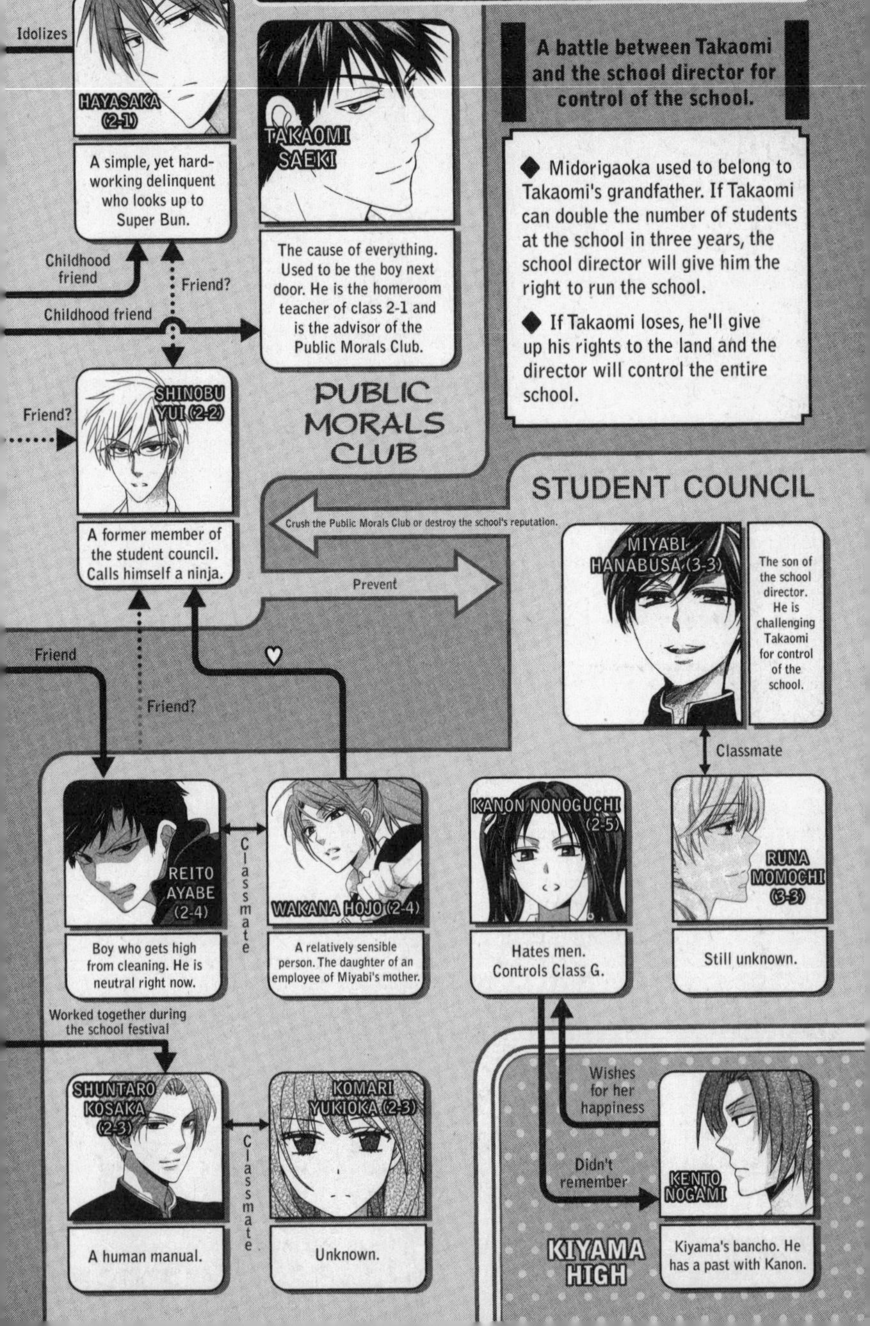
Idolizes
HAYASAKA (2-1)
A simple, yet hard-working delinquent who looks up to Super Bun.
TAKAOMI SAEKI
The cause of everything. Used to be the boy next door. He is the homeroom teacher of class 2-1 and is the advisor of the Public Morals Club.
A battle between Takaomi and the school director for control of the school.
◆ Midorigaoka used to belong to Takaomi's grandfather. If Takaomi can double the number of students at the school in three years, the school director will give him the right to run the school.
◆ If Takaomi loses, he'll give up his rights to the land and the director will control the entire school.
Childhood friend
Friend?
Childhood friend
Friend?
SHINOBU YUI (2-2)
A former member of the student council. Calls himself a ninja.
PUBLIC MORALS CLUB
STUDENT COUNCIL
Crush the Public Morals Club or destroy the school's reputation.
Prevent
MIYABI HANABUSA (3-3)
The son of the school director. He is challenging Takaomi for control of the school.
Friend
Friend?
♥
Classmate
REITO AYABE (2-4)
Boy who gets high from cleaning. He is neutral right now.
Classmate
WAKANA HOJO (2-4)
A relatively sensible person. The daughter of an employee of Miyabi's mother.
KANON NONOGUCHI (2-5)
Hates men. Controls Class G.
RUNA MOMOCHI (3-3)
Still unknown.
Worked together during the school festival
SHUNTARO KOSAKA (2-3)
A human manual.
Classmate
KOMARI YUKIOKA (2-3)
Unknown.
Wishes for her happiness
Didn't remember
KENTO NOGAMI
Kiyama's bancho. He has a past with Kanon.
KIYAMA HIGH

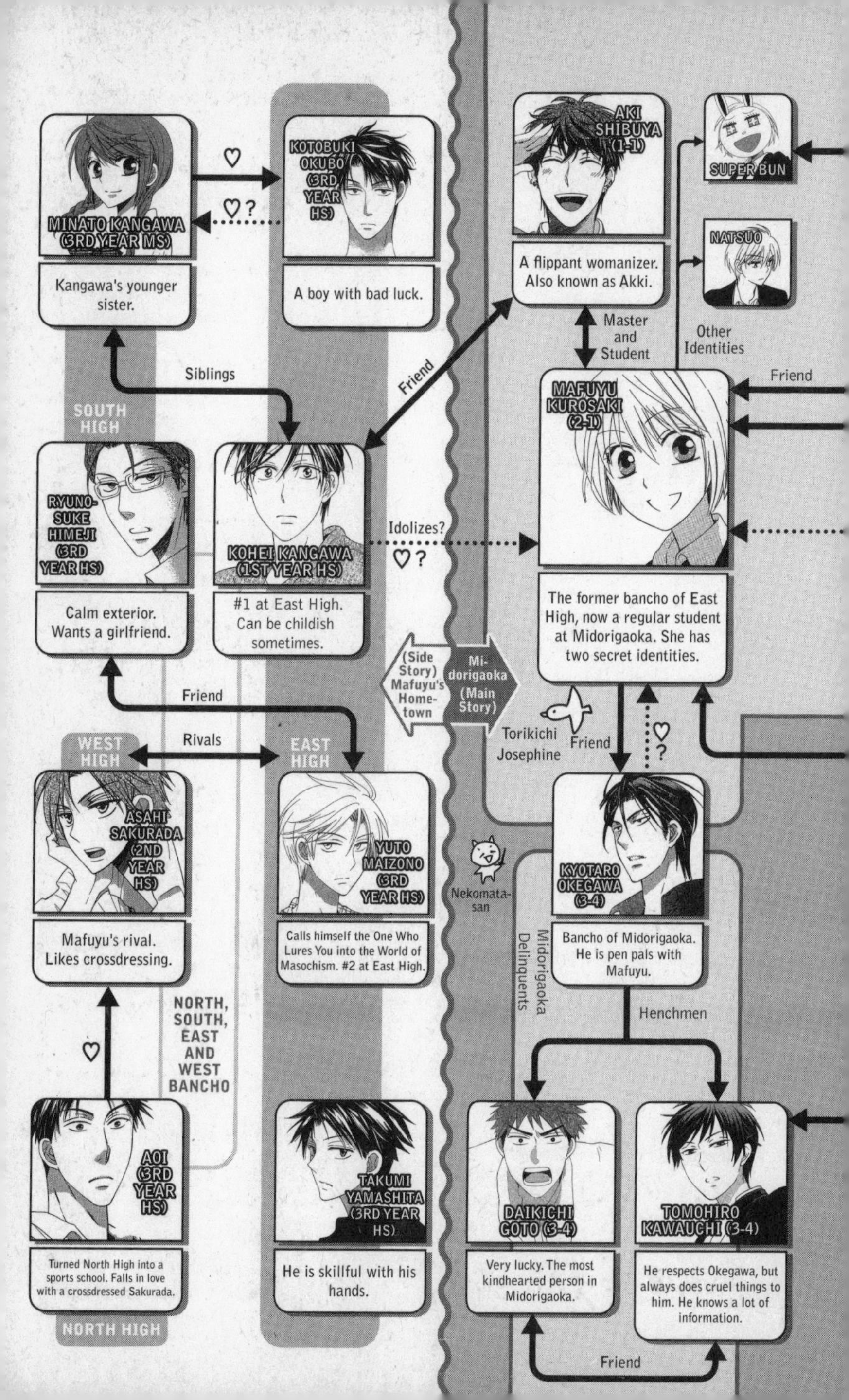
MINATO KANGAWA (3RD YEAR MS)
Kangawa's younger sister.
♡
♡?
KOTOBUKI OKUBO (3RD YEAR HS)
A boy with bad luck.
Siblings
SOUTH HIGH
RYUNOSUKE HIMEJI (3RD YEAR HS)
Calm exterior. Wants a girlfriend.
KOHEI KANGAWA (1ST YEAR HS)
#1 at East High. Can be childish sometimes.
Friend
Idolizes? ♡?
Friend
Rivals
WEST HIGH
EAST HIGH
ASAHI SAKURADA (2ND YEAR HS)
Mafuyu's rival. Likes crossdressing.
YUTO MAIZONO (3RD YEAR HS)
Calls himself the One Who Lures You into the World of Masochism. #2 at East High.
NORTH, SOUTH, EAST AND WEST BANCHO
♡
AOI (3RD YEAR HS)
Turned North High into a sports school. Falls in love with a crossdressed Sakurada.
TAKUMI YAMASHITA (3RD YEAR HS)
He is skillful with his hands.
NORTH HIGH
(Side Story) Mafuyu's Hometown
Midorigaoka (Main Story)
AKI SHIBUYA (1-1)
A flippant womanizer. Also known as Akki.
SUPER BUN
NATSUO
Other Identities
Master and Student
MAFUYU KUROSAKI (2-1)
Friend
The former bancho of East High, now a regular student at Midorigaoka. She has two secret identities.
Torikichi Josephine
Friend
♡?
KYOTARO OKEGAWA (3-4)
Bancho of Midorigaoka. He is pen pals with Mafuyu.
Nekomata-san
Midorigaoka Delinquents
Henchmen
DAIKICHI GOTO (3-4)
Very lucky. The most kindhearted person in Midorigaoka.
TOMOHIRO KAWAUCHI (3-4)
He respects Okegawa, but always does cruel things to him. He knows a lot of information.
Friend

Izumi Tsubaki began drawing manga in her first year of high school. She was soon selected to be in the top ten of *Hana to Yume*'s HMC (*Hana to Yume* Mangaka Course), and subsequently won *Hana to Yume*'s Big Challenge contest. Her debut title, *Chijimete Distance* (Shrink the Distance), ran in 2002 in *Hana to Yume* magazine, issue 17. She is currently working on the manga series *Oresama Teacher*.

ORESAMA TEACHER
Vol. 14
Shojo Beat Edition

STORY AND ART BY
Izumi Tsubaki

English Translation & Adaptation/JN Productions
Touch-up Art & Lettering/Eric Erbes
Design/Shawn Carrico
Editor/Pancha Diaz

ORESAMA TEACHER by Izumi Tsubaki © Izumi Tsubaki 2012
All rights reserved. First published in Japan in 2012 by HAKUSENSHA, Inc., Tokyo.
English language translation rights arranged with HAKUSENSHA, Inc., Tokyo.

The rights of the author(s) of the work(s) in this publication to be so identified
have been asserted in accordance with the Copyright, Designs and Patents Act
1988. A CIP catalogue record for this book is available from the British Library.

The stories, characters and incidents mentioned in this publication are
entirely fictional.

No portion of this book may be reproduced or transmitted in any form or
by any means without written permission from the copyright holders.

Printed in Canada

Published by VIZ Media, LLC
P.O. Box 77010
San Francisco, CA 94107

10 9 8 7 6 5 4 3 2 1
First printing, July 2013

www.viz.com   www.shojobeat.com

PARENTAL ADVISORY
ORESAMA TEACHER is rated T for Teen and
is recommended for ages 13 and up. This
volume contains violence.
ratings.viz.com

Kyoko Mogami followed her true love Sho to Tokyo to support him while he made it big as an idol. But he's casting her out now that he's famous enough! Kyoko won't suffer in silence—she's going to get her sweet revenge by beating Sho in show biz!

Vol. 1 ISBN: 978-1-4215-4226-3

Vol. 2 ISBN: 978-1-4215-4227-0

Vol. 3 ISBN: 978-1-4215-4228-7

Only $14.99 for each volume! ($16.99 in Canada)

Show biz is sweet...but revenge is sweeter!

Skip·Beat!

Story and Art by YOSHIKI NAKAMURA

In Stores Now!

Skip•Beat! © Yoshiki Nakamura 2002/HAKUSENSHA, Inc.

www.viz.com

A **Publisher's Weekly** bestseller!

What happens when the hottest boy in school
...is a girl?!?

Find out in these 3-in-1 collections of the hit shojo series!

Hana-Kimi

Story & Art by **HISAYA NAKAJO**

Mizuki Ashiya has such a crush on a track star named Izumi Sano that she moves from the U.S. to Japan to enroll in the all-male high school he goes to! Pretending to be a boy, Mizuki becomes Sano's roommate...

...but how can she keep such a big secret when she's so close to the guy she wants?

IN STORES NOW!

3-in-1 Vol. 1 ISBN: 978-1-4215-4224-9
3-in-1 Vol. 2 ISBN: 978-1-4215-4225-6
3-in-1 Vol. 3 ISBN: 978-1-4215-4229-4

Only **$14.99 US / $16.99 CAN** each!

Hanazakari no Kimitachi he
© Hisaya Nakajo 1996/HAKUSENSHA, Inc.

www.viz.com

Can love trump a cursed life?

Sawako's a shy, lonely, pure-hearted student who just happens to look like the scary girl in a famous horror movie! But when she manages to befriend the most popular boy in school, will her frightful reputation scare off her best chance for love?

kimi ni todoke
From Me to You

❉ By Karuho Shiina ❉

Find out in the *Kimi ni Todoke* manga—
BUY YOURS TODAY!

❉ Winner of the 2008 ❉ Kodansha Manga Award
(shojo category)

On sale at **www.shojobeat.com**
Also available at your local bookstore or comic store.

KIMI NI TODOKE © 2005 Karuho Shiina/SHUEISHA Inc.

Surprise!

You may be reading the wrong way!

It's true: In keeping with the original Japanese comic format, this book reads from right to left—so action, sound effects, and word balloons are completely reversed. This preserves the orientation of the original artwork—plus, it's fun! Check out the diagram shown here to get the hang of things, and then turn to the other side of the book to get started!

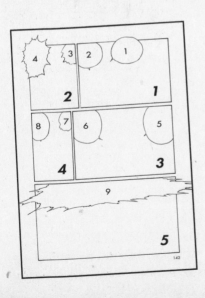

VIZMANGA
Read manga anytime, anywhere!

From our newest hit series to the classics you know
and love, the best manga in the world is now available
digitally. Buy a volume* of digital manga for your:

- iOS device (**iPad®**, **iPhone®**, **iPod®** touch)
  through the **VIZ Manga** app

- Android-powered device (**phone or tablet**)
  with a browser by visiting **VIZManga.com**

- **Mac or PC computer** by visiting **VIZManga.com**

VIZ Digital has loads to offer:

- 500+ ready-to-read volumes
- New volumes each week
- FREE previews
- Access on multiple devices! Create a log-in through the app
  so you buy a book once, and read it on your device of choice!*

To learn more, visit www.viz.com/apps

* Some series may not be available for multiple devices.
  Check the app on your device to find out what's available.

Aiwo Utauyori Oreni Oborero! Volume 1 © Mayu SHINJO 2010
DEATH NOTE © 2003 by Tsugumi Ohba, Takeshi Obata/SHUEISHA Inc.
NURARIHYON NO MAGO © 2008 by Hiroshi Shiibashi/SHUEISHA Inc.

viz.com/apps

from the director of Fruits Basket

You've read the manga,
Now relive the romance
in the anime!

Kamisama Kiss

Coming Soon to DVD and Blu-ray!
Watch NOW on FUNimation.com/Kamisama-Kiss

© Julietta Suzuki / Hakusensha-Kamisama Kiss Project. All Rights Reserved. Under License to FUNimation® Productions, Ltd. Produced by TMS ENTERTAINMENT CO., LTD.   FUNimation.

Don't Hide What's *Inside*

OTOMEN

by AYA KANNO

Despite his tough jock exterior, Asuka Masamune harbors a secret love for sewing, shojo manga, and all things girly. But when he finds himself drawn to his domestically inept classmate Ryo, his carefully crafted persona is put to the test. Can Asuka ever show his true self to anyone, much less to the girl he's falling for?

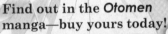

Find out in the *Otomen* manga—buy yours today!

On sale at www.shojobeat.com
Also available at your local bookstore and comic store.

RATED
T
FOR TEEN
ratings.viz.com

VIZ
MEDIA
www.viz.com

OTOMEN © Aya Kanno 2006/HAKUSENSHA, Inc.